Petulant and Contrary: Approaches by the Permanent Five Members of the UN Security Council to the Concept of 'threat to the peace' under Article 39 of the UN Charter

International Humanitarian Law Series

VOLUME 56

The International Humanitarian Law Series is a series of monographs and edited volumes which aims to promote scholarly analysis and discussion of both the theory and practice of the international legal regulation of armed conflict.

The series explores substantive issues of International Humanitarian Law including,

- protection for victims of armed conflict and regulation of the means and methods of warfare
- questions of application of the various legal regimes for the conduct of armed conflict
- issues relating to the implementation of International Humanitarian Law obligations
- national and international approaches to the enforcement of the law and
- the interactions between International Humanitarian Law and other related areas of international law such as Human Rights, Refugee Law, Arms Control and Disarmament Law, and International Criminal Law.

The titles published in this series are listed at *brill.com/ihul*

Petulant and Contrary: Approaches by the Permanent Five Members of the UN Security Council to the Concept of 'threat to the peace' under Article 39 of the UN Charter

By

Tamsin Phillipa Paige

BRILL
NIJHOFF

LEIDEN | BOSTON

Cover illustration: New York–UN Security Council chamber. ANP Robin Utrecht

Library of Congress Cataloging-in-Publication Data

Names: Paige, Tamsin Phillipa.
Title: Petulant and contrary: approaches by the permanent five members of the UN Security Council to the concept of 'threat to the peace' under Article 39 of the UN Charter / by Tamsin Phillipa Paige.
Description: Leiden ; Boston : Brill Nijhoff, 2019. | Based on author's thesis (doctoral - University of Adelaide Law School, 2017). | Includes bibliographical references and index.
Identifiers: LCCN 2018061473 (print) | LCCN 2019000282 (ebook) | ISBN 9789004391420 (ebook) | ISBN 9789004391390 (hardback : alk. paper)
Subjects: LCSH: Intervention (International law)--Decision making. | United Nations. Security Council--Decision making. | United Nations. Charter. Article 39.
Classification: LCC KZ6376 (ebook) | LCC KZ6376 .P35 2019 (print) | DDC 341.5/84--dc23
LC record available at https://lccn.loc.gov/2018061473

Typeface for the Latin, Greek, and Cyrillic scripts: "Brill". See and download: brill.com/brill-typeface.

ISSN 1389-6776
ISBN 978-90-04-39139-0 (hardback)
ISBN 978-90-04-39142-0 (e-book)

This book wouldn't have been possible without the support of my mentor Prof Rob McLaughlin, my adopted family Bernice, Deon, and Gwen Van Der Schyff, my dear friend Elizabeth Robards, and my puppy Admiral Tali'Zorah vas Normandy (or just Tali for short).

Contents

PART 3
Meta-synthesis

Annex

Foreword

When looking at the post-1945 legal order embodied in the UN Charter there is a clear tightening of the rules as to when states can use force in international relations, combined with a centralisation of authority in the Security Council, including the competence to take military action. This power can be unleashed when the Security Council determines that there is a 'threat to the peace', a much looser concept than its fellow terms in Article 39 – 'breach of the peace' or 'act of aggression', or indeed the trigger for a state's right of self-defence in Article 51, namely an 'armed attack'. The research contained in the book represents a different, interesting and convincing examination of the pivotal and elastic concept of 'threat to the peace'. It eschews doctrinal understandings and, instead, undertakes an empirical analysis of how each of the permanent members of the Security Council understands 'threat to the peace'. By delving deeply into such practice, the author draws some profound and valuable conclusions. While a dramatically different book such as this will draw plenty of criticism, there is no doubt in my mind that it makes a very valuable contribution to our knowledge and understanding of how the Security Council works and, more broadly, how international law functions.

Nigel D. White
Professor of Public International Law,
University of Nottingham, UK

Preface

Before I began my tertiary studies, I was a chef. Mostly I was French trained and although I trained in everything I specialised in dessert and pastry work. As a teenager learning to be a chef I discovered that there were two ways to learn to cook; you can learn all the recipes you need and when you need a new recipe you can do some research and learn that recipe, or you can learn the chemistry as to why a recipe works and behaves the way that it does and stop relying on recipes, using them as only a starting point. I was taught with, and consistently adopted, the second approach throughout that career and when I moved to the study of law I unconsciously transferred that principle to my approach to the law. For me black letter law represents the recipe; valuable, well-articulated, and readily applicable. Socio-legal approaches to how the law works represent the underlying principles and concern themselves less with what the law is (as this is simply a starting point for understanding) and instead focus on why the law works the way it does when put into practice (so that when new problems arise solutions can be found based on these understandings). I hope that this principle has been effectively implemented in this book.

The idea for this book came to me during the end of my undergraduate degree as I was preparing my applications for graduate school. At that stage I had to decide between doing this project and an examination of how international law was being applied in counter-piracy operations. I was advised to pursue the counter-piracy project first because the empirical data gathering was time sensitive, and the project was more conducive to discreet journal articles than a book. This advice was invaluable as it allowed me to be better prepared to write this volume through the experience I gained during the counter-piracy project, and because it allowed me to pursue this project during my doctoral studies without the distractions of teaching and other academic duties.

The experience I gained before I commenced this project also allowed me to secure support from the Australian Government in the form of an Endeavour Fellowship (which funded my time at Columbia Law School as a Visiting Scholar), and from the University of Adelaide in the form of an Australian Postgraduate Award and the Zelling Gray Scholarship. My time at the University of Nottingham and Columbia Law School as a Visiting Scholar, and my involvement in Prof Dianne Otto's *Queering International Law* volume honed my methodology and allowed me to produce this book, something that wouldn't have been possible had I pursued this project at the start of my academic career.

Acknowledgements

I would like to thank the following people for all of their assistance and support throughout the process of this project. First, I would like to thank Prof Dale Stephens, Dr Rebecca LaForgia, Prof Rob McLaughlin, Prof Nigel White and Dr Sarah Percy for their feedback on the manuscript. I'd also like to thank my Adelaide colleagues, in particular, Dr Angela Melville, Dr Stacey Henderson, Claire Williams, and Dr Gabrielle Golding. I would also like to thank my New York colleagues Prof Matthew Waxman, Prof Christina Tvarnø, Dr Şeyda Emek, Dr Rán Tryggvadóttir, Dr Amanda Geller, Dr Frank Giaoui, and Bella Kang.

I would also like to thank from my friends around the world for their support, in particular, Dr Geetanjali Rangekar, Sophie Beers, Claudette Yazbek, Mary-Anne and Cam Jack, Helen Travers, Trent Hansen, Patricia Hunt, Will and Amanda Nicholas, Erica Flannes, Ki Hunt, Caroline Compton, Jesse Barker-Gale, Christy Geromboux, Timothea Horn, Nonie Tuxen, Dr Katherine Grocott, Dr Robyn Goodwin, Amy Davies, Sze-Wei Chan, Evan Jewell, and Beatrix van Dissel.

Introductory Overview

In 1945, tremendous change occurred in the way states conducted themselves in relation to international law and security issues. With the end of World War II came the drafting and entry into force of the United Nations (UN) Charter, which was most significant in its creation of prohibition against the use of force.[1] This meant that states could no longer lawfully engage in proactively exercising military activity as a part of a dispute. This advent did not mean that states could no longer engage in the lawful use of force—indeed, Article 51 of the Charter specifically provides that states possess the right to engage in the use of force as part of collective or self-defence measures. However, this development meant that the only other ways in which states could lawfully engage in the proactive use of force were through consent, or an appropriate authorisation provided by the Security Council under Chapter VII of the Charter. The grounds on which the Security Council can authorise the use of force are articulated in Article 39 of the Charter:

> The Security Council shall determine the existence of any threat to the peace, breach of the peace, or act of aggression and shall make recommendations, or decide what measures shall be taken in accordance with Articles 41 and 42, to maintain or restore international peace and security.[2]

The notions of breach of the peace and an act of aggression (which must be distinguished from the crime of aggression more recently articulated in the Rome Statute of the International Criminal Court, although the definition of an act of aggression is contained with the crime)[3] both suggest clear positive acts to activate Security Council competence under Article 39. By contrast, the notion of threat is much less easily defined because of the subjective nature of what constitutes a threat. Reflecting this subjective nature is the fact that the

1 The vast amount of armed conflict after the introduction of the prohibition of the use of force demonstrates it's failure as a legal rule and need for a much more practical solution: N.D. White, *The United Nations and the Maintenance of International Peace and Security*, The Melland Schill Monographs in International Law (Manchester, UK.; New York, NY, USA: New York, NY: Manchester University Press; Distributed in the USA and Canada by St. Martin's Press, 1990), 47.

2 'Charter of the United Nations', 1 UNTS XVI (1945) Article 39.

3 'Amendment to the Rome Statute of the International Criminal Court on the Crime of Aggression, Articles 8bis, 15bis and 15ter', Pub. L. No. 11 June 2010, 2187 UNTS 90 Article 8bis.

 | DOI:10.1163/9789004391420_002

phrase was left intentionally undefined during the drafting of the UN Charter.[4] This has caused legal commentators to dismiss the phrase itself as being relatively undefinable, and criticising it for its general lack of consistency, ambiguity and flexibility in nature.[5] Further thought on this question has generally come to the conclusion that the only legal limitation on Security Council decisions is that they must accord with the UN's Purposes and Principles as dictated by the Charter, and the Security Council's mandate for the maintenance of international peace and security.[6]

I suggest that this hypothesis—that 'threat to the peace' is undefinable in nature—is wholly grounded in the manner in which commentators have explored the question. Previous legal commentators addressing this issue have explored the notion of 'threat to the peace' by examining resolutions that make such a finding. This is problematic in determining whether the Security Council's dealings with this concept have any pattern, consistency or grounding

4 See, for example, responses to the proposed Turkish Amendment to the Charter: 'Summary Report of Tenth Meeting of Committee III/2', *Documents on the United Nations Conference on International Organisations* 12, no. 72: 1–2; Christopher J. Le Mon and Rachel S. Taylor, 'Security Council Action in the Name of Human Rights: From Rhodesia to the Congo', *U.C. Davis Journal of International Law & Policy* 10, no. 2 (2004): 206; Leland M. Goodrich, *Charter of the United Nations; Commentary and Documents*, 3d and rev. ed (New York: Columbia University Press, 1969), 295–96.

5 Amy Eckert, 'The Non-Intervention Principle and International Humanitarian Interventions':, *International Legal Theory* 7, no. 1 (2001): 56; Le Mon and Taylor, 'Security Council Action in the Name of Human Rights', 198; Inger Österdahl, *Threat to the Peace: The Interpretation by the Security Council of Article 39 of the UN Charter* (Uppsala: Iustus, 1998), 103; Jennifer Welsh, Carolin Thielking, and S. Neil MacFarlane, 'The Responsibility to Protect: Assessing the Report of the International Commission on Intervention and State Sovereignty', *International Journal* 57 (2002): 502; N. D White, *Keeping the Peace: The United Nations and the Maintenance of International Peace and Security* (Manchester; New York; New York: Manchester University Press; Distributed exclusively in the USA and Canada by St. Martin's Press, 1993), 44.

6 Prosecutor v. Dusko Tadic a/k/a 'Dule' (Decision on the Defence Motion for Interlocutory Appeal on Jurisdiction), International Criminal Tribunal for the Former Yugoslavia, Appeals Chamber (International Criminal Tribunal for the Former Yugoslavia, Appeals Chamber 1995); The Prosecutor v Joseph Kanyabashi (Decision on the Defence Motion on Jurisdiction), International Criminal Tribunal for Rwanda (International Criminal Tribunal for Rwanda 1997); Phil Chan, 'A Keen Observer of the International Rule of Law? International Law in China's Voting Behaviour and Argumentation in the United Nations Security Council', *Leiden Journal of International Law* 26, no. 4 (2013): 880; Le Mon and Taylor, 'Security Council Action in the Name of Human Rights', 207; Daniel Pickard, 'When Does Crime Become a Threat to International Peace and Security?', *Florida Journal of International Law* 12, no. 1 (1998): 19–20; Österdahl, *Threat to the Peace*, 93; Phenyo Keiseng Rakate, 'The Characterisation of Conflicts in International Law: Applying Tadic to the Kosovo Crisis', *Stellenbosch L. Rev* 11 (2000): 278; White, *Keeping the Peace*, 45–46.

in approach, as these resolutions represent the Security Council's negotiated consensus rather than the reasoning applied by each key member to the decision itself. In common law terms, it is akin to reading the orders handed down by a court in relation to a case while wholly ignoring the substantive text of the judgement and facts that explain those orders. I instead propose that each member of the Permanent Five (P5) has their own internal working definition that is consistent through history and can be seen in how they justify their decisions regarding situations that may constitute a 'threat to the peace'. Such internal consistency thus discloses patterns of approach that possess a level of explanatory power regarding the general predictability of if and how the Security Council will act on security issues.

I intend to address this previously inadequately analysed question by engaging in a critical discourse analysis of meeting transcripts where the P5 members of the Security Council have substantially discussed the existence of a 'threat to the peace'. These investigations form a body of case studies that are then examined through meta-synthesis to determine if any key factors are used by each member of the P5 to make their decisions regarding 'threat to the peace'. The importance of these case studies is that they form individual instance qualitative data analysis case studies, each addressing the same question: 'What constitutes a threat?' This transformation of tens of thousands of pages of raw discourse data into usable case studies for the first time then allows for a meta-synthesis to be conducted. This not a mere descriptive process; rather, it is an iterative analysis that builds a picture of the ways in which the P5 approach the question of what constitutes a 'threat to the peace', which forms the foundations and context for the analysis conducted in the meta-synthesis and concluding chapters. This is also necessary because a meta-synthesis, by its very nature, requires numerous qualitative case studies on the same topic for the claims of patterns (or lack of patterns, as the case may be) to be valid and verifiable.[7] Further, the core principles of all critical theory state that all claims made must be grounded in evidence, and that this evidence must be verifiable, which, given the sheer volume of the raw data (in the form of meeting

7 Nicky Britten et al., 'Using Meta Ethnography to Synthesise Qualitative Research: A Worked Example', *Journal of Health Services Research and Policy* 7, no. 4 (October 2002): 210; Rona Campbell et al., 'Evaluating Meta-Ethnography: A Synthesis of Qualitative Research on Lay Experiences of Diabetes and Diabetes Care', *Social Science & Medicine* 56 (2003): 672; Denis Walsh and Soo Downe, 'Meta-Synthesis Method for Qualitative Research: A Literature Review', *Journal of Advanced Nursing* 50, no. 2 (2005): 205.

transcripts), means that to make any claim without including condensed case studies of this raw data would render those claims unverifiable and invalid.[8]

This will answer a core legal question relating to the UN Security Council and matters of international security, particularly the authorisation of the use of force—namely, how do the P5 understand the concept of threat in Article 39, and can this understanding amount to a working definition? However, this will be achieved through methods of legal sociology, rather than through a doctrinal law methodology (which in an international law context is articulated most succinctly by Article 38(1) of the International Court of Justice [ICJ] Statute).[9] The use of a legal sociology methodology is necessary as the previous studies that have attempted to define 'threat to the peace' using doctrinal legal methods have determined that such an approach is impossible.[10] This impossibility is noted by Österdahl when she asserts that doctrinal legal methods cannot assess situations where the Security Council has declined to make a finding of 'threat to the peace', as such situations do not produce a legal instrument.[11] She then points out that a large-scale historical, sociological analysis (such as the sort undertaken in this book) could address this limitation of doctrinal legal methods.[12] The primary goal of this volume is to determine if there can be any working definition of the phrase 'threat to the peace' through an empirical analysis of the P5's justificatory discourse when they have significantly discussed this question. This will reveal if there is any predictability and consistency of behaviour, understanding and justification within the P5 regarding the concept of 'threat to the peace', which will in turn provide greater capacity to predict when and how the Security Council will act.

This book is structured in three separate parts: theory and methodology, case studies and meta-synthesis results. The first part, theory and methodology, begins by addressing the importance of Article 39 of the UN Charter in

---

8 Roger Cotterrell, *Law's Community: Legal Theory in Sociological Perspective*, Oxford Socio-Legal Studies (Oxford: New York: Clarendon Press; Oxford University Press, 1995), 201–13.

9 'Statute of the International Court of Justice', 1 UNTS 993 (1945) Article 38(1).

10 Prosecutor v. Dusko Tadic a/k/a 'Dule' (Decision on the Defence Motion for Interlocutory Appeal on Jurisdiction), International Criminal Tribunal for the Former Yugoslavia, Appeals Chamber paragraph 29; Robert Cryer, 'The Security Council and Article 39: A Threat to Coherence?', *Journal of Armed Conflict* 1 (1996): 164; Eckert, 'The Non-Intervention Principle and International Humanitarian Interventions':, 56; Le Mon and Taylor, 'Security Council Action in the Name of Human Rights', 198; Österdahl, *Threat to the Peace*, 103; Karel Wellens, 'The UN Security Council and New Threats to the Peace: Back to the Future', *Journal of Conflict and Security Law* 8, no. 1 (2003): 33–34; Welsh, Thielking, and MacFarlane, 'The Responsibility to Protect', 502; White, *Keeping the Peace*, 44.

11 Österdahl, *Threat to the Peace*, 86.

12 Österdahl, 87.

the context of international law. After establishing the black letter law implications of Article 39, I then explore the notion that the law can be understood as more than simply treaties and custom—namely, that law in post-World War II society has become the *lingua franca* of diplomacy. This idea that law is actually the social interactions it creates, rather than simply black letter edicts, is not a new one in the field of legal sociology, as I demonstrate in Chapter 1; however, while not a new idea for legal sociology, it still needs to be established to give credence to the use of discourse analysis as a process of legal inquiry (as legal theory and general jurisprudence traditionally deny the applicability and role of empirically based sociological analysis to the discipline of law).[13] Finally, this analysis sets out how this understanding of law as the *lingua franca* of diplomacy allows for a critical discourse analysis of Security Council meeting transcripts to glean greater understanding of what constitutes a 'threat to the peace' under Article 39 of the Charter.

The second part of this book constitutes the bulk of it: the case study section. In this section, I engage in critical discourse analysis of numerous situations where the Security Council has substantively discussed whether a situation constitutes a 'threat to the peace' and publicly justified their reasons for these positions. Each case study possesses the same inherent structure: first, I address the context of the case study in relation to the overall project of understanding 'threat to the peace'; I then set out the factual context surrounding the statements being made by the P5 in the Security Council; finally, I analyse the justificatory discourse of each P5 member on the basis that international law is the language being used to articulate their arguments. Each of these case studies has been coded in line with grounded theory methods to then allow for the findings produced in the meta-synthesis—this process necessitates the volume of case studies included within the book. While it is impossible to include the coding within the book, the annexes at the end tabulate the results, and the analysis and results of this coding have been clearly signposted and summarised in each case study.

The value of this work is twofold. First, it creates a usable data set where previously only raw data that was functionally unusable existed, from which I can engage in a meta-synthesis to address the question of whether there is any working definition for how the P5 understands the concept of 'threat to the peace'. Second, it provides a sound demonstration of how viewing non-legal documents through a lens of legal sociology can be used by lawyers to provide great insight into ambiguous or contested legal documents. Perhaps most

13 Roger Cotterrell, *The Politics of Jurisprudence: A Critical Introduction to Legal Philosophy*, 2nd ed (Oxford; New York: Oxford University Press, 2003), 2–3.

importantly, a large-scale exploration of this sort into primary documents relating to the Security Council and 'threat to the peace' has not been previously conducted. Thus, regardless of what the primary sources reveal, the outcome of this empirical exploration represents a valuable and significant contribution to research on Article 39 of the UN Charter, as it will either show that long-held assumptions of undefinability due to arbitrariness are empirically sound, or demonstrate that the facts and history do not support such assumptions. Either of these outcomes will help shape thinking and action in relation to the Security Council and 'threat to the peace'.

The final section of this book is the meta-synthesis of the case studies to determine whether there is any consistency and definition to how each of the P5 approaches the question of 'threat to the peace'. Meta-synthesis is a relatively recent technique that has been deployed predominantly in medical sociology as a method of gaining greater understanding from qualitative data sets that all address the same issue, in much the same way that meta-analysis is used in quantitative data.[14] It can be employed in legal sociology, as it is a process concerned with method rather than subject matter; it is designed to analyse multiple related qualitative data case studies, rather than being designed to address medical specific data. By engaging in a meta-synthesis of the case studies, I demonstrate that although the Security Council as a whole has no discernible pattern or definition for what constitutes a 'threat to the peace', each individual P5 state does have a distinct methodology, definition and consistent decision-making framework for this issue. This finding runs counter to the intuitive but untested hypothesis of previous commentators,[15] and will lead to greater understanding of Security Council action in the future. Of particular significance to my conclusions in this final section is the manner in which I have categorised different case studies based upon the approaches and supported outcomes adopted by each individual P5 state, rather than by focusing upon the overall Security Council outcome. This approach radically changes thinking on Security Council action through the nuance inherent to this method. Rather than viewing the Security Council as a coherent

14 See generally: Britten et al., 'Using Meta Ethnography to Synthesise Qualitative Research'; Campbell et al., 'Evaluating Meta-Ethnography'; Janet Heaton, 'Secondary Analysis of Qualitative Data: An Overview', *Historical Social Research* 33, no. 3 (2008): 33; Walsh and Downe, 'Meta-Synthesis Method for Qualitative Research'.

15 Cryer, 'The Security Council and Article 39', 164; Eckert, 'The Non-Intervention Principle and International Humanitarian Interventions':, 56; Le Mon and Taylor, 'Security Council Action in the Name of Human Rights', 198; Österdahl, *Threat to the Peace*, 103; Welsh, Thielking, and MacFarlane, 'The Responsibility to Protect', 502; White, *Keeping the Peace*, 44.

monolithic entity, as approaches grounded in overall outcomes are prone to doing, and instead reading each situation and the meta-synthesis on the basis of individual state's supported outcome, greater insight is available into the positions of the P5 states. This in turn provides greater understanding of how each P5 member approaches the question of 'threat to the peace', and of their approaches to international law generally, especially in a security context.

While it touches on issues of legal issues and approaches to international law, and the individual incidents contained in each case study are influenced by issues of international relations, this volume is necessarily one of legal definition through sociological examination, not international relations theory or doctrinal law. 'Threat to the peace' in Article 39 was left intentionally undefined by the UN Charter drafters, and scholars have been unable to ascertain a working definition of the phrase through doctrinal legal analysis.[16] Thus, I turn to historical legal sociology to determine if the P5's practice, articulated through justificatory discourse in which international law is *lingua franca* of diplomacy, can yield any sort of functional definition. The importance of this inquiry is grounded in the premise that by understanding what constitutes a 'threat to the peace' more completely, we will have greater ability to predict how and when the Security Council will choose to act.

---

16 Cryer, 'The Security Council and Article 39', 164; Eckert, 'The Non-Intervention Principle and International Humanitarian Interventions':, 56; Le Mon and Taylor, 'Security Council Action in the Name of Human Rights', 198; Österdahl, *Threat to the Peace*, 103; Wellens, 'The UN Security Council and New Threats to the Peace', 33–34; Welsh, Thielking, and MacFarlane, 'The Responsibility to Protect', 502; White, *Keeping the Peace*, 44.

PART 1

Theory and Methodology

CHAPTER 1

Law and Politics in the Time of the Prohibition on the Use of Force

> While the 'act of aggression' is more amenable to a legal determination, the 'threat to the peace' is more of a political concept. But the determination that there exists such a threat is not a totally unfettered discretion, as it has to remain, at the very least, within the limits of the Purposes and Principles of the Charter.[1]

∵

The above statement from the International Criminal Tribunal for the Former Yugoslavia (ICTY) sets out the difficulty international lawyers have with Article 39 of the UN Charter and the discretion it provides the Security Council in determining the existence of a 'threat to the peace'.[2] Its difficulty as a legal concept is further highlighted and exacerbated by suggestions that such determinations by the Security Council are in no way justiciable, a fact raised by Alvarez and picked up on by the International Criminal Tribunal for Rwanda (ICTR) judges.[3] This difficulty is compounded by the fact that the Charter does not define what constitutes a threat to the peace, breach of the peace or act of aggression, allowing the Security Council wide discretion in its determinations.[4] As a result, commentators have suggested that the phrase 'threat to the

1 Prosecutor v. Dusko Tadic a/k/a 'Dule' (Decision on the Defence Motion for Interlocutory Appeal on Jurisdiction), International Criminal Tribunal for the Former Yugoslavia, Appeals Chamber (International Criminal Tribunal for the Former Yugoslavia, Appeals Chamber 1995).

2 'Charter of the United Nations', 1 UNTS XVI (1945) Article 39.

3 The Prosecutor v Joseph Kanyabashi (Decision on the Defence Motion on Jurisdiction), International Criminal Tribunal for Rwanda (International Criminal Tribunal for Rwanda 1997); Jose E. Alvarez, 'Judging the Security Council', *The American Journal of International Law* 90, no. 1 (1996): 1. The Namibia and Lockerbie ICJ cases, while related to Security Council activity, in no way questioned or made justiciable Security Council authority.

4 Attempts to limit or and define this power were rejected at the convention in which the UN Charter was drafted. See for example: 'Summary Report of Tenth Meeting of Committee III/2', *Documents on the United Nations Conference on International Organisations* 12, no. 72:

 | DOI:10.1163/9789004391420_003

peace' is undefinable in nature and that UN Security Council decisions surrounding the concept are 'fluid and arbitrary',[5] political in nature,[6] grounded in an ambiguous mandate,[7] lacking in consistency,[8] and flexible in nature.[9]

It has been suggested that if we want to grasp how the Security Council understands the phrase 'threat to the peace', then we should examine the practice of the Security Council itself to gain such insight.[10] The difficulty of doing this by only examining Security Council resolutions (the legal instrument that shows the end point of the Security Council's decision-making process, the examination of which has been the primary method employed to explore this issue) is the notoriously selective nature of Security Council action.[11] The only way to gain any real insight when examining how the Security Council defines the existence of a 'threat to the peace' is to examine the public record of the decision-making process in the form of meeting transcripts. That said, if Security Council decision-making processes are so arbitrary, inconsistent and political, the question then becomes: what role does international law have to play in such an examination? This chapter primarily seeks to answer that question.

A body of literature within international law also attempts to answer that question. The primary argument in this literature proposes that international law forms a regular and consistent part of mainstream international political discourse.[12] Johnstone and Koskenniemi have undertaken the majority of that

1–2; Christopher J. Le Mon and Rachel S. Taylor, 'Security Council Action in the Name of Human Rights: From Rhodesia to the Congo', *U.C. Davis Journal of International Law & Policy* 10, no. 2 (2004): 206; Leland M. Goodrich, *Charter of the United Nations; Commentary and Documents*, 3d and rev. ed (New York: Columbia University Press, 1969), 295–96.

5 Inger Österdahl, *Threat to the Peace: The Interpretation by the Security Council of Article 39 of the UN Charter* (Uppsala: Iustus, 1998), 103.

6 Jennifer Welsh, Carolin Thielking, and S. Neil MacFarlane, 'The Responsibility to Protect: Assessing the Report of the International Commission on Intervention and State Sovereignty', *International Journal* 57 (2002): 502.

7 Le Mon and Taylor, 'Security Council Action in the Name of Human Rights', 198.

8 Amy Eckert, 'The Non-Intervention Principle and International Humanitarian Interventions':, *International Legal Theory* 7, no. 1 (2001): 56.

9 N. D White, *Keeping the Peace: The United Nations and the Maintenance of International Peace and Security* (Manchester; New York; New York: Manchester University Press; Distributed exclusively in the USA and Canada by St. Martin's Press, 1993), 44.

10 Robert Cryer, 'The Security Council and Article 39: A Threat to Coherence?', *Journal of Armed Conflict* 1 (1996): 164.

11 Martii Koskenniemi, 'The Place of Law in Collective Security', *Michigan Journal of International Law* 17 (1996): 164.

12 Phil Chan, 'A Keen Observer of the International Rule of Law? International Law in China's Voting Behaviour and Argumentation in the United Nations Security Council', *Leiden Journal of International Law* 26, no. 4 (2013): 875–76; Ian Johnstone, 'Security Council Deliberations: The Power of the Better Argument', *European Journal of International Law* 14, no. 3 (2003): 439–40; Koskenniemi, 'The Place of Law in Collective Security', 475; China

work, which forms the foundation for my proposed suggestion to address this dilemma. In different ways, both argue that legal phraseology and principles are the way in which global political powers justify their decision-making in public forums where the self-interest of politics is not acceptable (a phenomena at which Lauterpacht hinted).[13] From this foundation, I propose that the law is not separate from political power, nor simply the 'gentle civiliser of national self-interest',[14] but rather the *lingua franca* of political discourse.

This chapter first explores the role Article 39 of the Charter plays in the international arena and the way in which the Security Council decisions surrounding Article 39 have been analysed. This exploration discusses academic explorations that form the landscape of understanding regarding the Security Council's approaches to the question of 'threat to the peace', highlighting the inability of doctrinal legal methods to define 'threat to the peace' in the context of Article 39. It also parses the legal limitations that operate upon the Security Council in relation to such decisions.

Following this overview of previous explorations into 'threat to the peace', I turn my attention to outlining the lens through which this book is conducted: the law as the language of power. In exploring this proposition, I examine the way in which wholly political processes have been characterised as legal in nature because of the use of legal norms within the process itself. This will allow me, while drawing upon the work of legal and social theorists, to examine the way in which the law has become the language of power in international political discourse. This examination, while predominantly a literature review, is of foundational importance, as it establishes the basis for using the methodology of critical discourse analysis to conduct a legal investigation to define the meaning of 'threat to the peace' in Article 39 of the UN Charter.

1 The Importance of Article 39 in International Law and the Current Landscape

> The Security Council shall determine the existence of any threat to the peace, breach of the peace, or act of aggression and shall make recommendations, or decide what measures shall be taken in accordance

Miéville, 'Multilateralism as Terror: International Law, Haiti and Imperialism', *London: Birkbeck EPrints*, 2009, 2, http://eprints.bbk.ac.uk/783.

13 Johnstone, 'Security Council Deliberations: The Power of the Better Argument', 435–54; Koskenniemi, 'The Place of Law in Collective Security', 477; Hersch Lauterpacht, *The Function of Law in the International Community*, 1st pbk. ed (Oxford; New York: Oxford University Press, 2011), 147.

14 George Kenman in Koskenniemi, 'The Place of Law in Collective Security', 489.

> with Articles 41 and 42, to maintain or restore international peace and security.[15]

Article 39 of the Charter vested in the Security Council the power to determine when the international community can consider a situation to represent a 'threat to the peace'. The importance of this article is that the Security Council's finding of threat to the peace, breach of the peace or act of aggression is the only legal avenue that authorises the use of force, aside from Article 51 of the Charter.[16] It has been noted by the ICTY that breach of the peace and act of aggression are easily amenable to legal definition, whereas 'threat to the peace' is somewhat more amorphous and undefinable in nature.[17] Of interest is the fact that all attempts to define 'threat to the peace' when the UN Charter was being drafted failed,[18] resulting in the phrase being left wholly undefined, something I attempt to address in this book.

The importance of understanding how the Security Council will interpret and define 'threat to the peace' and determine if such situations exist lies in the fact that it is within the Security Council's power and mandate to make binding decisions regarding the use of force.[19] It is worth noting that a breach of international law is not synonymous with a 'threat to the peace', and that the Security Council's mandate is to maintain international peace and security, not to enforce international law;[20] however, the Security Council must have a sound legal basis for its decisions, or else it risks jeopardising the legitimacy of all Security Council decisions.[21] It must be noted, though, that broader

15 Charter of the United Nations Article 39.

16 Charter of the United Nations Article 51.

17 Prosecutor v. Dusko Tadic a/k/a 'Dule' (Decision on the Defence Motion for Interlocutory Appeal on Jurisdiction), International Criminal Tribunal for the Former Yugoslavia, Appeals Chamber paragraph 29.

18 Cryer, 'The Security Council and Article 39', 163; Le Mon and Taylor, 'Security Council Action in the Name of Human Rights', 206.

19 Charter of the United Nations Art 25; Legal Consequences for States of the Continued Presence of South Africa in Namibia (South West Africa) Notwithstanding Security Council Resolution 276 (1970): Advisory Opinion of 21 June 1971, 1971 International Court of Justice Reports of Judgments, Advisory Opinions and Orders (International Court of Justice 1971).

20 Charter of the United Nations Art 24(1); Karel Wellens, 'The UN Security Council and New Threats to the Peace: Back to the Future', *Journal of Conflict and Security Law* 8, no. 1 (2003): 31–32.

21 Chan, 'A Keen Observer of the International Rule of Law?', 879; For a recent empirical study addressing the question of Security Council legitimacy see: Martin Binder and Monika Heupel, 'The Legitmacy of the UN Security Council: Evidence from Recent General Assembly Debates', *International Studies Quarterly* 59, no. 2 (2015): 238–50.

questions of Security Council legitimacy are beyond the scope of this book, which focuses on the question of defining 'threat to the peace'. In the past, the Security Council has decided to find a 'threat to the peace' in relation to a broad variety of situations, including apartheid in South Africa,[22] refugee concerns,[23] international armed conflict,[24] terrorism,[25] civil war,[26] and the defence of democracy.[27] While this list is far from exhaustive, it provides a solid example as to why understanding how the Security Council determines the existence of a 'threat to the peace' is of significant importance. While there have been numerous studies on the content and effect of individual 'threat to the peace' resolutions, there have been no successful significant studies of how 'threat to the peace' can be defined.

The significant studies already conducted into the question of what is meant by the phrase 'threat to the peace' focus on the Security Council's positive findings on the resolutions that follow.[28] Of these studies, Österdahl's is the most comprehensive, yet still restricts itself to Security Council resolutions that have followed the decision that a 'threat to the peace' exists. This is because the meeting transcripts constitute supplementary materials of limited legal status to the resolution itself, and are excluded from consideration when interpreting the meaning of Article 39 of the UN Charter through doctrinal legal methods.[29] Further, the perception that the Security Council's decision-making process is arbitrary and political in nature,[30] which renders it lacking in consistency, may also serve to encourage simply examining the Security

22 'Resolution 418 (1977)', S/RES/418 (1977) UN Security Council (1977).

23 'Resolution 918 (1994)', S/RES/918 (1994) UN Security Council (1994).

24 'Resolution 54 (1948)', S/RES/54 (1948) UN Security Council (1948); 'Resolution 186 (1964)', S/RES/186 (1964) UN Security Council (1964).

25 'Resolution 748 (1992)', S/RES/748 (1992) UN Security Council (1992); 'Resolution 1054 (1996)', S/RES/1054 (1996) UN Security Council (1996); 'Resolution 1368 (2001)', S/RES/1368 (2001) UN Security Council (2001).

26 'Resolution 713 (1991)', S/RES/713 (1991) UN Security Council (1991); 'Resolution 733 (1992)', S/RES/733 (1992) UN Security Council (1992).

27 'Resolution 841 (1993)', S/RES/841 (1993) UN Security Council (1993).

28 Cryer, 'The Security Council and Article 39'; Le Mon and Taylor, 'Security Council Action in the Name of Human Rights'; Österdahl, *Threat to the Peace*; Wellens, 'The UN Security Council and New Threats to the Peace'.

29 'Statute of the International Court of Justice', 1 UNTS 993 (1945) Article 38(1); 'Vienna Convention on the Law of Treaties', 1155 UNTS 18232 (1969) Articles 31–32.

30 Chan, 'A Keen Observer of the International Rule of Law?', 881; Michael J. Glennon, 'Why the Security Council Failed', *Foreign Affairs* 82 (2003): 16; Österdahl, *Threat to the Peace*, 103; Wellens, 'The UN Security Council and New Threats to the Peace', 30; Welsh, Thielking, and MacFarlane, 'The Responsibility to Protect', 502; White, *Keeping the Peace*, 49.

Council resolutions rather than digging into the resolution-making process.[31] The problem with making this distinction is that when dealing with international law, it is impossible to separate the legal from public and political policy, particularly in situations of armed conflict.[32] An alternate reading of the Security Council's political and arbitrary decision-making is that it is simply exercising the discretion granted to it by the UN Charter.[33]

While these previous studies are incomplete in nature and reluctant to consider the political element of international law-making, they form an incomparable and obvious starting point for any study on the concept of 'threat to the peace'. Significant insight can be gleaned into the Security Council's operation, and the interpretation of Article 39, from the work that has come before. It is suggested that at the time of drafting and for some time thereafter, the Security Council understood 'threat to the peace' to mean military threats to international peace and security.[34] This narrow interpretation of the phrase is supported by the fact that between 1946 and 1986, the Security Council only had seven positive findings of a 'threat to the peace'.[35] To put this number in context, it is estimated that 73 interstate conflicts occurred during this period, in addition to whatever intrastate conflicts occurred during the same time.[36] There are suggestions that Cold War politics rendered the Security Council deadlocked and impotent throughout this period.[37] Counter to this argument, others have posited that the existence of the veto to stymie activity where fundamental disagreements exist over the correct course of action is a design

31 Eckert, 'The Non-Intervention Principle and International Humanitarian Interventions':, 56; Wellens, 'The UN Security Council and New Threats to the Peace', 33–34; White, *Keeping the Peace*, 44.

32 Rob McLaughlin, '"Giving" Operational Legal Advice: Context and Method', *Military Law and the Law of War Review* 50 (2011): 100.

33 Simon Chesterman, 'An International Rule of Law?', *American Journal of Comparative Law* 56, no. 2: 351.

34 Le Mon and Taylor, 'Security Council Action in the Name of Human Rights', 208; Österdahl, *Threat to the Peace*, 18.

35 Resolution 54 (1948); 'Resolution 161 (1961)', S/RES/161 (1961) UN Security Council (1961); 'Resolution 232 (1966)', S/RES/232 (1966) UN Security Council (1966); 'Resolution 307 (1971)', S/RES/307 (1971) UN Security Council (1971); 'Resolution 353 (1974)', S/RES/353 (1974) UN Security Council (1974); Resolution 418 (1977); 'Resolution 573 (1985)', S/RES/573 (1985) UN Security Council (1985).

36 N.D. White, *The United Nations and the Maintenance of International Peace and Security*, The Melland Schill Monographs in International Law (Manchester, UK.; New York, NY, USA: New York, NY: Manchester University Press ; Distributed in the USA and Canada by St. Martin's Press, 1990), 47.

37 Koskenniemi, 'The Place of Law in Collective Security', 457.

feature, and that during this period, the Security Council was operating in accordance with this design safeguard.[38]

Analyses tend to find that since the end of the Cold War, the Security Council has taken a much more proactive and broad approach to interpreting Article 39, particularly the 'threat to the peace' component.[39] Österdahl argues that this is a result of, and consistent with, the democratisation of the Soviet Union, which saw the Security Council begin defining human rights issues and lack of democracy as a 'threat to the peace'.[40] Similarly, Koskenniemi posits that between 1988 and 1994, there was a qualitative development in the Security Council's understanding of its task to maintain international peace and security.[41] His suggestion is consistent with, and supported by, statements by the Security Council in January 1992 noting the broad discretion it possesses in relation to the existence of a 'threat to the peace'.[42] Koskenniemi caveats this suggestion by pointing out that Security Council interests do not reflect the UN as a whole, but rather the special interests and predominance of the United States (US) and its Western allies.[43] This is illustrated by the fact that the mechanism the Security Council opted to use for the Kuwaiti intervention was the authorisation of the US-led coalition,[44] rather than an Article 43 agreement.[45] Glennon supports this view by arguing that while the UN Charter purports to represent of universal law, the majority of UN states are unable to agree on when the use of force can be justified,[46] leading to a divide not only between the West and the rest of the world, but also between the US and the rest of the West.[47]

There are arguments both for and against this broad interpretation of 'threat to the peace' by the Security Council. It has been suggested that this broad interpretation has elevated Article 1(2) of the UN Charter[48] to the same level of importance as Article 1(1)[49] when considering the UN's principles and

38 Österdahl, *Threat to the Peace*, 99–100.
39 Wellens, 'The UN Security Council and New Threats to the Peace', 67–68.
40 Österdahl, *Threat to the Peace*, 88.
41 Koskenniemi, 'The Place of Law in Collective Security', 459.
42 United Nations Security Council, 'Note by the President of the Security Council' (United Nations, 31 January 1992), 3.
43 Koskenniemi, 'The Place of Law in Collective Security', 460–61.
44 'Resolution 678 (1990)', S/RES/678 (1990) UN Security Council (1990); Koskenniemi, 'The Place of Law in Collective Security', 461.
45 Charter of the United Nations Article 43.
46 Glennon, 'Why the Security Council Failed', 21.
47 Glennon, 21.
48 Charter of the United Nations Article 1(2).
49 Charter of the United Nations Article 1(1).

purposes.[50] It has also been tentatively suggested that the Security Council's expanded use of Article 39 created customary law that elevated democracy to a required form of government.[51] While the customary nature of democracy is questionable, what is clear is that since the expansion of Security Council action in the wake of the Cold War, 'threat to the peace' is no longer contained to military situations.[52] Social, political, economic, humanitarian, ecological and other non-military factors have now been seen to fall within the ambit of 'threat to the peace' under Article 39.[53] It has been posited that the basis of this trend is that war is an external manifestation of the violence of social institutions, and that peace begins with the eradication of poverty, social injustice, and the violation of civil rights.[54]

The end of the Cold War and the broader interpretation of 'threat to the peace' thus appear causally linked. It has been suggested that this is because during this period of expansion in the 1990s, there was a higher level of consensus within the Security Council and, consequently, greatly reduced use or threat of the veto by Russia and the US on ideological grounds.[55] This expansion of interpretation has been regarded both positively and negatively, often at the same time. It is proposed that the advantage of this expansion is that the Security Council is seen to be adapting to changing times and intervening more often when necessary.[56] The flipside of this potential positive outcome of the Security Council's broader interpretations of 'threat to the peace' is that the high level of consensus opens the door to abuse of power due to reduced usage of the veto.[57] It has been argued that this broader interpretation, combined with the greater level of consensus, has allowed the US to act through the Security Council rather than unilateral action, providing greater levels of legitimacy to both US and Security Council action;[58] however, this suggestion

50 Österdahl, *Threat to the Peace*, 25–26.

51 Österdahl, 34–35.

52 United Nations Security Council, 'Note by the President of the Security Council', 3; Le Mon and Taylor, 'Security Council Action in the Name of Human Rights', 208; Österdahl, *Threat to the Peace*, 18–19.

53 Österdahl, *Threat to the Peace*, 18–19.

54 Koskenniemi, 'The Place of Law in Collective Security', 459. I personally propose that peace is in fact the oppression of freedom. This is because that the existence of freedom is going to cause conflict of competing freedoms; however, this is not the venue to explore this notion.

55 Österdahl, *Threat to the Peace*, 21–22.

56 Österdahl, 21–22.

57 Österdahl, 21–22.

58 Österdahl, 22.

was made before the Kosovo campaign, the second Gulf War and the Afghanistan invasion,[59] all of which call this interpretation into question.

These events, in particular the second Gulf War, led to a great deal of questioning around the Security Council's consistency and efficacy. In relation to Kosovo, the questions centred on the veto and the likelihood that intervention into humanitarian crises would operate in the manner of seeking forgiveness rather than asking permission in such situations if the Security Council could not be liberated from the veto.[60] In relation to the second Gulf War, the US threats to act unilaterally should they not receive Security Council authorisation led to serious questions as to whether the Security Council could function at all without a second superpower to counterbalance US dominance.[61] Recently, China has emerged as a political opposition to the US and has begun exercising its veto more regularly;[62] this has arguably brought more balance to Security Council action. This rise of China has also been supported by the resurgence of Russia as a global political force.

It is evident that the end of the Cold War and the expansion of Security Council activity under Article 39 (and by extension under 'threat to the peace') are causally linked;[63] however, this insight is of little aid when attempting to define what 'threat to the peace' means—indeed, it makes the phrase somewhat more difficult to define because of the increased breadth in its application. These arguments and analyses focus on the instances when the Security Council has decided to intervene in a situation, or a veto has been exercised. The problem with this analysis is that the process by which the Security Council makes decisions has been dismissed as wholly political and not a question of law.[64] Therefore, there has been very little rigorous examination of the public

59 It must be noted that while the United States et al acted without a UN Security Council mandate in Afghanistan, they acted in accordance with the Art 51 collective self-defence measures that Resolution 1368 acknowledged as a right they possessed; Resolution 1368 (2001); Charter of the United Nations Article 51.

60 Louis Henkin, 'Kosovo and the Law of "Humanitarian Intervention"', *The American Journal of International Law* 93, no. 4 (October 1999): 827.

61 Glennon, 'Why the Security Council Failed', 16–18.

62 Since the inception of the Security Council China has exercised its veto on eleven occasions, eight of those since 2007; Dag Hammarskjöld Library, 'Security Council – Veto List', Dag Hammarskjöld Library Research Guides, 19 August 2018, http://research.un.org/en/docs/sc/quick/veto; Chan, 'A Keen Observer of the International Rule of Law?', 889.

63 Österdahl, *Threat to the Peace*, 21–22; Peter Wallensteen and Patrik Johansson, 'Security Council Decisions in Perspective', in *The UN Security Council: From the Cold War to the 21st Century*, ed. David E. Malone, 1st ed. (Boulder, London: Lynne Rienner Publishers, 2004), 28–29; Wellens, 'The UN Security Council and New Threats to the Peace', 67–68.

64 Prosecutor v. Dusko Tadic a/k/a 'Dule' (Decision on the Defence Motion for Interlocutory Appeal on Jurisdiction), International Criminal Tribunal for the Former Yugoslavia,

justification as to why the veto was exercised. I dispute this position, instead positing that law can address this question in the form of legal sociology, which will allow for analysis of the action taken and the associated justifications for it to ascertain why these resolutions were (or were not) made, through qualitative analysis of the justificatory discourse surrounding the decisions.

The probable cause of this lack of legal inquiry into the Security Council's decision-making is the lack of judicial oversight the Security Council enjoys in relation to its decision-making. Legal thought on this question has generally come to the conclusion that the only legal limitation on Security Council decisions is that they must be in accordance with the UN's Purposes and Principles as dictated by the Charter, and the Security Council's mandate for the maintenance of international peace and security.[65] The Security Council's ability to make decisions regarding what constitutes a 'threat to the peace' has been described as 'an unfettered discretion',[66] and not justiciable.[67] The most succinct description of the legal limits the Security Council faces is provided by Österdahl, who states: '[p]ut in simple terms, the Security Council may basically decide or do anything it wishes and it will remain within the limits of the legal framework for its action'.[68] Given the general lack of judicial oversight of Security Council action, the real question becomes, what place does law have in such a framework and can a legal phrase with such broad discretion be in any way defined?

Appeals Chamber paragraph 29; Glennon, 'Why the Security Council Failed', 16; Österdahl, *Threat to the Peace*, 103; Wellens, 'The UN Security Council and New Threats to the Peace', 30; Welsh, Thielking, and MacFarlane, 'The Responsibility to Protect', 502; White, *Keeping the Peace*, 49.

65 Prosecutor v. Dusko Tadic a/k/a 'Dule' (Decision on the Defence Motion for Interlocutory Appeal on Jurisdiction), International Criminal Tribunal for the Former Yugoslavia, Appeals Chamber paragraph 29; The Prosecutor v Joseph Kanyabashi (Decision on the Defence Motion on Jurisdiction), International Criminal Tribunal for Rwanda paragraph 20; Chan, 'A Keen Observer of the International Rule of Law?', 880; Le Mon and Taylor, 'Security Council Action in the Name of Human Rights', 207; Daniel Pickard, 'When Does Crime Become a Threat to International Peace and Security?', *Florida Journal of International Law* 12, no. 1 (1998): 19–20; Österdahl, *Threat to the Peace*, 93; Phenyo Keiseng Rakate, 'The Characterisation of Conflicts in International Law: Applying Tadic to the Kosovo Crisis', *Stellenbosch L. Rev* 11 (2000): 278; White, *Keeping the Peace*, 45–46.

66 Rakate, 'The Characterisation of Conflicts in International Law', 278.

67 The Prosecutor v Joseph Kanyabashi (Decision on the Defence Motion on Jurisdiction), International Criminal Tribunal for Rwanda paragraph 20; Although it must be noted that Alvarez argues that ICJ advisory opinions serve as a form of judicial review, their non-binding nature arguably causes them to fall short of true judicial review: Alvarez, 'Judging the Security Council'.

68 Österdahl, *Threat to the Peace*, 98.

The common conception regarding the place of law in Security Council operations is of the Security Council as a political body whose decisions have legal consequences that are often far-reaching.[69] The primacy of political interests in preference to the use of legal rules is enshrined in the UN Charter at Article 24 and 27.[70] Because of this, the Security Council 'is not obligated in to react in any predetermined way to any "breach of the peace, threat to the peace or act of aggression"'.[71] In fact, the Security Council intentionally goes out of its way to stress that its pronouncements are not precedent-setting in any way regarding what constitutes a 'threat to the peace'.[72] What this means is that 'saving people or removing a "threat to the peace", in one case is not wrong because no decision was taken to save people or remove a "threat to the peace" in another case'.[73] Although seemingly paradoxical, the Security Council's regular use of the political finding of a 'threat to the peace' to forcibly establish the rule of law in the situations where it chooses to intervene is nevertheless well established.[74] *Prima facie* it seems quite apparent that the law does not interact with the Security Council's ability to determine a 'threat to the peace' until after a legally binding resolution has been passed and is to be put into place. Given this state of affairs, there is little wonder that legal studies on 'threat to the peace' have focused upon resolutions rather than the public justification of decisions by Security Council members in their efforts to craft a working definition of 'threat to the peace'.

This approach taken to understanding the place of law in politics is understandable given the lack of judicial oversight and the legal process by which the decisions are made. It reflects what Koskenniemi suggests is the prevailing view—that law having a place in the high politics of international security is an abstract and utopian notion not worth indulging.[75] This is most certainly

69 Johnstone, 'Security Council Deliberations: The Power of the Better Argument', 452.

70 Charter of the United Nations Articles 24 & 27; Koskenniemi, 'The Place of Law in Collective Security', 463.

71 Koskenniemi, 'The Place of Law in Collective Security', 474.

72 Wellens, 'The UN Security Council and New Threats to the Peace', 33–34; The most glaring example of this was the Resolutions regarding piracy originating from Somalia; Tamsin Paige, 'Piracy and Universal Jurisdiction', *Macquarie Law Journal* 12 (2013): 149.

73 Österdahl, *Threat to the Peace*, 107.

74 Simon Chesterman, 'UNaccountable? The United Nations, Emergency Powers, and the Rule of Law', *Vanderbilt Journal of Transnational Law* 42 (2009): 1515; Jeremy Matam Farrall, 'Impossible Expectations? The UN Security Council's Promotion of the Rule of Law after Conflict', in *The Role of International Law in Rebuilding Societies after Conflict: Great Expectations*, ed. Hilary Charlesworth and Brett Bowden (Cambridge, UK; New York: Cambridge University Press, 2009), 134.

75 Koskenniemi, 'The Place of Law in Collective Security', 463.

true if one adopts a black letter approach to the conception of what constitutes law. Article 38(1) of the ICJ statute very clearly sets out the black letter approach as to what constitutes law and the hierarchy of these sources in the context of international law.[76] In the context of the ICJ, this is a helpful and appropriate approach to law; however, in the context of understanding Article 39 of the UN Charter and how it is interpreted by the Security Council, it is overly narrow and wholly inappropriate. This is evidenced by the fact that legal scholars considering this question have dismissed the process as political and arbitrary without in-depth examination of the justificatory discourse that has taken place to reach the decisions that have been made.[77]

While it is possible that these scholars are correct that the process is political, arbitrary and devoid of law, such assertions cannot reliably be formed until an in-depth examination is conducted of the manner in which the Security Council decisions are made. In this spirit, I now propose an alternative conception of law to be applied to the question of international security, but with broader application to international law and law as a discipline generally. I demonstrate that examining the public justifications of Security Council decisions regarding 'threat to the peace' viewed through this alternative lens as to what constitutes law allows for a greater understanding of how the Security Council approaches this question, and how each of the P5 defines 'threat to the peace'.

2 The Language of Power

The narrow, black letter conception of what constitutes law as articulated in Article 38(1) of the ICJ Statute,[78] and Articles 31–32 of the Vienna Convention on the Law of Treaties,[79] while the most common form of legal thinking, is far from the only approach to international law (as I intend to show). In relation to the work of the Security Council, the most detailed work on an alternate conception of law has been undertaken by Koskenniemi and Johnstone, although others have contributed. The common theme of this work is the interaction of law and political power within the Security Council, or similar international

76 Statute of the International Court of Justice Article 38(1).

77 Chan, 'A Keen Observer of the International Rule of Law?', 881; Glennon, 'Why the Security Council Failed', 16; Österdahl, *Threat to the Peace*, 103; Wellens, 'The UN Security Council and New Threats to the Peace', 30; Welsh, Thielking, and MacFarlane, 'The Responsibility to Protect', 502; White, *Keeping the Peace*, 49.

78 Statute of the International Court of Justice Article 38(1).

79 Vienna Convention on the Law of Treaties Articles 31–32.

relations activities or fora. Within this body of work, there is relative consensus that international law forms part of the normalised framework of discourse within global politics.[80] It is suggested that that the point where law became an accepted, normalised framework to express international political activity was in the wake of the Kosovo crisis.[81]

When applying this framework, international law and international geopolitical power are often conceived of as separate but entwined entities.[82] In one conception of this separate but entwined view of the nature of law and politics, law is viewed as a restraining entity on political power and self-interest, reigning in its excesses so it becomes socially and publicly palatable.[83] Under this framework, law and global geopolitical power are understood as two sides of the same coin, separate and coherent aspects of a unified reality that develop as analogous to each other in the context of the Security Council.[84] In line with this understanding, law is seen as an entirely separate entity from political power, acting to regulate these power interactions as the handmaiden or facilitator of political power.[85]

Using this framework, Koskenniemi argues that what law brings to international political decision-making is not the substantive responses, but rather the public justification and assumption of responsibility for the policies chosen.[86] He argues that 'law is what diplomats do when they debate the meaning of the UN charter, the competence of the Security Council, or Libya's duties

80 Chan, 'A Keen Observer of the International Rule of Law?', 875–76; Johnstone, 'Security Council Deliberations: The Power of the Better Argument', 439–40; Martti Koskenniemi, *The Gentle Civilizer of Nations: The Rise and Fall of International Law, 1870–1960* (Cambridge, UK ; New York: Cambridge University Press, 2002), 7; Koskenniemi, 'The Place of Law in Collective Security', 477; Martii Koskenniemi, 'The Mystery of Legal Obligation', *International Theory* 3, no. 2 (2011): 321–22; Miéville, 'Multilateralism as Terror: International Law, Haiti and Imperialism', 3.

81 Johnstone, 'Security Council Deliberations: The Power of the Better Argument', 466; Miéville, 'Multilateralism as Terror: International Law, Haiti and Imperialism', 3.

82 Chan, 'A Keen Observer of the International Rule of Law?', 879; Nicole Deitelhoff, 'The Discursive Process of Legalization: Charting Islands of Persuasion in the ICC Case', *International Organization* 63, no. 1 (Winter 2009): 35; Johnstone, 'Security Council Deliberations: The Power of the Better Argument', 475; Koskenniemi, 'The Place of Law in Collective Security', 475.

83 Deitelhoff, 'The Discursive Process of Legalization', 35; Ben Golder and Peter Fitzpatrick, *Foucault's Law* (Milton Park, Abingdon; New York: Routledge, 2009), 64–65; Koskenniemi, 'The Place of Law in Collective Security', 488.

84 Koskenniemi, 'The Place of Law in Collective Security', 475.

85 Koskenniemi, 488.

86 Koskenniemi, 478.

under particular Council resolutions'.[87] Through this understanding, the law operates as the public face of political power, separate from political aims and ends but invoked to sanitise for public consumption the self-interest inherent in those political goals.

From this conception, Koskenniemi argues that the law should not be viewed as a tool of self-interest and institutional phenomena of states, but rather as a cultural phenomenon.[88] Using this grounding rationale, he asserts that when examining international law, we should look beyond state practices to the culture that exists, the sensibilities that this culture imparts upon the practice of international law and the influence this then has upon the politics and society of the state in question.[89] Similarly, he argues that the act of creating international law is one of diplomacy and political negotiation.[90] The net effect of this framework is that law and geopolitics are completely separate entities that feed and influence one another, but never truly merge.

The problem with this framework is demonstrated in Deitelhoff's work on the formation of the statute of the International Criminal Court. Through a qualitative data study, she examines the way in which a coalition of nations not considered political powers were able to influence the nature of the statute through delegations and informal alliances focused upon legal issues.[91] Through her analysis, she concludes that the process of becoming highly versed and competent in legal expression allows these less powerful nations to mitigate and counteract the overwhelming political power of more traditionally strong nations.[92] The troubling part of this conclusion is the disassociation of using the law to achieve a desired political outcome and political power. It is unclear how deft manipulation of legal issues and concerns to achieve the desired outcome runs in opposition to political power rather than simply being an exercise of political power.

Johnstone puts forward a similar framework for understanding the role of law within situations of high politics, such as the UN Security Council. He suggests that law operates as a form of justificatory discourse among the participating actors.[93] He posits that the reason for this is twofold: first, states cannot avoid the collective judgement of other states and international organs, and public opinion, for their actions, and thus choose to use the framework

87 Koskenniemi, 478.
88 Koskenniemi, 489.
89 Koskenniemi, *The Gentle Civilizer of Nations*, 2.
90 Koskenniemi, 'The Mystery of Legal Obligation', 321–22.
91 Deitelhoff, 'The Discursive Process of Legalization'.
92 Deitelhoff, 55–56.
93 Johnstone, 'Security Council Deliberations: The Power of the Better Argument', 440.

of law to express this in the hope of avoiding negative judgement.[94] Second, they have an inherent interest in maintaining the international law system of justificatory discourse for political decision-making, as they rely upon the predictability and stability that it brings to the international order.[95] On its face, Johnstone's argument appears to be that law is the language of political power; however, it becomes clear that he views it as a method of expressing and justifying political power that is deployed because of its usefulness rather than being mandatory in nature.[96] While Johnstone conceives of law as separate but intertwined with political power, his work provides an invaluable foundation, in conjunction with Koskenniemi's work, to the notion of law as the *lingua franca* of international political power, rather than as the separate restraining entity that they conceive it to be.

By looking at the interaction of legal principles (in particular comity) and international practice, Johnstone notes that international law as a concept is very rarely enforced, but is usually obeyed by states.[97] As an extension of this, he argues that international law is in essence a discursive process of discourse.[98] Continuing this argument, he suggests that within international politics, the use of and reference to law to justify the political actions of states has resulted in a socialisation of international law as a norm of behaviour and discourse within international relations.[99] This socialisation has resulted in law becoming embedded in international political and bureaucratic processes, allowing each of them to operate as a parallel institutional check on the activities of the others.[100]

Stemming from this socialisation of international law as the norm of global political discourse, Johnstone argues that those engaged in international law practice and scholarship form an interpretive community (based on the work of Stanley Fish) for the landscape of international law.[101] This community provides a baseline, normative framework for the interpretation of international legal discourse and instruments.[102] The effect of this is significant but, most importantly—as a result of this socialisation of law as the norm of communicating international political decisions and the interpretive community that it

94 Johnstone, 441.
95 Johnstone, 441.
96 Johnstone, 452.
97 Johnstone, 441.
98 Johnstone, 441.
99 Johnstone, 441–42.
100 Johnstone, 442.
101 Johnstone, 443–44.
102 Johnstone, 443–44.

has created—good arguments can be distinguished from bad arguments readily and easily, forcing states to justify their actions with good legal arguments for the sake of credibility.[103]

Within this landscape of legal discourse, texts are constrained to the cultural assumptions that are used to approach both the text and the context within which it is situated.[104] These constraints on the cultural framework through which legal discourse is read not only colour how the interpretive community understands the text, but are also created through the history of the interpretive community engaging in international legal discourse.[105] Therefore, the work of international legal discourse is the search for an intersubjective understanding of the social and cultural norm in question. It is thus immaterial that the Security Council debates do not constitute a source of law from a black letter perspective. This is because the normative framework of Security Council debates is discussion regarding peace and security through the norm of legal discourse.[106]

Koskenniemi highlights (although does not support) that examining the use of legal norms as a form of communication within the Security Council could be viewed simply as a façade for the political plays of power, ideologies and interests.[107] While Koskenniemi may reject this understanding of the Security Council, Johnstone highlights that whether the use of legal norms is genuine or simply a strategic façade is completely irrelevant when considering the role of law as a cultural and social norm in global politics.[108] The reason for this rejection is that regardless of which intent is brought to the use of legal norms when communicating in global politics, the practice has effect independent of the intent—changing behaviour and culture regardless[109]—with good arguments cementing themselves and creating cultural change, and bad or unsupportable arguments being winnowed away.[110] From this position, Johnstone argues that when examining a macro landscape of discourse that has been used to justify 'high politic' positions, the effect of 'high politics' in each individual instance is irrelevant, as the consistent use of international law-based arguments that

103 Johnstone, 443.
104 Johnstone, 445.
105 Ibid 444–445.
106 Johnstone, 'Security Council Deliberations: The Power of the Better Argument', 456–57.
107 Koskenniemi, 'The Place of Law in Collective Security', 475–76.
108 Johnstone, 'Security Council Deliberations: The Power of the Better Argument', 453.
109 Johnstone, 455.
110 Johnstone, 460; Ingo Venzke, *How Interpretation Makes International Law: On Semantic Change and Normative Twists*, 1st ed (Oxford, United Kingdom: Oxford University Press, 2012), 40.

have been normalised by society creates a pattern of expectation and conduct within the users, regardless of the genuine political motivations behind each individual incident.[111] I have no quarrel with suggestions regarding the relationship between law and power that either Koskenniemi or Johnstone put forward; however, I suggest that these solid foundational notions do not adequately explain the interlinked, co-dependent nature of the relationship—namely, that law is the language of power.

'It's the characteristic of our Western societies that the language of power is law, not magic, religion, or anything else'.[112] Given that evidence suggests it is a characteristic of international law to represent the interests of Western societies predominantly,[113] it makes logical sense that law's relationship to power should follow these Western cultural paradigms. This proposition of law acting as a language of power rather than as power itself has been criticised for de-centring law and in essence expelling it from power relations,[114] suggesting that as a result of this premise, 'law is marginalised'.[115] These criticisms have been succinctly and consistently rebuffed as simplistic and as lacking in nuance,[116] it being noted that to understand the role and effect of law within society, 'it is necessary to de-centre the law from the outset'.[117] This is because '[l]aw, like language, is a social, not a natural product'.[118] While Venzke likens law to language,[119] Reisman notes that the process of international law

111 Johnstone, 'Security Council Deliberations: The Power of the Better Argument', 462–63.

112 Michel Foucault and Colin Gordon, *Power/Knowledge* (Harlow: Pearson Education: Longman, 1980), 201.

113 Glennon, 'Why the Security Council Failed', 21; Koskenniemi, 'The Place of Law in Collective Security', 460–61.

114 Alan Hunt and Gary Wickham, *Foucault and Law : Towards a Sociology of Law as Governance* (London; Boulder, Colo.: Pluto Press, 1994) the expulsion of the law through this premise is a recurring theme throughout this book; Bob Fine, *Democracy and the Rule of Law: Liberal Ideals and Marxist Critiques* (London: Pluto Press, 1984), 200; Paul Q Hirst, *Law, Socialism, and Democracy* (London; Boston: Allen & Unwin, 1986), 49–50; Duncan Kennedy, 'The Stakes of Law, or Hale and Foucault', *Legal Studies Forum* 15, no. 4 (1991): 354; Boaventura de Sousa Santos, *Toward a New Legal Common Sense: Law, Globalization, and Emancipation* (London: Butterworths LexisNexis, 2002), 5–6.

115 Hirst, *Law, Socialism, and Democracy*, 50.

116 Anthony Beck, 'Foucault and Law: The Collapse of Law's Empire', *Oxford Journal of Legal Studies* 16, no. 3 (1996): 489; François Ewald, 'Norms, Discipline, and the Law', *Representations* 30, no. Spring (1990): 158–59; Golder and Fitzpatrick, *Foucault's Law*, 11; Nikolas Rose and Mariana Valverde, 'Governed By Law?', *Social & Legal Studies* 7 (1998): 542.

117 Rose and Valverde, 'Governed By Law?', 545.

118 Venzke, *How Interpretation Makes International Law*, 40.

119 Although elsewhere Venzke acknowledges that international law is a language in its own right; Venzke, 1.

formation is communication and that all communication is political.[120] Consequently, there is a need to cease thinking of these two concepts as separate and in opposition and instead understand them as intertwined, co-dependent and inseparable.

Through the de-centred analysis of law, it is suggested that the law has not been expelled or become insignificant through this framework of approaching the law as the language of power; rather, it has become a more honest expression of its interdependent relationship with other forms of power.[121] The core of this argument is that the law stopped being a blunt weapon of the sovereign used to control society through fear and instead became a pliant instrument used to regulate and express non-legal forms of power that have affected control over modern society.[122] On this basis, it is suggested that with the rise of modernity, the law began to use non-legal forms of power to do its bidding,[123] and became the language for these non-legal forms of power[124]—evidenced most conspicuously by the proliferation of regulatory legislation in society,[125] and of treaty law in an international legal context.[126]

This shift in the way that law works has led to arguments to the effect that in modern society, the law operates in a completely horizontal, self-regulating and reciprocal framework of normalisation,[127] with a top-down parliamentary sovereignty framework of municipal law now being a fiction to ensure society's respect of this regulatory, normalising system.[128] The debate as to whether the law within a municipal context operates on a top-down sovereignty framework or a horizontal reciprocity framework is irrelevant in this instance, as international law most certainly does operate within a horizontal reciprocity

120 W. Michael Reisman, 'International Law-Making: A Process of Communication', *Yale Law School Faculty Scholarship Series* Paper 713 (1981): 105.

121 Beck, 'Foucault and Law', 493; Ewald, 'Norms, Discipline, and the Law', 138; Golder and Fitzpatrick, *Foucault's Law*, 26–27; Rose and Valverde, 'Governed By Law?', 543.

122 Ewald, 'Norms, Discipline, and the Law', 154–55; Golder and Fitzpatrick, *Foucault's Law*, 2 & 34; Rose and Valverde, 'Governed By Law?', 543.

123 Golder and Fitzpatrick, *Foucault's Law*, 24; Rose and Valverde, 'Governed By Law?', 543.

124 Michel Foucault, *The History of Sexuality*, vol. 1 (London: Penguin, 1990), 109; Golder and Fitzpatrick, *Foucault's Law*, 60–61; Rose and Valverde, 'Governed By Law?', 543.

125 Ewald, 'Norms, Discipline, and the Law', 155; Golder and Fitzpatrick, *Foucault's Law*, 64–65, 110–11 & 129; Hunt and Wickham, *Foucault and Law*, 59 & 67.

126 Duncan B. Hollis, 'Defining Treaties', in *The Oxford Guide to Treaties*, ed. Duncan B. Hollis, 1st ed. (Oxford, U.K: Oxford University Press, 2012), 43.

127 Ewald, 'Norms, Discipline, and the Law', 154–55; Foucault, *The History of Sexuality*, 1:144; Golder and Fitzpatrick, *Foucault's Law*, 110–11; Rose and Valverde, 'Governed By Law?', 542.

128 Ewald, 'Norms, Discipline, and the Law', 155.

framework.[129] As with all power relationships within society, horizontal does not mean equal; in all relationships within society, the levels of power that exist within the interaction are necessarily varied, with the end result being a product of the exertion of and resistance to power within that relationship.[130] This phenomenon is also present in international law when considering nation states—even though all states are theoretically sovereign equals,[131] 'sovereign equality may be the founding myth of the international legal order but remains a myth nonetheless'.[132]

The notion of law being the language of power is not a new one; it has existed within other disciplines for some time. Turk explores this notion in relation to sociology when considering the subject matter of terrorism, highlighting the way in which society encourages the notion that political violence in opposition to authority is both crazy and criminal rather than a potentially rational response of the powerless in a conflict situation,[133] thus demonstrating the way in which the language of law is used in politics as a weapon of the powerful.[134] From his analysis of this question, Turk suggests that the two languages of political power are the law and military force each operating with different implications and outcomes.[135] Foucault also raised this concept in relation to sociology on a number of occasions.[136]

As a concept, law being the language of power has been explored in criminology. In relation to the role of psychiatry in law, it has been argued that psychiatry has ingratiated itself into the law, using the language of law and legal process as a way of expressing its power and control over society.[137] Beyond the specifics of psychiatry in criminology, it has been contended more generally that the law and legality are a language used to define social behaviour as

129 Case Concerning the Arrest Warrant of 11 April 2000 (Democratic Republic of Congo v Belgium) (Joint separate opinion of Judges Higgins, Kooijmans and Buergenthal), ICJ Reports (International Court of Justice 2002) paragraph 51.

130 Michel Foucault, *Discipline and Punish : The Birth of the Prison* (London: Allen Lane, 1977), 27.

131 Gerry J. Simpson, *Great Powers and Outlaw States: Unequal Sovereigns in the International Legal Order*, Cambridge Studies in International and Comparative Law (Cambridge, UK; New York, NY: Cambridge University Press, 2004), 5.

132 Chesterman, 'An International Rule of Law?', 357.

133 Austin Turk, 'Sociology of Terrorism', *Annual Review of Sociology* 30 (2004): 274.

134 Turk, 274.

135 Turk, 280.

136 Foucault, *The History of Sexuality*, 1:109; Foucault and Gordon, *Power/Knowledge*, 201.

137 Foucault, *Discipline and Punish*, 21–22; Austin Turk, 'Psychiatry vs. The Law – Therefore?', *Criminologica* 5 (1968 1967): 32–33.

acceptable or not, and to control those without political power.[138] Further, it has been suggested that invoking and applying the law is an inherently political act, an exercise of political power, and that the law and politics are inseparable.[139] This is most succinctly put by Turk when he states:

> It is past time to drop the pretense and dream of consensus and 'the just order', admitting openly that 'justice' is 'rather than an unchanging, real or imagined state of affairs the permanently changing outcome of dialects of power and resistance'.[140]

The premise of law being the language of power has also existed within literary works throughout history. Although *Antigone* is often hailed for and cited as being a perfect example of the debate between positive and natural law theories (which it most certainly is), it is set to the background premise that the law is the expression of power.[141] This premise can be seen within the play, particularly through statements by Antigone,[142] Creon,[143] and Ismene.[144] From this position, Butler argues that black letter law is in fact a process of semiotic symbolism based upon the notion that law is the centre of all things.[145] She suggests that, rather, law is a discourse given force and power in its performative aspects, and that black letter law represents the symbolised ideal of this social norm and broader discourse.[146]

In more modern literature, the theme of law being the language of power is an undercurrent in *The Trial* by Kafka.[147] This theme is set up from the very beginning of the novel when Kafka insinuates that by recognising the legal rights and authority that others have over you, you concede power to those people.[148] This is seen directly in the interaction between K and his wardens at the time of his arrest, where there is an blithe acceptance that the law and

---

138 Foucault, *Discipline and Punish*, 23–24; Austin Turk, *Criminality and the Legal Order* (Chicago: Rand McNally & Company, 1969), 31–32.

139 Rose and Valverde, above n 132, 543; Turk, above n 154, 33.

140 Turk, 'Psychiatry vs. The Law – Therefore?', 34.

141 Judith Butler, *Antigone's Claim: Kinship between Life and Death*, The Wellek Library Lectures (New York: Columbia University Press, 2000), 5 & 9–10.

142 Sophocles, *The Three Theban Plays*, Penguin Classics (Harmondsworth, Middlesex, England; New York, N.Y: Penguin Books, 1984), 60 & 82.

143 Sophocles, 68.

144 Sophocles, 62.

145 Butler, *Antigone's Claim*, 20–21.

146 Butler, 21.

147 Franz Kafka, *The Trial*, trans. Idris Parry (London: Penguin, 2000).

148 Kafka, 2.

power are synonymous and unquestionable.[149] The interactions between K and the court, highlight the inherent power differential between those who have the ability and knowledge to express themselves with the language of legal discourse and those who don't.[150] The interrelationship between law and power is driven home most clearly at the completion of the novel when K is legally executed in a state of ignorance of his crimes as he lacked the language necessary to ever understand the charges laid against him and thus to defend himself.[151] K dies powerless in spite of his apparent affluence simply because he cannot communicate in the language of law.

The concept of needing language to express and exercise power is a core and central theme of *The Reader* by Bernhard Schlink.[152] While this theme plays out through the entire novel it is most apparent in part two when Schlink deals with Hanna's criminal trial.[153] Hanna's illiteracy (and by extension, her inability to communicate in the legal forum) leaves her being described as appearing filled with "confusion and helplessness",[154] having "no sense of context"[155] or "the rules of the game",[156] making it clear that by the end of the trial, she had simply given up.[157] It is suggested that because of these things the trial itself was not a proof of her guilt,[158] but rather an inability to mount any kind of defence through her inability to understand and wield the language necessary for effective communication.[159] The whole middle section of this novel harks back to the premise that the law is about the exercise of power and social control rather than justice, and that the exercise of this power is communicated through the medium of law.

While these examples represent only a limited selection of instances where law has been envisioned as the language of power, they demonstrate that as a lens for understanding discourses of power, the premise is widely accepted. Therefore, the next chapter outlines the materials that will be examined in the course of this book through this lens, and how they will be examined. As noted above, the reason for this examination is to attempt to glean how the

149 Kafka, 5.
150 Kafka, 30–38 & 48.
151 Kafka, 174–78.
152 Bernhard Schlink, *The Reader*, trans. Carol Brown Janeway (New York: Vintage Books, 1998).
153 Schlink, 83–162.
154 Schlink, 108.
155 Schlink, 109.
156 Schlink, 109.
157 Schlink, 135.
158 Schlink, 136.
159 Schlink, 136.

Security Council approaches and defines the concept of 'threat to the peace', how these approaches have developed over time and if there is any consistency in its practice.

3 Conclusion

This chapter has indicated the importance of understanding how the Security Council approaches the question of 'threat to the peace' under Article 39 of the UN Charter. This importance lies in the fact that 'threat to the peace' is a somewhat amorphous and undefined phrase that, when found to exist, opens the door to a myriad of potential consequences—including the use of military force. Numerous attempts have been made to understand this phenomenon, but all have fallen somewhat short. While they form an invaluable starting point for this project, they are ultimately inadequate as a complete methodology because they approach the question through the lens of formal legal analysis. They are restricted in their material scope to the legal instruments that have resulted from a finding of 'threat to the peace' by the Security Council—namely, UN Security Council resolutions. Consequently, none of them have engaged in any analysis of situations where the Security Council has discussed the possibility of a 'threat to the peace' existing, but declined to make such a finding. This renders an incomplete picture of how the Security Council approaches this question.

Following this assessment of the current legal landscape regarding the concept of 'threat to the peace', I have concluded this chapter by outlining the proposed lens through which I explore this same question over the course of this book. That lens does not assume that international law is entirely separate, and separable from, international politics, but rather conceives of the two as co-dependent and intertwined entities; law is the language through which international politics is expressed. The framework of this lens is drawn primarily from the work of Johnstone and Koskenniemi; however, it has also been shown that this lens exists within numerous disciplines outside of law. In the next chapter, I provide an overview of the methodology of critical discourse analysis and how the case studies that are being parsed through this methodology have been selected.

CHAPTER 2

Critical Discourse Analysis and Case Study Selection

1 Exploring 'Threat to the Peace' Through Critical Discourse Analysis

The primary goal of this volume is to determine if there can be any working definition of the phrase 'threat to the peace' through an empirical analysis of the P5's justificatory discourse when they have significantly discussed this question. This will reveal if there is any predictability and consistency of behaviour, understanding and justification within the P5 in relation to the concept of 'threat to the peace'. This is consistent with the primary goals and purposes of legal sociology as a discipline and methodology: to provide insight into and understanding of the law through an empirical study of its practice.[1] This analysis is achieved through a series of case studies where the concept has been debated. These examinations will restrict themselves to the P5 members of the Security Council (France, Russia, China, the UK and the US), as these are the only states certain to have been involved in every relevant case study. Further, because each of these states holds the right of veto,[2] they are in effect 'more equal than others'.[3] The combination of these two factors gives the public justifications and reasonings of these five states greater significance than any other state on this topic.

The most significant criticism of UN Security Council procedure is that substantive decision-making often happens behind closed doors and in secret.[4] While this does create both legitimacy and transparency concerns for the

1 Roger Cotterrell, *Law, Culture and Society: Legal Ideas in the Mirror of Social Theory*, Law, Justice, and Power (Aldershot, England; Burlington, VT: Ashgate Pub. Co, 2006), 130–31; Moshe Hirsch, 'The Sociology of International Economic Law: Sociological Analysis of the Regulation of Regional Agreements in the World Trading System', *European Journal of International Law* 19, no. 2 (2008): 280.

2 'Charter of the United Nations', 1 UNTS XVI (1945) Article 27(3).

3 George Orwell, *Animal Farm*, eBook, EBooks @ Adelaide (Adelaide: The University of Adelaide, 2008), 169.

4 Phil Chan, 'A Keen Observer of the International Rule of Law? International Law in China's Voting Behaviour and Argumentation in the United Nations Security Council', *Leiden Journal of International Law* 26, no. 4 (2013): 875–76; Martii Koskenniemi, 'The Place of Law in Collective Security', *Michigan Journal of International Law* 17 (1996): 485.

 DOI:10.1163/9789004391420_004

Security Council,[5] it has no material effect upon the project at hand. This is because regardless of what happens in those closed-door meetings where agreements and decisions are reached, all the states involved must publicly justify their decisions,[6] and the language of this justificatory discourse is the law (as demonstrated in Chapter 1).[7] The venue of these public justifications for political action, through the medium of law, is the Security Council meetings on any given issue.

These Security Council meetings thus become a rich source of qualitative data for examining how states have approached this question. While Security Council meetings and the concept of 'threat to the peace' may be grounded in politics,[8] as indicated above, the normative language of these politics is international law; thus, a large-scale historical analysis of this empirical data may provide significant insight into the P5's behaviour and their attitudes towards, and understanding of, Article 39.[9] Consequently, I explore this issue through a series of case studies looking at public justifications in the Security Council meeting transcripts of the P5 members where the question of 'threat to the peace' has been significantly considered. The purpose of each individual case study is to parse how each P5 member justified their position in relation to 'threat to the peace' when the question was significantly discussed. This provides a series of case studies all addressing the same question with the same actors, but with vastly different contexts, creating an iterative body of work for the meta-synthesis at the end. While it might be possible to simply tabulate the results of this analysis and subsequent coding, one of the greatest risks of legal sociology is bias in analysis—therefore, the analysis must be available for others to scrutinise as an assurance that no unconscious bias has skewed results.[10] Further, for a meta-synthesis to be successful, there must be sufficient volume of qualitative case studies upon which to draw.[11] As noted by Johnstone

5 Chan, 'A Keen Observer of the International Rule of Law?', 875–76; Koskenniemi, 'The Place of Law in Collective Security', 485.

6 Ian Johnstone, 'Security Council Deliberations: The Power of the Better Argument', *European Journal of International Law* 14, no. 3 (2003): 453–54.

7 Johnstone, 454–55.

8 Johnstone, 452; Inger Österdahl, *Threat to the Peace: The Interpretation by the Security Council of Article 39 of the UN Charter* (Uppsala: Iustus, 1998), 87.

9 Michael J. Glennon, 'Why the Security Council Failed', *Foreign Affairs* 82 (2003): 32; Österdahl, *Threat to the Peace*, 87.

10 Roger Cotterrell, *The Sociology of Law: An Introduction*, 2nd ed (London: Butterworths, 1992), 13–15.

11 Nicky Britten et al., 'Using Meta Ethnography to Synthesise Qualitative Research: A Worked Example', *Journal of Health Services Research and Policy* 7, no. 4 (October 2002): 210; Rona Campbell et al., 'Evaluating Meta-Ethnography: A Synthesis of Qualitative

above, this sort of macro-analysis of the justificatory discourse of situations influenced individually by 'high politicking' does not require a consideration of the political motives involved in each situation. This is because the consistent use of legal arguments to justify these political motivations creates a body of discourse grounded in acceptable argument, which in turn creates an expectation on the state in relation to its future behaviour.[12] In short, by taking the premise that law is the language of power and thus that international law is the *lingua franca* of diplomacy, we can subject the meeting statements regarding the nature of 'threat to the peace' to a legal sociology-based discourse analysis, which will allow the phrase 'threat to the peace' to be legally defined through the practice of the P5, something that doctrinal legal analysis has been unable to achieve.

A secondary benefit of this examination of Security Council meeting transcripts is that it has the potential to provide insight into how the P5 approach various issues of international law. Because these states are using the language of law to publicly justify their decisions, where contentious issues of international law arise, these statements will allow for further understanding of the approach being taken regarding the legal issue in question. An example of how this has already played out is in relation to interpreting the legality of third-party transfers of captured piracy suspects under Article 105 of the *United Nations Convention on the Law of the Sea*.[13] Such transfers were considered legally contentious until there was consistent UN Security Council praise for and endorsement of the practice.[14] In the same manner, examining the P5's legal discourse will facilitate a deeper understanding of how they conduct the practice of international law. Indeed, Hirch notes that '[s]ociological analysis may engender new insights into long-term processes of international law'.[15]

The difficulty with examining Security Council meeting transcripts effectively is providing sufficient context to the meetings and statements without distorting the content with hindsight and commentary. To ensure that the

---

Research on Lay Experiences of Diabetes and Diabetes Care', *Social Science & Medicine* 56 (2003): 672; Denis Walsh and Soo Downe, 'Meta-Synthesis Method for Qualitative Research: A Literature Review', *Journal of Advanced Nursing* 50, no. 2 (2005): 205.

12 Johnstone, 'Security Council Deliberations: The Power of the Better Argument', 460–63.

13 'United Nations Convention on the Law of the Sea', 1833 UNTS 3 (1982) Article 105.

14 'Resolution 1950 (2010)', S/RES/1950 (2010) UN Security Council (2010) Preamble; 'Resolution 2015 (2011)', S/RES/2015 (2011) UN Security Council (2011) Preamble; 'Resolution 2020 (2011)', S/RES/2020 (2011) UN Security Council (2011) Preamble; Paige, Tamsin Phillipa, 'The Impact and Effectiveness of UNCLOS on Counter-Piracy Operations', *Journal of Conflict and Security Law* 22, no. 1 (2017): 101, https://doi.org/10.1093/jcsl/krv028.

15 Moshe Hirsch, 'The Sociology of Interntional Law: Invitation to Study International Rules in Their Social Context', *University of Toronto Law Journal* 55, no. 4 (2005): 893.

factual context informing the analysis of these public justificatory statements is as free from bias as possible, I restrict the source material to the documents on public record as being used by all the members of the Security Council in each situation. This is important because, as noted above, one of greatest weaknesses of critical studies is the presence of unconscious or structural biases within studies and subsequent analysis, something that this decision (and the decision to include all the case study analysis rather than simply tabulate the results) is designed to mitigate. More often than not, this source material comprises the statements made within meetings by the Secretary-General or similar individuals reporting on the situation in question to the Security Council; however, on occasions, it also includes reports by the Secretary-General in relation to the situation in question. By restricting the factual source material to these documents, analysis of the meetings can be conducted with a similar factual matrix to the one that existed at the time of the debate, and thus be distanced from interpretive commentary on each of the decisions.

The analysis of the meetings themselves through the P5's statements focuses solely on the question of 'threat to the peace'. In each circumstance where this question is being examined, only those statements that clearly bear no relation to the question of 'threat to the peace' are excluded. If a statement cannot be excluded from the analysis because it is not self-evidently unrelated to the question of 'threat to the peace', then it is included until its relevance or irrelevance can be determined and explained. This research project is not so much concerned with what the Security Council did after finding a 'threat to the peace', but rather the process and reasoning by which that decision was made. Therefore, it is not material to this research project if the situation has been found to constitute a 'threat to the peace' but the Security Council has also chosen to take no action; the action that is taken (or not taken) after an Article 39 finding is beyond the scope of this volume. The results of the analysis and the coding that has been done for the meta-synthesis are restated and summarised at the end of each case study, providing a clear picture of how each P5 member approached and defined the concept of 'threat to the peace' (and as a secondary benefit, how they understood and conceptualised various concepts of international law).

This framework of text and discourse is analysed through critical discourse analysis methodology, in particular through the discourse-historical approach, which is a subset of critical discourse analysis.[16] The main difference between

16 Ruth Wodak and Michael Meyer, 'Critical Discourse Analysis: History, Agenda, Theory and Methodology', in *Methods of Critical Discourse Analysis*, ed. Ruth Wodak and Michael Meyer, 2nd ed (London; Thousand Oaks [Calif.]: SAGE, 2009), 27–31.

discourse-historical analysis and other methods of critical discourse analysis is the subject matter and primary materials being studied. While most forms of critical discourse analysis rely on interviews, observations and other forms of ethnography, allowing them to be micro or macro in scope, discourse-historical analysis relies on primary documents on public record (in this case, Security Council meeting transcripts) and is macro in nature and scope.[17] This methodology finds its foundation in the work of Foucault and Habermas regarding understandings of what constitutes discourse,[18] and the relationship between power and knowledge.[19] An important aspect of discourse analysis is to understand the difference between a text and the discourse within which it exists, a text being a single event within a broader discourse framework.[20] For example, the transcript of the speech by itself is a text, but when this text is placed with the broader context in which it was given, then that larger picture becomes a discourse.[21] In this project, the meeting transcripts are the texts, and they are given context by the Secretary-General's reports and statements, both existing within the broader discourse of legal expression and the institution of the Security Council.

While this approach 'leads to an understanding of law in terms of institutional practices and social processes rather than a system of rules, principles, judgement and doctrines',[22] the techniques used to achieve this are fundamentally the same as those used for black letter legal analysis. The primary difference is that black letter legal analysis is concerned with understanding 'mere' legal instruments such as treaties and judgements;[23] by contrast, discourse analysis approach does not restricted itself to these instruments (and it has been shown above that such a restriction is inappropriate for this kind of research project), and can be used to explore the legal debates at play behind the creation of the legal instruments of black letter law (in this case, UN Security Council resolutions).

17 Wodak and Meyer, 27; Martin Reisigl and Ruth Wodak, 'The Discourse-Historical Approach (DHA)', in *Methods of Critical Discourse Analysis*, ed. Ruth Wodak and Michael Meyer, 2nd ed (London; Thousand Oaks [Calif.]: SAGE, 2009), 89.

18 Reisigl and Wodak, 'The Discourse-Historical Approach (DHA)', 2–3.

19 Jan Blommaert and Chris Bulcaen, 'Critical Discourse Analysis', *Annual Review of Anthropology* 29 (2000): 451–52.

20 Reisigl and Wodak, 'The Discourse-Historical Approach (DHA)', 89–90.

21 Reisigl and Wodak, 89–90.

22 Reza Banakar, 'Can Legal Sociology Account for the Normativity of Law?', *University of Westminster School of Law Research Paper No.13-03*, 23, accessed 5 June 2014, http://papers.ssrn.com/sol3/papers.cfm?abstract_id=2229241.

23 'Statute of the International Court of Justice', 1 UNTS 993 (1945) Article 38(1).

The fundamental sameness of doctrinal legal analysis methodology and discourse analysis methodology resides in how they examine these documents. Both of these methodologies take the statements being made in the relevant text, place it within the context in which the statement existed and then seek to understand the meaning of those statements. For doctrinal legal analysis, this means taking the text of the legal instrument, creating context through understanding the object and purposes of the treaty or the facts of the case being argued and extrapolating legal meaning through this process.[24] Discourse analysis is no different in how it achieves this outcome;[25] however, it is not restrained to formal legal instruments.[26] It is with this methodological framework that I parse the qualitative data contained within the meeting transcripts and the other documents used to place them within their historical context.

2 How Case Study Selection Occurred

At its core, this book examines how the peak body of the UN—the body that can authorise the use of armed force—decides to address the weakness and folly of humanity and the suffering that stems from these failures. This section of the book thus outlines the process by which I selected case studies for inclusion within the project. I also highlight the materials that were considered within the investigation's scope, and the reason for their selection. Following the outline of the case study selection process, I then provide an overview of the process that was used to conduct each individual case study (beyond the methodology outlined above). This provides a broad perspective of how the case studies were chosen, the content included within each case study, the structure of all the case studies and the recurring themes within the case studies that require explanation, but that are not necessarily pertinent to the meta-synthesis at the end of the book.

Given the ongoing work of the Security Council, the first step in case study selection was determining a cut-off date for the project. As the project commenced in January 2014, the cut-off date for case studies was set at the end of the calendar year 2013 so that all the material within the investigation's scope would be complete, even if certain situations were ongoing. During the period

24 H.L.A. Hart, *The Concept of Law* (New York: Oxford University Press, 1972), 125–30.

25 Blommaert and Bulcaen, 'Critical Discourse Analysis', 448–49.

26 Teun A. Van Dijk, 'Critical Discourse Analysis', in *Handbook of Discourse Analysis*, ed. D. Tannen, D. Schiffrin, and H. Hamilton, Second Edition (Oxford: Blackwell, 2013), 353.

being studied (1946–2013), the Security Council conducted 7,091 meetings.[27] The vast amount of data contained within those meetings required that a method of narrowing down the possible case studies was necessary, as manually sifting through every meeting to determine its relevance was not a feasible option.

The *Repertoire of the Practice of the Security Council* served as the starting point for narrowing the data to be used within the case studies. This is possible because the *Repertoire of the Practice of the Security Council* routinely releases reports on Security Council action; included within these reports are situations where the Security Council engaged in significant, substantial or constitutive debates around the concept of 'threat to the peace'.[28] Examining these reports highlighted 47 possible case studies (27 positive of a finding of threat and 20

27 United Nations, 'Security Council Meeting Records: Meetings Conducted by the Security Council in 2013 (in Reverse Chronological Order)', 17 March 2016, http://www.un.org/en/sc/meetings/records/2013.shtml.

28 Repertoire of the Practice of the Security Council, 'Chapter XI: Considerations of Chapter VII the Charter (1946–51)'; Repertoire of the Practice of the Security Council, 'Chapter XI: Considerations of Chapter VII the Charter (1952–55)'; Repertoire of the Practice of the Security Council, 'Chapter XI: Considerations of Chapter VII the Charter (1956–58)'; Repertoire of the Practice of the Security Council, 'Chapter XI: Considerations of Chapter VII the Charter (1959–63)'; Repertoire of the Practice of the Security Council, 'Chapter XI: Considerations of Chapter VII the Charter (1964–65)'; Repertoire of the Practice of the Security Council, 'Chapter XI: Considerations of Chapter VII the Charter (1966–68)'; Repertoire of the Practice of the Security Council, 'Chapter XI: Considerations of Chapter VII the Charter (1969–71)'; Repertoire of the Practice of the Security Council, 'Chapter XI: Considerations of Chapter VII the Charter (1972–74)'; Repertoire of the Practice of the Security Council, 'Chapter XI: Considerations of Chapter VII the Charter (1975–80)'; Repertoire of the Practice of the Security Council, 'Chapter XI: Considerations of Chapter VII the Charter (1981–84)'; Repertoire of the Practice of the Security Council, 'Chapter XI: Considerations of Chapter VII the Charter (1985–88)'; Repertoire of the Practice of the Security Council, 'Chapter XI: Considerations of Chapter VII the Charter (1989–92)'; Repertoire of the Practice of the Security Council, 'Chapter XI: Considerations of Chapter VII the Charter (1993–95)'; Repertoire of the Practice of the Security Council, 'Chapter XI: Considerations of Chapter VII the Charter (1996–99)'; Repertoire of the Practice of the Security Council, 'Chapter XI: Considerations of Chapter VII the Charter (2000–03)'; Repertoire of the Practice of the Security Council, 'Chapter XI: Considerations of Chapter VII the Charter (2004–07)'; Repertoire of the Practice of the Security Council, '16th Supplement 2008–2009 Part VII: Actions with Respect to Threats to the Peace, Breaches of the Peace, and Acts of Aggression (Chapter VII of the Charter)'; Repertoire of the Practice of the Security Council, '17th Supplement 2010–2011 Part VII: Actions with Respect to Threats to the Peace, Breaches of the Peace, and Acts of Aggression (Chapter VII of the Charter)'; Repertoire of the Practice of the Security Council, '18th Supplement 2012–2013 Part VII: Actions with Respect to Threats to the Peace, Breaches of the Peace, and Acts of Aggression (Chapter VII of the Charter)'.

negative in relation to the existence of a threat)[29] within the timeframe. Of these potential case studies, four were immediately removed from the list: Somalia (1992), Burundi (early 1990s) and September 11, 2001, as these discussions were primarily conducted by states other than the P5 or because the substantive discussion occurred outside the materials being used within this project. Southern Rhodesia was also excluded because the formative debates around finding a 'threat to the peace' took place in conjunction with the Chapter VI resolution, unduly affecting the later justifications for the finding under Article 39,[30] which is the focus of this project. The table of the potential case studies can be found in the Annex at end of the book, which shows the large variety and historical variance of the subject matter.

With a list of potential case studies and relevant meeting transcripts narrowed through this process, I then set out to define the scope of the enquiry in each case study. To provide a defined scope for the context in which each set of debates occurred, I restricted the materials that could be used to provide factual context for the debates to those materials available to each Security Council member, as well as to the public at large. This meant that the factual context of each case study was provided by reports associated with Security Council debate and the oral briefings that had occurred within the debates themselves. This restricted the volume of data available on the context of each situation to a manageable level, while also ensuring that the used data were uniformly available to each of the P5 when they were making their decisions. This selection also proffers contextual data that is as free from national bias as possible. The P5's justificatory discourse was, likewise, restricted to the statements made in Security Council meetings and publicly available within the transcripts. This limitation ensured that the materials analysed were primary sources, and that all statements were being delivered to the same official audience: the rest of the Security Council, UN member states and the Secretariat.

Case studies were selected in a manner designed to provide a large cross-section of era and issues to provide insight into whether the P5's approaches to the concept of 'threat to the peace' had any pattern or predictability across these dimensions. In line with this approach, two of the case studies (weapons of mass destruction (WMD) non-proliferation, and piracy) combined multiple

29 A positive decision being one where the Security Council made a determination of 'threat to the peace' under Chapter VII, and a negative decision being one where the situation was not found to warrant Chapter VII action as a result of a 'threat to the peace'.

30 'Resolution 217 (1965)', S/RES/217 (1965) UN Security Council (1965); 'Resolution 232 (1966)', S/RES/232 (1966) UN Security Council (1966); See also for how the South Rhodesia decision was exceptional in nature and not reflective of Security Council practice: Österdahl, *Threat to the Peace*, 43–45.

situations that met the case study criteria because of the recurring similarities in theme and facts involved. Case studies were also selected to provide a balance between positive and negative decisions. Case studies continued until the point of conceptual saturation had occurred within the data.[31] At this point there were 22 case studies, addressing 26 of the identified situations. All case studies were organised chronologically, as this allowed for a stable and coherent structure of analysis to be maintained.

Each case study follows the same structural pattern. First, I provide an overview of why the case study is relevant to the overall project of testing the hypothesis that the P5's approaches to the concept of 'threat to the peace' in Article 39 of the Charter lack any consistency or pattern. Second, I outline the context in which the debates took place—this was usually derived from reports and oral briefings from the Secretariat, although, on occasion, had to be gleaned from the statements of the parties involved. Finally, the justificatory discourse of the P5 in relation to the situation is presented; this represents a condensed overview of how each of the individual P5 states justified their position in relation to the situation and whether it constituted a 'threat to the peace' under Article 39 of the Charter. The discourse analysis of these justifications considers all the reasoning, methods and tone the P5 used, as all these factors assist in understanding how the P5 approach and define the concept of 'threat to the peace'. The coding of these factors for the meta-synthesis is summarised at the end of each case study and tabulated in the Annex at the back of the book. It is important to note that the justificatory discourse only addresses those statements made within the Security Council and does not reflect positions or statements made in other venues. This is because this book addresses how the P5 justifies its determinations and assessments in the Security Council when dealing with the concept of 'threat to the peace' under Article 39; it does not address how the P5 states respond to the situation generally. Any such interrogations are welcome and valuable, but beyond the scope of this investigation.

Two recurring themes within the case studies must be clarified before the case studies themselves are presented. First, any reference to any P5 member's tone of speech is given on the basis of an internal comparison with the other P5 members and not based upon any external marker. In this manner, it must

31 See generally: Barney G. Glaser and Anselm L. Strauss, *The Discovery of Grounded Theory: Strategies for Qualitative Research* (New Brunswick: Aldine, 1967), 62–71; Mark Mason, 'Sample Size and Saturation in PhD Studies Using Qualitative Interviews', *Forum: Qualitative Social Research* 11, no. 3 (2010), http://www.qualitative-research.net/index.php/fqs/article/view/1428/3027.

be acknowledged that there is an element of subjectivity in this assessment and the description is entirely internally referential. Second, each member of the P5 regularly makes references to the right of self-determination found in the UN Charter. In making these arguments, they appear to be addressing not only non-self-governing people's postcolonial right of independence, but also Crawford's second interpretation of the right of self-determination—that it is an ongoing right of all states to determine their government free from interference from external forces—as an extension of the right of the non-interference in domestic affairs.[32]

Finally, as already noted, to facilitate an understanding of the approaches the P5 have taken over time in relation to this concept, the case studies are presented in chronological order. Where there is a time overlap between two case studies, the case study that was debated first in the Security Council appears before the latter. In line with this theme, the Soviet Union and its successor state, the Russian Federation, are simply referred to in this book as Russia. Similarly, Imperial China and Communist China are simply referred to as China. This is to provide a continuity of writing and reference throughout the project. While the effect of the governmental changes in Russia have been considered in their meta-synthesis chapter, there is insufficient data existed to track what, if any, effect the change from Imperial to Communist China had on the Chinese approach and definition of 'threat to the peace'.

32 James Crawford, *The Creation of States in International Law*, 2nd ed (Oxford: New York: Clarendon Press; Oxford University Press, 2006), 126.

PART 2

Case Studies

CHAPTER 3

Spain 1946 (Resolutions 4 (1946), 7 (1946) and 10 (1946))

1 Relevance to the Overall Project

The situation in Spain in 1946—the continued existence of the fascist regime under General Franco—represents the first occasion where the Security Council considered the meaning of 'threat to the peace' under Article 39 of the Charter. In this situation, a draft resolution brought under Articles 39 and 41 was defeated through insufficient votes (including votes against from China, the UK and the US—although these were not considered vetoes, as the resolution did not meet the required threshold to pass).[1] The *Repertoire of Practice of the Security Council* noted a significant discussion, particularly in meetings 34 and 46, on this issue and opted to include the fact-finding Sub-Committee's recommendation that the situation did not meet the threshold for action under Article 39.[2] The debate centred predominantly around the differences between Articles 34 and 39, and the point at which the Security Council was authorised to overrule Article 2(7) to fulfil its mandate for maintaining international peace and security.

2 Context of the Debates

The vast bulk of the context to the debates and statements on this situation was generated by the initial statements on the issue by Poland (which brought the matter before the Security Council), which drew heavily upon 'The White Book issued on 4 March 1946 by the State Department of the United States of America under the title "The Spanish Government and the Axis: Official German documents"'.[3] Using this source, Poland outlined the rise of the Franco regime in Spain with the support of the Axis powers, purportedly against the

1 Dag Hammarskjöld Library, 'Security Council – Veto List', Dag Hammarskjöld Library Research Guides, 19 August 2018, http://research.un.org/en/docs/sc/quick/veto.

2 Repertoire of the Practice of the Security Council, 'Chapter XI: Considerations of Chapter VII the Charter (1946–51)' (United Nations), 424–26.

3 United Nations Security Council, 'Security Council, First Year: 34th Meeting (S/PV.34)' (United Nations, 17 April 1946), 157–59.

 | DOI:10.1163/9789004391420_005

will of the Spanish people, prior to World War II.[4] Poland then outlined Spanish support for the Axis powers during World War II, commencing in August 1940.[5] With this background established, Poland tabled intelligence documents showing military activity by the Franco regime in the Pyrenees along the French border.[6] On the basis of this history (and the German use of Spanish industry to circumvent the Treaty of Versailles military construction bans)[7] and current activities, Poland requested the Security Council determine that the existence of the Franco regime constituted a 'threat to the peace' and that all UN members should sever diplomatic ties with Spain.[8] The Security Council formed a fact-finding sub-committee to investigate whether the situation indeed constituted a 'threat to the peace',[9] and their factual situation reports were consistent with the Polish statements.[10] The Sub-Committee found that although the Franco regime constituted a 'potential menace to international peace and security',[11] it failed to meet the threshold of 'threat to the peace'.[12] On the basis of the recommendations from the fact-finding mission, the draft resolution for Article 39 and 41 action against Spain failed to pass by a vote of seven against to four in favour (with China, the UK and the US voting against).[13]

3 Justificatory Discourse of the P5

The primary differences in the P5's justificatory discourse hinged on whether the concept of 'threat to the peace' could be grounded in political ideology, or if it was a question of factual conduct. Russia and France argued that a government's political ideology could, with sufficient grounds, lead to the existence

4 United Nations Security Council, 155–56.
5 United Nations Security Council, 157–59.
6 United Nations Security Council, 160.
7 United Nations Security Council, 163–65.
8 United Nations Security Council, 160–61.
9 'Resolution 4 (1946)', S/RES/4 (1946) UN Security Council (1946).
10 United Nations Security Council, 'The Report of the Sub-Committee on the Spanish Question Appointed by the Security Council on 29 April 1946' (United Nations, 1 June 1946); United Nations Security Council, 'Factual Findings Concerning the Spanish Situation: Supplementary Memorandum to the Report of the Sub-Committee Appointed by the Security Council on 29 April 1946' (United Nations, 1 June 1946).
11 United Nations Security Council, 'The Report of the Sub-Committee on the Spanish Question Appointed by the Security Council on 29 April 1946', para. 30.
12 United Nations Security Council, 'Security Council, First Year: 44th Meeting (S/PV.44)' (United Nations, 6 June 1946), 315.
13 United Nations Security Council, 'Security Council, First Year: 48th Meeting (S/PV.48)' (United Nations, 24 June 1946), 388.

of a 'threat to the peace' under Article 39. By contrast, China, the UK and the US argued that Article 2(7) meant that the question of governance of a state was beyond the scope of the Security Council's mandate and that 'threat to the peace' was a question of fact. These disagreements led to debate about the differences between Articles 34 and 39; it was generally agreed that the difference was one of threshold and not of imminence.

Russia made its conclusions very clear from the outset, stating that it was an indisputable fact that the Franco regime had come into being with the backing of fascist Germany and Italy; because of this, the regime's very existence in Spain constituted a threat to international peace and security.[14] Russia was swift to point out the Spanish alliance with the Axis powers through World War II as further justification for their position, stating: 'The Spanish soldiers sent by Franco to the Eastern Front were not sent there for winter sports, the more so because it is said they are indifferent skiers'.[15] They continued to argue that the existence of a fascist government in the wake of World War II ran in complete opposition to the principals of the UN and everything for which the Allied powers had fought in the war.[16] Their justificatory assertion that the existence of a fascist government was self-evidently a 'threat to the peace' occurred a number of times,[17] and is perhaps best summed up in the following statement:

> Peace-loving humanity will not understand a refusal on the part of the Security Council to take decisive measures to prevent the hydra of fascism, which has been decapitated a number of times by the United Nations, from rearing another head elsewhere.[18]

Regarding the question of non intervention in the domestic affairs of states, Russia argued that this did not apply to the Security Council when considering a 'threat to the peace'.[19] Further, they contended that the price of

14 United Nations Security Council, 'Security Council, First Year: 35th Meeting (S/PV.35)' (United Nations, 18 April 1946), 187.

15 United Nations Security Council, 188–89.

16 United Nations Security Council, 187.

17 United Nations Security Council, 'Security Council, First Year: 37th Meeting (S/PV.37)' (United Nations, 25 April 1946), 219–21; United Nations Security Council, 'Security Council, First Year: 39th Meeting (S/PV.39)' (United Nations, 29 April 1946), 242–43; United Nations Security Council, 'Security Council, First Year: 45th Meeting (S/PV.45)' (United Nations, 13 June 1946), 337; United Nations Security Council, '48th Meeting', 395.

18 United Nations Security Council, '35th Meeting', 193.

19 United Nations Security Council, 185.

non-intervention against fascism was all too well known: 'we all know now the price of this policy of non-intervention in respect of fascist states. It costs mountains of corpses and rivers of blood'.[20] This strong rhetoric continued when Russia pointed out that Stalin had warned the world about the threat of fascism prior to the outbreak of World War II and that the Allied powers had failed to heed his warnings.[21] Further, they argued:

> [The United Nations] should eradicate the last remnants of fascist regimes to deliver humanity from the fascist scourge, although at the moment some of us do not regard it as too dangerous at first sight. Nevertheless, as we see it, some of us are now urging the necessity of a policy of non-intervention with regard to fascism.[22]

In response to the Sub-Committee's recommendation for action under Article 34 and Chapter VI, Russia contended that the Sub-Committee's characterisation of the Franco regime in Spain as a potential threat created an overly narrow and erroneous interpretation of Article 39.[23] Russia asserted that distinguishing threat from potential threat lacked logic and led to incorrect conclusions, diminishing the Security Council's mandate.[24] They stated that '[t]he outcome is that a real threat to peace would only exist if fascist Spain took practical action of a military nature. But this would not be merely a threat to peace; it would be an act of aggression'.[25] Russia argued that the result of the Security Council's failure to act was the continued denial of Spain's democratic rights and freedoms.[26] When interrogated about the costs of a civil war to the Spanish people that might result from Security Council action, Russia stated, with

20 United Nations Security Council, 186.

21 'I want to recall to your attention that long before the Second World War, the Government of the USSR and Generalissimo Stalin warned the peoples and Governments of the world of the danger to the peace-loving countries of the development of fascism ... Unfortunately its warnings were not heeded by the Governments of certain States at the time'. United Nations Security Council, 191.

22 United Nations Security Council, 192.

23 United Nations Security Council, '45th Meeting', 337.

24 United Nations Security Council, 337.

25 United Nations Security Council, 337.

26 'It is the task of the United Nations to remove such a source of danger to international security as the existing fascist regime in Spain, at the same time help the people of Spain and the Spanish democratic forces to regain democratic freedoms which have been taken from them'. United Nations Security Council, '37th Meeting', 223.

reference to the American Civil War, that sometimes civil wars 'were not so bad after all'.[27]

France began by pointing out that its position on the current situation regarding the Franco regime had been known for some time: 'The position is that the continuation of the situation existing in Spain constitutes a threat to international peace and security'.[28] They argued that the continued existence of a fascist government was self-evidently a threat to international peace and security, given that 'the major aims unceasingly proclaimed by all United Nations leaders was to remove the Nazi and Fascist governments responsible for the world catastrophe'.[29]

On the question of non-interference in the domestic affairs of states, France argued that the Franco regime's existence in Spain constituted a violation of Article 2(7) by Germany and Italy and as a result continued to be a violation of Article 2(6) in relation to the Spanish people.[30] As to the question of non-intervention generally, France stated the following: 'Where did this policy take us? It led simply to the hazardous adventure in which world freedom and civilisation came very close to destruction. I hope we shall not readily forget this experience'.[31] When considering the Sub-Committee's recommendation for actions under Article 34 and Chapter VI, France argued that the Sub-Committee erroneously suggested that the difference between Articles 34 and 39 was one of imminence in relation to the threat, whereas their (correct) interpretation was one of gravity of the threat, because imminence as the major determining factor would often lead to a situation where action would be too late (specific reference was made to the Nazi forces and World War II in this context).[32] They particularly found the Sub-Committee's recommendation baffling, summarising that '[t]here is a threat which is not yet an actual threat, that is to say, which has not yet been translated to act of aggression but is a potential threat'.[33]

China was relatively silent on the question of Spain, only weighing in on two separate occasions throughout the entirety of the debates. Early in the debates, they stated that until the Security Council was satisfied that the facts surrounding the Franco regime (which it considered legitimate) constituted a 'threat to

27 United Nations Security Council, 222.

28 United Nations Security Council, '34th Meeting', 167–68.

29 United Nations Security Council, 168.

30 United Nations Security Council, 169.

31 United Nations Security Council, 'Security Council, First Year: 46th Meeting (S/PV.46)' (United Nations, 17 June 1946), 358.

32 United Nations Security Council, '44th Meeting', 322.

33 United Nations Security Council, '46th Meeting', 359.

the peace', it should not resort to any sort of collective action.[34] The other instance when they weighed in was in response to the defeated draft resolution calling for Chapter VII action. In this instance, they simply stated that a finding of 'threat to the peace' was a question of fact, and the Sub-Committee did not find enough evidence to warrant a Chapter VII declaration.[35] In accordance with this, they could not support a resolution demanding the severance of diplomatic relations with Spain, as this was a Chapter VII enforcement mechanism.[36]

The UK argued consistently that a determination under Article 39 was a question of fact and that in this situation of the Franco regime in Spain, the facts did not support a finding of 'threat to the peace'. Initially, their arguments were that the facts presented were grounded wholly in Spain's conduct before and during World War II,[37] which would not accurately reflect the facts since the end of the war. After the Sub-Committee presented its fact-finding reports, the UK contended that the factual scenario did not meet the gravity threshold required for an Article 39 determination by the Security Council,[38] and that Article 34 existed specifically for situations such as this, where attention was warranted but the situation was not grave enough for Chapter VII action. They reached this conclusion on the basis that the phrase 'likely to endanger' is a much lower threshold than the word 'threat'.[39] In response to claims that they were being legally pedantic, the UK made the following statement:

> I know it may be said that these are legal quibbles, but I cannot accept that. It seems to me to be of prime importance to define exactly the scope and powers of the United Nations in matters of this kind. We must base our actions on the Charter, and it would be tragic if the principal victim in this case was to be the Charter itself. No doubt it is true that in the course of time the Charter will have to be interpreted in the light of the procedure followed in various particular cases. The Charter cannot be so worded as to cover every conceivable situation in cases which may arise in the future. But in giving application to the various articles of the Charter, it seems to me most important that we should be on extremely solid ground.[40]

34 United Nations Security Council, '35th Meeting', 198–99.
35 United Nations Security Council, '48th Meeting', 387.
36 United Nations Security Council, 387.
37 United Nations Security Council, '35th Meeting', 182.
38 United Nations Security Council, '46th Meeting', 346.
39 United Nations Security Council, 346.
40 United Nations Security Council, 347.

Following on from this statement, and in light of constant disagreements over the interpretation of Articles 34 and 39, the UK suggested that the Security Council request an advisory opinion from the ICJ on these Articles' meaning and difference.[41] Throughout the debate, the UK consistently pointed out that Article 2(7) prevented them from taking action against the fascist regime in Spain on ideological grounds in the absence of a factually determined threat, no matter how distasteful they found the government.[42] Their reason for this was that international law did not prescribe a form of government to states and that the nature of the government of 'any given country is indisputably a matter of domestic jurisdiction'.[43]

The US appeared quite taciturn in relation to the question of Spain, and made its position on the Franco regime very clear at the commencement of the debates:

> My government has two broad objectives with regard to the situation in Spain. The first is that the Franco regime and its trappings and affiliated organisations, such as the Falange, be removed from power by the Spanish people at the earliest possible moment in order that Spain may resume its rightful place in the family of nations. Our second objective is, and I am sure this is also the earnest desire of every one of us here and of every Government of the United Nations, that this change in regime in Spain be accomplished by peaceful means and that the Spanish people be spared the horrors of a resumption of civil conflict, which would almost certainly have serious international repercussions.[44]

Beyond this broad statement regarding the US's ideological position, their only other statement was that an Article 39 determination was a question of fact and that their own internal intelligence did not provide evidence that such a threat existed.[45] It can be implied from their vote against the resolution imposing Chapter VII measures against the Franco regime in Spain that they agreed

41 United Nations Security Council, 347–48.

42 United Nations Security Council, '35th Meeting', 181; 'I must say that my government has grave doubts, indeed as to the judicial right of the Security Council to intervene in the internal affairs of a country unless there is a clear threat to the maintenance of international peace and security'. United Nations Security Council, '46th Meeting', 344–45.

43 United Nations Security Council, '35th Meeting', 181.

44 United Nations Security Council, '34th Meeting', 178.

45 United Nations Security Council, '37th Meeting', 217.

with the fact-finding Sub-Committee's recommendations that the facts did not meet the threshold required for an Article 39 determination.[46]

4 Summary of Coding

This case study had France and Russia support a finding of 'threat to the peace', with China, the US and the UK opposing such a finding. France supported the finding on the basis that the Franco regime stripped the Spanish people of their right of self-determination, that ideology can constitute a 'threat to the peace', that the situation was sufficiently grave that Article 2(7) was irrelevant to the facts. Russia's support was grounded in the defence of democracy, the notion that ideology can constitute a 'threat to the peace', that 'threat to the peace' was a question of law and that Article 2(7) was irrelevant on the facts. Chinese opposition to a finding of 'threat to the peace' was grounded in the notion that the situation was not sufficiently grave, that 'threat to the peace' was a question of fact, that Security Council actions would violate Spanish rights to self-determination and that the fact-finding recommendation stated that Chapter VII action would be inappropriate. Opposition from the US centred on the perception that the situation lacked sufficient gravity to be considered a 'threat to the peace', and that such a finding was a question of fact. The UK's opposition had them adopt a methodology of legal formalism, leading them to conclude that a 'threat to the peace' is a question of fact (unless the ICJ recommended otherwise), that Chapter VII action in this instance would violate Spain's rights to self-determination and non-interference and that a finding of 'threat to the peace' would run counter to fact-finding recommendations.

46 United Nations Security Council, '48th Meeting', 388.

CHAPTER 4

Palestine 1948 (Resolution 54 (1948))

1 Relevance to the Overall Project

Finding a 'threat to the peace' in UN Security Council *Resolution 54 (1948)*[1] in relation to the situation in Palestine constitutes the first-ever Article 39 finding, and finding of 'threat to the peace', by the Security Council. As such, it provides a valuable baseline for the P5's approaches to 'threat to the peace'. The *Repertoire Practice of the Security Council* for this period notes a significant amount of discussion regarding the question of whether a 'threat to the peace' within the scope of Article 39 of the UN Charter exists in Palestine in relation to the facts.[2] The vast majority of discussion hinged on whether the omission of the word 'international' in the phrase 'threat to the peace' in Article 39 was intentional, or an omission, and thus whether 'international' should be read into the article.

2 Context of the Debates

The situation in Palestine that led to the debates and the eventual finding of a 'threat to the peace' was escalating violence (leading to open conflict) in the build-up to the ceasing, and after the completion of, the UK Protectorate Mandate (the Mandate) over the Palestinian territory. Initially, the factual situation was provided via a written report from the UN Palestine Commission. This was then supplemented by the UK delegation's oral briefing to the Security Council based on intelligence reports from forces operating within Palestine as a part of the Mandate. After UK forces withdrew upon the Mandate's expiration, the majority of Security Council briefings consisted of intelligence telegrams regarding the situation from the truce commission. Towards the end of the debates, there was an oral briefing by the UN-appointed mediator to the conflict.

The initial reports from the UN Palestine Commission highlighted significant potential security issues in the Palestine area and the possible need for an international force to be deployed to the region upon the Mandate's

1 'Resolution 54 (1948)', S/RES/54 (1948) UN Security Council (1948).

2 Repertoire of the Practice of the Security Council, 'Chapter XI: Considerations of Chapter VII the Charter (1946–51)' (United Nations), 434–41.

 | DOI:10.1163/9789004391420_006

completion.[3] This was supplemented in their next report by a detailed description of the deteriorating situation in Palestine, and a quite detailed hypothesis (and in hindsight, also quite accurate) stating the likelihood of open conflict upon withdrawal of the Mandate.[4] The Chairman of the Palestine Commission also noted in oral briefings that the situation was chaotic and fuelled by 'violence and lawlessness',[5] highlighting the need to 're-establish a regime of law and establish an adequate measure of order and safety'.[6]

The UK then provided an extensive briefing (in its capacity as the Mandate power) on the continuing deterioration of the situation in Palestine in the build-up to their withdrawal at the end of the Mandate.[7] On the date the Mandate ended, the Security Council met. The meeting began with briefings on the outbreak of open conflict in Palestine between Jewish and Arab factions[8] (to which the Chinese delegate commented: 'We lament the fanaticism that has been shown by both sides in Palestine, but of course, we recognise that neither the Arabs nor the Jews have yet reached the stage of cannibalism'[9]).

From this point onwards, there were regular intelligence briefings noting the continuation of conflict and violence within the region.[10] These were then supplemented by oral briefings from the UN Mediator (who had been appointed by the P5 to negotiate a truce and eventual peace settlement) noting that even while the truce was in place, violence and incidents had continued to

3 United Nations Palestine Commission, 'Letter from the Chairman of the United Nations Palestine Commission to the President of the Security Council Dated 30 January 1948' (United Nations Security Council, 30 January 1948), 13.

4 United Nations Palestine Commission, 'Letter from the Chairman of the United Nations Palestine Commission to the President of the Security Council Dated 16 February 1948' (United Nations Security Council, 16 February 1948), 4–18.

5 United Nations Security Council, 'Security Council, Third Year: 253rd Meeting' (United Nations, 24 February 1948), 258.

6 United Nations Security Council, 258.

7 United Nations Security Council, 'Security Council, Third Year: 287th Meeting' (United Nations, 23 April 1948), 7–12.

8 United Nations Security Council, 'Security Council, Third Year: 292nd Meeting' (United Nations, 15 May 1948), 2–4.

9 United Nations Security Council, 15.

10 United Nations Security Council, 'Security Council, Third Year: 295th Meeting' (United Nations, 18 May 1948), 28; United Nations Security Council, 'Security Council, Third Year: 297th Meeting' (United Nations, 20 May 1948), 2–4; United Nations Security Council, 'Security Council, Third Year: 302nd Meeting' (United Nations, 22 May 1948), 64–65; United Nations Security Council, 'Security Council, Third Year: 305th Meeting' (United Nations, 26 May 1948), 42; United Nations Security Council, 'Security Council, Third Year: 308th Meeting' (United Nations, 28 May 1948), 37–38; United Nations Security Council, 'Security Council, Third Year: 310th Meeting' (United Nations, 29 May 1948), 16–17.

occur throughout the region, in violation of the ceasefire.[11] The mediator noted that this undermined any attempts for a negotiated peace as negotiations were affected by the daily tide of battle, and on this basis requested a 'firm and quick intervention by the Security Council'.[12]

3 Justificatory Discourse of the P5

The eventual finding of 'threat to the peace' with an abstention from China occurred when the Security Council voted on *Resolution 54 (1948)*. The build-up to this vote can be characterised by three different positions: the UK and China arguing that in spite of its absence, the word 'international' should be read into the concept of 'threat to the peace' when considering Article 39; France and Russia arguing that the facts made the existence of a 'threat to the peace' self-evident; and the US suggesting that the omission of the word 'international' from Article 39 was intentional to give the Security Council a mandate to act to prevent situations becoming international incidents. These positions are now explored in further detail.

The UK declined to engage much with the question of Security Council action in Palestine while still in their role as the Mandatory Power;[13] however, their arguments were based on a technical legal reading of Article 39 in the context of the UN Charter, particularly the Security Council's mandate for the maintenance of international peace and security. They argued that whenever peace was mentioned in the UN Charter, with the exception of Article 39, it was always prefaced with the word 'international'.[14] On this basis, they asserted that the omission of the word 'international' from Article 39 was a drafting oversight, rather than intentional, and thus the phrase should be read as 'threat to international peace'.[15] Given this interpretation of Article 39, the UK initially contended that, factually, an internal rather than international conflict was afoot, and as a result, the requirements for Security Council action under Chapter VII had not been met.[16] Further, the UK argued that they had been

11 United Nations Security Council, 'Security Council, Third Year: 317th Meeting' (United Nations, 10 June 1948), 37–38; United Nations Security Council, 'Security Council, Third Year: 333rd Meeting' (United Nations, 13 July 1948), 1–7.

12 United Nations Security Council, '333rd Meeting', 7.

13 United Nations Security Council, '253th Meeting', 270.

14 United Nations Security Council, 'Security Council, Third Year: 296th Meeting' (United Nations, 19 May 1948), 2–4.

15 United Nations Security Council, 3–4.

16 United Nations Security Council, 4.

engaged in the use of force to keep peace in Palestine for over 25 years and this had achieved very little,[17] so they saw no merit in perpetuating this failure through the Security Council,[18] demanding concrete details on any proposed enforcement plan.[19]

These positions led the UK to proffer an alternate resolution, which was adopted on 29 May 1948 as *Resolution 50 (1948)*.[20] The adopted text was different to the original US draft resolution that indicated a 'threat to the peace'. The compromise was paragraph 11, which stated that should either or both parties fail to comply with the ceasefire, the Security Council would consider further action under Chapter VII.[21] The failure of both sides to comply with this ceasefire, rather than a change in interpretation of Article 39, then led the UK to support *Resolution 54 (1948)* and the finding of a 'threat to the peace' in relation to Palestine.[22]

China had very little to say on the issue of the relationship between Palestine and the concept of 'threat to the peace' under Article 39 of the Charter. When the US first introduced the draft resolution designed around a finding of a 'threat to the peace', China made the following statement:

> [T]he broad purpose of the draft resolution introduced by the delegation of the United States is the restoration of peace in Palestine. It is a noble purpose, and one which is also the raison d'être of the United Nations in general and of the Security Council in particular. In the accomplishment of that purpose, my delegation has not been found and will not be found to lag one step, or even a half step, behind any other delegation.[23]

That being said, China argued that it could not find a legal basis for supporting a finding of 'threat to the peace' in relation to Palestine. This was because they agreed with the UK interpretation of the Charter on this issue, arguing that in all international documents, wherever the word 'peace' is used, it always refers to international peace.[24] As China did not see the ongoing violence

17 United Nations Security Council, '302nd Meeting', 45.
18 United Nations Security Council, 45.
19 United Nations Security Council, 'Security Council, Third Year: 309th Meeting' (United Nations, 29 May 1948), 10–11.
20 'Resolution 50 (1948)', S/RES/50 (1948) UN Security Council (1948).
21 Resolution 50 (1948), para. 11.
22 United Nations Security Council, '309th Meeting', 12–13; United Nations Security Council, 'Security Council, Third Year: 334th Meeting' (United Nations, 13 July 1948), 54–56.
23 United Nations Security Council, '296th Meeting', 19.
24 United Nations Security Council, 22.

and conflict in Palestine as international in nature, they could not support an interpretation of 'threat to the peace' that was not clearly international 'until the International Court of Justice decides otherwise. If we had an authority decision on that point, I certainly accept it'.[25] Further, China suggested that the use of force would not bring about peace (nor would it be within the Security Council's mandate), and instead advocated political negotiation to resolve the situation.[26] In the end, China opted to abstain from voting on *Resolution 54 (1948)* on the basis that they had doubts about the judicially correct application of a 'threat to the peace' finding in relation to Palestine;[27] however, they would 'in the interests of peace, fall in line, provided the resolution was otherwise satisfactory'.[28]

Russia declined to engage in the debate that preoccupied the US, UK and China regarding the necessity of the word 'international' in relation to Article 39. From the outset, they made their position very clear—they would not permit a threat to international peace to exist within Palestine.[29] From there, they proceeded to argue throughout the debates that the factual scenario occurring in Palestine made the existence of a 'threat to the peace' self-evident.[30] They noted that fighting in Palestine was 'not dying down, but continuing to spread'[31] and that 'Jews and Arabs are paying with their blood for the inability of the Security Council to take more or less effective steps to ensure the return of normal conditions in Palestine'.[32] This inability to agree on a way forward caused Russia to ask, '[i]s the Security Council so ineffectual and impotent that it is incapable of enforcing order in such a small country? If that is so, what is the use in talking of more serious matters?'[33] As the debates continued, Russia stated that 'what is happening in Palestine can only be described as military operations organised by a group of states against the new

25 Ibid.

26 United Nations Security Council, 'Security Council, Third Year: 271st Meeting' (United Nations, 19 March 1948), 171.

27 United Nations Security Council, 'Security Council, Third Year: 338th Meeting' (United Nations, 15 July 1948), 44.

28 United Nations Security Council, '334th Meeting', 34.

29 United Nations Security Council, 'Security Council, Third Year: 270th Meeting' (United Nations, 19 March 1948), 146.

30 United Nations Security Council, '295th Meeting', 40; United Nations Security Council, 'Security Council, Third Year: 306th Meeting' (United Nations, 27 May 1948), 17–18; United Nations Security Council, '309th Meeting', 8–9; United Nations Security Council, 'Security Council, Third Year: 336th Meeting' (United Nations, 14 July 1948), 29–30.

31 United Nations Security Council, '287th Meeting', 21.

32 United Nations Security Council, 21.

33 United Nations Security Council, 22.

Jewish state'.[34] As a result, they argued that the Security Council's fundamental task was to maintain international peace and security, and that in Palestine 'we are faced with an obvious threat to peace and security'.[35] In response to the question regarding the 'international' nature of the conflict, Russia suggested that while the extent of the threat and scale of the conflict could be debated, factually, there could be no doubt that there was an ongoing war in Palestine "and that, consequently, there exists a 'threat to the peace' within the meaning of Article 39 of the Charter".[36]

France stated very early in the debates that it believed the Security Council needed to determine whether a 'threat to the peace' existed in relation to Palestine before it could discuss the possibility of any action.[37] On this basis, France adopted the consistent position that the existence of a 'threat to the peace' was self-evident based on the available facts. In the build-up to the UK's withdrawal at the Mandate's completion, France argued that the alternative to a Security Council finding of 'threat to the peace' and corresponding action was to simply allow 'a general massacre'.[38] The most succinct summary of the French position on this issue was made in the 298th meeting:

> When fighting began in Palestine, we did not consider it to be a threat to the peace because it was a struggle between two sections of the Palestine population taking place inside one and the same country. When these operations then spread and when armed bands and irregular troops came from the outside and led hostilities to spread, we still did not consider that we had to note the existence of a threat to the peace or a breach of international peace, but the moment regular forces of several countries crossed the frontiers and entered territory which, whatever its status, was not their own, the moment fighting continued in these conditions and became more serious, we clearly had to deal with the question of international peace within the meaning of the Charter. In any case, fighting had assumed the character of a threat to international peace.[39]

34 United Nations Security Council, '309th Meeting', 2.
35 United Nations Security Council, 8–9.
36 United Nations Security Council, 9.
37 United Nations Security Council, 'Security Council, Third Year: 262nd Meeting' (United Nations, 5 March 1948), 22.
38 United Nations Security Council, 'Security Council, Third Year: 274th Meeting' (United Nations, 24 March 1948), 237.
39 United Nations Security Council, 'Security Council, Third Year: 298th Meeting' (United Nations, 20 May 1948), 17–18.

France also argued that Article 39, through its wording, placed a positive obligation upon the Security Council to make a determination of 'threat to the peace' where such a situation existed;[40] however, they noted that after making such a determination, the Security Council had wide discretion on the most appropriate action to be taken in any given situation.[41] In other statements, France continued to argue that the existence of a 'threat to the peace' was self-evident and therefore did not need further justification.[42]

The US began their arguments regarding Palestine by stating that the question of 'threat to the peace' was a constitutional question of the UN Charter, vis-a-vis the lengths and limits of the Security Council's power.[43] From there they argued that withdrawing the Mandate power would necessitate deploying non-Palestinian troops to the region, and that this factual scenario was clearly placed within the powers and mandate of the Security Council to maintain international peace and security.[44] Further, the US asserted that the Security Council had been granted broad powers under Articles 39–42 and that it should thus not shy away from using them to bring about peace.[45] In clarifying what they saw as the Security Council's mandate under the UN Charter, they argued that the Security Council's primary purpose is 'to save human life'.[46]

In justifying their position that the situation in Palestine constituted a 'threat to the peace', the US described events as 'the slaughter, the civil disobedience, the destruction of property and the anarchy which exists within the territory that is under a mandate'.[47] They also argued that this state of affairs, resulting from the conflict between Jews and Arabs in Palestine, had the potential to 'result in a threat to the peace of the world'.[48] As debates progressed, the US joined France and Russia in arguing that a 'threat to the peace' was self-evident on the basis of the facts.[49]

40 United Nations Security Council, 18; See also 'I do not think I have the right not to note that there now exists a threat to the peace' In 298th Meeting at 17.

41 United Nations Security Council, 18.

42 United Nations Security Council, '308th Meeting', 23 & 41; United Nations Security Council, '310th Meeting', 33; United Nations Security Council, '336th Meeting', 22.

43 United Nations Security Council, '253th Meeting', 266.

44 United Nations Security Council, 268.

45 United Nations Security Council, '271st Meeting', 167.

46 United Nations Security Council, 'Security Council, Third Year: 277th Meeting' (United Nations, 1 April 1948), 30.

47 United Nations Security Council, 31.

48 United Nations Security Council, 'Security Council, Third Year: 283rd Meeting' (United Nations, 16 April 1948), 10.

49 United Nations Security Council, 'Security Council, Third Year: 293rd Meeting' (United Nations, 17 May 1948), 2; United Nations Security Council, '296th Meeting', 6; United

In relation to the UK and Chinese arguments regarding the omission of the word 'international', the US contended that such an omission was intentional and placed a duty upon the Security Council to prevent the 'conflagration' of situations from becoming international in nature.[50] Further, they argued, in line with France, that the language of Article 39 places a positive burden upon the Security Council to make a determination as to when a 'threat to the peace' exists and that this applies to all threats, not only those that are international in nature.[51] Regarding the various draft resolutions making such a determination, they stated the following:

> But as the guardians of the peace of the world, it is our primary duty to find out, under Article 39, whether there exists any threat to the peace. That is the limit, the boundary, of the duty which the resolution offered by the United States delegation asked the Security Council to perform.[52]

Therefore, while the US relied on similar arguments to Russia and France, they engaged much more comprehensively with the theoretical question regarding the legal obligation placed upon the Security Council under Article 39.

4 Summary of Coding

This case study had China oppose a finding of 'threat to the peace', with the rest of the P5 supporting such a finding. China's opposition ultimately caused them to abstain from voting; however, this was grounded in arguments about the scope of the Security Council's mandate and the legal interpretation of 'threat to the peace' (including requests for an ICJ advisory opinion on this matter), a lack of faith in the proposed solution and the need for peaceful solutions. In reaching their support, the US adopted an approach of legal formalism. This had them conclude that the situation was of sufficient gravity for the Security Council to act and that the existence of a 'threat to the peace' was self-evident. They also argued that the situation was international in nature and thus within the Security Council's mandate. Russia made their arguments

Nations Security Council, '302nd Meeting', 41–43; United Nations Security Council, '306th Meeting', 14–15; United Nations Security Council, 'Security Council, Third Year: 307th Meeting' (United Nations, 28 May 1948), 19; United Nations Security Council, '334th Meeting', 99.

50 United Nations Security Council, '296th Meeting', 9–10.

51 United Nations Security Council, 7; United Nations Security Council, '307th Meeting', 19.

52 United Nations Security Council, '296th Meeting', 9.

in an extremely emotive manner, arguing that the situation was sufficiently grave and thus within the Security Council's mandate. Further, they argued that the existence of a 'threat to the peace' was self-evident and a question of fact. France adopted a process of formal legal argumentation to conclude that the situation was of sufficient gravity, and thus the existence of 'threat to the peace' was self-evident. They also argued that the situation was international in nature and, as a result, was within the Security Council's mandate. The UK also adopted a formal legal argument approach when concluding that the situation was within the scope of the Security Council's mandate, and thus a finding of 'threat to the peace' was a consequence of the action taken by the involved parties, while also arguing that the existence of a 'threat to the peace' was a question of law (and noting their lack of faith in the proposed solutions).

CHAPTER 5

Portuguese African Territories 1963 (Resolution 180 (1963))

1 Relevance to Overall Project

This case study explores the relationship between exercising the right of self-determination in the process of decolonisation and the concept of 'threat to the peace'. Much like the case study on Spain from 1946, the vast majority of the reasoning and arguments supporting a finding of 'threat to the peace' in this instance are grounded in ideology rather than the concrete facts of the situation. This situation also represents one of the few times during the Cold War period where the Security Council addressed the issue of the existence of a 'threat to the peace'. Although the *Repertoire of Practice of the Security Council* for the period including 1963 did not mention this situation as a significant discussion of the concept of 'threat to the peace',[1] the same situation arose in 1965 and gained mention in the *Repertoire of Practice of the Security Council* in that instance.[2] Closer examination of the draft resolution put before the Security Council in both instances shows the Security Council's 1965 discussion of the Portuguese African territories and the concept of 'threat to the peace' so strongly mirrored the 1963 incident that parsing the 1963 debates would be more relevant to this project than examining the repeated debates of 1965. This is especially so considering that operative paragraph 1 of *Resolution 218 (1965)*[3] mirrors the language of operative paragraph 4 of *Resolution 180 (1963)*.[4]

2 Context of the Debates

This situation came before the Security Council initially as a result of a request from Senegal in their letter to the Security Council after a border incident in

1 Repertoire of the Practice of the Security Council, 'Chapter XI: Considerations of Chapter VII the Charter (1959–63)'.
2 Repertoire of the Practice of the Security Council, 186.
3 'Resolution 218 (1965)', S/RES/218 (1965) UN Security Council (1965).
4 'Resolution 180 (1963)', S/5380 UN Security Council (1963).

 | DOI:10.1163/9789004391420_007

early April 1963.[5] The letter also referenced incidents between Senegal and Portuguese Guinea in 1961.[6] Senegal orally expanded upon claims made in the letter, incorporating claims of unlawful arrest against Senegalese nationals in Portuguese Guinea and extensive unlawful espionage by the Portuguese within Senegal.[7] Portugal immediately rebutted these claims, stating that the instances in question were mere misunderstanding as a result of navigational error, with the claims of damage sustained being fabricated or exaggerated by the Senegalese.[8] Portugal further denied any knowledge of the arrest in question,[9] and stated that any claims of espionage within Senegalese territory should be assessed in terms of conduct by governments other than Portugal.[10] Finally, Portugal claimed that by virtue of Article 33 of the UN Charter, the Security Council had no grounds for the involvement requested by Senegal on the basis that they had not attempted or pursued a peaceful negotiated settlement to the dispute before bringing it before the Security Council.[11] They contended that the Security Council was obliged to remain uninvolved until such time as attempts to peacefully resolve the situation had been undertaken in good faith.[12]

The debate reignited in July 1963, with a letter from 32 African states[13] addressing Portugal's failure to withdraw from African territories in accordance with *General Assembly Resolution 1514 (XV)*.[14] The letter before the Security Council included, inter alia, a request for a finding of 'threat to the peace' (although they used the phrase 'menace to the peace of the continent', the request for Chapter VII action on the basis of this finding makes it analogous to 'threat to the peace') against the Portuguese Government for their continued

5 Senegal, 'Letter Dated 10 April 1963 from the Acting Charge D'Affairs of the Permanent Mission of Senegal Addressed to the President of the Security Council' (United Nations, 10 April 1963).

6 Senegal.

7 United Nations Security Council, 'Security Council, Eighteenth Year: 1027th Meeting (S/PV.1027)', 17 April 1963, 9–10.

8 United Nations Security Council, 13–19.

9 United Nations Security Council, 20.

10 United Nations Security Council, 20.

11 United Nations Security Council, 12–13.

12 United Nations Security Council, 12–13.

13 Algeria et al., 'Letter Dated 11 July 1963 Addressed to the President of the Security Council by the Representatives of Algeria, Burundi, Cameroon, Central African Republic, Chad, Congo (Brazzaville), Congo (Leopoldville), Dahomey, Ethiopia, Gabon, Ghana, Guinea, Ivory Coast, Liberia, Libya, Madagascar, Mali, Mauritania, Morocco, Niger, Nigeria, Rwanda, Senegal, Sierra Leone, Somalia, Sudan, Tanganyika, Togo, Tunisia, Uganda, United Arab Republic and Upper Volta' (United Nations, 11 July 1963).

14 'Resolution 1514 (XV)', UN General Assembly (1960).

colonial occupation of African states, and also for wide-ranging trade bans to be implemented flowing from this finding.[15] A great deal of meeting time was dedicated to African states orally expanding upon the letter and its attached memorandum.[16] Brazil recounted its experience as a Portuguese territory;[17] Portugal vehemently rebutted these allegations.[18] Of particular note within the oral proceedings was Sierra Leone's veiled suggestion that should the Security Council not take action against Portugal, there could be an increase of violence designed to force the Security Council's hand in favour of acting to remove the Portuguese from Africa.[19] Ultimately, the resolution voted upon (which eventually became *Resolution 180 (1963)*[20]) removed the sanctions requests and the finding of 'threat to the peace',[21] presumably to avoid vetoes from France, the UK and the US (who abstained from voting).[22]

3 Justificatory Discourse of the P5

Within the P5, support for a finding of 'threat to the peace' came only from Russia, and it was heavily grounded in ideological principles. By contrast, the rest of the P5 saw Senegal's initial raising of the issue as lacking sufficient gravity to warrant Chapter VII action in response. The responses from China, France,

15 Algeria et al., 'Letter Dated 11 July 1963 Addressed to the President of the Security Council by the Representatives of Algeria, Burundi, Cameroon, Central African Republic, Chad, Congo (Brazzaville), Congo (Leopoldville), Dahomey, Ethiopia, Gabon, Ghana, Guinea, Ivory Coast, Liberia, Libya, Madagascar, Mali, Mauritania, Morocco, Niger, Nigeria, Rwanda, Senegal, Sierra Leone, Somalia, Sudan, Tanganyika, Togo, Tunisia, Uganda, United Arab Republic and Upper Volta', 5.

16 United Nations Security Council, 'Security Council, Eighteenth Year: 1040th Meeting (S/PV.1040)', 22 July 1963; United Nations Security Council, 'Security Council, Eighteenth Year: 1041st Meeting (S/PV.1041)', 23 July 1963; United Nations Security Council, 'Security Council, Eighteenth Year: 1046th Meeting (S/PV.1046)', 29 July 1963; United Nations Security Council, 'Security Council, Eighteenth Year: 1048th Meeting (S/PV.1048)', 30 July 1963.

17 United Nations Security Council, 'Security Council, Eighteenth Year: 1043rd Meeting (S/PV.1043)', 24 July 1963.

18 United Nations Security Council, 'Security Council, Eighteenth Year: 1042nd Meeting (S/PV.1042)', 24 July 1963; United Nations Security Council, 'Security Council, Eighteenth Year: 1047th Meeting (S/PV.1047)', 29 July 1963.

19 United Nations Security Council, '1041st Meeting', 8.

20 Resolution 180 (1963).

21 United Nations Security Council, 'Security Council, Eighteenth Year: 1044th Meeting (S/PV.1044)', 26 July 1963, 3–4.

22 United Nations Security Council, 'Security Council, Eighteenth Year: 1049th Meeting (S/PV.1049)', 31 July 1963, 4.

the UK and the US on the second occasion the incident was raised ranged from noncommittal to active rejection of the idea that the situation constituted a 'threat to the peace'.

China's response can be divided into two separate approaches split by the occasions on which the issue was raised. When dealing with the initial Portuguese border incursion into Senegal, China began by noting that both parties may have been telling the truth as they saw it, noting that military exercises conducted by Portugal near the Senegalese border could have resulted in stray ammunition and rocket fire, causing damage and loss of life in the Senegalese border village.[23] On this basis, China concluded that the Senegalese response in coming straight to the Security Council was an overreaction; however, they also saw it as an understandable one, because Senegal's recent independence would necessarily lead to heightened vigilance in relation to potential threats to their sovereignty and territorial integrity.[24] In response to this incident, however, China noted that should Portugal fail to respect Senegal's sovereignty and territorial integrity, then China would be willing to cooperate with Senegal to resolve the issue.[25]

In response to the request from the 32 African states to impose sanctions upon Portugal (to be lifted only upon their withdrawal from Africa), China first stated that it was against all forms of colonisation and foreign domination of states, and that they supported the aspiration of all non-self-governing peoples 'for independence and freedom'.[26] Regarding the claim that the situation constituted a 'threat to the peace', the China representative simply stated that he would 'not at this juncture go into a discussion as to whether a threat to international peace does or does not already exist. I content myself with the simple observation that the situation is potentially explosive'.[27] In spite of their refusal to engage with the question of 'threat to the peace', China did support the passing of *Resolution 180 (1963)*[28] under Chapter VI of the Charter (which, as noted above, was a compromise to avoid vetoes from France, the UK and the US).

Much like China, France's response to the overall situation is distinctly different when considering the initial incident that led to the Security Council's involvement, as well as the demands of the 32 African states that followed.

23 United Nations Security Council, 'Security Council, Eighteenth Year: 1033rd Meeting (S/PV.1033)', 24 April 1963, 15.
24 United Nations Security Council, 15.
25 United Nations Security Council, 16.
26 United Nations Security Council, 'Security Council, Eighteenth Year: 1045th Meeting (S/PV.1045)', 26 July 1963, 2.
27 United Nations Security Council, 4.
28 United Nations Security Council, '1049th Meeting', 4; Resolution 180 (1963), 180.

When discussing Portugal's border incursion into Senegal, France began by stating that its own internal intelligence gathering confirmed in their minds that the Senegalese report of the situation was the most accurate.[29] On this basis, France was of the opinion that the incident itself was not 'of such gravity that it could threaten the peace'.[30] That said, they did support any action that would be taken under Article 33 of the Charter and any resolutions that might help reduce tensions in a peaceful manner that respected Senegalese sovereignty and territorial integrity.[31]

In relation to the demands of the 32 African states in July 1963, France took a very different tack. They began by prefacing their position with an assertion that they supported the universal application of the right of self-determination in the current situation and all other situations where it may apply.[32] They then argued that '[a] distinction should, however, be drawn between what is desirable and what the Council can legitimately decide or even recommend'.[33] France contended that for the Security Council to force Portugal to grant independence within its colonial territories would constitute an interference in Portugal's internal affairs and be beyond the scope of legitimate Security Council action.[34] France argued that Portugal needed to consent to such a granting of independence to its colonies, and that France would greatly welcome this state of affairs.[35]

In both components of this situation, the UK approached its role in the Security Council and the Security Council's relationship to a determination of 'threat to the peace' in quite a legalistic and judicial manner. When addressing the border incursion into Senegal, they began by noting that the incident itself was relatively minor;[36] however, they argued that size is not the only relative consideration when addressing these sorts of situations, as minor instances can cascade into larger issues.[37] From there, the UK contended that for procedural reasons, the situation first needed to be addressed using all the options provided in Article 33 of the Charter before the Security Council could consider any direct action.[38] That said, they would be open to supporting stronger

29 United Nations Security Council, 'Security Council, Eighteenth Year: 1032nd Meeting (S/PV.1032)', 23 April 1963, 8–9.
30 United Nations Security Council, 9.
31 United Nations Security Council, 9.
32 United Nations Security Council, '1045th Meeting', 6.
33 United Nations Security Council, 6.
34 United Nations Security Council, 6.
35 United Nations Security Council, 6.
36 United Nations Security Council, '1033rd Meeting', 6.
37 United Nations Security Council, 6.
38 United Nations Security Council, 7.

responses from the Security Council should Article 33 options not succeed.[39] Further, as to the facts of the border incursion, the UK asserted strongly that the Security Council had a responsibility to determine the facts independently when the situation was unclear,[40] rather than rely upon statements by the parties involved; however, they also argued that the complainant had a higher responsibility for proving its position:

> As regards the investigation of facts, I believe that the Security Council has to exercise a quasi-judicial function. It would be wrong of course to be unduly legalistic and this Council is not a court of law … As in judicial proceedings, we cannot avoid the fact that the onus of proof must be on the party which brings the complaint, particularly complaints involving an alleged violent incursion across an international frontier.[41]

In relation to the later complaint by the 32 African states against the Portuguese, the UK commenced by stating that they opposed Portugal's denial of self-determination for African colonies, and that the Portuguese had created 'a situation capable of leading to international friction and the continuance of which is likely to endanger the maintenance of peace and security'.[42] From this position, the UK stated clearly that it could not support the threat of the use of force, or the use of force to end the Portuguese colonial regime, as they felt that it would have a negative effect rather than assist in resolving the situation;[43] however, they did support the possibility of Chapter VI action on the issue.[44] In response to Sierra Leone's suggestion that it would not be difficult to escalate violence to a point where there was sufficient bloodshed to create a 'threat to the peace', the UK stated the following, reinforcing their legalistic approach to the issue:

> This, I am bound to say, seems to us an exceptionally shocking argument. It is not only clearly contrary to the provisions and spirit of the Charter, but it offends against one of the most important and widespread

39 United Nations Security Council, 7.
40 United Nations Security Council, 7–8.
41 United Nations Security Council, 7.
42 United Nations Security Council, '1045th Meeting', 7.
43 'I repeat, our Organization is at all times an Organization of peace, and it is not permissible for this Council to urge or even to contemplate the use of non-peaceful means save in specific circumstances permitted and contemplated in the Charter itself'. United Nations Security Council, 8–9.
44 United Nations Security Council, 9.

> principles of natural justice, namely, that he who comes to a court of law seeking equity should come with clean hands.[45]

In the early stages of this dispute, the US highlighted that they did not see the Security Council as an effective venue for attempting to resolve the questions of self-determination that underpinned tensions between Portugal and the African states contiguous to Portuguese Guinea.[46] Therefore, the US resolved to not deal with the question of self-determination, but rather to address the immediate issue of Portugal's territorial incursions into Senegal.[47] While they acknowledged that Article 35 of the Charter gave Senegal the right to bring the matter before the Security Council, the US suggested that, in the first instance, the provisions of Article 33 should be used to attempt to resolve the dispute.[48] Nevertheless, the US voiced its support for potential Chapter VI Security Council action in response to the situation given the disparity of military equipment between Portugal and Senegal.[49]

With the escalation of the situation in July to focus squarely upon the right of self-determination and Portugal's continued colonial activity within Africa, the US began by acknowledging that the territories under Portuguese control in Africa met all the requirements within Chapter XI of the Charter to be considered non-self-governing territories; as such, the US supported their right of self-determination.[50] In response to the requested action from the 32 African states, the US argued that the question before them was how the Security Council could assist in bringing about peaceful change within the Portuguese African territories to aid in decolonisation and exercise of the right of self-determination.[51] In this vein, they rejected both the proposal that the situation be deemed a 'threat to the peace', and the call to implement trade sanctions against Portugal as a result.[52] The basis of this position was that the US considered that the UN and the Security Council were 'devoted to the reduction of international friction, to the maintenance of peace and security and therefore dedicated to peaceful change',[53] and that the proposed action would

45 United Nations Security Council, 9.
46 United Nations Security Council, '1033rd Meeting', 4.
47 United Nations Security Council, 4.
48 United Nations Security Council, 5.
49 United Nations Security Council, 5.
50 United Nations Security Council, '1045th Meeting', 12.
51 United Nations Security Council, 14.
52 United Nations Security Council, 16–17.
53 United Nations Security Council, 13.

not result in peaceful change.[54] While the US agreed that the continuation of Portuguese control of African territories would endanger international peace and security, they rejected the notion that a 'threat to the peace' was already in existence.[55] Further, they echoed and supported the UK's position on the idea of escalating violence within the territory to force a Security Council response on this matter.[56] After the passing of *Resolution 180 (1963)*, the US stated that its downgrading from Chapter VII to Chapter VI allowed them to avoid having to block the resolution, in spite of their inherent disagreement with some of the provisions.[57]

Russia began by stating that the Security Council was 'dealing with an act of undisguised aggression by Portugal against the young African state of Senegal'.[58] Russia continued by recounting the Portuguese history of aggression against Senegal since December 1961,[59] arguing that Portugal's dismissal of Senegal's claims as being 'rather trivial' was 'the logic of die-hard colonialists and racists who were once a law unto themselves'.[60] Further, they stated that Portugal was arguing that they had a '"right" to commit aggression'.[61] Russia maintained this ideological position throughout the debates; it was clearly encapsulated in the following statement:

> The Soviet delegation deems it necessary for the Security Council, as the main organ of the United Nations responsible for the maintenance of international peace and security, to take prompt and decisive action against the State which by trampling underfoot the Charter and the principles that form the very keystone of our Organization has created a serious threat to peace and security in Africa, a threat which is growing and assuming many new forms and increasingly dangerous proportions … The Soviet delegation will give full and unreserved support to any radical measures aimed at the resolute repression of Portugal's acts of aggression and the rigorous punishment of the aggressor.[62]

54 United Nations Security Council, 13–14.
55 United Nations Security Council, 16–17.
56 United Nations Security Council, 15.
57 United Nations Security Council, '1049th Meeting', 6–7.
58 United Nations Security Council, 'Security Council, Eighteenth Year: 1028th Meeting (S/PV.1028)', 18 April 1963, 19.
59 United Nations Security Council, 19–20.
60 United Nations Security Council, 20.
61 United Nations Security Council, 20.
62 United Nations Security Council, 25.

Further, Russia argued that the broader issue being addressed by the Security Council was 'the outcome and the practical manifestation of the inhumane, racist and aggressive nature of Portuguese colonialism'.[63] Building upon that sentiment, Russia contended that the real issue before the Security Council was actually the larger challenge of ending colonialism within Africa rather than addressing a simple border incident:

> The fundamental interests of the peoples of Africa—and not only of Africa—and the lofty principles of the United Nations Charter required that the struggle of the peoples of African countries for their freedom and independence and against colonialism and aggression should be supported by deeds.[64]

When the second stage of the situation commenced, Russia used the letter from the 32 African states requesting Security Council involvement on the issue of Portuguese colonial territories as evidence that their argument that the situation was not merely about an isolated border incident was correct.[65] Russia characterised Portuguese actions in Africa as a breach of the peace and 'as a threat to international peace and security'.[66] They argued that the coalition of African states' appeal was a legitimate demand upon the Security Council for action and that their concerns 'are undoubtedly shared by all peace loving and freedom loving countries and by all peoples of goodwill'.[67] Further, Russia engaged in an impassioned and lengthy soliloquy on how the North Atlantic Treaty Organization (NATO) and the Franco regime were actively supporting and assisting Portuguese colonial oppression.[68] In response to the arguments from France, the UK and the US against Chapter VII action, Russia stated: 'How can one go on about equality and democracy when the indigenous people of the Portuguese colonies are denied their sacred right to independence, their right to decide their destiny as they see fit?'[69] Finally, they argued that *Resolution 180 (1963)* was insufficient to deal with the situation:

> [I] t is entirely obvious that Portugal's policy in Africa, a policy characterised by acts of genocide, by growing provocation of the general armed

63 United Nations Security Council, '1033rd Meeting', 17.
64 United Nations Security Council, 19.
65 United Nations Security Council, '1041st Meeting', 8.
66 United Nations Security Council, 8–9.
67 United Nations Security Council, 9.
68 United Nations Security Council, 9–19.
69 United Nations Security Council, '1047th Meeting', 4.

> conflict in the continent and by obdurate and unprecedented disregard of all of the decisions adopted by various organs of our Organization, should receive the sterner judgement it deserves and that the Council should propose more drastic action by the United Nations than is recommended in the present draft resolution.[70]

4 Summary of Coding

This case study had only Russian support for a finding of 'threat to the peace', with the rest of the P5 opposing such a finding. Russia used emotive rhetoric to establish their support, which was grounded in the suggestion that ideology could constitute a 'threat to the peace', and the situation was thus sufficiently grave (with the existence of a 'threat to the peace' being self-evident). They also argued that in failing to withdraw from their African territories, Portugal were violating the Purposes and Principles of the Charter and denying the citizens of those territories their right of self-determination. China's opposition to a finding of 'threat to the peace' was grounded in their lack of faith in the facts; thus, they did not see the situation as having sufficient gravity to warrant Chapter VII action. France argued that the situation lacked sufficient gravity for Chapter VI action, and that a finding of 'threat to the peace' would therefore be beyond the scope of the Security Council's mandate and violate Portugal's right of non-interference. The UK adopted a formal legal approach—they likened the Security Council to a judicial body, and concluded that there was a need for UN fact-finding, as the facts presented were unreliable. This led them to surmise that the situation was not grave enough to constitute a 'threat to the peace'. The US adopted a formal legal approach that had them threaten to veto any Chapter VII action. This was because they saw the situation as lacking enough gravity to warrant Security Council action, that the proposed action was unlikely to improve the situation and because the situation needed to be resolved peacefully through negotiation.

70 United Nations Security Council, 2.

CHAPTER 6

Apartheid in South Africa 1963–77 (Resolutions 181, 182 (1963), 190, 191 (1964), 282 (1973), 311 (1972), 417 and 418 (1977))

1 Relevance to the Overall Project

The issue of apartheid was raised periodically for 14 years within the Security Council, with the question of whether the internal race policy of a state could constitute a 'threat to the peace' at the core of each of these debates. This issue was also raised in connection with the debates on the Portuguese African territories, Namibia and Southern Rhodesia. With the exception of Southern Rhodesia, these situations are dealt with in case studies elsewhere in this volume (Southern Rhodesia was excluded predominantly because the formative debates and finding of 'threat to the peace' took place in conjunction with a Chapter VI resolution making that finding, unduly affecting the later justifications for the finding under Article 39).[1] The question of apartheid is also significant in the UN Security Council's history as the first instance when the Security Council imposed mandatory sanctions against a Member State of the UN.[2] The *Repertoire of the Practice of the Security Council* noted significant debate about the concept of 'threat to the peace' in relation to the issue of apartheid in South Africa in the periods 1964–65[3] and 1975–80.[4] Of particular interest within this case study is the moment, following the events of Black Wednesday on 19 October 1977, when certain members of the P5 ceased considering the policy of apartheid to be a purely internal matter protected from Security Council interference.

1 'Resolution 217 (1965)', S/RES/217 (1965) UN Security Council (1965); 'Resolution 232 (1966)', S/RES/232 (1966) UN Security Council (1966).

2 United Nations Security Council, 'Security Council, Thirty-Second Year: 2045th Meeting (S/PV2045)' (United Nations, 31 October 1977), 1.

3 Repertoire of the Practice of the Security Council, 'Chapter XI: Considerations of Chapter VII the Charter (1964–65)', 185–86.

4 Repertoire of the Practice of the Security Council, 'Chapter XI: Considerations of Chapter VII the Charter (1975–80)', 399–400.

 | DOI:10.1163/9789004391420_008

2 Context of the Debates

The issue of apartheid was initially brought before the Security Council in the same meeting as the issue of Portuguese African territories, in 1963.[5] Debate upon the issue was delayed until the South African delegate could receive instructions from his government regarding how to proceed.[6] South Africa declined to attend the meetings addressing the issue, instead issuing a written response to the Security Council.[7] South Africa argued that any Security Council action at the behest of the African states with regards to apartheid amounted to illegal interference in South Africa's domestic affairs in violation of Article 2(7) of the UN Charter.[8] Further, they suggested that claims of oppression and neglect levelled against them were unfounded, as conditions in the Bantustans were significantly better in terms of housing and other social welfare aspects than any other African state.[9] This tack of declining to engage in Security Council debate and issuing a letter claiming that any Security Council action would be a violation of their rights to non-interference in domestic affairs continued to be the first option for South Africa, and was employed again in 1964 when the issue was further debated[10]—after which they did not even bother to send a response, instead simply declining to engage in the debate.

The issue of apartheid was added to the Security Council agenda as a result of a request of the Heads of African States after a unanimous decision at their conference to request that the Security Council impose a mandatory arms embargo against South Africa because of the policy of apartheid and the tension that it created within Africa.[11] This led to an expert panel being established to

5 Algeria et al., 'Letter Dated 11 July 1963 Addressed to the President of the Security Council by the Representatives of Algeria, Burundi, Cameroon, Central African Republic, Chad, Congo (Brazzaville), Congo (Leopoldville), Dahomey, Ethiopia, Gabon, Ghana, Guinea, Ivory Coast, Liberia, Libya, Madagascar, Mali, Mauritania, Morocco, Niger, Nigeria, Rwanda, Senegal, Sierra Leone, Somalia, Sudan, Tanganyika, Togo, Tunisia, Uganda, United Arab Republic and Upper Volta' (United Nations, 11 July 1963).

6 United Nations Security Council, 'Security Council, Eighteenth Year: 1040th Meeting (S/PV.1040)', 22 July 1963, 4.

7 United Nations Security Council, 'Security Council, Eighteenth Year: 1050th Meeting (S/PV.1050)' (United Nations, 31 July 1963), 2–3.

8 United Nations Security Council, 3.

9 United Nations Security Council, 3.

10 United Nations Secretary-General, 'Report of the Secretary-General in Pursuance of the Resolution Adopted by the Security Council at Its 1078th Meeting on 4 December 1963 (S/5471)' (New York: United Nations, 20 April 1964) 11.

11 Algeria et al., 'Letter Dated 11 July 1963 Addressed to the President of the Security Council by the Representatives of Algeria, Burundi, Cameroon, Central African Republic, Chad, Congo (Brazzaville), Congo (Leopoldville), Dahomey, Ethiopia, Gabon, Ghana, Guinea,

assess the effect of South Africa's apartheid policy on international relations.[12] These reports, presented in 1964, suggested that while the situation was dire (with any internal conflict arising from apartheid being likely to have serious international implications),[13] the point of no return at which conflict was inevitable had not yet been reached.[14] They also suggested on a number of occasions that the Security Council take Chapter VII enforcement action against South Africa to exert pressure with a view to ending apartheid.[15] The question of a Security Council response to apartheid continued to be raised until a final decision on 4 November 1977 to declare the policy of apartheid a 'threat to the peace' in *Resolution 418 (1977)*,[16] in response to the events of Black Wednesday on 19 October 1977.[17]

3 Justificatory Discourse of the P5

The justificatory discourse of the P5 in relation to apartheid was relatively stable throughout the debates. To varying degrees, Russia and China argued that the policy of apartheid violated the Purposes and Principles of the UN Charter, to which South Africa was bound to adhere by virtue of being a Member State of the UN. Until Black Wednesday, the US maintained that South Africa's

---

Ivory Coast, Liberia, Libya, Madagascar, Mali, Mauritania, Morocco, Niger, Nigeria, Rwanda, Senegal, Sierra Leone, Somalia, Sudan, Tanganyika, Togo, Tunisia, Uganda, United Arab Republic and Upper Volta'.

12 'Resolution 182 (1963)', S/5471 UN Security Council (1963).

13 United Nations Secretary-General, 'Report of the Secretary-General in Pursuance of the Resolution Adopted by the Security Council at Its 1078th Meeting on 4 December 1963 (S/5471)', para. 31.

14 United Nations Secretary-General, paras 122–123.

15 Special Committee on the Policies of Apartheid of the Government of the Republic of South Africa, 'Report of the Special Committee on the Policies of Apartheid of the Government of the Republic of South Africa' (New York: United Nations, 25 March 1964), para. 20; Special Committee on the Policies of Apartheid of the Government of the Republic of South Africa, 'Report of the Special Committee on the Policies of Apartheid of the Government of the Republic of South Africa' (New York: United Nations, 25 May 1964), para. Preamble & 15.

16 'Resolution 418 (1977)', S/RES/418 (1977) UN Security Council (1977); Tunisia, 'Letter Dated 20 October 1977 from the Permanent Representative of Tunisia to the United Nations Addressed to the President of the Security Council' (United Nations Security Council, 20 October 1977).

17 Black Wednesday saw the death in custody by torture of Steve Biko and the shutting down of numerous black newspapers and anti-apartheid organisations: United Nations Security Council, 'Security Council, Thirty-Second Year: 2037th Meeting (S/PV2037)' (United Nations, 25 October 1977), 4.

conduct lacked sufficient gravity to invoke Article 39. Until 1977, the French argued that as much as they found the policy of apartheid abhorrent, it constituted an internal affair of South Africa and was exempt from interference by virtue of Article 2(7) of the UN Charter; this position changed after Black Wednesday. The UK the argument against a finding of 'threat to the peace' was grounded in the notion that a mandatory embargo on all arms sales and transfers would constitute a violation of South Africa's Article 51 right of self-defence (an argument that, interestingly, also featured much later in the ICJ case regarding the Bosnia genocides),[18] and that military items that could only be used for external defence (such as the protection of shipping lanes) should be exempt from the embargo. Much like it was for the US and France, Black Wednesday was the turning point for the UK.

China, in its various statements, commenced by expressing disappointment that South Africa declined to participate in the Council deliberations, and in the South African invocation of Article 2(7) of the Charter.[19] They made it clear that their position on racial discrimination was one of stringent opposition: 'The attitude of the Chinese peoples towards the question of race find expressions in the teaching of Confucius that all men are brothers. For centuries, various ethnic groups in my country have lived in harmony and mutual respect'.[20] China also tied this ideal of a society striving to be free from racial discrimination to the Purposes and Principles of the UN Charter:

> My delegation has consistently maintained throughout the years that the promotion of human rights and fundamental freedoms are a paramount purpose of the United Nations, no less important than the maintenance of international peace and security. In our view, the two are intimately related. There can be no genuine peace and security if human rights and fundamental freedoms are not respected.[21]

Continuing, China noted that on issues of human rights and fundamental freedoms enshrined within the Charter, 'the competence of the United Nations is

18 Case Concerning Application of the Convention on the Prevention and Punishment of the Crime of Genocide (Bosnia and Herzegovina v Yugoslavia (Serbia and Montenegro)) – Preliminary Orders, 1993 International Court of Justice Reports of Judgments, Advisory Opinions and Orders (International Court of Justice 1993).

19 United Nations Security Council, 'Security Council, Eighteenth Year: 1053rd Meeting (S/PV.1053)' (United Nations, 5 August 1963), 13.

20 United Nations Security Council, 14.

21 United Nations Security Council, 13.

overriding'[22] and that it 'serves no useful purpose now to reopen the debate on the question of competence, which has long since been settled by an impressive number of precedents'.[23] Following on from this position, China articulated the view that racial discrimination in South Africa was distinct from racial discrimination in other states because South Africa had made it the official policy of the state, rather than working to abolish it.[24]

China then argued that Security Council action against South Africa was 'an inevitable sequel to General Assembly resolution 1761 (XVII)'[25] and that by taking initial measures short of Chapter VII enforcement, the door had been left open for peaceful change within South Africa.[26] As time progressed and South Africa continued to maintain the policy of apartheid, China contended that it was 'incumbent upon the Council take practical steps with a view to bring to an end the injustice imposed by the apartheid policies'.[27] Further, they argued that since the voluntary embargo recommended in *Resolution 181 (1963)* had not achieved any change, it was time for the embargo to be mandatorily and fully implemented.[28] These positions taken in 1963 and 1964 continued until *Resolution 418 (1977)* was passed, adopting Chapter VII enforcement against South Africa.

Russia began its comments on apartheid with 12 pages of emotive hyperbole, interspersed with observations regarding the facts of the situation.[29] This initial address to the Security Council set the tone for all Russia's interactions on this issue; Russia's fervent opposition to apartheid and the advocacy of Chapter VII action against South Africa was constant throughout the Security Council's deliberations. Russia argued that apartheid 'can be compared only with the barbarous policy of Nazi Germany, aimed at the extermination of

22 United Nations Security Council, 14.

23 United Nations Security Council, 14.

24 United Nations Security Council, 14; United Nations Security Council, 'Security Council, Eighteenth Year: 1077th Meeting (S/PV1077)' (United Nations, 3 December 1963), 5; United Nations Security Council, 'Security Council, Nineteenth Year: 1128th Meeting (S/PV1128)' (United Nations, 9 June 1964), 11; United Nations Security Council, '2037th Meeting', 4.

25 United Nations Security Council, 'Security Council, Eighteenth Year: 1056th Meeting (S/PV.1056)' (United Nations, 7 August 1963), 7.

26 United Nations Security Council, 7.

27 United Nations Security Council, '1077th Meeting', 5.

28 United Nations Security Council, 6; United Nations Security Council, 'Security Council, Twenty-Fifth Year: 1548th Meeting (S/PV1548)' (United Nations, 22 July 1970), 3; United Nations Security Council, '2037th Meeting', 6.

29 United Nations Security Council, 'Security Council, Eighteenth Year: 1054th Meeting (S/PV.1054)' (United Nations, 6 August 1963), 2–14.

whole groups of people on the grounds of so-called racial inferiority'.[30] This set the stage for Russia's response, aptly summarised in the following statement:

> The Soviet delegation, Mr. President, fully supports the just demands that the most effective economic, political and other sanctions be applied immediately against the government of the Republic of South Africa; the Soviet delegation fully agrees with the view the South African Government's systematic disregard of United Nations decisions, its systematic violation of the Principles of the United Nation's Charter and the Universal Declaration of Human Rights, places the Republic of South Africa beyond the bounds of our Organization. The Soviet Union does not and will not maintain any relations with the racist government of the Republic of South Africa.[31]

Russia also argued for South Africa to be expelled from the UN under Article 6 of the Charter.[32] They accused NATO and other colonial powers of being in cahoots with, and supporting, the policies of apartheid.[33] In connection with this accusation, they contended that apartheid policies violate 'the principles of equality and self-determination of peoples'.[34] Immediately before *Resolution 181 (1963)* was passed under Chapter VI of the Charter, Russia stated that it held a 'deep conviction for the need to adopt more radical measures against the racist regime in the Republic of South Africa'.[35] This position and the decision to articulate it through emotive rhetoric and hyperbole continued throughout the debates on this issue.[36]

30 United Nations Security Council, 2–3.
31 United Nations Security Council, 12.
32 United Nations Security Council, 13–14.
33 United Nations Security Council, 6–7.
34 United Nations Security Council, 12.
35 United Nations Security Council, '1056th Meeting', 2.
36 See generally: United Nations Security Council, 'Security Council, Eighteenth Year: 1078th Meeting (S/PV1078)' (United Nations, 4 December 1963), 9–11; United Nations Security Council, 'Security Council, Nineteenth Year: 1127th Meeting (S/PV1127)' (United Nations, 8 June 1964), 39; United Nations Security Council, 'Security Council, Nineteenth Year: 1130th Meeting (S/PV1130)' (United Nations, 12 June 1964), 15; United Nations Security Council, 'Security Council, Nineteenth Year: 1131st Meeting (S/PV1131)' (United Nations, 15 June 1964), 5–12; United Nations Security Council, 'Security Council, Nineteenth Year: 1135th Meeting (S/PV1135)' (United Nations, 18 June 1964), 7; United Nations Security Council, 'Security Council, Twenty-Fifth Year: 1547th Meeting (S/PV1547)' (United Nations, 21 July 1970), 2–3; United Nations Security Council, 'Security Council, Twenty-Fifth Year: 1549th Meeting (S/PV1549)' (United Nations, 23 July 1970), 4; United Nations Security Council, 'Security Council, Thirty-Second Year: 2039th Meeting (S/PV2039)' (United Nations, 26

The US began its arguments regarding apartheid by stating that the Security Council had a duty to engage in debate in a manner that sought practical results, and that the delegates had a duty to 'express our feelings with as much restraint as we can muster'.[37] They argued that racial discrimination was 'a disfiguring blight'[38] and that South Africa 'persists in seeing the disease as the remedy'.[39] Further, they stated that it was in everyone's interest 'to wipe out discrimination in our society' and that 'all members of the Organization have pledged themselves to take action, in co-operation with the Organization, to promote the observance of human rights, without distinction as to race'.[40] Nevertheless, in spite of all these objections to the policy of apartheid, the US consistently argued that mandatory sanctions under Chapter VII of the Charter were wholly inappropriate for dealing with the issue:[41]

> It is clear to my delegation that the application of sanctions under Chapter VII in the situation now before us would be both bad law and bad policy. It will be bad law because the extreme measures provided in Chapter VII where never intended and cannot reasonably be interpreted to apply to situations of this kind. The founders of the United Nations were very careful to reserve the right of the Organization to employ mandatory coercive measures in situations where there was an actuality of international violence or such a clear and present threat to peace as to leave no reasonable alternative but to resort to coercion. We do not have that kind of situation here.[42]

The US argued that the travesties of apartheid could be ended through 'a bridge of communication, of discussion and persuasion'.[43] Continuing this position, they later asserted that there could be no external solution for apartheid

October 1977), 5–6; United Nations Security Council, '2045th Meeting', 6–7; United Nations Security Council, 'Security Council, Thirty-Second Year: 2046th Meeting (S/PV2046)' (United Nations, 4 November 1977), 5.

37 United Nations Security Council, 'Security Council, Eighteenth Year: 1052nd Meeting (S/PV.1052)' (United Nations, 2 August 1963), 12.

38 United Nations Security Council, 12.

39 United Nations Security Council, 12.

40 United Nations Security Council, 14.

41 United Nations Security Council, '1078th Meeting', 12; United Nations Security Council, 'Security Council, Nineteenth Year: 1133rd Meeting (S/PV1133)' (United Nations, 16 June 1964), 9; United Nations Security Council, '1135th Meeting', 9; United Nations Security Council, '1549th Meeting', 2–3.

42 United Nations Security Council, '1052nd Meeting', 16.

43 United Nations Security Council, 16.

as it was an internal matter that needed to be resolved by the South Africans themselves; all external influence needed to be achieved by peaceful means, in accordance with the Charter.[44] They also argued that Security Council interference on the issue of apartheid would constitute an unlawful interference in the internal affairs of South Africa.[45]

The turning point for the US was the events of Black Wednesday on 19 October 1977, particularly the 'ending of all political expression by opponents of apartheid in South Africa' by the South African Government.[46] This action was, for the US, grave enough to cause the situation to now be significant enough to warrant a 'mandatory arms embargo under Chapter VII of the Charter'.[47] According to the US, the denial of all political participation presented 'dangers for peace'[48] and political dialogue within South Africa must thus include 'all peoples of South Africa [so as] to achieve a more just and stable society. Failing that, we can see only heightened danger and continuing threat to the security of all the region'.[49] After voting on *Resolution 418 (1977)* concluded, the US reiterated their position that supporting Chapter VII mandatory sanctions against South Africa was based upon measures adopted by the South African Government to suppress political expression by all opponents to apartheid;[50] it was the method by which South Africa chose to maintain apartheid, rather than the policy of apartheid itself, that led to the US supporting a finding of 'threat to the peace'.

The initial position adopted by the UK was that while they regarded it as self-evident that 'the policy of apartheid is evil'[51] and that 'this policy has now led to international friction',[52] they did not regard it as meeting the threshold sufficient for a finding of 'threat to the peace':

> We must, therefore, distinguish between a situation which has engendered international friction and one which constitutes a threat to peace. There is no evidence before us that the actions of the South African Republic, however repellent they may be to us all, are actions which threaten the territorial integrity of political independence of any member country

44 United Nations Security Council, '1078th Meeting', 12.
45 United Nations Security Council, '1128th Meeting', 8.
46 United Nations Security Council, '2045th Meeting', 2.
47 United Nations Security Council, 2.
48 United Nations Security Council, 2.
49 United Nations Security Council, 2.
50 United Nations Security Council, '2046th Meeting', 3.
51 United Nations Security Council, '1054th Meeting', 18.
52 United Nations Security Council, 18.

> … The Council does not in these circumstances have the power to impose sanctions. To attempt to do so would, as the representative of the United States has said, be both bad law and bad policy.[53]

Unlike the US and France, the UK did not consider Security Council action against apartheid to be a violation of the principle of non-interference in internal affairs. The basis of this position was that they regarded the policy of apartheid to be 'of such an extraordinary and exceptional nature as to warrant our regarding it and treating it as *sui generis*'.[54] They did, however, see a mandatory embargo upon all arms to South Africa as a violation of South Africa's right of self-defence under Article 51 of the Charter. They argued that by failing to exempt weapons that could only be used for external defence, and not the implementation of apartheid policies, such as naval hardware, the international community was denying South Africa its right to effectively defend shipping lanes[55] upon which the UK also relied.

The UK said very little regarding the explicit effect the events of Black Wednesday (19 October 1977) had on their changing of position. They simply argued that their support for the resolution and the finding of 'threat to the peace' was based upon South Africa's failure to 'pay heed to the voice of the international community' with regards to changing its policies of apartheid within the country.[56] They hoped that the embargo would bring about 'peaceful and democratic transformation' within South Africa.[57]

While France noted its disgust at the policy of apartheid, it argued that any action taken by the Security Council in relation to South Africa's apartheid policy would constitute a direct interference in matters falling wholly within the national jurisdiction of the state.[58] France asserted that it regarded 'this as a position of principle and believes it has shown the universal and permanent importance that attaches to it'.[59] They sympathised with the sentiments of the African nations and agreed that it was right for the Security Council to create

53 United Nations Security Council, 19–20.

54 United Nations Security Council, 19; see also: United Nations Security Council, '1078th Meeting', 2.

55 United Nations Security Council, '1056th Meeting', 8; United Nations Security Council, 'Security Council, Twenty-Fifth Year: 1546th Meeting (S/PV1546)' (United Nations, 20 July 1970), 3; United Nations Security Council, '1549th Meeting', 3–4.

56 United Nations Security Council, '2046th Meeting', 4.

57 United Nations Security Council, 4.

58 United Nations Security Council, '1054th Meeting', 21–22; United Nations Security Council, '1078th Meeting', 7–8; United Nations Security Council, '1135th Meeting', 11; United Nations Security Council, '1547th Meeting', 5.

59 United Nations Security Council, '1054th Meeting', 21.

moral pressure on South Africa to adjust its behaviour; however, they argued that any Chapter VII action taken would not fall within the mandate of the Security Council or the bounds of the Charter.[60] France did acknowledge that South Africa's 'reprehensible doctrine' put it at odds with the Purposes and Principles of the UN Charter.[61] Further, France argued that Chapter VII action against South Africa would inflame them and drive them into further isolation rather than persuade them to give in to the legitimate demands of the international community:[62] 'The isolation of societies has never made them more open. Quite the contrary. History teaches us that it has in fact led to the hardening of conflicting positions and to the blocking of any progress'.[63] Unrelated to the question of 'threat to the peace', France strongly argued that the policy of apartheid was in no way linked to Western colonial history.[64]

After the events of Black Wednesday, France argued that oppression by the South African Government under apartheid 'is the most flagrant denial of democracy'.[65] In connection with this suppression of political discourse of all opponents of apartheid, France contended that 'apartheid is no longer the internal affair of an individual state, but rather a matter of legitimate concern for the entire international community'.[66] For France, much like the US, it was not apartheid so much as the denial of democracy that stemmed from the manner in which South Africa had chosen to maintain the policy of apartheid that led to the French position that apartheid did, in fact, constitute a 'threat to the peace'.

4 Summary of Coding

The issue of apartheid led all P5 members (eventually) to support a finding of 'threat to the peace'; however, there was strong initial opposition from France, the US and the UK. Russia made its arguments through emotive rhetoric,

60 United Nations Security Council, 21–22; United Nations Security Council, '1078th Meeting', 7–8; United Nations Security Council, '1135th Meeting', 11; United Nations Security Council, '1547th Meeting', 5.

61 United Nations Security Council, '1078th Meeting', 7–8.

62 United Nations Security Council, '1128th Meeting', 10.

63 United Nations Security Council, 'Security Council, Thirty-Second Year: 1999th Meeting (S/PV1999)' (United Nations, 31 March 1977), 8.

64 United Nations Security Council, 8.

65 United Nations Security Council, 'Security Council, Thirty-Second Year: 2044th Meeting (S/PV2044)' (United Nations, 31 October 1977), 4; see also: United Nations Security Council, '1999th Meeting', 7.

66 United Nations Security Council, '2044th Meeting', 4.

highlighting that ideology can constitute a 'threat to the peace', and that apartheid violated human rights and the right of self-determination. China's support was grounded in the notion that apartheid violated human rights and the Purposes and Principles of the Charter. Further, they argued that the proposed sanctions would assist in bringing about a peaceful solution, and that these sanctions were a consequence of South Africa failing to comply with Security Council resolutions. The UK articulated its initial opposition through formal legal arguments, concluding that the situation was not grave enough to warrant Chapter VII action and thus was not within the scope of the Security Council's mandate, and that the proposed actions would violate South Africa's right of self-defence found in Article 51 of the Charter. Their eventual support was grounded in the notion that fact made Article 2(7) no longer relevant, and that the finding of 'threat to the peace' was a consequence of South Africa's actions. The US established its initial opposition through formal legal arguments that the situation was not sufficiently grave enough, and Chapter VII action would thus violate South Africa's right of non-interference while impeding a peaceful solution. Their eventual support was grounded in the defence of democracy and the protection of human rights and the Purposes and Principles of the Charter. Initial French opposition to a finding of 'threat to the peace' was centred on the perception that such a finding would violate South Africa's right of non-interference; Security Council action would thus be beyond their mandate and would violate the Purposes and Principles of the Charter. Their eventual support was formed on the basis that the situation had progressed to the point where Article 2(7) of the Charter was no longer a relevant concern.

CHAPTER 7

Vietnamese Intervention into Cambodia 1978–79

1 Relevance to Overall Project

The Vietnamese intervention into Cambodia on 25 December 1978, resulting in the fall of the Pol Pot regime in early January 1979, has been characterised as a legal and legitimate form of humanitarian intervention into mass atrocities.[1] This argument was never made by Vietnam or within the Security Council; however, the Vietnamese military incursion into Cambodia was discussed (albeit briefly) in terms of 'threat to the peace',[2] although the draft resolution was withdrawn without a vote.[3] There was also a veto of a Chapter VI draft resolution by Russia.[4] Of particular interest to this project is how the Security Council deals with a situation where no facts are offered as to the circumstances on the ground, leading them to deal only with the conjecture presented by those involved (although some indirectly) in the matter. Further, in this case study, two members of the P5, Russia and China, locked horns over the interpretation of the incident—leaving the West relatively absent from the debate. It must be noted that this issue was raised again a month after the meetings considered in this case study; however, these meetings were omitted from the case study, as they predominantly dealt with the Chinese military incursion into Vietnam in response to the Vietnamese military incursion into Cambodia, rather than the Vietnamese incursion directly.[5]

1 Aidan Hehir, 'NATO's "Humanitarian Intervention" in Kosovo: Legal Precedent or Aberration?', *Journal of Human Rights* 8 (2009): 254; J.E. Linter, 'Humanitarian Intervention: Legitimising the Illegal?', *Defence Studies* 5, no. 2 (June 2005): 282; Nicholas J. Wheeler, 'Reflections on the Legality and Legitimacy of NATO's Intervention in Kosovo', *The International Journal of Human Rights* 4, no. 3–4 (2000): 150.

2 United Nations Security Council, 'China: Draft Resolution', 11 January 1979.

3 United Nations Security Council, 'Security Council, Thirty-Fourth Year: 2112th Meeting (S/PV.2112)' (United Nations, 15 January 1979), 1.

4 United Nations Security Council, 1.

5 See generally: United Nations Security Council, 'Security Council, Thirty-Fourth Year: 2114th Meeting (S/PV.2114)' (United Nations, 23 February 1979); United Nations Security Council, 'Security Council, Thirty-Fourth Year: 2115th Meeting (S/PV.2115)' (United Nations, 24 February 1979); United Nations Security Council, 'Security Council, Thirty-Fourth Year: 2116th Meeting (S/PV.2116)' (United Nations, 25 February 1979); United Nations Security Council, 'Security Council, Thirty-Fourth Year: 2117th Meeting (S/PV.2117)' (United Nations, 27 February 1979); United Nations Security Council, 'Security Council, Thirty-Fourth Year: 2118th Meeting (S/PV.2118)' (United Nations, 28 February 1979); United Nations Security Council,

 | DOI:10.1163/9789004391420_009

2 Context of the Debates

On 31 December 1978, the Pol Pot Government in Cambodia informed the Security Council by telegram of Vietnamese military incursions into their territory and requested Security Council consideration and condemnation of the action.[6] This was followed by a telegram on 3 January 1979 requesting an urgent Security Council meeting to condemn Vietnamese aggression within their territory.[7] On 9 January, Vietnam presented a letter to the Security Council, ostensibly enclosing a telegram from the new government in Cambodia, declaring a change of government and stating that representatives of the Pol Pot regime had no standing on behalf of the country within the Security Council.[8] This was followed by a similar letter on 11 January informing the Security Council that should they be proceeding with a meeting on Vietnamese aggression in Cambodia, the new government representative would not be present to take part until 15 January.[9] When the meeting commenced, Russia objected to adopting the agenda on the basis that the request of the ousted Pol Pot Government was illegitimate, as they no longer had any standing within the UN (by virtue of the regime change) and that any Security Council action would amount to interference in Cambodia's internal affairs.[10] China argued that the meeting was not considering internal affairs in Cambodia, but rather Vietnamese aggression against another state, and thus was within the ambit of the Security Council's competence.[11] The then President (Jamaica) exercised their discretion to keep the matter on the agenda in spite of the change of government, on the basis of prior consultations.[12]

'Security Council, Thirty-Fourth Year: 2129th Meeting (S/PV.2129)' (United Nations, 16 March 1979).

6 Democratic Kampuchea, 'Telegram Dated 31 December 1978 from the Deputy Prime Minister in Charge of Foreign Affairs of Democratic Kampuchea Addressed to the President of the Security Council' (United Nations, 31 December 1978).

7 Democratic Kampuchea, 'Telegram Dated 3 January 1979 from the Deputy Prime Minister in Charge of Foreign Affairs of Democratic Kampuchea Addressed to the President of the Security Council' (United Nations, 3 January 1979).

8 Viet Nam, 'Letter Dated 9 January 1979 from the Permanent Representative of Viet Nam to the United Nations Addressed to the President of the Security Council' (United Nations Security Council, 9 January 1979).

9 Viet Nam, 'Letter Dated 11 January 1979 from the Permanent Representative of Viet Nam to the United Nations Addressed to the President of the Security Council' (United Nations Security Council, 11 January 1979).

10 United Nations Security Council, 'Security Council, Thirty-Fourth Year: 2108th Meeting (S/PV.2108)' (United Nations, 11 January 1979), 2.

11 United Nations Security Council, 2–3.

12 United Nations Security Council, 3.

Within the initial meetings, the representative of the ousted Pol Pot Government characterised the recent military activity as a continuation of a litany of Vietnamese military aggressions against Cambodia.[13] By contrast, Vietnam characterised the Security Council's recognition of the representative from the 'already defunct … Pol Pot-Ieng Sary regime' as a violation of Cambodia's Article 2(7) Charter rights to self-determination.[14] Further, Vietnam characterised their military activity as an exercise of their Article 51 'sacred right of self-defence of peoples in the face of aggression',[15] citing numerous border incursions dating back to 1975 between Vietnam and the Pol Pot Government in Cambodia.[16] Russia characterised the ousting of the Pol Pot Government as an uprising of '[t]he Kampuchean patriots' who overthrew 'the criminal Pol Pot clique',[17] with minimal reference to the Vietnamese military incursion (which they characterised as an act of self-defence by Vietnam).[18] As noted above, China characterised the incident as purely Vietnamese aggression against Cambodia.[19]

3 Justificatory Discourse of the P5

The justificatory discourse of France, the UK and the US was fairly similar in nature—each of their brief statements focused upon rights of territorial integrity. Russia consistently characterised its objections to Security Council action on the basis of non-intervention in the internal affairs of another state. China characterised its arguments as necessary action against unlawful aggression by Vietnam against Cambodia.

France began its argument by stating that since the beginning of conflict between the two states, France had pushed for peaceful settlement.[20] Further, they noted their consistent condemnation of the Pol Pot regime's conduct with regards to human rights violations against its own citizens.[21] In relation to the current situation, they argued that the consistent human rights violations

13 United Nations Security Council, 7–9.
14 United Nations Security Council, 11.
15 United Nations Security Council, 13.
16 United Nations Security Council, 12–17.
17 United Nations Security Council, 4.
18 United Nations Security Council, 16.
19 United Nations Security Council, 5.
20 United Nations Security Council, 'Security Council, Thirty-Fourth Year: 2109th Meeting (S/PV.2109)' (United Nations, 12 January 1979), 4.
21 United Nations Security Council, 4.

being committed by the government against its own citizens did not justify foreign intervention and forcible regime change:

> The notion that because a regime is detestable foreign intervention is justified and forcible overthrow is legitimate is extremely dangerous. That could ultimately jeopardise the very maintenance of international law and order and make the continued existence of various regimes dependent on the judgement of their neighbours. It is important for the Council to affirm, without any ambiguity, that it cannot condone the occupation of a sovereign country by a foreign Power.[22]

France closed its statements by expressing their hope that the Security Council would take a stand, ensuring a Vietnamese withdrawal and assisting Cambodia to move forward with a 'genuinely independent, democratic and peaceful regime'.[23]

In its statements, the US tried to tread a thin line between protecting human rights and rejecting the use of force against another state:

> The invasion by Viet Nam of Kampuchea presents to the Council difficult political and moral questions. The issue is affected by history, rival claims and Charter principles. It appears complex because several different provisions of the Charter are directly relevant to deliberations. These are that: the fundamental principles of human rights must be respected by all governments, one State must not use force against the territory of another State, a State must not interfere in the affairs of another State, and, if there is a dispute between States that must be settled peaceably.[24]

With that said, the US, while noting their consistent condemnation of human rights violations in Cambodia,[25] then proceeded to characterise the issue at hand for the Security Council as how to respond to the invasion and toppling of the government by a foreign state.[26] Once this characterisation had taken place, they made their response and position abundantly clear:

22 United Nations Security Council, 4.

23 United Nations Security Council, 4.

24 United Nations Security Council, 'Security Council, Thirty-Fourth Year: 2110th Meeting (S/PV.2110)' (United Nations, 13 January 1979), 7.

25 United Nations Security Council, 7–8.

26 United Nations Security Council, 7.

> [M]y Government believes we must look at one essential, contemporary fact. The troops of one country are now occupying the territory of another, and have imposed a new government appointed by force of arms. That fact led us to the conclusion that the solution to the problem we are discussing is clear: Viet Nam must immediately withdraw its armed forces from Kampuchea, must respect that country's territorial integrity and must make credible its intention to respect the territorial integrity of other States in the region.[27]

The UK began by noting their consistently voiced 'grave concern at the inhumanities which had taken place in Kampuchea'.[28] While they noted that the human rights concerns had featured heavily within the debates, they argued that the Pol Pot regime's violation of human rights against own citizens did not provide justification for Vietnam's actions:

> Whatever is said about human rights in Kampuchea, it cannot excuse Viet Nam, whose own human rights record is deplorable, for violating the territorial integrity of Democratic Kampuchea, an independent State Member of the United Nations … Respect for the sovereignty, territorial integrity and political independence of Member States is one of the cornerstones of the Charter and of the United Nations system.[29]

The UK closed by saying that it was firmly opposed to the Vietnamese use of force against Cambodia and the human rights violations that had been committed by the ousted Pol Pot regime, stating that the UK stood 'ready to support any action by the Council to give effect to [these issues]'.[30]

China began its arguments by stating that the ousted Pol Pot Government was the only legal authority in Cambodia, a fact affirmed by the General Assembly of the UN.[31] They then proceeded to argue that the new government was the result of Vietnamese aggression and Russian political manoeuvring aimed at creating a puppet state in the region.[32] Further, they argued that the telegrams the Vietnamese Government had forwarded to the Security Council were in fact Vietnamese or Russian forgeries originating in New York designed

27 United Nations Security Council, 7.
28 United Nations Security Council, 6.
29 United Nations Security Council, 6–7.
30 United Nations Security Council, 7.
31 United Nations Security Council, '2108th Meeting', 4.
32 United Nations Security Council, 5.

to fool the international community.[33] China asserted that Vietnam's invasion and annexation of Cambodia was 'an important step in Viet Nam's strategy of establishing a colonial empire called the "Indo-Chinese Federation" under its armed control for further expansion of its sphere of influence in South-East Asia'.[34] Further, they argued that the new government was merely a front established to legitimise the Vietnamese aggression in a manner that 'was the habitual practice of Adolf Hitler'.[35] China contended that the Security Council had a duty to respond to Vietnamese aggression in Cambodia, according to the UN Charter, on the basis of the Security Council bearing the primary responsibility for maintaining international peace and security.[36] They also suggested that Security Council action to remove Vietnam from Cambodia and restore the Pol Pot Government was in the interests of peace and justice:

> The Chinese government and people and the people of other countries in the Asia-Pacific region certainly cannot tolerate the gangsterism of the Vietnamese authorities and the grave situation arising therefrom. Therefore, it is the incumbent duty of all peace-loving and justice-upholding countries to stop Viet Nam's aggression, support the Kampuchean people's struggle and save peace in South-East Asia.[37]

China later withdrew its draft resolution, the preamble of which characterised the situation as 'a threat to international peace and security',[38] most likely due to the threat of a veto from Russia. They characterised Russia's veto of the Chapter VI draft resolution, and the situation generally, as a part of Russia's political goals for global hegemony.[39] Finally, they argued that Security Council action against Vietnam was essential for all 'peoples of the world that cherish their own independence and security in opposing external domination and hegemony, outside aggression to the acquisition of territory and in defending national independence and international peace and security'.[40]

Russia began by characterising the change in government in Cambodia as the result of an intolerable situation against which the Khmer people 'took up arms and overthrew that criminal regime to preserve the lives of their people

33 United Nations Security Council, 5.
34 United Nations Security Council, 10.
35 United Nations Security Council, 10.
36 United Nations Security Council, 11.
37 United Nations Security Council, 10.
38 United Nations Security Council, '2112th Meeting', 1.
39 United Nations Security Council, 3.
40 United Nations Security Council, 4.

and restore their national heritage and the unity of their state'.[41] They also argued that the ousted government was 'the criminal regime of Pol Pot' that had been expelled 'because of its massive repression and aggressive adventurism'.[42] On this basis, Russia argued that removing the Pol Pot regime was an 'internal affair of the people of that country, and should not be a subject for consideration in the Security Council'.[43] Further, they suggested that the new government's 'foreign policy provides for the building of an independent, democratic and non-aligned Kampuchea, the establishment of trade with neighbouring countries and the strengthening of peace and stability in South-East Asia and throughout the world'.[44]

In response to China's draft resolution, Russia suggested that it 'attempts to prod the Council towards intervention in the affairs of Kampuchea, a State Member of the United Nations'.[45] They also argued that it was a smokescreen to distract from the human rights violations that had occurred under the Pol Pot regime:

> It would appear that in this way certain persons are attempting to divert the attention of the world public opinion from the monstrous crimes committed by this clique against people of their own country and their acts of aggression against neighbouring states, which have led to the undermining of stability in international security in the area ... In a country with a population of 8 million, the rulers destroyed, according to statistics reported in, among others, the Western press, from 2 to 3 million people. The vocabulary used in international practice to describe mass violations of human rights is simply inadequate to describe these monstrous crimes.[46]

Russia suggested that the Pol Pot regime was globally acknowledged to be 'in an organised way and systematically pursuing a policy of mass murder, arbitrary terror and lawlessness'.[47] Further, they suggested that Chinese assertions that the new government was a Russian and Vietnamese puppet were slanderous:

> Peking's propaganda slanders the Kampuchean Patriots. That slander cannot hide an obvious fact: the Khmer people has waged a struggle in its

41 United Nations Security Council, '2108th Meeting', 4.
42 United Nations Security Council, 4.
43 United Nations Security Council, 4.
44 United Nations Security Council, 4.
45 United Nations Security Council, 14.
46 United Nations Security Council, 14–15.
47 United Nations Security Council, 15.

> territory for its own freedom. If there is an intervention from outside in the internal affairs of Kampuchea it is and continues to be carried out by the Peking hegemonists.[48]

In response to the Vietnamese military incursion into Cambodia, Russia characterised this as simply an exercise of self-defence against a foreign aggressor.[49] To support this, Russia cited the Pol Pot regime's commencement of hostilities against Vietnam in January 1978,[50] and the history of the Pol Pot regime's border incursions into Thailand.[51] When defending its veto of the Chapter VI draft resolution, Russia stated that the push for Security Council action in Cambodia was an attempt to cover up Pol Pot's genocide through interference in Cambodia's internal affairs.[52] They also stated that the new government would make a 'valuable contribution to the cause of the strengthening of international peace and security'.[53] Finally, in response to Chinese accusations, Russia stated that China's arguments and assertions amounted to 'slanderous fabrications'[54] and that the Pol Pot regime was directly related to Chinese imperialism:[55]

> The massive destruction of people in Kampuchea was the Chinese 'Cultural Revolution' in its Kampuchean version. The Kampuchean people has now put an end to the experiment and has opened up the way to democracy, peace and true independence for the country.[56]

4 Summary of Coding

In this case study, only Russia opposed a finding of 'threat to the peace'. Russia's opposition (and veto) was because such a finding would violate the Khmer people's right of self-determination and right of non-interference, and would violate the Vietnamese right of self-defence. They also stated that their opposition was grounded in the protection of human rights and the defence of democracy. French support was because they saw Vietnam's actions as a violation

48 United Nations Security Council, 17.
49 United Nations Security Council, 16.
50 United Nations Security Council, 16.
51 United Nations Security Council, 16.
52 United Nations Security Council, '2112th Meeting', 4.
53 United Nations Security Council, 5.
54 United Nations Security Council, 4.
55 United Nations Security Council, '2108th Meeting', 17.
56 United Nations Security Council, '2112th Meeting', 4.

of the right of non-interference. The UK used formal legal arguments to reach the same conclusion as France. The US characterised Vietnam's actions as a violation of international law and the right of non-interference amounting to a 'threat to the peace'. China argued that Vietnam's actions were a violation of the right of non-interference, and thus the situation was within the scope of the Security Council's mandate.

CHAPTER 8

US–Iran Hostage Crisis 1979 (Resolutions 457 and 461 (1979))

1 Relevance to the Overall Project

Towards the end of 1979 and at the beginning of 1980, the Security Council considered whether Iranian militants' taking of the US Embassy and holding of Embassy staff as hostages could fall within the ambit of 'threat to the peace'. A further contributing factor in these considerations was the ICJ's provisional orders, which found that Iran had violated numerous obligations under international law, and the subsequent order requiring the immediate release of the hostages and return of the Embassy to US control.[1] The question before the Security Council hinged on whether such violations of the core principles of diplomatic relations under international law, and the refusal to comply with ICJ orders, led to the existence of a 'threat to the peace'. The matter came to a close in the Security Council when the draft resolution from the US,[2] determining an Article 39 finding and Article 41 enforcement measures was rejected by a vote of 10 in favour, two against (including a veto from Russia) and two abstentions;[3] with China declining to engage in the vote.[4] The *Repertoire of Practice of the Security Council* highlights that this was the only instance between 1975 and 1980 where the concept of 'threat to the peace' was significantly discussed by the Council, with the sticking point being that the Council's proposed action was not commensurate with the violation committed by Iran.[5] While this certainly was one of the considerations in the debates, it was by no means the only one, as the justificatory discourse explored below demonstrates.

---

1 Case Concerning United States Diplomatic and Consular Staff in Tehran (United States of America v. Iran): Request for the Indication of Provisional Measures, 1979 International Court of Justice Reports of Judgments, Advisory Opinions and Orders (International Court of Justice 1979).

2 United Nations Security Council, 'United States of America: Draft Resolution' (United Nations, 10 January 1980).

3 United Nations Security Council, 'Security Council, Thirty-Fifth Year: 2191st Meeting (S/PV.2191)' (United Nations, 11 January 1980), 14.

4 United Nations Security Council, 14.

5 Repertoire of the Practice of the Security Council, 'Chapter XI: Considerations of Chapter VII the Charter (1975–80)', 400–01.

 DOI:10.1163/9789004391420_010

2 Context of the Debates

The Iranian perspective on events was represented to the Security Council in a letter to the Secretary-General dated 13 November 1979.[6] The letter generally outlined US interference and manipulation of Iran's internal affairs, requested public examination of the Shah's guilt and the US Government's return of his assets to Iran (as he and his family were residing in the US at the time). These were expressed as pre-conditions to releasing the hostages.[7] The Secretary-General then briefed the Security Council on Iranian militants' seizure of the US Embassy in Tehran, noting that this had been achieved with the support of the new Iranian Government.[8] The Secretary-General stated that the seizure of the Embassy, in contravention of international law and diplomatic relations, 'threaten[s] the peace and stability of the region and could well have great consequences for the entire world'.[9] The Secretary-General outlined the international response to the Embassy seizure, stating that 'it was in light of these developments and of the escalation of tension that I concluded that the present crisis poses a serious threat to international peace and security'.[10] This led to the unanimous passing of *Resolution 457 (1979)*, requesting that the Secretary-General attempt to mediate a resolution to the crisis.[11]

On 22 December 1979, the Secretary-General provided an update report to the Security Council on the progress of the crisis.[12] The report summarised the Secretary-General's actions on the issue and Iran's refusal to comply with the ICJ's orders to release the hostages and return the Embassy to the US.[13] The Secretary-General concluded, in oral briefings to the Security Council regarding the report, that there was no foreseeable end to the crisis.[14]

6 Iran, 'Letter Dated 13 November 1979 from the Charge D'Affairs of the Permanent Mission of Iran to the United Nations Addressed to the Secretary-General' (United Nations, 13 November 1979).

7 Iran, 3.

8 United Nations Security Council, 'Security Council, Thirty-Fourth Year: 2172nd Meeting (S/PV.2172)' (United Nations, 27 November 1979), 1.

9 United Nations Security Council, 1.

10 United Nations Security Council, 1.

11 United Nations Security Council, 'Security Council, Thirty-Fourth Year: 2178th Meeting (S/PV.2178)' (United Nations, 4 December 1979), 2.

12 United Nations Secretary-General, 'Report of the Secretary-General Concerning Implementation of Security Council Resolution 457 (1979)' (United Nations Security Council, 22 December 1979).

13 United Nations Secretary-General.

14 United Nations Security Council, 'Security Council, Thirty-Fourth Year: 2182nd Meeting (S/PV.2182)' (United Nations, 29 December 1979).

This led to the passing of *Resolution 461 (1979)*, by a vote of 11 for, zero against and four abstentions, threatening Security Council action under Articles 39 and 41 should Iran continue to refuse to comply with the ICJ's orders.[15] On 11 January 1980, the US raised the question of Articles 39 and 41 action in the form of wide-ranging sanctions against Iran because of their continued non-compliance.[16] Although the US had significant support within the Security Council, the draft resolution bringing about the sanctions and declaring the situation to be a 'threat to the peace' was defeated by a veto from Russia.[17] The issue was not raised again in the Security Council, as all focus on Iran shifted to the Iran–Iraq war.

3 Justificatory Discourse of the P5

For the most part, the P5's justificatory discourse coalesced around the gravity of the violations of international law Iran had committed by seizing the Embassy and taking Embassy staff as hostages. However, with the exception of the US, supportive P5 members were reluctant to find the situation to be a 'threat to the peace'. This reluctance was evident in the push for peaceful resolution through Chapter VI action, with the threat of further action under Articles 39 and 41 should Iran not comply, before the possibility of Chapter VII action was ever really considered. Russia flatly rejected the possibility of Chapter VII action on the basis that they saw the situation as purely bilateral and not within the scope of the Security Council's mandate.

Unsurprisingly, the US was the driving force behind attempts to characterise the situation in Iran as a 'threat to the peace'. They began their arguments by highlighting that diplomatic protections are by far the most basic obligation of international law,[18] and that although Iran claimed to have violated them in an effort to obtain redress for human rights violations, the US asserted that 'no country can break and ignore the law while seeking its benefits'.[19] After Iran's failure to comply with the ICJ's preliminary orders to release the hostages and return the Embassy, the US argued that Iran 'has placed itself in conflict with the structure of law and with the machinery of peace all of us have

15 United Nations Security Council, 'Security Council, Thirty-Fourth Year: 2184th Meeting (S/PV.2184)' (United Nations, 31 December 1979), 6.
16 United Nations Security Council, 'Draft Resolution (S/13735)'.
17 United Nations Security Council, '2191st Meeting', 14.
18 United Nations Security Council, 'Security Council, Thirty-Fourth Year: 2175th Meeting (S/PV.2175)' (United Nations, 1 December 1979), 2.
19 United Nations Security Council, 2.

painstakingly built'.[20] In this vein of characterising the dispute as one of Iran against the whole world legal order, rather than a bilateral state dispute, the US built upon their arguments by stating that '[t]he time has come for the world community to act, firmly and collectively, to uphold international law and to preserve international peace. We must give practical meaning to the principles and purposes of the Charter'.[21]

After Iran's continued failure to comply with the ICJ's orders and *Resolution 461 (1979)*, the US continued to characterise the situation as larger than a simple bilateral dispute:

> I should like to close by reminding the council of something I have said on a number of occasions: this is not a quarrel between the United States and Iran. In my judgement, it is a dispute between Iran and the international community. The continued viability of cherished and heretofore universally observed principles of international law is at stake.[22]

Continuing to assert that the potential breakdown of the international laws of diplomatic relations was a global issue that constituted a 'threat to the peace', along with Iran's continued failure to comply with orders to release the hostages and return the Embassy, the US argued that '[t]he time therefore has come for the Security Council to adopt effective measures against Iran under Articles 39 and 41 of the Charter that are required by paragraph 6 of Resolution 461 (1979)'.[23]

France was a clear supporter of the US position, albeit with hints of reluctance in their statements. Initially, France voiced their support for the Iranian's right of self-determination as provided for under the Charter, while highlighting that their current exercise of this right in terms of seizing the Embassy and taking hostages constituted a gross violation of international law.[24] They called for the situation to be resolved peaceably and in accordance with international legal norms.[25] Their position evolved to be in favour of the US argument for finding a 'threat to the peace' after Iran's failure to comply with ICJ's orders. At this point, France again called for the immediate release of the hostages and the return of the Embassy, noting that should Iran fail to comply, 'there will be nothing left for the Council to do but resort to measures laid down in Chapter VII

20 United Nations Security Council, '2182nd Meeting', 2.
21 United Nations Security Council, 2.
22 United Nations Security Council, '2191st Meeting', 4.
23 United Nations Security Council, 3.
24 United Nations Security Council, '2175th Meeting', 5–6.
25 United Nations Security Council, 6.

of the Charter'.[26] After Iran's continued failure to comply with the ICJ's orders and Security Council's calls for the release of the hostages, France stated that the Security Council had no alternative but to implement measures under Articles 39 and 41 of the Charter in an effort to resolve the situation.[27]

The only direct support the UK showed in terms of finding that the situation constituted a 'threat to the peace' was their vote in favour of the draft resolution in meeting 2191 (the draft resolution ultimately being vetoed by Russia).[28] Prior to the ICJ issuing its orders, the UK asserted that the Security Council should remain seized of the situation because of the violations of international law; however, they argued simply for peaceable settlement to the dispute.[29] After Iran's failure to comply with the ICJ's orders, the UK adopted the same characterisation of the situation as the US, stating that 'this is not simply a diplomatic crisis, a dispute between two countries. It touches deep humanitarian springs'.[30] Further, they argued that they had no quarrel with Iran beyond the 'flagrant violation of the Vienna Convention on Diplomatic Relations, of other United Nations conventions, of general international law and long-standing diplomatic practices of States',[31] and that because of these violations, they would stand with the US on this issue.[32]

China began its statements on this issue by highlighting (with reference to the coup in Iran) that 'we always hold that the internal affairs of each country should be managed by its own people and there should be no interference in the internal affairs of other countries'.[33] After stating this support for Iranian self-determination, China argued that diplomatic protections must be universally respected and called for the immediate release of the hostages within Iran.[34] After Iran's failure to comply with the ICJ's orders to release the hostages, China asserted that should this situation continue, they broadly supported the notion of future Articles 39 and 41 action provided for in operative paragraph 6 of *Resolution 461 (1979)*; however, they also called for prudence and proportionality should this road be taken.[35] When the draft resolution for action against Iran under Articles 39 and 41 was put to a vote, China declined to

26 United Nations Security Council, '2182nd Meeting', 5.
27 United Nations Security Council, '2191st Meeting', 13.
28 United Nations Security Council, 14.
29 United Nations Security Council, '2175th Meeting', 4.
30 United Nations Security Council, '2182nd Meeting', 3.
31 United Nations Security Council, 3.
32 United Nations Security Council, 3.
33 United Nations Security Council, '2175th Meeting', 10.
34 United Nations Security Council, 10.
35 United Nations Security Council, '2184th Meeting', 3.

participate (it is unclear why they refused to vote instead of simply abstaining) on the basis that they felt the action in the draft resolution was disproportionate and would exacerbate rather than resolve the situation.[36] Further, they used this opportunity to accuse Russia of attempting to make cheap political capital in the Islamic world by using the veto as a cover for their large-scale aggression within Afghanistan, which China argued posed 'a grave threat to the independence and security of Iran'.[37]

While Russia supported the calls to end the hostage situation, and characterised that situation as a gross violation of international law, they staunchly disagreed with the US and UK position that through these violations, Iran had placed itself in conflict with the entire world. Russia began its statements by highlighting the long-term conflict between the US and Iran, but nevertheless acknowledging that even in situations of conflict, diplomatic privileges must be respected.[38] Further, Russia indicated its support for the coup within Iran and Iran's 'interests, democratic rights, and its genuine independence'.[39] However, while Russia endorsed the motives behind the Embassy seizure—redressing violations committed by the previous, US-supported regime—they argued that taking hostages 'constitutes an act that is contrary to international law',[40] and called for a swift and peaceable resolution.[41] After Iran's failure to comply with the ICJ's orders, and the push for Chapter VII action that followed, Russia noted that tensions between the US and Iran as a result of the situation had the potential for 'great consequences for international peace and security',[42] and called for the parties to resolve their disputes 'by peaceable means in such a manner that international peace and security, and justice, would not be endangered'.[43] Russia asserted that the dispute itself was simply bilateral in nature and that any form of Chapter VII action by the Security Council 'could only serve to exacerbate the situation and create a threat to peace'.[44] This position was starkly underlined by Russia's veto of the draft resolution ordering action under Articles 39 and 41 against Iran,[45] with Russia stating that

36 United Nations Security Council, '2191st Meeting', 15.
37 United Nations Security Council, 15.
38 United Nations Security Council, '2175th Meeting', 7.
39 United Nations Security Council, 7.
40 United Nations Security Council, 7–8.
41 United Nations Security Council, 8.
42 United Nations Security Council, '2184th Meeting', 3.
43 United Nations Security Council, 3.
44 United Nations Security Council, 4.
45 United Nations Security Council, '2191st Meeting', 14.

> [T]he Soviet delegation has said on every occasion that it is wrong to allege that, as a result of the actions of Iran, a threat had been created to international peace and security. Attempts to represent matters in this light distort the actual state of affairs. What is happening between the United States and Iran is a bilateral dispute that does not fall within the purview of Chapter VII of the Charter. Attaching to this dispute the question of any kind of sanctions is unjustified. To apply sanctions or take any kind of physical action against Iran could only serve to exacerbate the situation and create a threat to peace.[46]

Finally, Russia defended its actions in Afghanistan against China's accusations by noting that it was simply providing assistance to an ally.[47]

4 Summary of Coding

This case study had support for a finding of 'threat to the peace' from France, the US and the UK, and opposition from China and Russia. The UK argued that the situation was sufficiently grave enough to warrant Chapter VII action (which they maintained would aid in finding a peaceful resolution) and that Iran's violations of international law constituted a 'threat to the peace'. France agreed with the UK that Iran's violations of international law constituted a 'threat to the peace', while also asserting that Chapter VII action was a consequence of Iran's actions (and that such action would help facilitate a peaceful resolution). The US used formal legal arguments to conclude that the situation was grave enough for a finding of 'threat to the peace', and that such a finding was the consequence of Iran's actions. They also argued that Iran's actions violated the Purposes and Principles of the Charter and of international law more generally, which amounted to a 'threat to the peace'. Chinese opposition to such a finding was grounded in upholding Iran's right of non-interference and their lack of faith in the proposed solution. Russia's opposition (and veto) was based on their desire for a peaceful solution and their lack of faith that the proposed solution would achieve that aim. They also argued that the situation lacked sufficient gravity for a finding of 'threat to the peace', and that such a finding may be in opposition to Iran's right of self-determination.

---

46 United Nations Security Council, 5.

47 United Nations Security Council, 16.

CHAPTER 9

Namibian Occupation by South Africa 1981–83 (Resolutions 532 and 539 (1983))

1 Relevance to the Overall Project

This case study examines the consequences of South Africa's failure comply with *Resolution 439 (1978)*, which guaranteed Chapter VII action as a result of non-compliance.[1] It is simultaneously concerned with Namibia's right of independence and self-determination in connection with the South African occupation of Namibian territory. This case study acts as a counterpoint to the Afghanistan case study (see Chapter 15), where failure to comply with Security Council resolutions was a contributing factor to a finding of 'threat to the peace'. Further, this situation had four vetoes each from France, the UK and the US (a total of 12 vetoes).[2] Given these factors, it is worthwhile attempting to understand why, in this instance, failure to comply with Security Council resolutions that promised Chapter VII action as a result of non-compliance was not considered sufficient for a finding of 'threat to the peace' and Chapter VII action. The *Repertoire of Practice of the Security Council* for this period notes significant discussion on the question of 'threat to the peace' in 1981 in relation to Namibia,[3] but omits the discussions that occurred in two separate sets of debates in 1983. Examining all sets of debates reveals a strong call for a finding of 'threat to the peace' in relation to the South African occupation of Namibia, rather than the question being simply restricted to 1981 debates, as suggested by the *Repertoire of Practice of the Security Council.*

2 Context of the Debates

In all three sets of debates, a Secretary-General's report regarding South Africa's ongoing occupation of Namibia was tabled and acted as the catalyst for the

1 'Resolution 439 (1978)', S/RES/439 (1978) UN Security Council (1978), para. 6.
2 United Nations Security Council, 'Security Council, Thirty-Sixth Year: 2277th Meeting (S/PV.2277)' (United Nations, 30 April 1981), 3.
3 Repertoire of the Practice of the Security Council, 'Chapter XI: Considerations of Chapter VII the Charter (1981–84)', 324–25.

 | DOI:10.1163/9789004391420_011

debates themselves. In the first set of debates in 1981, the Secretary-General's report notes the timetable set out for Namibian independence by the end of 1981,[4] and South Africa's unwillingness to agree to a ceasefire and implement this timetable.[5] In oral briefings regarding this report, the Secretary-General also mentions a letter from South Africa[6] accusing the UN of supporting terrorism and exhibiting bias in relation to settling the Namibia question.[7] The debates ended with the UK, US and France vetoing four different draft resolutions that would have been made under Chapter VII (three stating that the situation was a 'threat to the peace' and one stating that a 'breach of the peace' had occurred).[8]

When the question was raised again in 1983, the report that prompted this renewed round of debates notes that independence for Namibia was still not in sight,[9] while also highlighting that Namibian independence was essential for peace and security within the region.[10] This series of debates led to the passing of *Resolution 532 (1983)* under Chapter VI of the Charter, condemning the occupation and indicating that the Security Council remained seized of the matter.[11] A further report, sparking the debates at the end of 1983, cited the South African Government's continued unwillingness to negotiate a peace settlement and withdrawal from the territory,[12] while also arguing that peacefully settling the issue of Namibian independence was crucial to stability within the region.[13] The result of this set of debates was the passing of *Resolution 539*

---

4 United Nations Secretary-General, 'Further Report of the Secretary-General Concerning the Implementation of Security Council Resolutions 435 (1978) and 439 (1978) Concerning the Question of Namibia' (New York; New York: United Nations Security Council, 19 January 1981), para. 1.

5 United Nations Secretary-General, para. 19.

6 United Nations Security Council, 'Security Council, Thirty-Sixth Year: 2263rd Meeting (S/PV.2263)' (United Nations, 30 January 1981), 1–2.

7 South Africa, 'Letter Dated 28 January 1981 from the Permanent Representative of South Africa to the United Nations Addressed to the Secretary-General', 29 January 1981, 8.

8 United Nations Security Council, '2277th Meeting', 3.

9 United Nations Secretary-General, 'Further Report of the Secretary-General Concerning the Implementation of Security Council Resolutions 435 (1978) and 439 (1978) Concerning the Question of Namibia' (New York; New York: United Nations Security Council, 19 May 1983), para. 16.

10 United Nations Secretary-General, para. 20.

11 'Resolution 532 (1983)', S/RES/532 (1983) UN Security Council (1983).

12 United Nations Secretary-General, 'Further Report of the Secretary-General Concerning the Implementation of Security Council Resolutions 435 (1978) and 439 (1978) Concerning the Question of Namibia' (New York; New York: United Nations Security Council, 29 August 1983), para. 25.

13 United Nations Secretary-General, para. 27.

(*1983*) under Chapter VI,[14] echoing *Resolution 532* (*1983*) in content, with 14 votes and an abstention from the US (on the grounds that they could not support the implied future Chapter VII action contained within the resolution).[15]

3 Justificatory Discourse of the P5

The P5's justificatory discourse for this issue ranged from strong support for Chapter VII action against South Africa as a result of their continued occupation of Namibia, to insistence upon a solution involving the Security Council only through negotiation and peaceful means. Of the P5, Russia most strongly advocated for a finding of 'threat to the peace' (or, in one instance, a finding of 'breach of the peace') on the grounds that South Africa had violated Security Council resolutions with their occupation; Russia received strong support for this position from China. The counterpoint to these positions was adopted by the US, UK and France, all of which placed a negotiated peaceful settlement at the centre of efforts to ensure peace and stability within the region. This position was held most strongly by the US, which abstained from voting on *Resolution 539* (*1983*) on the basis that they could not support the implication of future Chapter VII action found within the resolution.

The US position on the South African occupation of Namibia was initially quite noncommittal; they simply stated that they supported the Secretary-General's efforts to bring about a peaceful and acceptable solution to the issue. Shortly afterwards, they noted that Namibian independence was their only goal,[16] and the lack of success in negotiations so far was no reason to seek a more forceful solution.[17] Further, they criticised the ability of a Security Council resolution to have any meaningful effect on the situation:

> But I think that if we are realistic—and if we are not realistic we waste our time and that of everyone else present—then we will understand the that resolutions do not solve problems, sanctions do not solve problems. Declarations do not make peace, declarations do not secure independence. Is it not past time that we have considered here, realistically, the practical

14 'Resolution 539 (1983)', S/RES/539 (1983) UN Security Council (1983).

15 United Nations Security Council, 'Security Council, Thirty-Eighth Year: 2492nd Meeting (S/PV.2492)' (United Nations, 28 October 1983), 6–7.

16 United Nations Security Council, '2263rd Meeting', 17.

17 United Nations Security Council, 'Security Council, Thirty-Sixth Year: 2271st Meeting (S/PV.2271)' (United Nations, 23 April 1981), 12.

> actual alternatives to a continuing search for an internationally acceptable solution in Namibia?[18]

The US position—that sanctions and other Chapter VII action against South Africa would be counterproductive towards Namibian independence and peace and stability in the region—was consistent throughout all subsequent deates.[19] The US argued that the only realistic solution to the problem outside of a negotiated South African withdrawal was armed intervention (for which they inferred a lack of support).[20] This assertion that a peaceful settlement was the only real solution for South African occupation of Namibia resulted in four vetoes of Chapter VII action,[21] and an abstention from a Chapter VI resolution,[22] which the US believed held 'allusions to possible future action under Chapter VII of the Charter',[23] and that they consequently found unacceptable. Further, the US suggested that their continued engagement with Security Council involvement in Namibia was contingent on a negotiated peaceful South African withdrawal being the only solution ('We will remain engaged in this effort as long as appears as a chance for a peaceful solution').[24]

UK's statements on the issue of Namibian independence were relatively terse in most debates, while maintaining clear consistency in respect of their position. They characterised South Africa's refusal to agree to a ceasefire as a 'regrettable setback' to the eventual goal of Namibian independence;[25] however, they argued that the progress that had been made towards peaceful settlement of the issue should not be thrown away by rash action.[26] Further, they argued consistently that sanctions against South Africa through Chapter VII action 'will not bring closer of the independence of Namibia internationally acceptable basis',[27] and that '[t]he United Kingdom does not believe that the

18 United Nations Security Council, 12; See also: 'Solving problems is much more difficult than adopting resolutions. But the problem of an independent, stable, self-governing, democratic Namibia will be solved because it must be solved. And it will be solved, eventually, only by force of arms or by exercise of reason'. United Nations Security Council, 13.

19 United Nations Security Council, '2277th Meeting', 6; United Nations Security Council, 'Security Council, Thirty-Eighth Year: 2484th Meeting (S/PV.2484)' (United Nations, 24 October 1983), 6.

20 United Nations Security Council, '2271st Meeting', 13.

21 United Nations Security Council, '2277th Meeting', 3.

22 United Nations Security Council, '2492nd Meeting', 6.

23 United Nations Security Council, 7.

24 United Nations Security Council, '2484th Meeting', 6.

25 United Nations Security Council, '2263rd Meeting', 15.

26 United Nations Security Council, 15.

27 United Nations Security Council, '2271st Meeting', 9; see also: United Nations Security Council, '2277th Meeting', 4.

problems of South Africa can or should be resolved by violence'.[28] While they characterised South Africa's occupation of Namibia as unlawful, and depriving the Namibian people of their right of self-determination,[29] they stated that the Security Council had a responsibility to pass a resolution that would reinforce a peaceful negotiated settlement to the question.[30] This position that Chapter VII action would exacerbate the situation rather than assist in facilitating Namibian independence was solidified by the four vetoes the UK cast on this issue.[31]

France began its statements by arguing that the parties involved had failed to take advantage of opportunities to resolve the situation in Namibia through peaceful negotiations, and France would thus only support a peaceful solution to the question:[32] 'My delegation is convinced that the time for negotiation has not passed. The positions of the parties are not so far apart that no hope remains'.[33] Beyond this, France was relatively silent on the question of Security Council involvement in Namibia. They consistently argued that sanctions against South Africa would undermine efforts to peacefully negotiate settling the question of Namibian independence.[34] They also stated that 'nothing will be resolved by force, either in Namibia or elsewhere'.[35] Further, they contended that any external interference in Namibian independence movements would not yield positive outcomes, and they could in no way support such a notion.[36] Like the UK and the US, they exercised their veto on four occasions to block Chapter VII action against South Africa on this issue.[37]

China began by strongly condemning South Africa, an approach that continued throughout the debates. They characterised the presence of the 'South African racist authorities' in Namibia as an 'illegal occupation',[38] and their refusal to agree to a ceasefire as demonstrating a lack of good faith on their

28 United Nations Security Council, '2492nd Meeting', 6.

29 United Nations Security Council, 'Security Council, Thirty-Eighth Year: 2439th Meeting (S/PV.2439)' (United Nations, 23 May 1983), 9.

30 United Nations Security Council, 9.

31 United Nations Security Council, '2277th Meeting', 3.

32 United Nations Security Council, '2263rd Meeting', 14.

33 United Nations Security Council, 'Security Council, Thirty-Sixth Year: 2275th Meeting (S/PV.2275)' (United Nations, 28 April 1981), 7.

34 United Nations Security Council, 6; United Nations Security Council, '2277th Meeting', 4; United Nations Security Council, 'Security Council, Thirty-Eighth Year: 2447th Meeting (S/PV.2447)' (United Nations, 27 May 1983), 8–9.

35 United Nations Security Council, '2447th Meeting', 9.

36 United Nations Security Council, 'Security Council, Thirty-Eighth Year: 2485th Meeting (S/PV.2485)' (United Nations, 25 October 1983), 6.

37 United Nations Security Council, '2277th Meeting', 3.

38 United Nations Security Council, '2263rd Meeting', 15.

part.[39] They argued that South Africa was insincere regarding the possibility of a peaceful settlement in Namibia,[40] and that moves to internally settle the question of Namibian independence was a smokescreen to maintain South African occupation.[41] China made it clear from the outset that they would support reasonable Security Council action against South Africa to bring about Namibian independence, including sanctions under Chapter VII.[42] As the debates progressed, they reiterated their support for the 'reasonable demands enunciated by the ministers on behalf of the African states and people'.[43] Further, they held South Africa solely responsible for the failure to implement Security Council resolutions for Namibian independence, in accordance with their right of self-determination:[44] 'The crux of the problem lies with the total lack of good faith on the part of the racist regime of South Africa to solve the question of Namibia, and that explains why resolution 435 (1978) remains unimplemented thus far'.[45]

Russia commenced its statements by noting their concern 'over the provocative refusal of South Africa to proceed with the implementation of the Namibian settlement'.[46] Further, Russia noted that 'Namibia is a territory illegally occupied by the South African racists',[47] while also highlighting their concern regarding the trend of attaching the label 'international terrorists' to all liberation movements that were not to the liking of the parties involved.[48] Russia argued that '[t]he right of the people of Namibia to freedom, independence and self-determination is, once again, according to United Nations decisions, their inalienable right'.[49] On this basis, they viewed the South African occupation as representing 'a serious threat to international peace and security'.[50] Russia continued to press this line, stating that 'peace-loving States'[51] had shown considerable patience and restraint regarding the occupation and that 'the

39 United Nations Security Council, 15.
40 United Nations Security Council, 15.
41 United Nations Security Council, 16.
42 United Nations Security Council, 16; United Nations Security Council, 'Security Council, Thirty-Sixth Year: 2272nd Meeting (S/PV.2272)' (United Nations, 24 April 1981), 3; United Nations Security Council, '2447th Meeting', 6.
43 United Nations Security Council, '2272nd Meeting', 2.
44 United Nations Security Council, 2–3.
45 United Nations Security Council, '2447th Meeting', 5.
46 United Nations Security Council, '2263rd Meeting', 6.
47 United Nations Security Council, 6.
48 United Nations Security Council, 6.
49 United Nations Security Council, 6.
50 United Nations Security Council, 6.
51 United Nations Security Council, 6.

Security Council should take decisive action under Chapter VII of the Charter to ensure the people of Namibia achieved genuine independence'.[52] Throughout the debates, Russia continued this support of Chapter VII action against South Africa to end of their occupation of Namibia,[53] characterising Namibian independence as 'one of the most urgent international tasks'.[54] In addition, Russia stated that it supported the possibility of Angola, Namibia and other neighbouring South African states exercising their Article 51 right of self-defence against 'South African aggressors'.[55] Russia argued that the vetoes exercised to block Chapter VII action, and the resolutions made under Chapter VI, denied justice for the people of Namibia.[56]

4 Summary of Coding

This case study featured opposition to a finding of 'threat to the peace' from France, the UK and the US, with support from China and Russia. China used emotive rhetoric to argue that South Africa's continued occupation of Namibia was a violation of Namibia's right of self-determination, and that a finding of 'threat to the peace' would be a natural consequence of South Africa's actions. Russia was similarly emotive in their arguments that South Africa's action constituted a violation of international law and Namibia's right of self-determination, amounting to a 'threat to the peace'. French opposition (and vetoes) were grounded in their desire to see a peaceful solution and their lack of faith in the proposed solution achieving that outcome. Similarly, the UK's opposition (and vetoes) were based on their desire to see a peaceful solution to the situation. The US opposition (and vetoes, and abstention from the Chapter VI resolution) was for the same reasons as France: a desire to see a peaceful solution, and their lack of faith in the proposed solution achieving such an outcome.

52 United Nations Security Council, 6.

53 United Nations Security Council, 6; United Nations Security Council, '2271st Meeting', 7; United Nations Security Council, 'Security Council, Thirty-Eighth Year: 2448th Meeting (S/PV.2448)' (United Nations, 27 May 1983), 14; United Nations Security Council, 'Security Council, Thirty-Eighth Year: 2488th Meeting (S/PV.2488)' (United Nations, 26 October 1983), 5.

54 United Nations Security Council, '2448th Meeting', 12.

55 United Nations Security Council, '2488th Meeting', 5.

56 United Nations Security Council, '2277th Meeting', 6; United Nations Security Council, '2492nd Meeting', 6–7.

CHAPTER 10

Repression of a Civilian Population—Iraq 1991 (Resolution 688 (1991))

1 Relevance to Overall Project

This case study considers under what circumstances the treatment of a state's citizens by its government can constitute a 'threat to the peace'. While the relationship between a state and citizens is ostensibly protected from external interference by Article 2 (7) of the UN Charter,[1] *Resolution 688 (1991)*, which notes in operative paragraph 1 that the Iraqi Government's treatment of its civilian population 'threatened international peace and security in the region',[2] suggests that this protection may be mutable. The question of whether a government's purely internal affairs in relation to its citizens can constitute a 'threat to the peace' has received very little Security Council consideration and substantive debate, with this case study being one of few such instances. It is important to note that while this situation was certainly influenced by the Iraq/Kuwait conflict and subsequent US-led Security Council intervention, it sits distinct and separate from this situation. The *Repertoire of Practice of the Security Council* noted this situational distinction between the Iraq/Kuwait conflict,[3] and 'the repression of a civilian population, constituting a threat to the peace',[4] dealing with each as separate issues in the 1989–92 volume.

2 Context of the Debates

On 2 April 1991, Turkey requested that the Security Council address the issue of refugees massing on their border as a result of the Iraqi Government taking military action against its own civilian population in the region.[5] This

1 'Charter of the United Nations', 1 UNTS XVI (1945) Article 2(7).

2 'Resolution 688 (1991)', S/RES/688 (1991) UN Security Council (1991), para. 1.

3 Repertoire of the Practice of the Security Council, 'Chapter XI: Considerations of Chapter VII the Charter (1989–92)', 882.

4 Repertoire of the Practice of the Security Council, 883.

5 Turkey, 'Letter Dated 2 April 1991 from the Permanent Representative of Turkey to the United Nations Addressed to the President of the Security Council' (United Nations, 2 April 1991).

 DOI:10.1163/9789004391420_012

request was supported by a letter from France on 4 April 1991.[6] The Permanent Representative of Turkey provided a briefing to the Security Council at the beginning of the meeting. They began by noting that the Iraqi military was engaged in putting down insurgencies in the northern parts of the country with 'indiscriminate use of deadly firepower'.[7] Turkey stated that between 200,000–300,000 Iraqi civilians had already been driven to the Turkish border, with reports of another 600,000 currently en route.[8] They pointed out that the vast majority of the civilians were from religious and ethnic minorities. Iran also noted an influx of approximately 180,000 refugees because of the Iraqi Government's military action.[9] Iraq argued that these refugees were a result of ongoing bombing campaigns being conducted by the US-led UN 'aggression against the Iraqi people'.[10] Further, Iraq argued that the resolution being voted upon, and all previous resolutions, constituted 'a flagrant, illegitimate intervention in Iraq's internal affairs and the violation of Article 2 of the Charter of the United Nations, which prohibits intervention in the internal affairs of other States'.[11] Voting on *Resolution 688 (1991)* led to 10 votes in favour, three against and two abstentions, including an abstention from China.[12]

3 Justificatory Discourse of the P5

In this instance, the P5's justificatory discourse generally hinged on the relationship between the right of non-interference in domestic affairs and the transboundary and international effects of such affairs. It was concluded by all but China that when internal affairs have repercussions beyond state borders, then Article 2(7) of the UN Charter is mutable. Lesser arguments were also made to the effect that even if the right of non-interference in domestic affairs prevailed, the Iraqi Government's conduct amounted to either war crimes or crimes against humanity, and these internationally wrongful acts rendered the

6 France, 'Letter Dated 4 April 1991 from the Charge D'Affaires A.I. of the Permanent Mission of France to the United Nations Addressed to the President of the Security Council' (United Nations, 4 April 1991).

7 United Nations Security Council, 'Security Council, Forty-Sixth Year: 2982nd Meeting (S/PV.2982)' (United Nations, 5 April 1991), 4–5.

8 United Nations Security Council, 6.

9 United Nations Security Council, 12.

10 United Nations Security Council, 16.

11 United Nations Security Council, 17.

12 United Nations Security Council, 52.

principle of non-interference in domestic affairs irrelevant. All P5 statements were made after the voting on *Resolution 688 (1991)*.

France began by suggesting that the Iraqi Government's conduct was such that the Security Council was obliged to take specific action to protect human rights. 'The Security Council … would have been remiss in its task had it stood idly by, without reacting to the massacre of entire populations, the extermination of civilians, including women and children'.[13] France also noted the history of 'brutal repression' of the civilian population, particularly those of Kurdish ethnicity, in Iraq.[14] Regarding the question of non-interference in domestic affairs, France argued that '[v]iolations of human rights, such as those now being observed, become a matter of international interest when they take on such proportions that they assume the dimension of a crime against humanity'.[15] Finally, France justified their vote on the basis that 'the increasing number of massacres are arousing indignation and threaten international peace and security in the region'.[16]

China's statements were incredibly brief (12 lines in total), and explain the basis of their abstention from voting in this instance. China began by noting the international aspects of the question at hand, in the form of refugee movements across borders into Turkey and Iran;[17] however, they were unconvinced that this was an international matter, 'because the internal affairs of a country are also involved'.[18] China's interpretation of the events taking place characterised the situation as Iraq's internal affair having an international effect, and thus they abstained from voting: 'According to paragraph 7 of article 2 of the Charter, Security Council should not consider or take action on questions concerning the internal affairs of any state … Based on the position I have just set out, we abstained in the vote on the resolution'.[19]

The US began by arguing that the current situation in Iraq had arisen because of the Iraqi Government's reflexive brutality 'in the aftermath of the Gulf crisis'.[20] They also asserted that the resolution expressed 'the council's condemnation of the Iraqi Government's continued violence towards its own people. The resolution insists that Iraq meet its humanitarian responsibilities'.[21] As

13 United Nations Security Council, 53.
14 United Nations Security Council, 53.
15 United Nations Security Council, 53.
16 United Nations Security Council, 53.
17 United Nations Security Council, 54–55.
18 United Nations Security Council, 54–55.
19 United Nations Security Council, 56.
20 United Nations Security Council, 57.
21 United Nations Security Council, 58.

to the question of non-interference in a state's internal affairs, the US argued that the transboundary effects of the current situation trumped that principle:

> It is not the role or the intention of the Security Council to interfere in the internal affairs of any country. However, it is the Council's legitimate responsibility to respond to the concerns of Turkey and the Islamic Republic of Iran, concerns increasingly shared by other neighbours of Iraq, about the massive numbers of people fleeing, or disposed to flee, from Iraq across international frontiers because of the repression and brutality of Saddam Hussein. The transboundary impact of Iraq's treatment of its civilian population threatens regional stability. That is what the Council has addressed today.[22]

Russia's justificatory discourse focused solely on the question of the international effect of the current situation and how that overcame the principle of non-interference:

> The Soviet Union reacted with understanding and concern to the appeal made to the Security Council by Turkey and Iran in connection with the extremely alarming situation that has come about on the borders with Iraq and the threat it has created to international peace and security in the region.[23]

Russia argued that the principle of non-interference in states' internal affairs, articulated in Article 2(7) of the Charter, must be respected, as must Iraq's territorial integrity, sovereignty and political independence;[24] however, Russia defended its vote on the basis of the transboundary effects Iraq's internal affairs were having through refugee spillover into neighbouring countries, 'creating a destabilising situation in the area and posing the threat of a new international conflict'.[25] Russia argued that the transboundary nature of the refugee situation in conjunction with the humanitarian violations taking place gave the Security Council competence on this issue.[26]

The UK commenced by criticising the Security Council for taking so long 'to respond to the human tragedy which has been unfolding before our eyes

22 United Nations Security Council, 58.
23 United Nations Security Council, 59–60.
24 United Nations Security Council, 61.
25 United Nations Security Council, 61.
26 United Nations Security Council, 61–62.

in the mountains of northern Iraq during recent days'.[27] They contended that the principle of non-interference in states' internal affairs does not apply to situations of mass human rights violations (noting Security Council action in response to apartheid in South Africa as an example of this principle).[28] Further, they argued that the flow of refugees across borders into Turkey and Iran enlivened a 'very real threat here to international peace and security. The huge surge of refugees is destabilising to the whole region'.[29] The UK closed its statement by arguing for the appropriateness of Security Council action on this issue given the Iraqi Government's violations of Article 3 of the Geneva Conventions of 1949 'to protect, in the cases of internal armed conflicts, all innocent civilians from violence of all kinds to life and person'.[30]

4 Summary of Coding

The only member of the P5 to oppose a finding of 'threat to the peace' in this situation was China. China argued that any Chapter VII action would be a violation of Iraq's right of non-interference; however, they abstained from voting in acquiescence to the majority view that a 'threat to the peace' existed. The UK, Russia, and the US all argued that a finding of 'threat to the peace' was necessary to protect human rights. They all also asserted that this situation was international in nature, and thus Article 2(7) was not relevant. France adopted a similar position, arguing that the facts made Article 2(7) irrelevant, and that a finding of 'threat to the peace' was necessary to protect human rights.

27 United Nations Security Council, 63.
28 United Nations Security Council, 64–65.
29 United Nations Security Council, 64–65.
30 United Nations Security Council, 66.

CHAPTER 11

Civil War in Yugoslavia 1991 (Resolution 713 (1991))

1 Relevance to the Overall Project

Security Council action in Yugoslavia is fundamental in the history of international law and the Security Council itself. This case study represents the starting point of that history, which, among other things, helped achieve mainstream acceptance of individual criminal responsibility at an international law level for violations of *jus cogens* norms other than piracy, with the ICTY being created in 1993.[1] Further, this situation also evidenced the Security Council's willingness to take action in what it identified as a purely internal matter, while still doing everything it could to not be seen as interfering. The *Repertoire of the Practice of the Security Council* for the period notes significant discussion of whether an internal armed conflict could amount to a 'threat to the peace',[2] highlighting that a number of states noted the international dimension of the conflict, which had already begun to spill into neighbouring states.[3]

2 Context of the Debates

This meeting began with the tabling of what would become *Resolution 713 (1991)*, to be made under Chapter VII, implementing a blanket arms embargo on Yugoslavia and thus inferring the existence of a 'threat to the peace'. The draft resolution noted the violation of two separate ceasefires that had been made in the months prior to the Security Council meeting as part of its justification for the embargo. *Resolution 713 (1991)* was passed unanimously, and all P5 statements occurred after voting. The oral briefing given to the Security Council before voting was delivered by the Permanent Representative of Yugoslavia to the UN,[4] as part of the Yugoslav Government's request for Security

1 'Resolution 827 (1993)', S/RES/827 (1993) UN Security Council (1993).

2 Repertoire of the Practice of the Security Council, 'Chapter XI: Considerations of Chapter VII the Charter (1989–92)', 883–84.

3 Repertoire of the Practice of the Security Council, 884.

4 United Nations Security Council, 'Security Council, Forty-Sixth Year: 3009th Meeting (S/PV.3009)' (United Nations, 25 September 1991), 6–16.

 | DOI:10.1163/9789004391420_013

Council assistance with ending the hostilities.[5] He commenced the briefing by noting that Yugoslavia was a founding member of the UN and, ironically, now needed help 'to defend ourselves from ourselves'.[6] He described the conflict in Yugoslavia as '[c]omplex and multifaceted',[7] stating that 'Yugoslavia is in conflict with itself'.[8] He pointed out that no party to the conflict was free from blame or guilt, nor had they lived up to their responsibilities; however, he argued that '[i]t would be neither possible nor useful at this juncture to deal with all of its causes'.[9] The continuation of the armed conflict after ceasefire agreements was noted,[10] as was the need for international support to restore stability—particularly economic and social stability in the post-conflict transition period.[11] Finally, he acknowledged that '[a]fter all that has happened in recent years and months, Yugoslavia can no longer be simply repaired. It should now be redefined'.[12]

3 Justificatory Discourse of the P5

The P5's justificatory discourse was reasonably varied in response to this resolution. For the most part, justification hinged on the Yugoslav Government's invitation to the Security Council to take action regarding the internal conflict. This argument was often buttressed by concerns about fighting spilling across international borders and transboundary refugee flows, giving the internal conflict an international dimension and placing it within Security Council competence. In the case of the US, this was the primary rather than secondary argument strengthening the Yugoslav Government's invitation. Unlike the rest of the P5, France characterised the Security Council resolution as supporting the rights of self-determination held by the various states within Yugoslavia that were party to the conflict.

China predominantly justified its vote by referencing that Security Council action was being undertaken 'with agreement explicitly given by the Yugoslav

5 Yugoslavia, 'Letter Dated 24 September 1991 from the Permanent Representative of Yugoslavia to the United Nations Addressed to the President of the Security-Council' (New York: United Nations, 24 September 1991).
6 United Nations Security Council, '3009th Meeting', 6.
7 United Nations Security Council, 7.
8 United Nations Security Council, 6.
9 United Nations Security Council, 7.
10 United Nations Security Council, 12.
11 United Nations Security Council, 16.
12 United Nations Security Council, 11.

government'.[13] When expanding upon this statement, they noted that the resolution's purpose was to facilitate peaceful dialogue between the parties to the conflict with the aim of restoring peace and stability to the country:[14] 'We hope that this action by the Security Council will contribute to the restoration of domestic peace and stability through Yugoslavia's internal peaceful negotiations'.[15] China went to great lengths to clarify that this vote did not represent a change in the Chinese Government's position regarding the concept of non-interference in internal affairs:

> Here I wish to reiterate and emphasise that it is the consistent position of the Chinese Government that a country's internal affairs should be handled by the people in that country themselves. According to the relevant provisions of the United Nations Charter, the United Nations, including the Security Council, should refrain from involving itself interfering in the internal affairs of any Member State. This principled position of the Chinese Government remains unchanged.[16]

Finally, China called for any assistance given by the international community to be done in accordance with all relevant international law:

> In our view, the international community, in its endeavours to restore peace and stability in Yugoslavia, must strictly abide by the relevant principles contained in the charter and international law, scrupulously respect the sovereignty of Yugoslavia and refrain from interfering in its internal affairs.[17]

Russia began its statements by highlighting its 'profound alarm' at the state of affairs in Yugoslavia, welcoming the Security Council's efforts to help restore peace.[18] They quickly placed on record their view that this state of affairs was international in nature and worthy of Chapter VII action: 'If this fratricidal, depressing conflict, which has begun to spill over national borders, continues, it will constitute a direct threat to international peace and security'.[19] Russia

13 United Nations Security Council, 49.
14 United Nations Security Council, 49.
15 United Nations Security Council, 49.
16 United Nations Security Council, 50.
17 United Nations Security Council, 51.
18 United Nations Security Council, 51.
19 United Nations Security Council, 51.

then argued that the only way to resolve these conflicts was by peacefully negotiating a political settlement:

> We are convinced that the only way to resolve the Yugoslav problems, as well as the problems of many other multinational states, is through honest negotiation and patient dialogue so as to find mutually acceptable solutions, new forms of cohabitation and cooperation within a shared economic and legal area, retaining ties that have justified themselves historically.[20]

Russia stated that support for the arms embargo was grounded in the fact that continuing to ship weapons to the area would further exacerbate the conflict,[21] and that restricting the flow of weapons was done with 'the consent given by Yugoslavia' and designed to prevent further bloodshed.[22] Finally, Russia argued that the current conflicts in Yugoslavia were endemic of the new challenges facing Europe in the post-Cold War era: 'We Europeans are now facing the challenge of trying to fashion a new Europe to replace blocs, a Europe that is fully democratic, where human rights are observed everywhere'.[23]

From the outset, the UK made their conjoined arguments, based on Yugoslav consent and the international effects of the conflict, the basis for Security Council competence:

> The background to this meeting is one of months of torment for the peoples of Yugoslavia. The system under which the country was governed has, to a large extent, disintegrated, ambitions have conflicted and, often, there have been unwise actions that have led to violent explosions of force. These explosions have spread, and unless checked they will spread further ... Against that background, our aim has not been to interfere or try to impose a solution—that would not be possible. Rather, we have sought to respond to the pleas of the Yugoslav parties to help them to find a peaceful way through their differences. That plea is symbolised by the presence of a Yugoslav colleague here today.[24]

20 United Nations Security Council, 52.
21 United Nations Security Council, 52–53.
22 United Nations Security Council, 52.
23 United Nations Security Council, 54–55.
24 United Nations Security Council, 54–55.

The UK argued that numerous breaches of international law were patent in the conflict, particularly noting unlawful use of force and attempts to change state borders through use of force.[25] When noting these instances, and the breaches of multiple ceasefire agreements, the UK asserted that all parties must abide by all relevant international law.[26] At the end of their statement, they defended the decision to engage in Chapter VII action at this early stage of the conflict by highlighting the transboundary harm that would be faced if the conflict continued:

> I know that some people had suggested in the last few days, it was premature to use the language of Chapter VII. It is a fact that this conflict which we are discussing has a strong international dimension. The patchwork of nationalities and minorities throughout Central and Eastern Europe means that full-scale war might not be confined easily to a single territory. This action which we have taken will, I hope, serve as a strong reminder to all those in positions of responsibility in Yugoslavia that the attention of the world is fixed on them. They have a responsibility to their own people, of course, but also to the ideals which the United Nations embodies.[27]

The US opened its statements by highlighting the gravity of the situation in Yugoslavia, commenting that it easily 'characterises open warfare'.[28] This tack of simply addressing the gravity of the conflict and the potential for its effects to reach beyond Yugoslavia's internal territory was evident throughout the US statements:

> This violent conflict threatens all the peoples of Yugoslavia with terrible economic and social strife, with sharp deterioration in the most fundamental human rights and freedoms and, above all, with massive bloodshed and loss of life … We are equally concerned about the dangerous impact on Yugoslavia's neighbours, who face refugee flows, energy shortfalls and the threat of spillover in the fighting. It is this danger of escalation, on which I know we all agree, which makes this a matter of prime concern to this Council.[29]

---

25 United Nations Security Council, 56.
26 United Nations Security Council, 56.
27 United Nations Security Council, 57.
28 United Nations Security Council, 58.
29 United Nations Security Council, 58.

The US acknowledged that all parties to the conflict had guilt in some measure; however, they argued that the Yugoslav federal military and the Serbian Government were the most culpable of all of parties to the conflict, and primarily responsible for the ceasefire violations.[30] They contended that fighting already being well underway in Croatia and beginning to take hold of Bosnia clearly made the situation 'a direct threat to international peace and security'.[31] Finally, the US argued that the attempts to change Yugoslavia's internal state borders constituted a violation of the UN Charter.[32]

France took a very different approach to the rest of the P5, primarily arguing that Security Council action was justified, and competence enlivened, in the name of defending states' right of self-determination:

> What are the facts of the problem before us? Several of the Yugoslav republics are calling for their independence. In the Europe of today, after the wave of freedom it has just experienced, the right of peoples to self-determination cannot be challenged anywhere.[33]

France then buttressed this argument by noting that the close ethnic affiliations that had once justified the creation of Yugoslavia were now the cause of this internal conflict, which would have serious internal and international consequences.[34] France stated the Security Council's historic responsibility was to assist Yugoslavia in ending the cycle of violence evident in the internal conflict and to bring about 'peace and cooperation without recourse to force for the settlement of disputes'.[35] While France did not argue for a need to overcome the right of non-interference in internal affairs, they were aware that the questions of non-interference and self-determination were intrinsically linked:

> 'Strength without justice is tyrannical', said Pascal, 'but justice without strength is helpless'. We are helping peace in Yugoslavia by supporting the efforts to organise and develop a dialogue between the Yugoslavs themselves, who have the primary responsibility, as well as the effort to find solutions acceptable to all parties.[36]

30 United Nations Security Council, 58–59.
31 United Nations Security Council, 59.
32 United Nations Security Council, 59.
33 United Nations Security Council, 65.
34 United Nations Security Council, 66.
35 United Nations Security Council, 66.
36 United Nations Security Council, 67.

4 Summary of Coding

In this situation, every P5 member supported a finding of 'threat to the peace'. For China, this support was wholly grounded in the state's consent for Security Council action. Russia supported this finding based on the situation being international in nature, their desire to see a peaceful solution and the state's consent. French support was based on the desire for a peaceful solution, the fact that the situation was international in nature and their endorsement of self-determination for the people of Yugoslavia. The UK supported this finding because they determined that the situation was international in nature (and thus Article 2(7) was irrelevant), the state had given consent and the international law violations that were occurring amounted to a 'threat to the peace'. The US supported a finding of 'threat to the peace' because of the gravity of the situation and the international law violations taking place (which, to their mind, made the existence of a 'threat to the peace' self-evident), in addition to the situation's international nature.

CHAPTER 12

The Coup in Haiti 1991–93 (Resolution 841)

1 Relevance to Overall Project

The 1991 coup in Haiti, which was declared a 'threat to the peace' in 1993,[1] is a valuable addition to this project, as it involved the Security Council taking action on what could be characterised (and was by China) as a purely internal matter.[2] It also indicates how the majority of the P5 had come to equate democracy with the right of self-determination.[3] Additionally, this situation raises questions about the validity of governments within international law, as the Security Council still accepted the government elected in UN-monitored democratic elections as the lawful authority in Haiti even while they were exiled and had no effective control of their territory. For the 1989–92 period, the *Repertoire of Practice of the Security Council* did not consider that the Haiti situation received substantive discussions of 'threat to the peace' during the 1991 debates; however, they did consider the 1993 debates to contain significant discussion on this issue (according to the 1993–95 report).[4]

2 Context of the Debates

The initial meeting that brought the coup in Haiti to the attention of the Security Council was requested by the government in exile of Haiti.[5] Oral briefings were provided by the President in exile of Haiti, noting that the coup occurred on 29 September 1991.[6] The President characterised the coup committed by the Haitian Armed Forces as a crime against democracy,[7] while also pointing out

1 'Resolution 841 (1993)', S/RES/841 (1993) UN Security Council (1993).
2 United Nations Security Council, 'Security Council, Forty-Eighth Year: 3238th Meeting (S/PV.3238)' (United Nations, 16 June 1993), 20–21.
3 United Nations Security Council, 'Security Council, Forty-Sixth Year: 3011th Meeting (S/PV.3011)' (United Nations, 3 October 1991), 19–20, 22, 29–32, 34 & 48.
4 Repertoire of the Practice of the Security Council, 'Chapter XI: Considerations of Chapter VII the Charter (1993–95)', 1097.
5 Haiti, 'Letter Dated 30 September 1991 from the Permanent Representative of Haiti to the United Nations Addressed to the President of the Security Council' (New York: United Nations, 30 September 1991).
6 United Nations Security Council, '3011th Meeting', 4–5.
7 United Nations Security Council, 6.

 | DOI:10.1163/9789004391420_014

the release of former armed forces personnel who were guilty of mass murder and torture.[8] The President argued that the people of Haiti were not in favour of the coup and the new military government,[9] and recalled the role the international community had played (in the form of UN election monitors) in ensuring the free and democratic elections that had occurred on 16 December 1990, bringing his government to power.[10]

The 1993 meeting that led to the adoption of *Resolution 841 (1993)* occurred at the request of the President in exile of Haiti.[11] In a letter requesting this meeting, the President asked the Security Council to make the sanctions that had been imposed by the Organization of American States mandatory and universal while the military government was still in place.[12] The basis for this request was that 20 months had passed since the coup had taken place, and Haiti was still no closer to having a democratically elected government restored to power.[13] In response to this request, France, the US and Venezuela submitted a draft resolution (which eventually became *Resolution 841 (1993)*) giving effect to these pleas.[14]

3 Justificatory Discourse of the P5

With the exception of China, the P5's justificatory discourse centred on reinstating the democratically elected government in Haiti, either in terms of municipal constitutional legal order or in terms of the right of self-determination recognised in the UN Charter. By contrast, China argued that this constituted an internal matter for Haiti, which they were willing to support because of the request from Haiti's recognised government.

France began by characterising the coup by the Haitian Armed Forces as a denial of the 'freely expressed will of the Haitian people to rejoin the community of democratic states'.[15] They asserted that the Haitian Armed Forces' ousting of the democratically elected government was an 'unjustifiable act',

8 United Nations Security Council, 6.
9 United Nations Security Council, 7.
10 United Nations Security Council, 8.
11 Haiti, 'Letter Dated 7 June 1993 from the Permanent Representative of Haiti to the United Nations Addressed to the President of the Security Council' (New York: United Nations, 16 June 1993).
12 Haiti.
13 Haiti.
14 United Nations Security Council, '3238th Meeting', 3–5.
15 United Nations Security Council, '3011th Meeting', 19–20.

and that the military's repression as part of the coup put Haiti in 'very serious danger'.[16] France proceeded to 'strongly' condemn the coup,[17] characterising the military government as illegitimate and calling for and supporting the restoration of the democratically elected government to power:[18]

> The Head of the sovereign State, legally elected in a free and democratic ballot monitored by the United Nations, is personally addressing the international community to request its support. For its part, France is ready to respond to this appeal. It is ready, out of friendship for Haiti—to which it is united by longstanding close ties of language and history—because our Organization, which lent its assistance during the elections and its guarantee for the conduct of the voting in the fairness of the results, cannot remain passive went today the will of the Haitian voters is flouted; and because, finally, the international community can no longer, in an era when throughout the world democracy and respect for human rights are being reaffirmed, accept the flagrant violation of these values.[19]

After the unanimous passing of *Resolution 841 (1993)*, France stated that the de facto government's refusal to restore power to the legitimately elected democratic government meant that it was time for the Security Council to act.[20] They suggested that the sanctions were designed to put pressure on the coup's perpetrators to return to the negotiating table to 'restore constitutional order in Haiti'.[21]

Russia's comments were limited to the initial meeting in 1991; they declined to comment after their vote in favour of *Resolution 841 (1993)*. Russia's arguments hinged very strongly on the defence of democracy, and inferred that such political processes were how the right of self-determination is materialised. Russia opened its comments with statements of support for the government in exile: 'On behalf of the Soviet Union we convey to President Aristide our support, our sympathy and our conviction that the cause of democracy in Haiti will triumph'.[22] Russia then proceeded to condemn 'the overthrow of the government legally and democratically elected on the basis of the free

16 United Nations Security Council, 19–20.
17 United Nations Security Council, 21.
18 United Nations Security Council, 21.
19 United Nations Security Council, 22.
20 United Nations Security Council, '3238th Meeting', 9.
21 United Nations Security Council, 9.
22 United Nations Security Council, '3011th Meeting', 28–30.

expression of the will of the Haitian people',[23] arguing that this coup demonstrated that 'democratic processes are still vulnerable in the face of the force of terror and weapons'.[24] Finally, they argued that '[t]he urgent need for international resistance to inhumane actions is perfectly clear. Such actions, wherever they may occur, undermined the constitutional order'.[25]

The US began by condemning, and refusing to recognise, the government that took control of Haiti as a result of the Haitian Armed Forces coup:[26] 'Let no one doubt where the United States stands. The United States condemns this assault on Haiti's democratically elected Government and on the people of Haiti who elected that Government, and we condemned the violence committed against innocent people'.[27] The US clearly linked the maintenance of democratically elected governments with the right of self-determination: 'This unconstitutional and violent seizure of power denies the people of Haiti their right of self-determination. These violent and illegal action must not, and will not, succeed. The inalienable right of all of the people of Haiti to democracy and constitutional rule must be restored'.[28] Further, the US argued that while the military junta maintained power in Haiti, they would be without friends or support.[29] After the passing of *Resolution 841 (1993)*, the US asserted that the Security Council had shown strong and decisive leadership in line with the international community's demand to restore democracy.[30] While they acknowledged that sanctions would not guarantee the return of the democratically elected government, they viewed sanctions as a positive step that would put pressure on those who opposed such an outcome.[31] Finally, the US stated that it was time for 'democracy to be returned to this long-suffering land'.[32]

The UK made only one very brief statement in the initial 1991 meeting, declining to comment after the unanimous passing of *Resolution 841 (1993)*. The statement broadly characterised democratic government as the exercise of the right of self-determination.[33] Further, they made statements of support for the restoration of Haiti's democratically elected government:[34]

23 United Nations Security Council, 29–30.
24 United Nations Security Council, 31.
25 United Nations Security Council, 31.
26 United Nations Security Council, 32.
27 United Nations Security Council, 31–32.
28 United Nations Security Council, 34.
29 United Nations Security Council, 33.
30 United Nations Security Council, '3238th Meeting', 18.
31 United Nations Security Council, 19.
32 United Nations Security Council, 19.
33 United Nations Security Council, '3011th Meeting', 48.
34 United Nations Security Council, 48.

> Those elections brought democracy to the second last country in the hemisphere not to choose its rulers through the ballot box. The democratic movement throughout Latin America must not now be reversed. That is why so much rides on the restoration of President Aristide and his government. The British government will work with others in this council and the General Assembly to bring the restoration about.[35]

China's only statement on this issue came after the passing of *Resolution 841 (1993)* introducing universal and mandatory sanctions against the military junta in Haiti. They commenced by noting the efforts, and their hope in those efforts' success, for a peaceful resolution to the crisis.[36] China then unequivocally stated that they viewed the crisis in Haiti as a particularly internal matter: 'The crisis in Haiti is essentially a matter which falls within the internal affairs of that country, and therefore should be dealt with by the Haitian people themselves'.[37] With that position made clear, China then explained that they were able to support the resolution introducing sanctions, as it was in accordance with the request from the legitimate government of the country affected, and designed to facilitate a peaceful, political solution to the crisis.[38] China also noted that support for sanctions in relation to Haiti's internal affairs 'should not be regarded as constituting any precedent for the future'.[39] They chose to use the conclusion of their statement to reiterate their position regarding sanctions and Security Council involvement in states' internal affairs:

> The Chinese delegation, as its consistent position, does not favour the Security Council's handling matters which are essentially internal affairs of a member state, nor does it approve of resorting lightly to such mandatory measures as sanctions by the Council. We wish to point out that the favourable vote the Chinese delegation cast just now does not mean any change in that position.[40]

35 United Nations Security Council, 48.
36 United Nations Security Council, '3238th Meeting', 19.
37 United Nations Security Council, 20.
38 United Nations Security Council, 20–21.
39 United Nations Security Council, 21.
40 United Nations Security Council, 21.

4 Summary of Coding

This situation garnered support from all P5 members for a finding of 'threat to the peace'. For China, this support was grounded in the state's consent and the desire for a peaceful solution. France support was based on the defence of democracy, the state's consent, their support for the right of self-determination and the protection of human rights and their belief that the facts made Article 2(7) irrelevant. Russia and the UK supported a finding of 'threat to the peace' based upon the defence of democracy and support for the right of self-determination. The US supported the finding to protect human rights, uphold the right of self-determination and defend democracy.

CHAPTER 13

Extradition of Pan Am Flight 103 Bombing Suspects and Access to Information Related to UTA flight 772 Bombing, 1992 (Resolutions 731 and 748 (1992))

1 Relevance to the Overall Project

The *Repertoire of Practice of the Security Council* characterised the debates surrounding Resolutions 731 and 748 (1992) as 'insufficient action by State against terrorism constituting a threat to the peace'.[1] Given the subject of these debates—the extradition of suspects in relation to the bombing of Pan Am flight 103 and UTA flight 772—it would be easy to assume that this constituted the core of the debates about, and justification of, the inferred finding of 'threat to the peace' in *Resolution 748 (1992)*.[2] In fact, the reality is much more interesting and lends greater credence to this case study's inclusion in this project. A significant amount of justification for *Resolution 748 (1992)* hinged on Libya's failure to comply with *Resolution 731 (1992)*,[3] a situation mirrored in the preamble of *Resolution 1267 (1999)*.[4] Given the propensity of international lawyers to dismiss the Security Council's understanding of 'threat to the peace' as ad hoc, arbitrary and fickle,[5] the existence of two unrelated incidences being characterised as counterterrorism, but being justified as a result of Security Council defiance, calls this assessment into question.

2 Context of the Debates

The debates began with letters from France, the UK and the US requesting that the Security Council compel Libyan cooperation in relation to Pan Am flight 103 and UTA flight 772. Regarding UTA flight 772, France requested

1 Repertoire of the Practice of the Security Council, 'Chapter XI: Considerations of Chapter VII the Charter (1989–92)', 887.
2 'Resolution 748 (1992)', S/RES/748 (1992) UN Security Council (1992).
3 'Resolution 731 (1992)', S/RES/731 (1992) UN Security Council (1992).
4 'Determining that the failure of the Taliban authorities to respond to the demands in paragraph 13 of resolution 1214 (1998) constitutes a threat to international peace and security': 'Resolution 1267 (1999)', S/RES/1267 (1999) UN Security Council (1999), para. Preamble.
5 See Chapter 1.

 DOI:10.1163/9789004391420_015

that the Security Council compel Libya to cooperate by providing access to evidence and witnesses, including allowing relevant members of the Libyan Government to answer questions.[6] Regarding Pan Am flight 103, the UK and the US requested that Libya extradite suspects for prosecution in accordance with the Lord Advocate of Scotland's statement of charges[7] and a Grand Jury indictment, respectively.[8] In response to these requests, Libya argued that the US and UK indictments provided no supporting evidence for the involvement of Libyan nationals, and that the request for extradition thus ran counter to the rule of law and merely constituted a set of baseless accusations.[9] Further, Libya characterised the indictments as 'hostile official statements' that go 'so far as to threaten military and economic aggression'.[10] They also asserted that their attempts to investigate the crimes and their own citizens' involvement were stymied by a lack of cooperation from the UK, the US and France.[11] Libya also stated that should any of their nationals have been involved in either of these bombings, then Libya had competent jurisdiction to try them for such crimes.[12] Finally, Libya argued that the question at hand was one of jurisdiction over the bombings, and as such was a legal question and thus outside the Security Council's purview.[13] Subsequently, the Secretary-General's report, in in accordance with *Resolution 731 (1992)*, highlighted Libya's willingness to conduct prosecutions of their nationals in accordance with the Libyan legal system, with observer judges from France, the UK and the US;[14] however, they

6 France, 'Letter Dated 20 December 1991 from the Permanent Representative of France to the United Nations Addressed to the Secretary-General' (New York: United Nations, 20 December 1991).

7 United Kingdom of Great Britain and Northern Island, 'Letter Dated 20 December 1991 from the Permanent Representative of United Kingdom of Great Britain and Northern Ireland to the United Nations Addressed to the Secretary-General' (New York: United Nations, 20 December 1991).

8 United States of America, 'Letter Dated 23 December 1991 from the Acting Permanent Representative of United States of America to the United Nations Addressed to the Secretary-General' (New York: United Nations, 23 December 1991).

9 United Nations Security Council, 'Security Council, Forty-Seventh Year: 3033rd Meeting (S/PV.3033)' (United Nations, 21 January 1992), 6.

10 United Nations Security Council, 7.

11 United Nations Security Council, 8–11.

12 United Nations Security Council, 11–12.

13 United Nations Security Council, 13–15.

14 United Nations Secretary-General, 'Report of the Secretary-General Pursuant to Paragraph 4 of Security Council Resolution 731 (1992)' (United Nations Security Council, 11 February 1992); United Nations Secretary-General, 'Further Report of the Secretary-General Pursuant to Paragraph 4 of Security Council Resolution 731 (1992)' (United Nations Security Council, 3 March 1992).

refused to extradite suspects, claiming that this would violate their municipal law.[15] Libya again argued that the dispute in question was legal, which would render Chapter VII action inappropriate, as a legal dispute could not meet the threshold Article 39.[16]

3 Justificatory Discourse of the P5

With the exception of China's statements just prior to abstaining from voting on *Resolution 748 (1992)*, all of the P5's statements on this issue were made after the resolutions had been passed. While the issue of counterterrorism was present in both sets of debates, the justification from all voting members of the P5 regarding the inferred finding of 'threat to the peace' in *Resolution 748 (1992)* was Libya's failure to comply with the Security Council's counterterrorism-themed dictates in *Resolution 731 (1992)*.

China began by condemning the bombings in question. While calling for the issue to be resolved by transparent application of law and due process, China emphasised that

> The Chinese government's principal position on the question of terrorism is known to all. We have persistently opposed, and condemned all forms of terrorism, because terrorism endangers innocent lives. We deeply deplore the bombings of Pan Am flight 103 and UTA flight 772 and their serious consequences. Such a tragedy, in our view, should never be repeated, and we are in favour of conducting earnest, fair, objective and thorough investigations on the bombing instances, in accordance with the Charter of the United Nations and the principles of international law, and inflicting due punishment on those accused, if proved guilty.[17]

China asserted that the difference of approach to the investigations, and legal proceedings, between the US, UK, France and Libya should be resolved through 'prudent and appropriate' negotiations rather than 'high-pressure approaches'.[18] They argued that resolving these differences 'by peaceful consultation through diplomatic channels' would 'contribute to the maintenance of

15 United Nations Secretary-General, 'Further Report of the Secretary-General Pursuant to Paragraph 4 of Security Council Resolution 731 (1992)', para. 4(a).

16 United Nations Security Council, 'Security Council, Forty-Seventh Year: 3063rd Meeting (S/PV.3063)' (United Nations, 31 March 1992), 18–20.

17 United Nations Security Council, '3033rd Meeting', 84–85.

18 United Nations Security Council, 86.

regional peace and security as well upholding the United Nations Charter and the principles of international law'.[19] In relation to the sanctions being made under Chapter VII in *Resolution 748 (1992)*[20] (and thus, by implication, a related finding of 'threat to the peace'), China argued that such a response would not help the question, but rather complicate the issues at hand and further inflame regional tensions.[21] On this basis, China decided to abstain from voting on this issue.[22]

The UK began by characterising the bombings as the 'most horrific acts of terrorism the world has seen'.[23] Further, they argued that the Security Council involvement was taking place to address 'the clear indication of Libyan Government involvement [in the bombings]'.[24] The nexus leading to Security Council involvement in acts of terrorism was the circumstances of state involvement in terrorist activities.[25] Regarding the extradition of Libyan nationals as suspects for the bombing of Pan Am flight 103, the UK noted that they had sufficient evidence for a prosecution, and that this was not an assertion of guilt; it was merely an assertion that these nationals should stand trial for these crimes, which implicated a conspiracy within the Libyan intelligence service.[26] The UK went on to argue that Libya had issued no 'effective response' to the request to make the accused available for trial, and that the Security Council was not dealing with the dispute between two parties to the Montréal Convention, but rather Libya's failure to respond to accusations of state involvement in terrorism.[27] The UK asserted that as the ICJ had no criminal jurisdiction, and as there was no international tribunal with competent jurisdiction to try the accused, then the US and the UK—as the two nations with a territorial jurisdiction over the incident—were the most appropriate venues for prosecution.[28] They noted Libya's complaint that their own law did not allow for extradition in the absence of a treaty, but countered this argument by stating that international law provides no such preclusion, and that when this factor was

19 United Nations Security Council, 87.
20 Resolution 748 (1992), paras 3–8.
21 United Nations Security Council, '3063rd Meeting', 61.
22 United Nations Security Council, 61.
23 United Nations Security Council, '3033rd Meeting', 102.
24 United Nations Security Council, 102.
25 United Nations Security Council, 103.
26 United Nations Security Council, 103.
27 United Nations Security Council, 104.
28 United Nations Security Council, 105.

combined with a lack of faith in the impartiality of the Libyan courts, then the Libyan arguments against extradition were unconvincing.[29]

After voting in favour of *Resolution 748 (1992)*, the UK emphasised that 10 weeks had passed since the adoption of *Resolution 731 (1992)* compelling the Libyan Government to cooperate with France, the UK and the US, and that 'no serious steps towards compliance with these requests' had taken place.[30] The UK then argued (citing a long history of Libyan vessels being used to transport weapons and explosives to terrorist groups)[31] that the Libyan Government's support of terrorism posed a 'threat to the peace' and that the sanctions were a proportional and inevitable response to that threat.[32] In response to Libya's claim that the Security Council was acting beyond its purview, the UK argued that the Security Council was fully entitled to deal with issues of terrorism and, indeed, that any other position would undermine the Security Council's responsibility to maintain international peace and security.[33]

'The Russian Federation unreservedly condemns all acts of international terrorism without exception, constituting as they do an open threat to international peace and security'.[34] This statement formed the foundation for Russia's positions on the dispute between the UK, US and France and Libya, in relation to jurisdiction over prosecutions for the bombings of Pan Am flight 103 and UTA flight 772. Russia's statements were anchored in the observance of international law, noting that the jurisdictions for any prosecutions in relation to the bombings belonged to the state to which the downed aircraft belonged and the state in which the crime was physically committed.[35] Russia thus supported the requests of the UK, the US and France regarding Libyan cooperation with the prosecutions of Libyan nationals who were suspects,[36] while also calling for these trials to be open and transparent.[37] Further, they stressed that Security Council involvement was necessary to consolidate the international community's efforts in response such a transnational challenge.[38] Regarding the passing of *Resolution 748 (1992)*, Russia noted Libya's refusal to comply with

29 United Nations Security Council, 105–06.
30 United Nations Security Council, '3063rd Meeting', 68.
31 United Nations Security Council, 71.
32 United Nations Security Council, 69.
33 United Nations Security Council, 68–69.
34 United Nations Security Council, '3033rd Meeting', 87.
35 United Nations Security Council, 88.
36 United Nations Security Council, 88.
37 United Nations Security Council, 88.
38 United Nations Security Council, 89.

the demands for cooperation found in *Resolution 731 (1992)*.[39] 'Accordingly, the Security Council had no alternative but to adopt another resolution providing for enforcement action to ensure compliance with the resolution it had previously adopted'.[40]

France began their arguments by stating that Libyan authorities had not responded satisfactorily to requests regarding legal proceedings for the bombings of Pan Am flight 103 and UTA flight 772.[41] France noted that they consistently denounced international terrorism as 'a scourge that in itself constitutes a threat to international peace and security'.[42] They also argued that the bombings were 'a clear-cut case of international terrorism' and that the 'exceptional gravity of these attacks and considerations connected with the restoration of law and security justified this action in the Security Council'.[43] After the passing of *Resolution 748 (1992)*, France contended that the decision to turn to the Security Council for action against Libya after their refusal to handover terrorist suspects was based on respect for the rule of law.[44] Further, they stated that the Security Council's imposition of sanctions against Libya was a 'balanced and appropriate' approach, given Libya's refusal to comply with *Resolution 731 (1992)*.[45]

The US commenced by arguing that the passing of *Resolution 731 (1992)* showed the Security Council's commitment to its responsibilities to maintain international peace and security.[46] The US characterised the bombings as 'ghastly' and that as a result, 'standard [legal] procedures are clearly inapplicable'.[47] Further, they asserted that '[t]he issue at hand is not some difference of opinion or approach that can be mediated or negotiated. It is, as the Security Council has just recognised, conduct threatening to us all, and directly a threat to international peace and security'.[48] The US also contended that *Resolution 731 (1992)* simply called upon Libya to conduct itself in accordance with the law and to thus handover 'its officials who have been indicted

39 United Nations Security Council, '3063rd Meeting', 79–80.
40 United Nations Security Council, 79–80.
41 United Nations Security Council, '3033rd Meeting', 81.
42 United Nations Security Council, 82.
43 United Nations Security Council, 82.
44 United Nations Security Council, '3063rd Meeting', 73.
45 United Nations Security Council, 74.
46 United Nations Security Council, '3033rd Meeting', 78.
47 United Nations Security Council, 78.
48 United Nations Security Council, 79.

are implicated in these bombings … to the judicial authorities of the governments which are competent under international law to try them'.[49]

After the passing of *Resolution 748 (1992)*, the US characterised Libya's involvement in the bombings as 'a serious breach of international peace and security'.[50] They also argued that Libya's refusal to comply with *Resolution 731 (1992)* was a denial of justice on this issue.[51] The US contended that the sanctions imposed by the resolution were 'tailored to fit the offence—Libya's wanton and criminal destruction of civil aviation—and designed to penalize the Government of Libya, not its neighbours or any other State'.[52] Further, they contended that the sanctions were an appropriate response under the UN Charter 'for dealing with a threat to international peace and security'.[53] Finally, the US argued that the resolution was 'the surest guarantee the United Nations Security Council, using its specific, unique powers under the charter, will preserve the rule of law and ensure peaceful resolution of threats to international peace and security now and in the future'.[54] The US closed their statements by stating that they hoped that Libya would heed the message and comply with *Resolution 731 (1992)*.[55]

4 Summary of Coding

Of the P5, only China opposed a finding of 'threat to the peace' here. China's opposition was based on their desire to find peaceful solutions and their lack of faith in the proposed solution to achieve such outcomes. China also argued that Security Council action needed to accord with all relevant laws and that a finding of 'threat to the peace' would violate Libya's right of non-interference; however, China abstained from voting in acquiescence to the support for a finding by the rest of the P5. France argued that the gravity of the situation made the existence of a 'threat to the peace' self-evident and that such a finding was a consequence of Libya's actions and supported the rule of law. The US used emotive rhetoric to argue that the existence of a 'threat to the peace' was self-evident, and such a finding was a consequence of Libya's actions. They also argued that the situation was within the Security Council's mandate,

49 United Nations Security Council, 79.
50 United Nations Security Council, '3063rd Meeting', 66.
51 United Nations Security Council, 66.
52 United Nations Security Council, 67.
53 United Nations Security Council, 67.
54 United Nations Security Council, 67.
55 United Nations Security Council, 68.

supported the rule of law and was consistent with all relevant laws. The UK used a combination of formal legal arguments and emotive rhetoric to state that the situation was within the Security Council's mandate and that a finding of 'threat to the peace' was in accordance with all relevant laws and a consequence of Libya's actions. Russia used formal legal arguments to conclude that the situation was international in nature and that the existence of a 'threat to the peace' was self-evident, a consequence of Libya's actions and in accordance with all relevant laws.

CHAPTER 14

Rwandan Civil War and Genocide 1993–94 (Resolutions 812 (1993), 846 (1993), 872 (1993), 893 (1994), 909 (1994), 912 (1994), and 918 (1994))

1 Relevance to Overall Project

The Civil War and genocide in Rwanda represents a significant moment in the Security Council's history and its approach to the concept of 'threat to the peace'. Perhaps the most significant aspect of this is how the situation became part of mainstream international law, with the establishment of the ICTR and the idea of individual criminal responsibility for *jus cogens* violations that began with that establishment (in conjunction with the establishment of the ICTY). While the repercussions of this development on international law and international relations have been almost overwhelming, perhaps more important to this project is the Security Council's reversal of its position on Rwanda and a 'threat to the peace' finding between 21 April and 17 May 1994. While the details of the justifications for this change are addressed shortly, in summary, when the genocide commenced, the Security Council opted to treat the situation as an internal matter, withdrawing UN peacekeeping forces and reducing their mandate to facilitate a political ceasefire between the parties involved.[1] Four weeks later, they reversed this position, which led to a finding of 'threat to the peace' and the deployment of a peacekeeping force under Chapter VII.[2] While the *Repertoire of the Practice of the Security Council* for this period recognises the decision in *Resolution 918 (1994)* to make a positive 'threat to the peace' finding in relation to Rwanda, it does not feel that the discussions were substantive enough to be considered 'constitutional discussions' for this issue.[3]

1 'Resolution 912 (1994)', S/RES/912 (1994) UN Security Council (1994); United Nations Secretary-General, 'Special Report of the Secretary-General on the United Nations Assistance Mission for Rwanda' (New York: United Nations, 20 April 1994), 15–18.

2 'Resolution 918 (1994)', S/RES/918 (1994) UN Security Council (1994).

3 Repertoire of the Practice of the Security Council, 'Chapter XI: Considerations of Chapter VII the Charter (1993–95)', 1099–101.

 DOI:10.1163/9789004391420_016

2 Context of the Debates

Security Council considerations of Rwanda began with the letter of request (containing the ceasefire agreement) from the Rwandese Government to assist in implementing the peace accords. This request was supplemented by a briefing from Rwanda regarding the Civil War's effect on the country. They highlighted that the 'particularly atrocious war' commenced on 1 October 1990, with ceasefire agreements put in place on 17 February 1991, 16 September 1991 and 12 July 1992. They also noted recent ceasefire violations on 7 and 8 February 1993. Rwanda noted that numerous international humanitarian law (IHL) violations had occurred, as well as large flows of displaced persons:

> Many civilians are still being killed and others mutilated, not to speak of the thousands who are being displaced and haunted by the spectre of death. National and international public opinion are greatly concerned by the 1 million who have been displaced…
>
> Please allow me to offer—if only briefly—a few examples of the atrocities that exacerbate the situation: calling farmers to a meeting before massacring them with machine gun fire; shutting up scores of people in a house before killing them with grenades or explosives; disembowelling women and old people; shootings in the displaced persons camps; dismemberment, gouging out of eyes and cutting off the breasts; binding people hand and foot; and so on.[4]

Because of these atrocities and continued ceasefire violations, the Rwandese Government requested assistance in the form of 'a multipurpose international force' to guarantee the safety of displaced persons in a demilitarised zone, and help guarantee the ceasefire:[5] 'May the Rwandese nation's distress and its call for help be worthy of the compassion of the Security Council, the last hope for the triumph of reason over the arguments of the gun'.[6] *Resolution 812 (1993)*, requesting that the Secretary-General investigate the role the UN could play in supporting the peace process in Rwanda, was unanimously passed at the end of that meeting.

4 United Nations Security Council, 'Security Council, Forty-Eighth Year: 3183rd Meeting (S/PV.3183)' (United Nations, 12 March 1993), 6.
5 United Nations Security Council, 7.
6 United Nations Security Council, 7.

From the commencement of the Secretary-General's involvement until the outbreak of violence on 6 April 1994, the factual situation that informed the Security Council's decisions was presented in reports by the Secretary-General. The initial report suggested deploying an observer mission to help facilitate the peace process and provide humanitarian assistance while overseeing the continuation of the ceasefire.[7] This was supported by the unanimous passing of *Resolution 846 (1993)*, creating the United Nations Observer Mission Uganda—Rwanda (UNOMUR).[8] This was followed by the recommendation to deploy a full UN mission to Rwanda to help facilitate the peace process in a demilitarised zone,[9] resulting in the unanimous passing of *Resolution 872 (1993)*, establishing United Nations Assistance Mission for Rwanda (UNAMIR).[10] The next report emphasised that reducing the force numbers of the observer mission could jeopardise the peace process,[11] and that while the ceasefire was holding for the most part (minor violations were noted), both sides were being relatively inflexible in negotiating a long-term peace deal in spite of negotiations taking place in relative good faith.[12] Further, the reports made consistent note of rising ethnic tensions in conjunction with the heavy influx of, and easy access to, weapons in and around refugee camps.[13] Just prior to the resumption of widespread violence in April, in conjunction with the plane crash that killed the presidents of Rwanda and Burundi, the Secretary-General's reports noted increased political violence and ethnic-based violence.[14]

Following the plane crash and death of the presidents of Burundi and Rwanda, the Secretary-General issued a special report outlining the conditions in Rwanda and three alternate strategies that the Security Council could adopt. The report noted that in the wake of the plane crash, the ceasefire had ended, resulting in mass violence throughout the country that was both political and

7 United Nations Secretary-General, 'Interim Report of the Secretary-General on Rwanda' (New York: United Nations, 20 May 1993), paras. 19–23.

8 United Nations Security Council, 'Security Council, Forty-Eighth Year: 3244th Meeting (S/PV.3244)' (United Nations, 22 June 1993), 3–5.

9 United Nations Secretary-General, 'Report of the Secretary-General on Rwanda' (New York: United Nations, 24 September 1993), para. 63.

10 United Nations Security Council, 'Security Council, Forty-Eighth Year: 3288th Meeting (S/PV.3288)' (United Nations, 5 October 1993), 19.

11 United Nations Secretary-General, 'Special Report of the Secretary-General on the United Nations Assistance Mission for Rwanda', para. 30.

12 United Nations Secretary-General, para. 28.

13 United Nations Secretary-General, paras. 16 & 29.

14 United Nations Secretary-General, 'Second Progress Report of the Secretary-General on the United Nations Assistance Mission for Rwanda' (New York: United Nations, 30 March 1994), paras. 26(f)-27 & 36.

ethnic in nature.[15] The alternatives the Secretary-General offered for the UNAMIR mandate were as follows. Alternative one proposed a massive increase in force deployment, changes to the mandate to place it under Chapter VII and allowing peacekeepers to use force in an effort to enforce peace in the region. This was the option requested by the governments of Rwanda and Uganda.[16] Alternative two suggested a reduction in UNAMIR's numbers to a barebones security force mandated only to protect the force commander, who was to continue attempting to broker a ceasefire between the parties.[17] Alternative three was the complete withdrawal of UNAMIR.[18] While the report strongly inferred a recommendation for alternative one, the Security Council unanimously passed *Resolution 912 (1994)*, adopting alternative two from the Secretary-General's report.[19]

Four weeks later, the Secretary-General issued another report updating the Security Council on the situation in Rwanda. The report noted the continued heavy fighting, in addition to militias engaging in the mass killing of civilians throughout the country.[20] It also noted that there were now around two million displaced persons as a result of the resumed fighting.[21] The report proposed a new force of approximately 5,500 troops, with constabulary use of force engagement orders (UNAMIR II), and a mandate to provide humanitarian assistance and civilian safe zones.[22] *Resolution 918 (1994)*, which created UNAMIR II and an arms embargo under Chapter VII for Rwanda (at Russia's insistence, given the absence of a ceasefire), was passed, with Rwanda voting against the Chapter VII arms embargo contained in Section B of the resolution.[23]

3 Justificatory Discourse of the P5

Until *Resolution 918 (1994)*, the P5's justificatory discourse hinged very strongly on peace through political negotiation without external interference. This

15 United Nations Secretary-General, 'Special Report of the Secretary-General on the United Nations Assistance Mission for Rwanda', paras. 1–3.
16 United Nations Secretary-General, paras. 13–14.
17 United Nations Secretary-General, paras. 15–18.
18 United Nations Secretary-General, para. 19.
19 United Nations Security Council, 'Security Council, Forty-Ninth Year: 3368th Meeting (S/PV.3368)' (United Nations, 21 April 1994), 6.
20 United Nations Secretary-General, 'Report of the Secretary-General on the Situation in Rwanda' (New York: United Nations, 13 May 1994), para. 3.
21 United Nations Secretary-General, para. 3.
22 United Nations Secretary-General, paras. 11–15.
23 United Nations Security Council, 'Security Council, Forty-Ninth Year: 3377th Meeting (S/PV.3377)' (United Nations, 16 May 1994), 10–11.

position was most strongly vocalised by France, which opted to make statements in more meetings than any other member of the P5 on this issue. The decision to make a finding of 'threat to the peace' was generally justified on the basis of trying to foster the conditions necessary for a peaceful settlement to the conflict in the face of the humanitarian crisis.

China opted to make statements about Rwanda on two separate occasions, the first being after the passing of *Resolution 872 (1993)* creating UNAMIR under Chapter VI of the Charter. The second was before voting on *Resolution 918 (1994)*, which resulted in the creation of UNAMIR II and the finding of 'threat to the peace'. With the initial UNAMIR mission, China argued that the peace process in Rwanda was at a crucial stage that relied upon the continued cease-fire and stability to proceed. China called upon both parties to 'start forthwith the cantonment and demobilisation of their troops so as to create necessary conditions for the establishment of the transitional institutions and the holding of general elections on schedule'.[24] Further, China noted that support for creating UNAMIR was entirely grounded in the mandate of the mission to promote compliance with the peace agreements in conjunction with the request of both parties for such support from the UN.[25]

Before voting on *Resolution 918 (1994)*, China stated that

> the conflicting Rwandese parties should cease forthwith massacring each other and agree to an effective and lasting cease-fire so as to create the conditions necessary for an improvement in the humanitarian situation and the settlements of the conflict through negotiation.[26]

Following this statement, China made it clear that support for *Resolution 918 (1994)* was '[b]ased on humanitarian considerations'[27] and 'sincere desire to create conditions for the early restoration of peace and security in that country'.[28] Finally, China argued that the already agreed-upon peace accords was the framework to which both parties should adhere when establishing peace and new government within the country.[29]

Russia's statements on this issue mirrored China's—they opted only to articulate their position after the passing of *Resolution 872 (1993)*, and before voting on *Resolution 918 (1994)*. In relation to the creation of UNAMIR, Russia

24 United Nations Security Council, '3288th Meeting', 24.
25 United Nations Security Council, 24.
26 United Nations Security Council, '3377th Meeting', 9.
27 United Nations Security Council, 9.
28 United Nations Security Council, 9.
29 United Nations Security Council, 9.

argued that the mission and its mandate should assist both parties in Rwanda to comply with the peace agreements to assist in facilitating lasting peace for the nation.[30] Russia also stated that it believed the Security Council's role in situations such as this was to support the effort of regional organisations to end conflict.[31] Their support for UNAMIR's creation under Chapter VI was grounded in these positions.

Before voting on *Resolution 918 (1994)*, Russia argued that the gravity of the situation in Rwanda since the fighting had resumed demanded a Security Council response. Russia stated that they supported the expansion of UNAMIR's mission under the new UNAMIR II tag because of the 'severe humanitarian crisis' that was now underway in Rwanda.[32] Further, their support for the peacekeeping mission was based on the fact that the draft resolution now addressed their concerns about taking into account the basic criteria for carrying out peacekeeping operations, which the Security Council had confirmed by presidential statement on 3 May 1994.[33] Further, they insisted upon imposing an arms embargo, necessitating the finding of a 'threat to the peace' and Chapter VII action by the Security Council, because of the lack of a functioning and effective ceasefire.[34] They argued that this would help foster the necessary conditions for a successful peacekeeping operation.[35] In spite of this, Russia highlighted the importance of the 'unconditional cooperation of both Rwandese parties' if the peacekeeping mission was to be successful.[36]

The UK's only statements on this situation were made after voting on Resolutions 872 (1993) and 918 (1994). In relation to the initial deployment of UNAMIR, the UK argued that the UN's role in Rwanda was that of facilitator, and that peace would only be achieved when 'an African solution was found to an African problem'.[37] On this note, the UK contended that the responsibility for ending the protracted conflict and creating an atmosphere that allowed displaced persons to resettle within Rwanda lay with the Rwandese Government and Rwandan Patriotic Front (RPF).[38] After making these positions clear,

30 United Nations Security Council, '3288th Meeting', 26.

31 United Nations Security Council, 26.

32 United Nations Security Council, '3377th Meeting', 9.

33 United Nations Security Council, 10. Interestingly, the Presidential Statement in question (S/PRST/1994/23) made in relation to Bosnia and Herzegovina made no direct mention of peacekeeping criteria. It is possible that Russia were referring to statements regarding aerial surveillance and the use of force to be used against safe zone violators.

34 United Nations Security Council, 10.

35 United Nations Security Council, 10.

36 United Nations Security Council, 10.

37 United Nations Security Council, '3288th Meeting', 21.

38 United Nations Security Council, 21.

the UK noted that they were strongly in favour of the international community providing support for these endeavours.[39]

This position of supporting the RPF and the Rwandese Government to end the violence in the Rwandan conflict continued in the UK's statement after the passing of *Resolution 918 (1994)*:

> The world has been appalled by the scale of tragedy which has occurred in Rwanda. It is not tragedy to which there is an easy international response. The United Nations cannot impose an end to bloodshed. But neither can it stand idly by ... The focus of this expanded United Nations operation will rightly be humanitarian.[40]

The UK then proceeded to state that the only way to end to bloodshed and establish peace was for the parties involved to take responsibility for their actions and resume a politically negotiated settlement: 'The Arusha Agreement remains the only viable basis for national reconciliation in Rwanda'.[41]

The US position throughout this situation was that the responsibility for establishing peace in Rwanda lay with the Rwandese people, who were parties to the conflict. When making statements after the passing of *Resolution 872 (1993)*, the US highlighted that their support for deploying UNAMIR was grounded in the fact that 'it will advance the goals of peaceful conflict resolution and democratization, and allow the return of hundreds of thousands of those that fled their homes'.[42] After emphasising this basis for action, the US expressed their concern at the burden the Security Council was shouldering, noting that it was important to ensure the mission remained focused on a tight mandate.[43] Regarding the question of peace within Rwanda, the US stated that it was 'up to the Rwandese themselves to ensure that the transition to democracy moves forward'.[44]

Just prior to the resumption of violence on 6 April 1994, the US raised their concerns over delays by the parties involved in terms of implementing transitional institutions, noting that the Secretary-General suggested that such delays posed a threat to peace and security in the region.[45] The US argued that

39 United Nations Security Council, 21.
40 United Nations Security Council, '3377th Meeting', 12.
41 United Nations Security Council, 12.
42 United Nations Security Council, '3288th Meeting', 22.
43 United Nations Security Council, 23.
44 United Nations Security Council, 22.
45 United Nations Security Council, 'Security Council, Forty-Ninth Year: 3358th Meeting (S/PV.3358)' (United Nations, 5 April 1994), 6.

their support for Chapter VII action in *Resolution 918 (1994)* was premised upon the basis that '[t]he sheer magnitude of the humanitarian disaster in that tragic country demands action. This Council has struggled to formulate a response that is both appropriate and effective'.[46] While supporting Security Council action on the basis of the disaster's magnitude, the US was clear in their position that 'whatever efforts the United Nations may undertake, the true key to the problems in Rwanda is in the hands of the Rwandese people'.[47] Finally, the US stated that continued international assistance in Rwanda was contingent upon both parties to the conflict demonstrating a willingness and ability to cooperate with the peacekeeping forces and bringing about an end the violence.[48]

France opted to speak at every possible opportunity regarding this situation. The core of their argument throughout these statements was that the only way to achieve peace in Rwanda was through a politically negotiated settlement between the parties to the conflict.[49] France asserted that the UN should support these processes, but that the majority of the work had be performed by the Rwandese Government and the RPF.[50] After the passing of *Resolution 872 (1993)*, France stated that they only supported establishing UNAMIR because it was being done with the cooperation of both parties to the conflict.[51] Before UNAMIR troops were withdrawn in the wake of resumed conflict on 6 April 1994, France argued that the 'continuation of United Nations action in Rwanda depends directly on the efforts they are prepared to make to restore peace definitively to Rwanda in the wake of a conflict that has, alas, claimed all too many victims'.[52] This position proved relatively accurate given the passing of *Resolution 912 (1994)*, which significantly reduced the scope of the mandate and UNAMIR force numbers. France again used this opportunity to restate their position that there was no military solution possible in Rwanda, and that only a political solution could bring about peace in the region.[53] They also reiterated their notion that should the parties not agree to a ceasefire, the UN would have to reconsider UNAMIR having a continued presence in Rwanda at all.[54]

46 United Nations Security Council, '3377th Meeting', 12.
47 United Nations Security Council, 13.
48 United Nations Security Council, 13.
49 United Nations Security Council, '3244th Meeting', 4–5; United Nations Security Council, '3358th Meeting', 6.
50 United Nations Security Council, '3183rd Meeting', 15.
51 United Nations Security Council, '3288th Meeting', 20.
52 United Nations Security Council, 'Security Council, Forty-Ninth Year: 3326th Meeting (S/PV.3326)' (United Nations, 6 January 1994), 11.
53 United Nations Security Council, '3368th Meeting', 7.
54 United Nations Security Council, 7.

After the finding of 'threat to the peace' in *Resolution 918 (1994)*, France justified support for Security Council action on the basis of the gravity of the humanitarian situation further unfolding in Rwanda: 'Faced with a humanitarian catastrophe on such magnitude, the international community could not fail to react'.[55] France also opted to defend its vocal support for withdrawing the majority of UNAMIR after fighting had resumed, arguing that the Security Council was 'compelled to make troop reductions'[56] and 'took that decision reluctantly'.[57] Given France's previous threats that continued UN support in Rwanda depended upon the Rwandese people making progress in the peace process, such justifications regarding UNAMIR's withdrawal seem disingenuous at best. France closed its statements by arguing that UNAMIR II's mission was to protect the civilian population and deliver humanitarian assistance, as peace in Rwanda could only be attained by resuming the peace process that had already been politically agreed upon.[58]

4 Summary of Coding

All P5 members supported a finding of 'threat to the peace' in this situation; however, France initially opposed Security Council involvement. The US supported a finding because of the gravity of the situation, and because a finding would support regional solutions. The UK and Russia supported a finding because of the gravity of the situation, and because a finding would assist with peaceful solutions (Russia also pointed out that the situation was clearly within the Security Council's mandate). China supported a finding because they saw the existence of a 'threat to the peace' as self-evident and because a finding would assist with peaceful solutions. France initially opposed a finding of 'threat to the peace' in favour of advocating for peaceful regional solutions; since these did not occur, France argued that withdrawing Security Council support was a consequence of the actions of the parties involved. They eventually supported a finding because of the gravity of the situation and the need for a peaceful solution.

55 United Nations Security Council, '3377th Meeting', 11.
56 United Nations Security Council, 11.
57 United Nations Security Council, 11.
58 United Nations Security Council, 11.

CHAPTER 15

Afghanistan 1999 (Resolution 1267)

1 Relevance to Overall Project

In 1998, the Security Council, acting under Chapter VI, demanded 'that the Taliban stop providing sanctuary and training for international terrorists and their organisations, and that all Afghan factions cooperate with efforts to bring indicted terrorists to justice'.[1] Ten-and-a-half months later, the Security Council determined 'that the failure of the Taliban authorities to respond to the demands in paragraph 13 of *Resolution 1214 (1998)* constitutes a threat to international peace and security',[2] resulting in Chapter VII action. The justification, *prima facie*, seems to have been that the failure to meet a Security Council demand resulted in the situation being characterised as a 'threat to the peace'. The alternate reading is that in spite of the language used in the preamble to *Resolution 1267 (1999)*, the resolution is very simply a counterterrorism one. The *Repertoire of Practice of the Security Council* picks up on this subject matter within the resolution and the debates, and focuses solely upon that alternate reading as the justification for the finding.[3] The value of this case study to the overall project is that it allows for interrogation of a situation that raised the question of whether the stated justification—a consequence of the Security Council's defiance, as suggested in the preamble—was consistent with the P5's justificatory discourse.

2 Context of the Debate

In the build-up to *Resolution 1214 (1998)*, the Secretary-General produced a report for the UN (both General Assembly and Security Council) on the situation in Afghanistan.[4] The only mention of terrorism in this report is in paragraph 13, which discusses the presence of Osama bin Laden, allegations of his responsibility for the bombings of US embassies in Kenya and Tanzania and retaliatory

1 'Resolution 1214 (1998)', S/RES/1214 (1998) UN Security Council (1998), para. 13.
2 'Resolution 1267 (1999)', S/RES/1267 (1999) UN Security Council (1999), para. Preamble.
3 Repertoire of the Practice of the Security Council, 'Chapter XI: Considerations of Chapter VII the Charter (1996–99)', 1123.
4 United Nations Secretary-General, 'The Situation in Afghanistan and Its Implication for International Peace and Security' (United Nations, 23 November 1998).

 | DOI:10.1163/9789004391420_017

US missile strikes on purported terrorist training camps in Afghanistan.[5] The report makes no links between the Taliban and the terrorism allegations, although this linkage does seem to be the basis for paragraph 13 in *Resolution 1214 (1998)*. In the meetings that led to *Resolution 1267 (1999)* being adopted, oral briefings focused on the overall situation in Afghanistan. The briefings contained confirmed and unconfirmed reports of various IHL violations by the Taliban, including forced displacement of people,[6] targeting of civilians[7] and the use of child soldiers.[8] The report also suggested that all parties to the conflict were guilty of using child soldiers,[9] deploying landmines,[10] and targeting civilians with impunity.[11] The questions of terrorism and Taliban support for terrorism were not raised in these oral briefings (although the use of Pakistani religious schools as a recruiting ground for the Taliban was confirmed);[12] however, the Afghan delegate did accuse the Pakistani Inter-Services Intelligence of training terrorists who were being used in support of Taliban activities.[13]

3 Justificatory Discourse of the P5

Statements from all P5 members on this issue were relatively brief, and focused primarily on the ongoing civil war rather than on the terrorism issue that led to the declaration of 'threat to the peace'. Of the P5, only the US and China opted to make statements in the meeting in which *Resolution 1267 (1999)* was unanimously passed. As mentioned above, the *Repertoire of Practice of the Security Council* suggests that the basis for this resolution was one of counterterrorism. Alternatively, the resolution itself suggests that the finding was grounded in escalating consequences for defying previous Security Council resolutions. Examining the P5's justificatory discourse shows the real situation to be something of a hybrid of these two rationales, supplemented by counter-narcotics trafficking goals.

---

5 United Nations Secretary-General, para. 13.
6 United Nations Security Council, 'Security Council, Fifty-Fourth Year: 4039th Meeting (S/PV.4039)', 27 August 1999, 3.
7 United Nations Security Council, 2–3.
8 United Nations Security Council, 3.
9 United Nations Security Council, 3.
10 United Nations Security Council, 4.
11 United Nations Security Council, 3.
12 United Nations Security Council, 3.
13 United Nations Security Council, 6–7.

Russia's position was most aligned with the wording of *Resolution 1267 (1999)*. Russia argued openly that a message needed to be sent to those who would defy the Security Council, and that such defiance was actually directed at the international community at large and would result in consequences for the short-sightedness it demonstrated.[14] This strongly echoes the last section of the preamble to *Resolution 1267 (1999)*. More generally, Russia also spoke strongly against Taliban support for international terrorism and the production and trafficking of narcotics out of areas under their control.[15] Further, Russia raised concerns about IHL and human rights violations occurring generally within Afghanistan as a byproduct of the civil war.[16]

China advocated for a strong arms embargo with an adaptable and effective monitoring system as an appropriate response to the ongoing situation in Afghanistan.[17] In doing so, they also called for the immediate cessation of foreign military assistance to the various factions of Afghanistan, called for political settlements and for the international community to respect whatever outcomes would emerge from those political settlements.[18] In direct relation to their support of *Resolution 1267 (1999)*, China made a very clear and succinct statement summarising their entire position:

> China is against all forms of terrorism. It was on the basis of this principled position that we participated in the consultations on the resolution that has just been adopted, during which we requested the text be limited to the question of combating international terrorism. At the same time, we have taken note of the fact that the text of this resolution reiterates commitment to the sovereignty, independence and territorial integrity of Afghanistan, as well as respect for its cultural and historic traditions.[19]

The majority of the UK's statement pertaining to *Resolution 1267 (1999)* was related to its perception of Taliban violations of IHL.[20] Continuing in this vein, the UK called for all parties to engage in negotiations for peace, and particularly highlighted Pakistan's role in this, given their relationship with the

14 United Nations Security Council, 9.
15 United Nations Security Council, 9.
16 United Nations Security Council, 9.
17 United Nations Security Council, 10.
18 Ibid.
19 United Nations Security Council, 'Security Council, Fifty-Fourth Year: 4051st Meeting (S/PV.4051)', 15 October 1999, 5.
20 United Nations Security Council, '4039th Meeting', 14.

Taliban.[21] The UK's only comment relating directly to justifying the Security Council's 'threat to the peace' declaration in *Resolution 1267 (1999)* was their suggestion that continued conflict in Afghanistan would have global ripple effects because of the threat of terrorism and narcotics trafficking from within the region.[22]

France's brief statements delineated their view that the situation in Afghanistan was deteriorating rather than improving.[23] They attributed this to the Taliban's unwillingness to engage in peace negotiations,[24] and inferred that foreign military interference in Afghanistan was also a major contributing factor.[25] As to the finding of 'threat to the peace', France pointed out that the Security Council made very clear demands of the Taliban in *Resolution 1214 (1998)* to cease and desist harbouring and training terrorist groups.[26] France expanded upon this in their statements, calling for a halt to producing and trafficking narcotics from Taliban-controlled areas, and for the Taliban to respect, and conform to, IHL and human rights norms.[27]

The US statements contained the strongest counterterrorism rhetoric, particularly in relation to Osama bin Laden; however, the US also used this opportunity to speak broadly about ending external interference and IHL violations in the Afghan Civil War.[28] They stated that the US goal was to grow and strengthen representative democracy and civil society in accordance with international norms, especially those regarding transnational organised crime and human rights.[29] The US joined Russia in speaking about the consequences of defying the Security Council: 'If, in defiance of Security Council resolutions, the Taliban fails to end their protection of terrorists, the international community should bring increasing and certain pressure to bear on them'.[30] They reiterated this sentiment in their statements immediately prior to the unanimous adoption of *Resolution 1267 (1999)*, arguing that this resolution 'will send a direct message to Osama bin Laden, and terrorists everywhere, "you can run, you can hide, but you will be brought to justice"'.[31] This rhetoric of justice for

21 United Nations Security Council, 14.
22 United Nations Security Council, 14.
23 United Nations Security Council, 13.
24 United Nations Security Council, 14.
25 United Nations Security Council, 14.
26 United Nations Security Council, 14.
27 United Nations Security Council, 14.
28 United Nations Security Council, 12.
29 United Nations Security Council, 13.
30 United Nations Security Council, 13.
31 United Nations Security Council, '4051st Meeting', 2–3.

terrorism continued with the US calling on the Taliban to surrender bin Laden 'to authorities in a country where he will be brought to justice'.[32] Further, they asserted that should the Taliban choose not to surrender bin Laden, the sanctions would be targeted specifically upon them and not the Afghan people, inferring that this was a form of justice.[33]

4 Summary of Coding

This situation garnered the support of all P5 members for a finding of 'threat to the peace'. The US used emotive rhetoric to argue that the finding supported the rule of law and defence of democracy, while also being a direct consequence of the Taliban's failure to comply with previous Security Council resolutions. The UK supported a finding because they perceived the situation as international in nature and believed the finding would assist in bringing about a peaceful solution, and because the violations of international law occurring amounted to a 'threat to the peace'. Russia argued that a finding of 'threat to the peace' was a direct consequence of the Taliban's failure to comply with previous Security Council resolutions. Further, they saw this finding as justified because of the international law violations occurring, and to protect human rights. China supported a finding of 'threat to the peace' because of the international law violations occurring, and in the hope that it would aid in facilitating peaceful solutions for the situation. France characterised the finding of 'threat to the peace' as a direct consequence of the Taliban's failure to comply with previous Security Council resolutions, and justified this with the ongoing international law violations that were taking place.

32 United Nations Security Council, 3.

33 United Nations Security Council, 3.

CHAPTER 16

East Timor Intervention 1999 (Resolution 1264)

1 Relevance to Overall Project

The value of examining the East Timor (now Timor Leste) intervention debates from 1999 lies not in the level of debate that was undertaken, or the contentious nature of that debate, but rather in the high level of consensus that existed within the P5, and the fact that the existence of a 'threat to the peace' was assumed to be a given rather than a possibility. The East Timor situation was considered so uncontentious with regards to Article 39 that the *Repertoire for the Practice of the Security Council* for 1996 to 1999 stated that 'no substantive issues relating to the provision of Article 39 were raised'.[1] Although the East Timor intervention did not feature in the *Repertoire for the Practice of the Security Council* for the period, it is included here as a baseline and uncontroversial finding of 'threat to the peace' to demonstrate the P5's varied approaches to reaching a consensus that was never in question. This case study provides very little in the way of argumentative debate and differing positions regarding what is considered a 'threat to the peace'; however, it does offer insight into the differences in justification that the various P5 states use, even when they agree that a 'threat to the peace' exists.

2 Context of the Debates

On 5 May 1999, Indonesia and Portugal, in conjunction with the UN, finalised the agreements to allow for a democratic and popular consultation by the East Timorese people (both within and external to the territory) to determine the future nature of the territory's government.[2] The options in play were special autonomy within the aegis of the Republic of Indonesia, or a transition, with the UN as handmaiden, to full independence.[3] The agreement also provided for the establishment of a UN Mission in East Timor to facilitate the popular

1 Repertoire of the Practice of the Security Council, 'Chapter XI: Considerations of Chapter VII the Charter (1996–99)', 1118.

2 United Nations Secretary-General, 'Question of East Timor: Report of the Secretary-General', 5 May 1999, para. 1.

3 United Nations Secretary-General, para. 1.

 | DOI:10.1163/9789004391420_018

consultation.[4] Under the 5 May 1999 agreements, Indonesia retained responsibility for maintaining law and order within East Timor during the build-up to the popular consultation, and while it was being undertaken.[5]

On 3 September 1999, the Secretary-General reported to the Security Council that East Timor had registered 451,792 voters.[6] The vote took place on 30 August 1999 and the result was 94,388 (21.5%) in favour of special autonomy and 344,580 (78.5%) in favour of full independence.[7] According to the Secretary-General, this result marked the end of 24 years of conflict in East Timor and represented a clear call for a peaceful and orderly transition to independence.[8] Shortly after these statements by the Secretary-General, the President of the Security Council made a statement on behalf of the whole Security Council condemning the pre- and post-30 August 1999 election violence that had occurred in East Timor, and called upon all people involved to work together to implement the democratic decision for independence.[9] Further, the Security Council asked the Indonesian Government to take steps to prevent further violence and to maintain peace and security in East Timor in accordance with the 5 May 1999 agreements.[10]

On 11 September 1999, the Secretary-General again addressed the Security Council and provided an overview of the situation in East Timor. It was suggested that the ballot conditions were less than ideal, and that shortly after the ballot was conducted, East Timor began a 'descent into chaos'.[11] The Secretary-General stated that '[t]he scale of violence, death and destruction has been far beyond what any international observers anticipated'.[12] In spite of the efforts of the UN Mission in East Timor, the security situation had deteriorated to the point where all non-essential UN staff had been relocated out of the region.[13] 'Lawlessness and disorder have reigned in Dili this week, despite a significant presence of the Indonesian police and military who are unwilling or unable to

4 United Nations Secretary-General, para. 1.

5 United Nations Secretary-General, para. 4; 'East Timor Popular Consultation' (1999) Articles 1 & 4.

6 United Nations Security Council, 'Security Council, Fifty-Fourth Year: 4041st Meeting (S/PV.4041)', 3 September 1999, 2.

7 United Nations Security Council, 2.

8 United Nations Security Council, 2.

9 United Nations Security Council, 'Security Council, Fifty-Fourth Year: 4042nd Meeting (S/PV.4042)', 3 September 1999, 2.

10 United Nations Security Council, 2–3.

11 United Nations Security Council, 'Security Council, Fifty-Fourth Year: 4043rd Meeting (S/PV.4043)', 11 September 1999, 2.

12 United Nations Security Council, 2.

13 United Nations Security Council, 3.

control the situation'.[14] This summary of the situation by the Secretary-General was followed by calls for the Indonesian Government to seek help from the international community to fulfil its responsibility for maintaining peace and security within East Timor in accordance with the 5 May 1999 agreements.[15]

3 Justificatory Discourse of the P5

The P5's justificatory discourse for this situation occurred over two separate meetings. The first was the 4043rd meeting, on 11 September 1999, which led directly to the intervention in East Timor; the second was in the 4057th meeting, on 25 October 1999, which addressed the progress of the UN Mission in East Timor. Of particular interest throughout these meetings is that, as noted above, the question of whether a 'threat to the peace' existed was never raised, but rather was taken as assumed to exist, although justified differently by the P5 states. Even given this consensus on the existence of a 'threat to the peace' and the need for intervention, an examination of the meeting transcripts reveals that the justifications were quite varied.

The US began its justification for the intervention by likening the situation in East Timor to the then recent situation in Kosovo.[16] After drawing these parallels, the US delegate suggested that the democratic election process that had taken place was a process consistent with the traditions of the UN Charter.[17] Given that democracy and democratic traditions are not mentioned within the UN Charter, this is most likely a US cultural interpretation of Article 1(2) of the Charter,[18] rather than a statement of international law (although, as noted in Chapter 1, there have been suggestions that democracy as a required form of government is emerging customary law although I personally do not support such a position). After drawing on rhetoric supporting the primacy of democracy within international law, the US then pointed to the ongoing violence in East Timor with the same level of rhetorical intensity: 'militia—clearly backed by elements of the military of Indonesia—took to the streets and began a murderous rampage'.[19] Regarding reports of ongoing violence, the US stated that 'we are consumed by images of brutality, violence and mayhem'.[20]

---

14 United Nations Security Council, 3.
15 United Nations Security Council, 3.
16 United Nations Security Council, 7.
17 United Nations Security Council, 7.
18 'Charter of the United Nations', 1 UNTS XVI (1945) Article 1(2).
19 United Nations Security Council, '4043rd Meeting', 8.
20 United Nations Security Council, 8.

What was very clear from these meetings was that the US Government held Indonesia directly and wholly responsible for this situation, threatening diplomatic relations with Indonesia unless it 'reverses course immediately' in its support of violent militias.[21] This was followed by clear statements calling on the Indonesian Government to allow an international peacekeeping force to enter East Timor to restore peace and security. The basis for this call was the fact that the Indonesian Government could not be entrusted with maintaining peace and security in East Timor, as required by the 5 May 1999 agreements, because of their support of the militias operating in East Timor.[22] The US statement concluded with an appeal for the Security Council to protect democracy.[23] These statements, presented in the 4057th meeting, strongly mirrored the statements made in the 4043rd meeting in their appeals for action to support the protection of democracy and the cessation of violence.[24] Of interest, though, is the inference made in this meeting regarding the rule of law, 'justice' and the investigation of IHL and international human rights law (IHRL) violations as essential components of re-establishing of peace and security within the region.[25]

The French adopted a very similar approach to the US on these issues, although employed less rhetorical flourish in describing their position.[26] The French inferred that the derailing of the democratic process in East Timor, and the rebellion-style violence that followed, made the existence of a 'threat to peace' self-evident.[27] They repeated these appeals to self-determination and democratic process in the 4057th meeting.[28] France also concurred with the US likening the situation to Kosovo and expanded upon this by characterising the situation as on a par with the Rwanda genocide.[29] While France acknowledged ties between the militia groups and segments of the Indonesian military, they did not hold the Indonesian Government directly responsible for the violence and peace and security lapses in the region;[30] however, they did call into question the Indonesian Government's ability to fulfil their commitments to

21 United Nations Security Council, 8.
22 United Nations Security Council, 8.
23 United Nations Security Council, 9.
24 United Nations Security Council, 'Security Council, Fifty-Fourth Year: 4057th Meeting (S/PV.4057)', 25 October 1999, 17.
25 United Nations Security Council, 17–18.
26 United Nations Security Council, '4043rd Meeting', 9–10; United Nations Security Council, '4057th Meeting', 16.
27 United Nations Security Council, '4043rd Meeting', 9.
28 United Nations Security Council, '4057th Meeting', 16.
29 United Nations Security Council, '4043rd Meeting', 9.
30 United Nations Security Council, 9.

maintaining order and security in accordance with the 5 May Agreements.[31] Their appeals for a Security Council-mandated international security presence in East Timor relied upon the facts the Secretary-General had presented, assuming and presupposing that a 'threat to the peace' under Article 39 had already been accepted.[32]

The UK joined France and the US in calling for the defence of democracy and mitigation of the humanitarian crisis.[33] While their use of language was more subdued than the US, it was no less strong, which became clear when they stated that the 'international community must stand by the people of East Timor and ensure that their democratic choice is turned into a political reality'.[34] Their comments on the primacy of democratic institutions in the international order, and their requirements for social progress, peace and security, were abundantly evident by the close of their statement in the 4043rd meeting,[35] and throughout their statements in the 4057th meeting.[36] In the latter meeting, this position was supplemented by strong inferences regarding the necessity of the rule of law and strong governmental bureaucracies in peace and security.[37]

While the UK made very frank statements about the violence taking place in East Timor, they seemed to dispassionately recount of the facts when compared with the rhetoric the US employed.[38] While the UK called for Indonesia to suppress violence and restore peace and security to the region, acts that should be supplemented by an international force if Indonesia was incapable of doing so, at no point was Indonesia held directly and wholly responsible for the situation.[39] Again, the assumption was clearly that a 'threat to the peace' under Article 39 was already in existence at the time of the debate, the thus only concern permeating the arguments being made was that action now had to be authorised.[40]

In discussing the situation in East Timor, Russia restricted its comments to the acts of violence that had taken place since the ballot.[41] In doing so, Russia

31 United Nations Security Council, 9.
32 United Nations Security Council, 10.
33 United Nations Security Council, 13.
34 United Nations Security Council, 13.
35 United Nations Security Council, 14.
36 United Nations Security Council, '4057th Meeting', 12.
37 United Nations Security Council, 12.
38 United Nations Security Council, '4043rd Meeting', 13.
39 United Nations Security Council, 14.
40 United Nations Security Council, 13–14.
41 United Nations Security Council, 14–15.

made very little reference to the details of the violence, keeping all of its statements abstract in nature and simply remarking that attacks had been made on civilians and 'murders of completely innocent people' had occurred.[42] They were of the view that the international community should support Indonesia in restoring peace and security to the region through Security Council action, as the evidence suggested Indonesia was unable to do so alone.[43] While their preference was clearly for Indonesian consent to such action, they were comfortable with issuing a Security Council mandate for peacekeeping in the absence of this consent.[44]

While Russia focused on the violence and avoided all questions of self-determination, China did the exact opposite, emphasising the right of self-determination and making minimal reference to the violence happening in East Timor.[45] Even though the Chinese made strong appeals to everyone involved to 'respect the will of the people', there was no reference to concepts of democracy in these statements.[46] The closest China came to mentioning democracy was to refer to the process in East Timor as a popular consultation,[47] a term that was used in the 5 May Agreements.[48] They supported the concept of an intervention to restore peace and security for implementing the East Timorese right of self-determination;[49] however, they stated that maintaining peace and security was a responsibility that should be borne by the Security Council in accordance with the Charter, rather than one that lay with the Indonesian Government in accordance with the 5 May Agreements.[50] China clearly established that its preference was for such a peacekeeping force to be deployed with the Indonesian Government's consent, avoiding questions about whether it would support such an intervention if such consent was not present.[51]

42 United Nations Security Council, 9.
43 United Nations Security Council, 9–10.
44 United Nations Security Council, 9–10.
45 United Nations Security Council, 13; United Nations Security Council, '4057th Meeting', 13.
46 United Nations Security Council, '4043rd Meeting', 13; United Nations Security Council, '4057th Meeting', 13.
47 United Nations Security Council, '4043rd Meeting', 13.
48 United Nations Secretary-General, 'Question of East Timor', para. 1; 'Agreement between the Republic of Indonesia and the Portuguese Republic on the Question of East Timor' (1999) Article 1.
49 United Nations Security Council, '4043rd Meeting', 13.
50 United Nations Security Council, 13.
51 United Nations Security Council, 13.

4 Summary of Coding

All P5 members supported a finding of 'threat to the peace' in this case study. France argued that the existence of a 'threat to the peace' was self-evident and in accordance with all relevant law while supporting the right of self-determination and the defence of democracy. China argued that the finding accorded with all relevant law and supported the right of self-determination and regional solutions. Russia argued that the situation was within the Security Council's mandate because of its gravity, and that a finding of 'threat to the peace' supported regional solutions and the right of self-determination. The UK argued that the existence of a 'threat to the peace' was self-evident and supported the protection of human rights, the defence of democracy and the rule of law. The US used emotive rhetoric to argue that a finding of 'threat to the peace' supported the rule of law and the defence of democracy.

CHAPTER 17

Small Arms Trade (Resolution 2117 (2013) and the Arms Trade Treaty)

1 Relevance to the Overall Project

The Security Council debates regarding the illicit trade in small arms and light weapons commenced in 1999 and were ongoing until 2013, culminating with the passing of *Resolution 2117 (2013)*[1] and the finalisation of the *Arms Trade Treaty* (ATT).[2] Periodically, the Secretary-General and various rotating Security Council members sought to place findings that the illicit trade in small arms constituted a 'threat to the peace' on the agenda. This is consistent with the *Repertoire of Practice of the Security Council's* analysis, which shows a strong push by rotating members in the 2004–07 period for the illicit small arms trade to be considered a 'threat to the peace'.[3] While numerous references throughout these debates were made regarding the effect of the illicit small arms trade on peace and security, of the P5, only France argued that this trade was of sufficient gravity to constitute a 'threat to the peace'.[4] Of further interest to this overall project of understanding the P5's approaches to the concept of 'threat to the peace' is that *Resolution 2117 (2013)* (passing with 14 votes, and an abstention from Russia)[5] declared the illicit trade in small arms to be a 'threat to the peace';[6][7] however, as this declaration was made under Chapter VI, the use of the phrase 'threat to the peace' is insufficient for it to be considered a positive determination in relation to Article 39—highlighting the importance of a sound understanding of international legal nuance when analysing international political discourse because of the interrelated nature of these two distinct authorisational bases.

1 'Resolution 2117 (2013)', S/RES/2117 (2013) UN Security Council (2013).

2 'The Arms Trade Treaty', UNTC Chapter XXVI 8 (2013).

3 Repertoire of the Practice of the Security Council, 'Chapter XI: Considerations of Chapter VII the Charter (2004–07)', 33–34.

4 United Nations Security Council, 'Security Council, Sixty-Third Year: 5881st Meeting (S/PV.5881)' (United Nations, 30 April 2008), 11.

5 United Nations Security Council, 'Security Council, Sixty-Eighth Year: 7036th Meeting (S/PV.7036)' (United Nations, 26 September 2013), 5–6.

6 Resolution 2117 (2013), para. Preamble.

7 *Resolution 2117 (2013) 2013* (UN Security Council) Preamble.

 | DOI:10.1163/9789004391420_019

2 Context of the Debates

The eight debates on the issue of the illicit small arms trade took place over 14 years (1999–2013),[8] with the largest gap between debates being five years. In that time, the Security Council made 16 presidential statements generally addressing the issue (each of these statements acknowledged the effect of the illicit small arms trade on conflict and post-conflict regions),[9] and one resolution[10] (and a treaty occurring outside of, but informing, the Security Council

8 United Nations Security Council, 'Security Council, Fifty-Fourth Year: 4048th Meeting (S/PV.4048)' (United Nations, 24 September 1999); United Nations Security Council, 'Security Council, Fifty-Sixth Year: 4355th Meeting (S/PV.4355)' (United Nations, 2 August 2001); United Nations Security Council, 'Security Council, Fifty-Seventh Year: 4623rd Meeting (S/PV.4623)' (United Nations, 11 October 2002); United Nations Security Council, 'Security Council, Fifty-Ninth Year: 4896th Meeting (S/PV.4896)' (United Nations, 19 January 2004); United Nations Security Council, 'Security Council, Sixtieth Year: 5127th Meeting (S/PV.5127)' (United Nations, 17 February 2005); United Nations Security Council, 'Security Council, Sixty-First Year: 5390th Meeting (S/PV.5390)' (United Nations, 20 March 2006); United Nations Security Council, '5881st Meeting'; United Nations Security Council, '7036th Meeting'.

9 United Nations Security Council, 'Statement by the President of the Security Council (S/PRST/1999/21)' (United Nations, 8 July 1999); United Nations Security Council, 'Statement by the President of the Security Council (S/PRST/1999/28)' (United Nations, 24 September 1999); United Nations Security Council, 'Statement by the President of the Security Council (S/PRST/2000/10)' (United Nations, 23 March 2000); United Nations Security Council, 'Statement by the President of the Security Council (S/PRST/2001/21)' (United Nations, 31 August 2001); United Nations Security Council, 'Statement by the President of the Security Council (S/PRST/2002/30)' (United Nations, 31 October 2002); United Nations Security Council, 'Statement by the President of the Security Council (S/PRST/2002/31)' (United Nations, 31 October 2002); United Nations Security Council, 'Statement by the President of the Security Council (S/PRST/2004/1)' (United Nations, 19 January 2004); United Nations Security Council, 'Statement by the President of the Security Council (S/PRST/2005/7)' (United Nations, 17 February 2005); United Nations Security Council, 'Statement by the President of the Security Council (S/PRST/2006/38)' (United Nations, 9 August 2006); United Nations Security Council, 'Statement by the President of the Security Council (S/PRST/2007/3)' (United Nations, 21 February 2007); United Nations Security Council, 'Statement by the President of the Security Council (S/PRST/2007/24)' (United Nations, 29 June 2007); United Nations Security Council, 'Statement by the President of the Security Council (S/PRST/2007/42)' (United Nations, 6 November 2007); United Nations Security Council, 'Statement by the President of the Security Council (S/PRST/2008/43)' (United Nations, 19 November 2008); United Nations Security Council, 'Statement by the President of the Security Council (S/PRST/2009/20)' (United Nations, 10 July 2009); United Nations Security Council, 'Statement by the President of the Security Council (S/PRST/2010/6)' (United Nations, 19 March 2010); United Nations Security Council, 'Statement by the President of the Security Council (S/PRST/2012/16)' (United Nations, 25 April 2012).

10 Resolution 2117 (2013).

activity).[11] The Secretary-General (usually through his representatives) regularly called upon the Security Council to take more significant action on curbing the illicit trade of small arms,[12] and on three occasions referred to the illicit trade in small arms as posing a threat to international peace and security while briefing the Security Council.[13] This appears to have been done as a strategic manoeuvre to put pressure upon the Security Council to make an Article 39 'threat to the peace' declaration in relation to this issue, rather than a request, as seen in the report recommendations in relation to sexual violence as a tactic of war.[14] The briefings themselves consistently argued that the illicit trade in small arms exacerbated ongoing conflicts, derailed post-conflict rebuilding and supported terrorism and transnational organised crime.[15]

3 Justificatory Discourse of the P5

The P5's justificatory discourse on this issue is of interest because of what is not said rather than what is said. Of the P5, only France took the position that the illicit trade in small arms did in fact constitute a 'threat to the peace', and they only did this explicitly on one occasion. By contrast, the US and China took the clear position that the illicit trade in small arms is outside the Security Council's mandate when not directly related to a particular conflict. Russia and

11 The Arms Trade Treaty.

12 United Nations Security Council, '4048th Meeting', 3; United Nations Security Council, '4355th Meeting', 3–4; United Nations Security Council, '4623rd Meeting', 3; United Nations Security Council, '4896th Meeting', 3; United Nations Secretary-General, 'Small Arms: Report of the Secretary-General' (United Nations, 7 February 2005), para. 68; United Nations Security Council, '5390th Meeting', 3; United Nations Secretary-General, 'Small Arms: Report of the Secretary-General' (United Nations, 17 April 2008), paras. 65–69 & 73–74.

13 In this instance it was referred to as a 'grave scourge' and 'a grave threat to international peace and security' United Nations Security Council, '4355th Meeting', 3; United Nations Security Council, '5390th Meeting', 2; 'The threat to international peace and security posed by the uncontrolled trade in small arms and their excessive accumulation and proliferation cannot be overemphasized' United Nations Security Council, '5881st Meeting', 2.

14 United Nations Secretary-General, 'Report of the Secretary-General Pursuant to Security Council Resolution 1820 (2008)' (United Nations Security Council, 20 August 2009), para. 56(c).

15 United Nations Security Council, '4048th Meeting', 2; United Nations Security Council, '4355th Meeting', 3–4; United Nations Security Council, '4623rd Meeting', 2; United Nations Security Council, '4896th Meeting', 2–3; United Nations Security Council, '5127th Meeting', 2–3; United Nations Security Council, '5390th Meeting', 2–3; United Nations Security Council, '7036th Meeting', 2.

the UK, to varying degrees, took noncommittal positions in between these two perspectives.

China made it clear from the outset that they did not consider the illicit trade in small arms generally to be within the Security Council's mandate. They argued that the Security Council should pay 'due attention'[16] to the issue, but their efforts should focus upon international peace and security; the small arms trade should be addressed by other competent UN bodies.[17] China expanded upon this by stating that all endeavours to solve the problems caused by the illicit trade in small arms needed to be cognisant of respect for state sovereignty,[18] particularly the right of self-defence under Article 51 of the UN Charter,[19] and must refrain from interfering in states' internal affairs.[20] That said, China did accept that the illicit trade in small arms could affect issues of security and peace,[21] and acknowledged that the Security Council should be prepared to act on a case-by-case basis when directly confronted with an issue within its mandate for maintaining international peace and security.[22] China's willingness to act on a case-by-case basis was tempered by their statement that 'National Governments shoulder the primary responsibility in combating the illicit traffic in small arms and light weapons'.[23] In addition, China continued:

> [we] should further clarify that States bear the primary responsibility for combating the illicit trade in small arms and light weapons so as to prompt them to enhance their capacity and institution building accordingly, strengthen the management and control of small arms and light weapons, and prevent outflow of such weapons to illegal channels.[24]

---

16 United Nations Security Council, '4048th Meeting', 14.

17 United Nations Security Council, 14; United Nations Security Council, '4623rd Meeting', 8; United Nations Security Council, '5390th Meeting', 8; United Nations Security Council, '5881st Meeting', 18.

18 United Nations Security Council, '4048th Meeting', 14.

19 United Nations Security Council, 15.

20 United Nations Security Council, 14.

21 United Nations Security Council, '4355th Meeting', 14; United Nations Security Council, '4896th Meeting', 15–16; United Nations Security Council, '5127th Meeting', 14; United Nations Security Council, '5390th Meeting', 7; United Nations Security Council, '5881st Meeting', 17.

22 United Nations Security Council, '4048th Meeting', 15; United Nations Security Council, '4355th Meeting', 14; United Nations Security Council, '4896th Meeting', 16; United Nations Security Council, '5127th Meeting', 14–15; United Nations Security Council, '5390th Meeting', 8.

23 United Nations Security Council, '5127th Meeting', 14.

24 United Nations Security Council, '5390th Meeting', 7–8.

This clear trajectory of reasoning continued in the wake of adopting the ATT, when China called upon the international community to commit itself to resolving disputes through political and diplomatic means as a safeguard for international peace,[25] while pointing out once again that 'National Governments bear the primary responsibility to fight the illicit trade in arms'.[26]

The US response to the idea that the Security Council take an active role in combating the illicit trade in small arms as a separate and independent agenda to any specific conflict was consistently negative. Generally speaking, the US argued that combating the illicit trade of small arms was a matter for individual states and domestic law, and not within the Security Council's ambit.[27] When confronted with suggestions that the Security Council should be more involved in situations where the small arms trade was clearly fuelling ongoing conflict, they swiftly rebuffed this idea, stating that further Security Council involvement in situations where there has been complete or nearly complete breakdown of civil order would be unhelpful at combating the small arms trade because 'hard cases do not make good law'.[28] While the US regularly acknowledged that the illicit trade in small arms exacerbated conflicts, terrorism and transnational organised crime,[29] they argued that all Security Council involvement had be practical and effective,[30] and conducted on a case-by-case basis.[31] They stated that a blanket response to the illicit trade in small arms as an independent agenda item would be unhelpful because '[u]ltimately, a simple one-size-fits-all solution is unlikely to be effective in dealing with this complex problem'.[32] The US also had further concerns regarding Security Council action on this issue generally, as they felt that such engagement would impinge upon states' lawful rights to possess arms, and upon their citizens' constitutional right to possess arms.[33] This was particularly illustrated

25 United Nations Security Council, '7036th Meeting', 17.
26 United Nations Security Council, 17.
27 United Nations Security Council, '5127th Meeting', 5; United Nations Security Council, '5881st Meeting', 15.
28 United Nations Security Council, '5881st Meeting', 15.
29 United Nations Security Council, '4048th Meeting', 20; United Nations Security Council, '4623rd Meeting', 12; United Nations Security Council, '5390th Meeting', 14; United Nations Security Council, '5881st Meeting', 14–15.
30 United Nations Security Council, '4355th Meeting', 4.
31 United Nations Security Council, '4623rd Meeting', 13; United Nations Security Council, '5127th Meeting', 5.
32 United Nations Security Council, '5127th Meeting', 6.
33 United Nations Security Council, '7036th Meeting', 16.

by their clarification that all their statements on this issue related only to military weapons and excluded 'firearms such as hunting rifles and pistols'.[34]

Russia's response to the question of the illicit trade in small arms and 'threat to the peace' can arguably be categorised as one of radical support, but dissatisfaction with the practical outcomes proposed. Russia commenced its first statements on this issue by arguing that 'the broad proliferation of small arms and light weapons may represent a threat to regional peace and security'.[35] However, this general position was qualified by the assertion that

> With respect to the role of the Security Council, it is our conviction that the Council must focus its attention primarily on those instances in which the illicit trade in small arms and light weapons is directly linked to conflict situations that are on the Council's agenda.[36]

This can be read as a practical concern rather than one of principle, with Russia contending that the lack of international consensus on how to address the illicit small arms trade combined with 'the dearth of necessary political will also makes it impossible to regulate that sphere appropriately'.[37] This practical concern regarding Security Council action generally on the illicit trade in small arms was further evidenced in Russia's calls for any action taken to be practical and incremental,[38] and that it respect that the right of self-defence under Article 51 of the UN Charter implies that states have a right to access arms.[39] This is further evidenced by Russia's justification for abstaining from voting on *Resolution 2117 (2013)* on the basis that they felt the resolution failed to adequately address the issue.[40] Therefore, while Russia did not support a finding of 'threat to the peace' in relation to the illicit trade in small arms, their statements suggest that should the facts surrounding this change, they could support such a finding.

The UK was quite vocal in their support for Security Council action to address the illicit trafficking in small arms as an issue, independent of any particular conflict. However, their language used to vocalise this support fell short

34 United Nations Security Council, '5390th Meeting', 16.

35 United Nations Security Council, '4048th Meeting', 11.

36 United Nations Security Council, '4623rd Meeting', 17; See also: United Nations Security Council, '4355th Meeting', 14; United Nations Security Council, '4896th Meeting', 8; United Nations Security Council, '5127th Meeting', 12; United Nations Security Council, '5390th Meeting', 14.

37 United Nations Security Council, '5881st Meeting', 12.

38 United Nations Security Council, '4048th Meeting', 11.

39 United Nations Security Council, '4355th Meeting', 13.

40 United Nations Security Council, '7036th Meeting', 4–5.

of asserting that a 'threat to the peace' existed. The UK argued that addressing small arms supply was crucial to securing peace, justifying this position on the basis that

> In the last decade alone, conflicts fought with only small arms have killed over 3 million people, overwhelmingly unarmed civilians. Against that enormous death toll, we really need a different phrase than 'small arms'. There has been nothing 'small' about the misery they have brought to the families or the disruption they have brought to societies.[41]

The UK also stated that 'by fuelling conflict, crime and terrorism, the proliferation of small arms and light weapons, undermines peace and greatly hinders development',[42] that the 'serious threat to security caused by the uncontrolled proliferation of small arms and light weapons is all too well known'[43] and that 'the threat of small arms and light weapons is real and relevant to the mandate of the Security Council'.[44] In their support for general Security Council action on this issue, the UK argued not only in favour of destroying firearms in post-conflict situations,[45] but also of controlling the global production and flow of firearms.[46] They contended that both of these things were necessary because '[i]n large parts of the world, small arms and light weapons are weapons of mass destruction, killing perhaps as many as half a million people a year'.[47] Their decision not to push for the illicit trafficking in small arms to be considered a 'threat to the peace' can perhaps be seen as strategic, given the lack of support from the US and China. This is evidenced in their 2008 statements publicly pushing for the adoption of a treaty designed to regulate the arms trade,[48] and then in their statements following the adoption of *Resolution 2117 (2013)* regarding how the resolution bolsters the ATT.[49]

France was the strongest P5 proponent for Security Council action to deal with the trafficking of small arms; however, only on one occasion (in 2008) did

41 United Nations Security Council, '4048th Meeting', 5.
42 United Nations Security Council, '5390th Meeting', 8.
43 United Nations Security Council, '4623rd Meeting', 20.
44 United Nations Security Council, '5390th Meeting', 9.
45 United Nations Security Council, '4048th Meeting', 5.
46 United Nations Security Council, 5; United Nations Security Council, '4355th Meeting', 12; United Nations Security Council, '4623rd Meeting', 21; United Nations Security Council, '4896th Meeting', 4; United Nations Security Council, '5881st Meeting', 16.
47 United Nations Security Council, '4896th Meeting', 4.
48 United Nations Security Council, '5881st Meeting', 16.
49 'Resolution 2117 (2013) gives us the chance to strengthen our joint efforts to tackle the issue and help secure peace and stability. A key part of that work, as the resolution recognizes, is the Arms Trade Treaty'. United Nations Security Council, '7036th Meeting', 9.

France state outright that it considered the illicit trade of small arms to be a 'threat to the peace'. In this instance, France simply stated that 'the trafficking in small arms and light weapons poses a threat to peace'.[50] This position was continued by implication in the wake of the ATT and the passing of *Resolution 2117 (2013)*, when they argued that the Security Council's work in relation to the small arms trade is 'absolutely indispensable to world peace'.[51] France advocated for greater Security Council action to regulate the small arms trade,[52] and asserted that the Security Council needed to stop making distinctions between the small arms trade generally and the individual contexts in which it occurred.[53] Further, they voice their support for a treaty regulating the small arms trade in 2006.[54] France also argued that the small arms trade was intrinsically linked with the rise of internal conflicts conducted by irregular militias using guerrilla tactics, further blurring the lines of distinction between combatants and civilians.[55]

4 Summary of Coding

A finding of 'threat to the peace' was supported here by France and the UK, and opposed by the US, China and Russia. France and the UK argued that gravity of the harm caused by the small arms trade made the existence of a 'threat to the peace' self-evident. China argued that the situation was outside the Security Council's mandate and that such a finding would violate states' rights to non-interference and self-defence. Russia (which abstained from voting) argued that the small arms trade was outside the Security Council's mandate and that the proposed solutions would be ineffective at addressing the issue. The US used formal legal arguments to contend that the small arms trade was outside the Security Council's mandate and that a finding of 'threat to the peace' would violate states' rights to non-interference, while also being ineffective at solving the problem.

50 United Nations Security Council, '5881st Meeting', 11.

51 United Nations Security Council, '7036th Meeting', 10.

52 United Nations Security Council, '4048th Meeting', 4; United Nations Security Council, '4623rd Meeting', 18–19; United Nations Security Council, '5390th Meeting', 16; United Nations Security Council, '5881st Meeting', 11; United Nations Security Council, '7036th Meeting', 10.

53 United Nations Security Council, '5390th Meeting', 16.

54 United Nations Security Council, 16.

55 United Nations Security Council, '4048th Meeting', 3; United Nations Security Council, '5881st Meeting', 11; United Nations Security Council, '7036th Meeting', 9–10.

CHAPTER 18

AIDS Epidemic in Africa and Peacekeeping Operations 2000–05

1 Relevance to the Overall Project

The issue of AIDS in Africa (which later became AIDS in Africa and its relationship to peacekeeping operations) represented the first time the Security Council addressed a non-traditional threat in its meetings.[1] This fact alone merits this case study's inclusion here, but of additional interest is the way in which the scope of the Security Council discussions narrowed from the AIDS epidemic in Africa generally down to its relationship with peacekeeping operations. The *Repertoire of Practice of the Security Council* for 2000–03 noted significant discussion in relation to the concept of 'threat to the peace' and the AIDS epidemic in Africa generally,[2] but the discussion relating to peacekeeping was apparently not considered significant enough to warrant note.[3] The issue itself received no mention in the *Repertoire of Practice of the Security Council* for 2004–07.[4] *Resolution 1308 (2000)* noted in the preamble that 'the HIV/AIDS pandemic, if unchecked, may pose a risk to stability and security'.[5] This is as close as the formal language came to 'threat to the peace', in spite of advocacy from the US and the UK.

2 Context of the Debates

The Secretary-General originally set the context of these debates in his oral briefing to the Council during the first debate on this issue. During this briefing, he noted that 90% of all orphans as a consequence of AIDS were African

1 United Nations Security Council, 'Security Council, Fifty-Fifth Year: 4087th Meeting (S/PV.4087)', 10 January 2000, 2.
2 Repertoire of the Practice of the Security Council, 'Chapter XI: Considerations of Chapter VII the Charter (2000–03)', 929.
3 Repertoire of the Practice of the Security Council, 922–34.
4 Repertoire of the Practice of the Security Council, 'Chapter XI: Considerations of Chapter VII the Charter (2004–07)', 8–34.
5 'Resolution 1308 (2000)', S/RES/1308 (2000) UN Security Council (2000), para. Preamble.

 | DOI:10.1163/9789004391420_020

children.[6] Further, he recognised that while AIDS was affecting other areas of the world, with particularly alarming rates of spread in Asia and Eastern Europe, the only place where it had 'become a threat to economic, social and political stability' was in southern and eastern Africa,[7] where '[l]ast year, AIDS killed about 10 times more people in Africa than did armed conflict'.[8] He justified this position with the following statement:

> By overwhelming the continent's health services, by creating millions of orphans and by decimating health workers and teachers, AIDS is causing social and economic crises, which in turn threaten political stability. It also threatens good governance through high death rates among the elites, both public and private.[9]

The Secretary-General argued that this 'cocktail of disasters' provided a recipe for further conflict, which in turn proffered the ingredients required for further infections, creating an unending spiral.[10] In later meetings, the Executive Director of the Joint United Nations Programme on HIV/AIDS (UNAIDS) and the Under-Secretary-General for Peacekeeping Operations provided oral briefings to the Security Council. They argued that the social and economic gains throughout Africa over the last several decades hung in the balance as a result of the AIDS epidemic,[11] and that the disease needed to be viewed as an issue of human security to allow everyone to grapple with its effects and how it was exacerbated by conditions of poverty and vulnerability.[12] It was noted that a number of UN peacekeeping personnel were likely HIV positive prior to deployment, and that there was a lack of data on HIV/AIDS in areas were the peacekeepers were deployed, as well as on the prevalence of HIV among peacekeepers.[13] These briefings also noted that conflict and post-conflict environments remained high-risk areas for the spread of HIV/AIDS.[14]

---

6 United Nations Security Council, '4087th Meeting', 4.

7 United Nations Security Council, 4.

8 United Nations Security Council, 5.

9 United Nations Security Council, 5.

10 United Nations Security Council, 5.

11 United Nations Security Council, 'Security Council, Fifty-Fifth Year: 4172nd Meeting (S/PV.4172)', 17 July 2000, 2.

12 United Nations Security Council, 'Security Council, Fifty-Sixth Year: 4259th Meeting (S/PV.4259)', 19 January 2001, 6–7.

13 United Nations Security Council, 2–3.

14 'War is one of the instruments of AIDS, as rape is one of the instruments of war'. United Nations Security Council, '4087th Meeting', 11; United Nations Security Council, 'Security Council, Sixtieth Year: 5228th Meeting (S/PV.5228)', 18 July 2005, 2.

3 Justificatory Discourse of the P5

The P5's justificatory discourse on this issue ranged from strong support for a finding of 'threat to the peace' and Security Council action to scepticism about the Security Council's role in this issue. The US led the push for a positive finding by the Security Council, with support from the UK. By contrast, France was the most openly sceptical that this was a Security Council issue, with Russia and China both declining to speak on it until the fourth and fifth meetings (in 2003 and 2005, respectively), when the issue had already been debated for three years.

The US made their position on this issue clear before the first oral briefing was delivered to the Security Council, taking the opportunity when they introduced the topic in their capacity as rotating Security Council President: 'We tend to think of a threat to security in terms of war and peace. Yet no one can doubt that the havoc wreaked and the toll exacted by HIV/AIDS do threaten our security'.[15] This position continued with statements made in their capacity as the US rather than as Security Council President. The US argued that AIDS was a borderless threat and that '[w]e owe ourselves and each other the upmost commitment to act against AIDS on a global scale, and especially where the scourge is greatest. AIDS is a global aggressor that must be defeated'.[16] They also pre-emptively dealt with the possible criticism that the Security Council was not the appropriate venue to deal with the question of AIDS:

> AIDS is one of the most devastating threats to ever confront the world community ... The United Nations was created to stop wars. Now we must wage and win a great and peaceful war of our time—the war against AIDS.[17]

They were quite critical of the objections some Council members raised suggesting that the Security Council was not an appropriate venue in which to address the issue of the AIDS epidemic.[18] At one point, the US even asked, 'how could it not be a threat to international peace and security?'[19] They also argued that its widespread effects upon the younger members of society and future generations made it even more clearly a 'threat to the peace'.[20]

15 United Nations Security Council, '4087th Meeting', 2.

16 United Nations Security Council, 5.

17 United Nations Security Council, 7.

18 United Nations Security Council, '4259th Meeting', 9–10.

19 United Nations Security Council, 'Security Council, Fifty-Eighth Year: 4859th Meeting (S/PV.4859)', 17 November 2003, 10.

20 United Nations Security Council, 10.

The UK began its statements by arguing that the prevalence of AIDS in Africa was a failure of humanity: 'The fact is that the prevalence of AIDS in Africa is a symbol of the comparative failure of development, security and education in Africa. That is an African failure, and it is an international failure'.[21] While they argued that this was not an issue that needed to be primarily dealt with by the Security Council, they did see the Security Council as playing a key role in organising systematic cooperation between UN organs and the international community in response.[22] When the focus shifted from AIDS generally to AIDS in peacekeeping, the UK became much more supportive of Security Council involvement, while still highlighting that the general issue of AIDS should be addressed by the UN as a whole and not simply the Security Council.[23] They stated that AIDS 'is a global crisis which, by creating an environment in which political and ethnic tensions can worsen, will contribute to the proliferation of armed conflict'.[24] The UK also argued that it was important for the Security Council to remain focused on AIDS in the peacekeeping context as part of its primary responsibility for maintaining international peace and security, to ensure that peacekeepers would not become an infection vector for the virus, thus undermining their peacekeeping role.[25] Continuing in this approach, the UK asserted that

> The massive and rapid spread of HIV/AIDS is not just a health issue. It is a human development issue, an equity and equality issue and a significant threat to international peace and security. It therefore needs the co-ordinated response of the United Nations bodies, including the Security Council.[26]

The UK also noted that within the Africa general population, rates of HIV/AIDS infection could be as high as 37%, with civilian and military security personnel infection rates often being between two and five times greater than those of general population.[27] They argued that '[n]ot only does this pose a risk to national security and stability, it also undermines the potential for regional peacekeeping operations in the worst affected areas'.[28]

21 United Nations Security Council, 'Security Council, Fifty-Fifth Year: 4087th Meeting (S/PV.4087) (Resumption 1)', 10 January 2000, 7.
22 United Nations Security Council, 7.
23 United Nations Security Council, '4172nd Meeting', 9.
24 United Nations Security Council, 10.
25 United Nations Security Council, 10.
26 United Nations Security Council, '4259th Meeting', 20.
27 United Nations Security Council, '4859th Meeting', 9.
28 United Nations Security Council, '4859th Meeting'.

France began by acknowledging that AIDS constitutes 'a lasting health, economic and political crisis in Africa';[29] however, their arguments generally hinged on the fact that this was a development issue to be addressed by the Secretariat and General Assembly rather than a security issue:

> Thus, I believe that, thanks to the commitment that the Secretary-General has shown as a moral authority and, I stress, as a political authority—thanks to the commitment and to the efforts that we will be called upon to make today because of his initiative—in this way we might find it possible to drive back the disease and to provide prospects of the genuine sustainable development of the African countries.[30]

The French arguments continued along the same lines even when the Security Council focus narrowed to AIDS and peacekeeping operations, rather than AIDS generally. They contended that AIDS was a major cause of social and economic decline in the developing world, as well as supporting the restriction of Security Council action to the relationship between AIDS and peacekeeping operations, in interaction with other relevant UN organs.[31] Elsewhere, France referred to the fight against AIDS as a 'collective endeavour' led by the Secretary-General.[32] Further, they acknowledged that while links were evident between AIDS and a decline in peace and security, the issue as a whole was outside the Security Council's mandate.[33]

Russia, as noted above, was relatively taciturn on this issue, opting to only make statements in two of the five meetings that took place. Russia took the position that it was appropriate for the Security Council to address the issue of HIV/AIDS in peacekeeping operations,[34] stating that 'HIV/AIDS is one of the most serious non-military threats to peace and security'.[35] They also argued that 'it ultimately had a negative impact on international peace and stability'.[36] When addressing the issue of HIV/AIDS generally, Russia was of the opinion

29 United Nations Security Council, '4087th Meeting', 17.

30 United Nations Security Council, 18.

31 United Nations Security Council, '4859th Meeting', 17; United Nations Security Council, '5228th Meeting', 15.

32 United Nations Security Council, '4859th Meeting', 17–18.

33 United Nations Security Council, 17–18.

34 United Nations Security Council, 13; United Nations Security Council, '5228th Meeting', 9.

35 United Nations Security Council, '5228th Meeting', 9.

36 United Nations Security Council, 9; See also: United Nations Security Council, '4859th Meeting', 13.

that this was predominantly an issue for other UN organs, particularly the General Assembly, the Economic and Social Council and the Secretariat.[37]

China, like Russia, opted to speak only in two of the five meetings that occurred on the issue of AIDS in Africa. China acknowledged that AIDS in relation to peacekeeping merited 'the Council's serious consideration'[38] and constituted 'one of the contemporary world's most salient non-traditional security issues'.[39] Indeed, they argued that in the context of peacekeeping, AIDS was one of the most important issues before the Security Council:

> AIDS has not only constituted a major threat to human life and health, but seriously affected the economic development and social stability of the countries and regions concerned. Thus it has become one of the most important non-traditional security issues. The Security Council in accordance with its mandate has therefore been devoting increased attention to the issue of peacekeepers and HIV/AIDS and the impact of AIDS on peace and security.[40]

As this statement suggests, China clearly believed that the issue of AIDS, from the Security Council's perspective, did not extend beyond its relationship to peacekeeping operations so as not to go beyond the Security Council's mandate for maintaining international peace and security.[41] They argued that AIDS was a general issue to be addressed by other 'relevant international bodies'.[42]

4 Summary of Coding

The only P5 member that supported a finding of 'threat to the peace' in this case study was the US. They argued that the gravity of the situation made the existence of a 'threat to the peace' self-evident. By contrast Russia, France and the UK all argued that the situation was beyond the scope of the Security Council's mandate (the UK did this through formal legal argumentation). China also argued that the situation was beyond the scope of the Security Council's mandate, while also arguing that as the situation lacked sufficient gravity for Security Council involvement, regional solutions would be preferable.

37 United Nations Security Council, '4859th Meeting', 13; United Nations Security Council, '5228th Meeting', 10.
38 United Nations Security Council, '4859th Meeting', 16.
39 United Nations Security Council, 16.
40 United Nations Security Council, '5228th Meeting', 14.
41 United Nations Security Council, '4859th Meeting', 16.
42 United Nations Security Council, 16.

CHAPTER 19

Non-Proliferation of WMDs: Resolutions 1441 (2002), 1540 (2004), 1696 (2006), 1718 (2006)

1 Relevance to the Overall Project

This case study actually encapsulates four separate instances of the Security Council discussing (and then handing down resolutions on) the issue of non-proliferation of WMDs. With the exception of the discussions around *Resolution 1540 (2004)*[1] (in which WMDs were discussed generally without any specific focus on particular types), the debates focused primarily upon nuclear non-proliferation (the debate on Iraq touched on non-nuclear WMDs, but the focus was on nuclear weapons). Conversely, *Resolution 2118 (2013)*[2] on chemical weapons was very specific and unique—consequently, this instance is not addressed in this case study, but is dealt with elsewhere.[3] Understanding the P5's justificatory discourse in relation to the issue of non-proliferation—particularly nuclear non-proliferation, given that all of the P5 possess a nuclear arsenal—is of value not only because of the gravity of the potential consequences, but also because the Security Council has considered it on numerous occasions; indeed, on at least four separate occasions, all addressed here, the *Repertoire of Practice of the Security Council* has considered the debate in relation to 'threat to the peace' on this issue as significant.[4]

2 Context of the Debates

The first instance considered is the debates surrounding *Resolution 1441 (2002)*. This situation focused upon whether Iraq's continued non-compliance with disarmament obligations, dating back to 1991, constituted a 'threat to the peace'. A representative of the Secretary-General confirmed this non-compliance in

1 'Resolution 1540 (2004)', S/RES/1540 (2004) UN Security Council (2004).
2 'Resolution 2118 (2013)', S/RES/2118 (2013) UN Security Council (2013).
3 See Chapter 24: 'Chemical Weapons (2013): Resolution 2118' case study for details.
4 Repertoire of the Practice of the Security Council, 'Chapter XI: Considerations of Chapter VII the Charter (2000–03)', 923–26; Repertoire of the Practice of the Security Council, 'Chapter XI: Considerations of Chapter VII the Charter (2004–07)', 18–19, 28–30 & 30–32.

 | DOI:10.1163/9789004391420_021

oral briefings on 16 October 2002,[5] 17 days before *Resolution 1441 (2002)* was voted upon. The second instance, *Resolution 1540 (2004)*, was a general debate and pre-emptive resolution aimed at stopping the proliferation of WMDs to non-state actors before it became a significant situation.[6] The third instance, *Resolution 1696 (2006)*, comprises statements following the 14 votes for and one vote against (by Qatar) that had the resolution passed.[7] The background to this resolution was Iran's continued non-compliance with International Atomic Energy Agency (IAEA) inspectors in relation to their nuclear program.[8] The final instance was statements following the unanimous adoption of *Resolution 1718 (2006)*[9] in the wake of the Democratic People's Republic of Korea's (DPRK) self-declared nuclear test on 9 October 2006,[10] their assertion that this nuclear test was a positive step towards dismantling their nuclear weapons program,[11] and their formal declaration of war against the US.[12]

3 Justificatory Discourse of the P5

The justificatory discourse of France, the UK, and the US in relation to non-proliferation generally centred upon the position that the proliferation of nuclear weapons and WMDs in and of itself constituted a 'threat to the peace'. This was often supplemented by a subtext that non-proliferation goals were clearly supported by international law and accorded with the Purposes and Principles of the UN Charter. The reverse was true for China, which argued

5 United Nations Security Council, 'Security Council, Fifty-Seventh Year: 4625th Meeting (S/PV.4625)', 16 October 2002, 3–4.

6 See generally: United Nations Security Council, 'Security Council, Fifty-Ninth Year: 4950th Meeting (S/PV.4950)', 22 April 2004; United Nations Security Council, 'Security Council, Fifty-Ninth Year: 4956th Meeting (S/PV.4956)', 28 April 2004.

7 United Nations Security Council, 'Security Council, Sixty-First Year: 5500th Meeting (S/PV.5500)', 31 July 2006, 2.

8 See generally: United Nations Secretary-General, 'Letter Dated 8 March 2006 from the Secretary-General Addressed to the President of the Security Council' (United Nations, 9 March 2006), 3–13; United Nations Security Council, 'Note by the President of the Security Council' (United Nations, 28 April 2006), 3–10.

9 United Nations Security Council, 'Security Council, Sixty-First Year: 5551st Meeting (S/PV.5551)', 14 October 2006, 2.

10 Democratic People's Republic of Korea, 'Letter Dated 11 October 2006 from the Representative of the Democratic People's Republic of Korea Addressed to the President of the Security Council' (United Nations, 11 October 2006), 2.

11 Democratic People's Republic of Korea, 2.

12 Democratic People's Republic of Korea, 3.

primarily along international law lines, with WMD proliferation as a 'threat to the peace' being a subtext rather than the core of the argument. Russia's arguments focused on international law, referencing pre-existing regional instability (in relation to the state specific situations of concern) or counterterrorism (for *Resolution 1540 (2004)*).

The UK's statements in all of these instances drew heavily on the fact that, from their perspective, '[p]reventing the proliferation of weapons of mass destruction is one of the Security Council's vital roles in carrying out his responsibility for maintaining international peace and security'.[13] In relation to Iraq, they suggested that WMD disarmament was a clear path to, and indicator of, peace,[14] and that to ignore Iraq's quest to acquire WMDs 'would be an abdication of responsibility',[15] while also stressing the need for peaceful resolution where possible.[16] They supplemented this position with the legal argument that Iraq was in material breach of its disarmament obligation under *Resolution 687 (1991)*.[17] When discussing this in the context of *Resolution 1540 (2004)* and the Security Council taking proactive action to prevent non-state actors acquiring WMDs, the UK argued that the prospect of a terrorist organisation acquiring WMDs was 'a real, urgent and horrific threat',[18] and that the Security Council 'should not have to wait for such a tragedy in order to act'.[19] In this instance, the UK again contended that such action was clearly a Security Council responsibility. Oddly, the UK suggested at the time that this was the first-ever resolution on the issue of WMD non-proliferation.[20]

In relation to Iran, the UK highlighted its years of failure to comply with IAEA inspections,[21] the threat that WMD proliferation posed to the world,[22] and the need for peaceful resolution tempered by the possibility of further action should Iran continue to reject peaceful settlement of the issue.[23] Finally,

13 United Nations Security Council, '5500th Meeting', 4.
14 United Nations Security Council, 'Security Council, Fifty-Seventh Year: 4644th Meeting (S/PV.4644)', 8 November 2002, 5.
15 United Nations Security Council, 'Security Council, Fifty-Seventh Year: 4625th Meeting (S/PV.4625 Resumption 3)', 17 October 2002, 8.
16 United Nations Security Council, 7–9; United Nations Security Council, '4644th Meeting', 4–5.
17 United Nations Security Council, '4625th Meeting (Resumption 3)', 7; United Nations Security Council, '4644th Meeting', 4.
18 United Nations Security Council, '4956th Meeting', 7.
19 United Nations Security Council, '4950th Meeting', 12.
20 United Nations Security Council, '4956th Meeting', 7.
21 United Nations Security Council, '5500th Meeting', 4.
22 United Nations Security Council, 4.
23 United Nations Security Council, 4.

when responding to the DPRK's missile tests, the UK argued that such actions were 'provocative and irresponsible'[24] and a 'threat to international peace and security'.[25] Further, they asserted that the resolution's purpose and targeting was to further non-proliferation of WMDs; it was not intended as a punitive measure against the North Korean people.[26]

The US asserted a fairly consistent thread of argument to the effect that Security Council action in relation to non-proliferation 'is responding appropriately to what we all agree is a clear and present threat to global peace and security: the proliferation of nuclear, chemical and biological weapons and their means of delivery, especially to non-State actors, including terrorists'.[27] While this statement was made particularly in relation to *Resolution 1540 (2004)* and the non-proliferation of WMDs to non-state actors, the only hint of justification as to why non-state actors posed more of a threat than states with WMDs was the idea that 'terrorist use of WMD would punish all of us, strong and weak alike'.[28] Further, the US suggested that Chapter VII was the most appropriate type of action for non-proliferation issues, as it would send a clear political message regarding the gravity of the threat to international peace and security that WMD proliferation represented.[29]

When speaking about Iraq, the US argued that the threat at hand was Iraq's 'drive towards an arsenal of terror and destruction',[30] suggesting that preventing this outcome was a common goal for broader peace and security in the Middle East.[31] The US also relied very heavily on the suggestion that Iraq's failure to comply with non-proliferation activities constituted a material breach of the peace accords and *Resolution 687 (1991)*.[32] They clearly stated that Iraq's continued non-compliance would result in military action:[33] 'one way or another, Iraq will be disarmed'.[34] Regarding Iran, the US asserted that '[t]he pursuit of nuclear weapons by Iran constitutes a direct threat to international peace and security and demands a clear statement from the Council in the

24 United Nations Security Council, '5551st Meeting', 5.
25 United Nations Security Council, 5.
26 United Nations Security Council, 5.
27 United Nations Security Council, '4956th Meeting', 5.
28 United Nations Security Council, '4950th Meeting', 17.
29 United Nations Security Council, 17.
30 United Nations Security Council, '4625th Meeting (Resumption 3)', 10.
31 United Nations Security Council, 10–11.
32 United Nations Security Council, 10–11; United Nations Security Council, '4644th Meeting', 3.
33 United Nations Security Council, '4625th Meeting (Resumption 3)', above n 1003, 11–12.
34 United Nations Security Council, '4644th Meeting', 3.

form of a binding resolution'.[35] They buttressed this statement with arguments that Iran's pursuit of a nuclear weapons program was a violation of its obligations under the Treaty on the Non-Proliferation of Nuclear Weapons, and the obligations set forth by the IAEA.[36] When addressing the DPRK's nuclear tests, the US proclaimed that the test 'unquestionably poses one of the greatest threats to international peace and security that the Council has ever had to confront'.[37] They then made further statements addressing the threat posed by WMD proliferation,[38] while also recounting the DPRK's history of defying the international community, and their support for transnational organised crime, as grounds for US support of *Resolution 1718 (2006)*.[39]

The French made it clear that they had consistently considered the proliferation of WMDs to be a threat to peace and security;[40] however, they approached the issue very differently when dealing with states as opposed to when dealing with the prospect of WMDs being acquired by non-state actors. In the three situations considered here that deal directly with individual states, France consistently called for respect for international law when dealing with non-proliferation, and peaceful resolutions and avoiding the use of force where possible.[41] In relation to Iraq, this is most evident in France's statements that all of their 'diplomatic efforts in recent weeks were directed towards giving peace a chance',[42] and '[w]ar can only be the last recourse ... If Iraq wants to avoid confrontation it must understand that this is the last opportunity'.[43] This approach was repeated for Iran, with France stating that their support of *Resolution 1696 (2006)* was solely to bring Iran's nuclear program into compliance with IAEA requests, and that should Iran fail to comply, France would support

35 United Nations Security Council, '5500th Meeting', 3.

36 United Nations Security Council, 3.

37 United Nations Security Council, '5551st Meeting', 2.

38 United Nations Security Council, 2.

39 United Nations Security Council, 2–3.

40 'The proliferation of weapons of mass destruction and their delivery systems, in Iraq or elsewhere, constitutes a serious threat to international security': United Nations Security Council, '4625th Meeting (Resumption 3)', 12; United Nations Security Council, '4950th Meeting', 8–9; 'The proliferation of weapons of mass destruction and their means of delivery is a threat to international peace and security': United Nations Security Council, '4956th Meeting', 2; United Nations Security Council, '5500th Meeting', 7; United Nations Security Council, '5551st Meeting', 3.

41 United Nations Security Council, '4625th Meeting (Resumption 3)', 14; United Nations Security Council, '4644th Meeting', 5; United Nations Security Council, '5500th Meeting', 7; United Nations Security Council, '5551st Meeting', 3–4.

42 United Nations Security Council, '4644th Meeting', 5.

43 United Nations Security Council, 5.

further Security Council action.[44] In relation to the DPRK nuclear test, France simply stated that *Resolution 1718 (2006)* evidenced universal condemnation for the nuclear tests,[45] while calling on international law to be respected and conformed with when dealing with this issue.[46]

This very tempered approach stands in stark contrast to France's statements regarding the proliferation of WMDs to non-state actors. While France did note that when dealing with this issue, all relevant aspects of international law and state sovereignty had to be respected,[47] there seemed to be a hint of panic in their statements. This is most apparent in their assertion that 'we are now living in an era of wholesale terrorism in which the most dangerous technologies have become accessible and are being trafficked'.[48] It is further evident in the French argument that the reason for passing *Resolution 1540 (2006)* under Chapter VII (as opposed to Chapter VI), was because 'the reference provides as a basis for the Council in this area the notion that there is indeed a threat to international peace and security'.[49] These two statements imply an air of panic and fear, as their tone runs counter to France's statements regarding WMDs and state actors. France's further insistence that the prospect of terrorists acquiring WMDs 'is a serious threat' adds to this tone of fear.[50] The latter statement indicates the possibility that France considered the resolution to be clearly preemptive in nature, but that a Security Council declaration that such a threat existed would provide a factual basis for France's position of fear and panic.

While Russia supported each of these resolutions, their support for the state specific resolutions presents as reluctant, grounded in the context of the broader issue at hand rather than in the idea of WMD proliferation being a 'threat to the peace'. Russian support for *Resolution 1540 (2004)* centred on the potential terrorist threat posed by WMDs in the hands of non-state actors. When examining the situation in Iraq, Russia began by stating that the circumstances leading to the need for further Security Council action were caused by both Iraq and the Security Council in equal measure,[51] referencing ambiguity in the criteria the Security Council set down in *Resolution 1284*

44 United Nations Security Council, '5500th Meeting', 7.
45 United Nations Security Council, '5551st Meeting', 3.
46 United Nations Security Council, 4.
47 United Nations Security Council, '4950th Meeting', 9.
48 United Nations Security Council, 8. They did not specify what an era of retail terrorism would look like.
49 United Nations Security Council, 8–9.
50 United Nations Security Council, 9.
51 United Nations Security Council, '4625th Meeting (Resumption 3)', 20–21.

(*1999*).[52] Further, Russia stated that while they supported Iraqi disarmament in principle, they had received no credible evidence of Iraq's WMD possession.[53] They also clearly stated that they saw no possibility for the Security Council to authorise the use of force in relation to Iraq, and that resolving this issue must be achieved through political settlement.[54] Finally, Russia made it apparent that although they supported the resolution, they had serious issues with the language used,[55] and felt the timelines being laid down were unrealistic.[56]

In relation to Iran, Russia made it clear that its support for *Resolution 1696 (2006)* was based on a desire to see the Iranian nuclear program meet IAEA requirements for transparency.[57] While they acknowledged that if Iran failed to comply with the resolution, further Security Council action would be necessary,[58] this was tempered by a call for other Security Council members not to take unilateral action against Iran in the event of non-compliance.[59] Russia's support for *Resolution 1718 (2006)* was grounded in Russia's belief that the DPRK's nuclear test was 'irresponsible and destabilising'.[60] They argued that the test itself escalated pre-existing threats to peace, security and stability in the region,[61] in addition to undermining regional non-proliferation regimes.[62] Russia pointed out that while it did not support the use of sanctions generally, this was an extraordinary situation that required an extraordinary response.[63]

Russia's reluctance to support these non-proliferation resolutions was not evident in their statements regarding *Resolution 1540 (2004)*. While Russia's statements in this instance began with a blanket statement that WMD proliferation constituted a serious threat to international peace and security,[64] further reading indicates that this was directly related to the concept of WMDs and non-state actors. This is evident in Russian references to multiple terrorist

52 United Nations Security Council, 21.
53 United Nations Security Council, 21.
54 United Nations Security Council, 22.
55 United Nations Security Council, '4644th Meeting', 8.
56 United Nations Security Council, 9.
57 United Nations Security Council, '5500th Meeting', 5.
58 United Nations Security Council, 5.
59 United Nations Security Council, 5.
60 United Nations Security Council, '5551st Meeting', 5.
61 United Nations Security Council, 5.
62 United Nations Security Council, 5.
63 United Nations Security Council, 5–6.
64 United Nations Security Council, '4950th Meeting', 16.

attacks in the three years leading up to these debates,[65] and in their assertion that *Resolution 1540 (2004)* was a natural extension of, and in the same vein as, *Resolution 1373 (2001)* made in response to the September 11, 2001 terrorist attacks.[66] Russia's clearest statement on this issue came immediately after the unanimous passing of *Resolution 1540 (2004)*: 'we believe that the problem of the acquisition of weapons of mass destruction by non-State actors, primarily for terrorist purposes, is becoming one of the crucial threats to international peace and security'.[67]

China's position on non-proliferation was clear and consistent across all of the instances being examined. In each situation, China argued that non-proliferation of WMD promoted peace and security worldwide,[68] articulating this most explicitly when they stated that '[t]he fundamental purpose of non-proliferation is to maintain and promote international and regional peace, stability and security'[69] in relation to WMDs and non-state actors, and in relation to the DPRK, that '[t]his [nuclear test] is not conducive to peace and stability in North-East Asia'.[70] China regularly noted that '[t]he Security Council bears the primary responsibility for the maintenance of international peace and security—a responsibility that is entrusted to it by the Charter'.[71] In each circumstance, China argued that non-proliferation efforts needed to respect international law,[72] be achieved through peaceful means (of particular note was their dissent regarding the inspection of cargo going to and from the DPRK

65 United Nations Security Council, 16.

66 United Nations Security Council, 16.

67 United Nations Security Council, '4956th Meeting', 6.

68 United Nations Security Council, '4644th Meeting', 12; United Nations Security Council, '5500th Meeting', 6.

69 United Nations Security Council, '4956th Meeting', 6.

70 United Nations Security Council, '5551st Meeting', 4.

71 United Nations Security Council, '4644th Meeting', 13; See also: United Nations Security Council, '4625th Meeting (Resumption 3)', 10; United Nations Security Council, '4950th Meeting', 6; United Nations Security Council, '5500th Meeting', 6; United Nations Security Council, '5551st Meeting', 4.

72 United Nations Security Council, '4625th Meeting (Resumption 3)', 10; United Nations Security Council, '4644th Meeting', 12; 'In implementing the resolution, it is essential that we achieve our non-proliferation goals by peaceful means; undertake international cooperation on the basis of equality, mutual trust and strict compliance with international law': United Nations Security Council, '4956th Meeting', 6; 'According to Article 25 of the United Nations Charter, all United Nations Member States are obligated to accept and carry out Security Council resolutions'.: United Nations Security Council, '5500th Meeting', 6; United Nations Security Council, '5551st Meeting', 4.

because of the likelihood that such actions would inflame tensions rather than contribute to peace)[73] and be conducted through political and diplomatic dialogue.[74]

4 Summary of Coding

All of the P5 members supported the notion that the proliferation of WMDs constituted a 'threat to the peace'. The US argued that the international law violations and the gravity associated with the use of WMDs made the existence of a 'threat to the peace' self-evident, and the findings a natural consequence of the actions of those involved. The UK argued that the proliferation of WMDs was self-evidently a 'threat to the peace' and clearly within the Security Council's mandate, and that such a finding was a natural consequence of the actions of those involved. They also advocated strongly for peaceful solutions to the situations. Russia argued that the international law violations and the gravity associated with the use of WMDs made the existence of a 'threat to the peace' self-evident, and the findings a natural consequence of the actions of those involved. They also argued that the findings accorded with all relevant laws, while advocating for peaceful solutions. China argued that the proliferation of

73 'A number of countries, especially the Arab States, have also expressed their strong for wish for peace, not war'.: United Nations Security Council, '4625th Meeting (Resumption 3)', 9–10; United Nations Security Council, '4644th Meeting', 12; 'To effectively push non-proliferation efforts forward, we must guarantee the legitimate rights of all countries – including developing countries – to utilize and share dual-use scientific and technological advances and products for peaceful purposes'.: United Nations Security Council, '4950th Meeting', 6; United Nations Security Council, '4956th Meeting', 6; United Nations Security Council, '5500th Meeting', 5–6; United Nations Security Council, '5551st Meeting', 4.

74 'We believe also that the international community should work tirelessly to seek a comprehensive settlement of the Iraqi question through political and diplomatic means': United Nations Security Council, '4625th Meeting (Resumption 3)', 9; United Nations Security Council, '4644th Meeting', 13; 'To gain the understanding and support of the overwhelming majority of the international community, it is essential that we ensure a fair, rational and non-discriminatory non-proliferation regime. Both the improvement of the existing regime and the establishment of a new one should be based on universal participation by all countries and be based on decisions made by means of democratic process'.: United Nations Security Council, '4950th Meeting', 6; 'Dialogue and negotiations are the only way out'.: United Nations Security Council, '5500th Meeting', 6; United Nations Security Council, '5551st Meeting', 4.

WMDs was self-evidently a 'threat to the peace' and clearly within the Security Council's mandate, while advocating for peaceful solutions in accordance with all relevant laws. France used emotive rhetoric to argue that the international law violations associated with WMD use and proliferation make the existence of a 'threat to the peace' self-evident, while also advocating for peaceful solutions in accordance with all relevant laws.

CHAPTER 20

UK and US Use of Force against Iraq 2003

1 Relevance to the Overall Project

The US- and UK-led military incursion into Iraq in 2003 represents a rare example of a situation where the actions of multiple P5 members were placed under close scrutiny by the Security Council. While there was not so much as a draft resolution addressing this issue (most likely because it would have been vetoed out of hand), there was discussion regarding the relationship between the use of force in Iraq and the concepts of 'threat to the peace' and aggression. Of particular interest are the P5's competing legal interpretations of the situation used to either justify or condemn the actions taken, which lend great insight to this overall project. The *Repertoire of Practice of the Security Council* notes in detail numerous occasions on which this topic was addressed within the Security Council in relation to Article 39;[1] however, it is notable that the vast majority of discussion was conducted by non-permanent members, or states not presently sitting on the Security Council at the time of the debates. While the situation flows on from the non-proliferation case study in Chapter 19 (Iraq's perceived non-compliance, with weapons inspections the primary justification provided for the use of force), it is distinct in that the non-proliferation case study assessed the justification behind finding Iraq's perceived possession of WMDs and non-compliance with inspectors as a 'threat to the peace'. This case study instead assesses the relationship between military action by the US- and UK-led coalition in Iraq without Security Council support, and the concept of 'threat to the peace'.

2 Context of the Debates

Prior to the use of military force against Iraq, there was significant debate within the Security Council, spearheaded by the non-aligned movement, raising concern at the prospect of action in Iraq in response to the perceived failure

1 Repertoire of the Practice of the Security Council, 'Chapter XI: Considerations of Chapter VII the Charter (2000–03)', 926–28.

 | DOI:10.1163/9789004391420_022

of weapons inspections.[2] South Africa became directly involved in the weapons inspections process on the basis that their own disarmament program had been considered best international practice by the global community, and in an effort to prevent any use of force in Iraq.[3] Just over a month after these concerns were raised in the Security Council, the Secretary-General provided an oral briefing to the Council on the effect of the US- and UK-led military action in Iraqi territory.[4] The Secretary-General noted that the action was contentious from a legal standpoint, particularly as it had not been undertaken with Security Council consensus.[5] The Secretary-General also highlighted the responsibility of the belligerent forces within Iraq to provide for the humanitarian needs of the areas under their effective control, and to comply with all armed conflict laws.[6] He closed his briefing with the following appeal to Security Council with respect to future action:

> For my part, I would emphasise two guiding principles, on which I believe there is no disagreement, and which should underpin all your efforts or your future decisions on Iraq. The first principle is respect for Iraq sovereignty, territorial integrity and independence. The second, which flows logically from the first, is respect for the right of the Iraqi people determine their own political future and control their own natural resources.[7]

3 Justificatory Discourse of the P5

The P5's justificatory discourse was clearly divided into two separate approaches. The US and the UK strongly argued that their military action in Iraq was multilateral and lawful under the 1990 Security Council resolution for collective

2 United Nations Security Council, 'Security Council, Fifty-Eighth Year: 4709th Meeting (S/PV.4709)' (United Nations, 18 February 2003); United Nations Security Council, 'Security Council, Fifty-Eighth Year: 4709th Meeting (S/PV.4709) (Resumption 1)' (United Nations, 19 February 2003); United Nations Security Council, 'Security Council, Fifty-Eighth Year: 4717th Meeting (S/PV.4717)' (United Nations, 11 March 2003); United Nations Security Council, 'Security Council, Fifty-Eighth Year: 4717th Meeting (S/PV.4717) (Resumption 1)' (United Nations, 12 March 2003).

3 United Nations Security Council, '4709th Meeting', 3–5.

4 United Nations Security Council, 'Security Council, Fifty-Eighth Year: 4726th Meeting (S/PV.4726)' (United Nations, 26 March 2003), 3.

5 United Nations Security Council, 3.

6 United Nations Security Council, 3.

7 United Nations Security Council, 4.

action in Iraq. The rest of the P5 rejected this argument and characterised the use of force as a violation of the Purposes and Principles of the UN Charter, and a violation of other aspects of international law to varying degrees.

The UK began its arguments by stating that the action occurring in Iraq was an inevitable consequence of the Iraqi Government's continued defiance of Security Council resolutions and demands.[8] Further, they argued that the Security Council and UN's response had 'not succeeded in drawing the right conclusions about the consequences of that [defiance]'.[9] Stemming from their view that the Security Council had failed to act in the correct manner in response to Iraqi defiance of weapons disarmament resolutions, the UK position was that '[i]nternational peace and security cannot be maintained with responsibility by avoiding hard decisions',[10] and that their military action was a difficult decision, but a responsibility they were forced to undertake.[11] In spite of the Secretary-General having highlighted that the action was taken without Security Council consensus or support, the UK argued that they were acting in accordance with all of the relevant Security Council resolutions on Iraq:

> The actions that the United Kingdom is now taking with its coalition partners to uphold United Nations resolutions is both legitimate and multilateral. The use of force is authorized in the current circumstances and Security Council resolutions, 678 (1990), 687 (1991) and 1441 (2002). A broad coalition of well over 40 states is supporting this action materially or politically.[12]

The US response and justification strongly echoed the UK's statements. They argued that '[t]he responsibility for the current situation lies in the hands of the Iraqi regime, a regime which launched two bloody wars and which has refused for 12 years to give up weapons of mass destruction and join its neighbours in peace'.[13] The US characterised the military action as regrettable and as 'not a war against the people of Iraq, but rather against a regime that has denied the will of the international community for more than 12 years'.[14] Like

---

8 United Nations Security Council, 'Security Council, Fifty-Eighth Year: 4726th Meeting (S/PV.4726) (Resumption 1)' (United Nations, 27 March 2003), 22–23.
9 United Nations Security Council, 23.
10 United Nations Security Council, 23.
11 United Nations Security Council, 23.
12 United Nations Security Council, 23.
13 United Nations Security Council, 25.
14 United Nations Security Council, 25.

the UK, the US argued that they had full Security Council authorisation for the use of force under extant Security Council resolutions:

> The coalition response is legitimate and not unilateral. Resolution 687 (1991) imposed a series of obligations on Iraq that were conditions of the ceasefire. It has long been recognized and understood that a material breach of these obligations removes the basis of the ceasefire and revives the authority to use force under resolution 678 (1990). Resolution 1441 (2002) explicitly found Iraq in continuing material breach. In view of Iraq's additional material breaches, the basis of the existing ceasefire has been removed and the use of force is authorised under resolution 678 (1990).[15]

Of the P5 that disagreed with the military action in Iraq, France adopted the most moderate tone. They argued strongly that the most correct and viable approach to dealing with Iraqi disarmament was through peaceful means of inspection and political negotiation, rather than military force.[16] In spite of the US and the UK insistence that they were acting with Security Council authorisations afforded under previous but still extant resolutions, France characterised their military action as regrettable and lacking UN support.[17] Following from this position, France argued that they 'will continue to act to ensure that crises that threaten international peace and security find fair solutions through collective action in the framework of the United Nations'.[18] France also strongly asserted that Iraq's sovereignty and territorial integrity needed to be respected, as '[t]hese principles are enshrined in the Charter and recalled in resolution 687 (1991) and subsequent resolutions. They must be fully respected'.[19] Finally, they argued that frameworks used to facilitate the end of the crisis must be employed with full respect for Iraqi sovereignty and the right of self-determination.[20]

China commenced its statement by condemning the military action of the US- and UK-led coalition, characterising this as a 'sidestepping of the Security Council'.[21] Further, China argued that 'such an action constitutes a violation of the basic principles of the Charter of the United Nations and of international

15 United Nations Security Council, 25.
16 United Nations Security Council, 28.
17 United Nations Security Council, 28.
18 United Nations Security Council, 29.
19 United Nations Security Council, 29.
20 United Nations Security Council, 29.
21 United Nations Security Council, 28.

law'.[22] China argued that the decision to engage in war was bound to bring about a humanitarian disaster and would have a negative effect on safety, stability and development in the region.[23] China also took this opportunity to remind everyone that the Security Council is the institution entrusted with primary responsibility for maintaining international peace and security.[24] They closed their arguments with the following statement:

> Opposition to war and the maintenance of peace are the common aspirations of the world's peoples. The Chinese Government has been consistently committed to the maintenance of international peace and security, advocated the settlement of international disputes by political means and opposed the use or threat of force in international affairs. We strongly call on the countries concerned to halt their military action and to return to the proper path of the political settlement of the Iraqi issue.[25]

Russia began by condemning the actions of the US and the UK, stating that '[a]n unprovoked military action has been undertaken, in violation of international law and in circumvention of the Charter, against Iraq, a sovereign state and member of the United Nations'.[26] Russia contended that the action created a 'looming threat of a humanitarian, economic and ecological disaster'.[27] They also noted that the military action was illegal and was already having an effect in countries throughout the region, and upon the Muslim world and international relations generally.[28] Russia argued that the decision to engage in military action 'in violation of Security Council resolutions'[29] occurred at the moment that the IAEA and the United Nations Monitoring, Verification and Inspection Commission was about to provide an objective answer on the question of Iraq's possession of WMDs,[30] inferring that it was at times such as to prevent these findings from hindering an already determined course of action. Further, they argued that 'those countries are unable to provide any proof to support the allegation regarding Iraq's possession of weapons of mass destruction and Baghdad's support of international terrorism—or with regard

22 United Nations Security Council, 28.
23 United Nations Security Council, 28.
24 United Nations Security Council, 28.
25 United Nations Security Council, 28.
26 United Nations Security Council, 26.
27 United Nations Security Council, 26.
28 United Nations Security Council, 26.
29 United Nations Security Council, 26.
30 United Nations Security Council, 26.

to a threat to the countries of the region or to international security emanating from Iraq'.[31] Finally, Russia stated that 'it is clear to everyone the use of force against Iraq in an effort to change the political regime of the sovereign state runs totally counter to the fundamental principles contained within the Charter of the United Nations'.[32]

4 Summary of Coding

In this case study, the US and UK opposed a finding of 'threat to the peace', while France, China and Russia supported one. The US opposition was based solely on their position that their use of force against Iraq was a direct consequence of Iraq's failure to comply with previous Security Council resolutions. The UK mirrored this position that their use of force against Iraq was a direct consequence of Iraq's failure to comply with previous Security Council resolutions, while also arguing that the gravity of the situation warranted such use of force. Russia supported a finding on the basis that the gravity of the US and UK's use of force amounted to a 'threat to the peace', while also arguing that it constituted a violation of the Purposes and Principles of the Charter and of international law more generally. Further, Russia argued that the situation was clearly international in nature, that the facts upon which the US and UK were relying were unreliable and that a finding of 'threat to the peace' would be a direct consequence of the US and UK's actions. China supported a finding on the basis that the use of force against Iraq constituted a violation of the Purposes and Principles of the Charter and of international law more generally, placing it firmly within the Security Council's mandate. France argued that the use of force against Iraq constituted a violation of the Purposes and Principles of the Charter and of Iraq's rights of self-determination and non-interference, making a finding of 'threat to the peace' consistent with all relevant law.

31 United Nations Security Council, 27.

32 United Nations Security Council, 27.

CHAPTER 21

Sexual Violence as a Tactic of War: 'Women and Peace and Security', and 'Children and Armed Conflict' (Resolutions 1820 (2008), 1882 (2009), 1888 (2009), and 1960 (2010))

1 Relevance to the Overall Project

The topic of sexual violence as a tactic of armed conflict has received significant attention from the Security Council,[1] with reports and meeting transcripts on this issue totalling 681 pages between 2008 and 2010 (inclusive).[2] This material

1 For a more complete examination of Security Council activity on this issue see: Tamsin Phillipa Paige, 'The Maintenance of Heteronormativity', in *Queering International Law: Possibilities, Alliances, Complicities, Risk*, ed. Dianne Otto (Routledge, 2017) which was an expansion of the material contained within this chapter.

2 United Nations Security Council, 'Security Council, Sixty-Third Year: 5916th Meeting (S/PV.5916)' (United Nations, 19 June 2008); United Nations Security Council, 'Security Council, Sixty-Third Year: 5916th Meeting (S/PV.5916) (Resumption 1)' (United Nations, 19 June 2008); United Nations Security Council, 'Security Council, Sixty-Third Year: 6005th Meeting (S/PV.6005)' (United Nations, 29 October 2008); United Nations Security Council, 'Security Council, Sixty-Third Year: 6005th Meeting (S/PV.6005) (Resumption 1)' (United Nations, 29 October 2008); United Nations Security Council, 'Security Council, Sixty-Fourth Year: 6114th Meeting (S/PV.6114)' (United Nations, 29 April 2009); United Nations Security Council, 'Security Council, Sixty-Fourth Year: 6114th Meeting (S/PV.6114) (Resumption 1)' (United Nations, 29 April 2009); United Nations Security Council, 'Security Council, Sixty-Fourth Year: 6180th Meeting (S/PV.6180)' (United Nations, 7 August 2009); United Nations Security Council, 'Security Council, Sixty-Fourth Year: 6180th Meeting (S/PV.6180) (Resumption 1)' (United Nations, 7 August 2009); United Nations Security Council, 'Security Council, Sixty-Fourth Year: 6195th Meeting (S/PV.6195)' (United Nations, 30 September 2009); United Nations Security Council, 'Security Council, Sixty-Fifth Year: 6302nd Meeting (S/PV.6302)' (United Nations, 27 April 2010); United Nations Security Council, 'Security Council, Sixty-Fifth Year: 6411th Meeting (S/PV.6411)' (United Nations, 26 October 2010); United Nations Security Council, 'Security Council, Sixty-Fifth Year: 6411th Meeting (S/PV.6411) (Resumption 1)' (United Nations, 26 October 2010); United Nations Security Council, 'Security Council, Sixty-Fifth Year: 6453rd Meeting (S/PV.6453)' (United Nations, 16 December 2010); United Nations Security Council, 'Security Council, Sixty-Fifth Year: 6453rd Meeting (S/PV.6453) (Resumption 1)' (United Nations, 17 December 2010); Permanent Mission of the United Kingdom of Great Britain and Northern Ireland to the United Nations, 'Women Targeted or Affected by Armed Conflict: What Role for Military Peacekeepers? (Conference Summary)' (United Nations, 18 June 2008); United Nations Secretary-General, 'Women and Peace and Security: Report of the Secretary-General' (United Nations Security Council, 25 September 2008); United Nations

 DOI:10.1163/9789004391420_023

discloses attempts by certain parties to have the Security Council take action in relation to Article 39 and 'threat to the peace'; however, all relevant resolutions were made under Chapter VI.[3] The *Repertoire of Practice of the Security Council* for 2008–11 highlights significant discussion of the relationship between sexual violence as a tactic of war and the concept of 'threat to the peace' in relation to the 'Women and Peace and Security' debates.[4] Although not commented upon by the *Repertoire of Practice of the Security Council*, the contemporaneous debates relating to 'Children and Armed Conflict' also addressed this issue.[5] The volume of material dedicated to this issue within the Security Council in and of itself illustrates the significance of Security Council consideration of the relationship between sexual violence as a tactic of armed conflict and the concept of 'threat to the peace', and the importance of including it in this project. This importance is buttressed by the fact that the Secretary-General's reports on the issue of sexual violence as a tactic of war provide data for instances in 10 current (at the time the report was written) non-international armed conflicts already on the Security Council agenda,[6] and an additional three such conflicts that the Security Council was not at that time addressing.[7] Further, the Secretary-General deemed it appropriate to recommend that the Security Council find within this general situation a 'threat to the peace', which emphasises

Secretary-General, 'Children and Armed Conflict: Report of the Secretary-General' (United Nations, 26 March 2009); United Nations Secretary-General, 'Report of the Secretary-General Pursuant to Security Council Resolution 1820 (2008)' (United Nations Security Council, 20 August 2009); United Nations Secretary-General, 'Women and Peace and Security: Report of the Secretary-General' (United Nations Security Council, 6 April 2010); United Nations Secretary-General, 'Women and Peace and Security: Report of the Secretary-General' (United Nations Security Council, 28 September 2010); United Nations Secretary-General, 'Report of the Secretary-General Pursuant to Security Council Resolutions 1820 (2008) and 1888 (2009)' (United Nations Security Council, 24 November 2010).

3 'Resolution 1820 (2008)', S/RES/1820 (2008) UN Security Council (2008); 'Resolution 1882 (2009)', S/RES/1882 (2009) UN Security Council (2009); 'Resolution 1888 (2009)', S/RES/1888 (2009) UN Security Council (2009); 'Resolution 1960 (2010)', S/RES/1960 (2010) UN Security Council (2010).

4 Repertoire of the Practice of the Security Council, '16th Supplement 2008–2009 Part VII: Actions with Respect to Threats to the Peace, Breaches of the Peace, and Acts of Aggression (Chapter VII of the Charter)' (United Nations), 19–21; Repertoire of the Practice of the Security Council, '17th Supplement 2010–2011 Part VII: Actions with Respect to Threats to the Peace, Breaches of the Peace, and Acts of Aggression (Chapter VII of the Charter)' (United Nations), 27–29.

5 United Nations Security Council, '6114th Meeting', 29 April 2009; United Nations Security Council, '6114th Meeting', 29 April 2009.

6 United Nations Secretary-General, 'Children and Armed Conflict: Report of the Secretary-General', paras. 17, 22, 24–26, 33, 36–37, 44–45, 55, 57, 66, 97 & 104.

7 United Nations Secretary-General, paras. 117, 126 & 143.

the significance the organ responsible for most of the Security Council's fact-finding placed upon this issue.[8] Given this importance, the robust debate that has occurred and the consistent finding that sexual violence as a tactic of war does not constitute a 'threat to the peace', this case study offers a wealth of insight into how the various P5 members approach the question of 'threat to the peace'. While the issue continued to be debated beyond 2010, this has no longer been in the context of consideration of a 'threat to the peace', as it had become clear that any efforts to take Chapter VII action on sexual violence would be met with a veto. Consequently, the debates beyond 2010 have been omitted from this case study.

2 Context of the Debates

The UK brought the issue of sexual violence as a tactic of armed conflict before the Security Council in response to a conference held in Sussex, UK, on 27–29 May 2008 aimed at addressing 'the prevention of widespread and systematic sexual violence in conflict and post-conflict contexts'.[9] The debate that followed led to the unanimous adoption of *Resolution 1820 (2008)*,[10] the first Security Council resolution that focused solely upon the issue of sexual violence as a tactic of war. *Resolution 1820 (2008)* included a provision requiring the Secretary-General to monitor and report on progress in relation to the issue.[11] This was followed by the Secretary-General's annual report on 'Women and Peace and Security' for 2008, which describes (in the critical themes section) use of sexual violence as a tactic of armed conflict as a systematic security concern in need of Security Council action.[12] This highlighting of the need to fight and prevent sexual violence in armed conflict is a key conclusion in the report,[13] and the Secretary-General summarised these key findings at the commencement of the meeting.[14]

8 See United Nations Secretary-General, para. 5 for an overview of the measures taken to ensure that the information presented is as accurate as possible.

9 Permanent Mission of the United Kingdom of Great Britain and Northern Ireland to the United Nations, 'Women Targeted or Affected by Armed Conflict', 2.

10 United Nations Security Council, '5916th Meeting', 19 June 2008, 40.

11 Resolution 1820 (2008), para. 15.

12 United Nations Secretary-General, 'Women and Peace and Security: Report of the Secretary-General', 25 September 2008, paras. 5–7.

13 United Nations Secretary-General, paras. 96 & 97(c).

14 United Nations Security Council, '6005th Meeting', 29 October 2008, 2–4.

This issue was also addressed in the Secretary-General's report on 'Children in Armed Conflict' in 2009. While this report generally considers issues surrounding children's involvement in armed conflicts, it also notes the use of sexual violence as a tactic of war in ongoing conflicts in Afghanistan, Burundi, Central African Republic, Chad, Colombia, Côte d'Ivoire, Democratic Republic of the Congo, Haiti, Iraq, the Philippines, Somalia, Sudan, and Uganda.[15] The report also includes a section addressing issues of sexual violence in armed conflict as it specifically relates to children.[16] The issue was again highlighted in 2009, with the presentation of the Secretary-General's report pursuant to *Resolution 1820 (2008)*. The report itself notes, inter alia, that the use of sexual violence as a tactic of war was often found in conjunction with other crimes against humanity;[17] that this conduct constituted violations of IHL, IHRL and ICL;[18] that municipal law was inadequate in states where this crime occurred in the context of armed conflict and how this compounded impunity issues;[19] how the majority of amnesties in conjunction with peace negotiations undermined efforts to combat impunity on this issue;[20] that support systems for survivors of wartime sexual violence were inadequate;[21] the fact that this tactic was used by both state and non-state actors in conflict;[22] and the need for the Security Council to address the issue under Chapter VII as a 'threat to the peace'.[23]

Meeting 6302 included an oral briefing by the recently appointed Special Representative of the Secretary-General on Sexual Violence in Conflict, Ms Margot Wallström, who highlighted that

> From the Trojan War to the nuclear age, rape has existed in symbiotic relationship with armed conflict. And yet, it's a relationship we are just beginning to understand. History has perpetuated the ancient myth of 'arms and the man', prioritising the plight of soldiers on the front lines while relegating women to the sidelines.[24]

15 United Nations Secretary-General, 'Children and Armed Conflict: Report of the Secretary-General', paras. 17, 22, 24–26, 33, 36–37, 44–45, 55, 57, 66, 97 & 104.

16 United Nations Secretary-General, paras. 154–160.

17 United Nations Secretary-General, 'Report of the Secretary-General Pursuant to Security Council Resolution 1820 (2008)', paras. 15–16.

18 United Nations Secretary-General, para. 22.

19 United Nations Secretary-General, para. 23.

20 United Nations Secretary-General, para. 28.

21 United Nations Secretary-General, para. 30.

22 United Nations Secretary-General, para. 45.

23 United Nations Secretary-General, para. 56(c).

24 United Nations Security Council, '6302nd Meeting', 2.

She also noted that 'our approach to rape in places where peace and order prevailed no more equips us to address systematic rape as a war strategy than our approach to murder prepares us for genocide … the crimes are incomparable'.[25] Finally, in the oral briefings connected to the passing of *Resolution 1960* (*2010*), the Secretary-General noted that '[s]exual violence is one of the only crimes where the victims—and not the perpetrators—are left with stigma',[26] and '[h]istorically, sexual violence by soldiers was prosecuted with a view to restoring military discipline, rather than upholding women's rights'.[27]

3 Justificatory Discourse of the P5

The P5's justificatory discourse ranged from open assertions that sexual violence as a tactic of war in and of itself constituted a 'threat to the peace' (by the UK),[28] implied support for the notion (by the French), non-commitment (by the US) and disagreement with the notion as a whole (by Russia and China, albeit for different reasons). While each P5 state's position was thus individual and distinct, on the relationship between sexual violence as a tactic of war and the concept of 'threat to the peace', each P5 member was consistent across all debates in the justificatory discourse used to substantiate and articulate their position. All arguments centred on the relationship between gender-based violence in armed conflict and the Security Council's mandate to maintain international peace and security, and its role in gender-equality politics generally.

The UK made its position on this issue clear from the outset (beyond their instigation of this issue being raised in Security Council). They stated openly 'that widespread and systematic sexual violence can pose a threat to international peace and security',[29] and that acts of sexual violence as a warfare tactic were 'unacceptable abuses that threaten international peace and security'.[30] Further, the UK pre-emptively addressed the argument that sexual violence in conjunction with armed conflict had always existed:

25 United Nations Security Council, 2.
26 United Nations Security Council, '6453rd Meeting', 16 December 2010, 3.
27 United Nations Security Council, 5.
28 While the positions of the P5 regarding 'threat to the peace' varied greatly, all States supported Security Council action on this issue generally; Resolution 1820 (2008); Resolution 1882 (2009); Resolution 1888 (2009); Resolution 1960 (2010).
29 United Nations Security Council, '5916th Meeting', 19 June 2008, 14.
30 United Nations Security Council, '6453rd Meeting', 16 December 2010, 10–11.

> But some, of course, will say, what is new about this? After all, it is true that rape and sexual violence have been associated with conflict since before records began to be kept. Three things have changed. First, sexual violence is now being used as a tool of warfare, rather than it being a tragic by-product of conflict, and is taking place on a much larger scale than we have seen before. Secondly, we now have a better understanding of how sexual violence damages the prospects of post-conflict recovery. And, thirdly, and perhaps most importantly, we have the means to tackle this problem within our reach.[31]

The UK argued that the Security Council needed to take a leadership role by proposing practical measures that all parties (including peacekeepers and belligerents) could take in response to armed conflicts to prevent such tactics, and to ensure that those who committed sexual violence in conflict 'are brought to justice'.[32] In relation to its call for the Security Council to lead on this issue, the UK heavily criticised the UN for lack of gender equality in peacekeeping operations, particularly given evidence that deploying female peacekeepers had significantly assisted in addressing issue of sexual violence.[33]

The UK's articulation strongly demonstrated that, to their mind, this issue was not simply one of gender equality, but was also one of peace and security. This was clear on two separate fronts. The first was their insistence that sexual violence monitoring and reporting mechanisms should be expanded to include children in addition to women.[34] Second, the UK argued that '[i]f we are serious about preventing and resolving conflict, then we need to be serious about addressing conflict-related sexual violence',[35] and that sexual violence in armed conflict 'is not a women's issue. It is a peace and security issue'.[36] They asserted that the key to ending sexual violence as a tactic of war in the long term was to establish and develop the rule of law in areas of armed conflict and post-conflict recovery,[37] and to end impunity for perpetrators.[38]

31 United Nations Security Council, '5916th Meeting', 19 June 2008, 14.
32 United Nations Security Council, 15.
33 United Nations Security Council, '6005th Meeting', 29 October 2008, 24–25.
34 United Nations Security Council, '6114th Meeting', 29 April 2009, 28.
35 United Nations Security Council, '6180th Meeting', 7 August 2009, 23.
36 United Nations Security Council, '6302nd Meeting', 7.
37 United Nations Security Council, '6180th Meeting', 7 August 2009, 23.
38 United Nations Security Council, '6114th Meeting', 29 April 2009, 28; United Nations Security Council, '6195th Meeting', 8; United Nations Security Council, '6411th Meeting', 26 October 2010, 23–24.

> The message from today's meeting should be that women can never be truly empowered while they remain threatened by sexual violence, and that peace cannot take root when half the community—the female half—lives in fear and trepidation. The Security Council must take up its responsibilities and never again relegate the question of systematic sexual violence to being a secondary issue. It is not. The measures we have adopted over the last two years, including today's resolution, now have to be pursued and implemented.[39]

The UK made their position on implementation extraordinarily clear: 'this requires more than just warm words; it requires meaningful actions that will ultimately make a difference to the situation of women on the ground'.[40]

The French position on the issue of sexual violence in armed conflict was evident in their opening statement in the first meeting on this issue: 'The history of men has long been the history of their violence. In that intermarriage of blood and history, the war of men has all too often also been the story of violence against women'.[41] This clarity of linkage continued through all of the debates on the issue, although France only implied their support for an Article 39 'threat to the peace' finding through their statement of full support for the Secretary-General's report recommendations, which included that the Security Council should take Chapter VII action on this issue.[42] This apparent hesitancy was not apparent, however, when France addressed whether the Security Council should act specifically on sexual violence as a tactic of armed conflict:

> Doubts have at times been raised: should a debate on the issue of sexual violence in armed conflict be included on the agenda of the Security Council, which debates issues of peace and war? For France, that debate has been decided. One cannot establish peace by remaining silent on the subject of rape and violence done to women.[43]

France further argued that 'in light of the effect on the maintenance of international peace and security',[44] they wholly supported implementing all the Secretary-General's recommendations for the Security Council and the General

39 United Nations Security Council, '6195th Meeting', 9.

40 United Nations Security Council, '6411th Meeting', 26 October 2010, 24.

41 United Nations Security Council, '5916th Meeting', 19 June 2008, 16.

42 United Nations Security Council, '6180th Meeting', 7 August 2009, 8.

43 United Nations Security Council, '5916th Meeting', 19 June 2008, 16.

44 United Nations Security Council, '6302nd Meeting', 15.

Assembly for addressing the issue.[45] They then stated that '[t]he worldwide fight against this scourge is a priority of France's foreign policy',[46] and that the key to ending sexual violence as a tactic of war was the end of impunity,[47] proposing that it be added to the criteria examined when considering the imposition of sanctions.[48] Beyond ending impunity, France also suggested that '[f]ocus needs to be placed on the prevention of sexual violence, particularly to ensure that such violence does not become a systematic tactic of warfare'.[49]

The US position on the Security Council's involvement in addressing sexual violence in armed conflict as a specific issue was very clear and consistent: 'When women and girls are preyed upon and raped, the international community cannot be silent or inactive. It is our responsibility to be their advocates and their defenders'.[50] Further, they asserted that '[the US is] proud that today we can respond to the lingering question with a resounding "yes". This world body now acknowledges that sexual violence in conflict zones is, indeed, a security concern',[51] and that 'our shared responsibility for the maintenance of international peace and security includes a profound responsibility to safeguard the lives and security of women and girls, who make up at least half of humankind'.[52] However, this clarity regarding the relationship between sexual violence in armed conflict and Security Council activity did not extend to situations where the issue was insufficiently grave to constitute a 'threat to the peace'. At no point in the eight debates dedicated to this issue did the US specify their position regarding whether sexual violence as a tactic of war should be considered a 'threat to the peace'; rather, they simply stated that 'the fight to end sexual violence has yet to be universally recognised as central to securing international peace and security',[53] and that the international community should 'share the responsibility to protect all of the world's children

45 United Nations Security Council, '6180th Meeting', 7 August 2009, 8; United Nations Security Council, '6195th Meeting', 7; United Nations Security Council, '6302nd Meeting', 15; United Nations Security Council, '6411th Meeting', 26 October 2010, 20.

46 United Nations Security Council, '6195th Meeting', 6.

47 United Nations Security Council, '5916th Meeting', 19 June 2008, 17; United Nations Security Council, '6114th Meeting', 29 April 2009, 14; United Nations Security Council, '6411th Meeting', 26 October 2010, 20.

48 United Nations Security Council, '6453rd Meeting', 16 December 2010, 13.

49 United Nations Security Council, '6302nd Meeting', 15.

50 United Nations Security Council, '5916th Meeting', 19 June 2008, 4.

51 United Nations Security Council, 3.

52 United Nations Security Council, '6453rd Meeting', 16 December 2010, 25.

53 United Nations Security Council, 24.

and provide them with a future of promise and opportunity, not one of war and abuse'.[54]

This position on sexual violence as a tactic of armed conflict and the Security Council's role was matched by a consistent assertion regarding the underpinning ideal for how the issue should be resolved. For the US, the path to ending sexual violence in armed conflict was through ending impunity.[55] Further, they asserted, amnesties as a component of peace negotiations were a 'troubling dynamic of men with guns forgiving other men with guns for crimes committed against women. If peace processes are to succeed and endure, they must avoid this pitfall'.[56] Finally, the US saw ending sexual violence as a tactic of war as a significant issue of cultural and social change:

> It is time for all of us to assume our responsibility to go beyond condemning this behaviour and take concrete steps to end it, to make it socially unacceptable, to recognise that it is not cultural; it is criminal. And the more we say that, over and over and over again, the more we will change attitudes and create peer pressure and the conditions for the elimination of this violation.[57]

While Russia supported each of the resolutions that dealt specifically with sexual violence as a tactic of war, and made it apparent that 'in conflict as in peacetime, sexual violence is a detestable crime that requires condemnation and strict sanctioning',[58] they gave this support under protest. They repeatedly argued that dealing with a particular type of violence against women and children in isolation from the other threats they faced in armed conflict 'significantly reduces'[59] appreciation of the concurrent protection issues—ending

54 United Nations Security Council, '6114th Meeting', 29 April 2009, 17.

55 United Nations Security Council, '6180th Meeting', 7 August 2009, 4–5; United Nations Security Council, '6195th Meeting', 3; '[We are eager to work] to ensure a coordinated approach to addressing a series of critical issues, ending the cycle of impunity, helping national authorities strengthen the rule of law ... providing assistance to victims and creating a framework to prevent emerging or recurring outbreaks of violence or to provide early warning if they cannot be staved off': United Nations Security Council, '6302nd Meeting', 9; United Nations Security Council, '6453rd Meeting', 16 December 2010, 25.

56 United Nations Security Council, '6180th Meeting', 7 August 2009, 5.

57 United Nations Security Council, '6195th Meeting', 4.

58 United Nations Security Council, '5916th Meeting', 19 June 2008, 26.

59 United Nations Security Council, '6005th Meeting', 29 October 2008, 15.

poverty and the inequalities that lead to conflict, and gender equality[60]—stating that

> The United Nations should, as a priority, respond to systematic mass violence against women and children. Equal attention should be given to all categories of such violence in conflicts. Of serious concern are cases in which women and children are killed or injured, including as a result of indiscriminate or excessive use of force.[61]

Further, Russia argued that since other UN agencies were addressing issues of sexual violence, and that the Security Council's role was to maintain international peace and security, Security Council work on this issue would be a 'hardly optimal'[62] use of resources.[63] In conjunction with this position, Russia queried whether '[s]hould we really turn a blind eye to other grievous crimes against civilians, including women and children? In that connection, the proposals of the Secretary-General merit careful study, perhaps in a broader context'.[64] Continuing their criticism of the focus on sexual violence as a tactic of war, Russia argued that to address the issue in isolation in this way failed to take into account the interwoven and complicated nature of addressing women's involvement in peace processes and post-conflict rebuilding, in addition to other issues of gender equality and protection during times of armed conflict.[65]

China acknowledged that '[i]n the many conflicts underway today, women continue to be the most direct victims, and violence against women remains an extremely grave concern'.[66] China also pointed out that sexual violence

60 United Nations Security Council, '5916th Meeting', 19 June 2008, 26; United Nations Security Council, '6005th Meeting', 29 October 2008, 14–15; United Nations Security Council, '6195th Meeting', 11; United Nations Security Council, '6302nd Meeting', 16; United Nations Security Council, '6411th Meeting', 26 October 2010, 28; United Nations Security Council, '6453rd Meeting', 16 December 2010, 21.

61 United Nations Security Council, '6005th Meeting', 29 October 2008, 15.

62 United Nations Security Council, '5916th Meeting', 19 June 2008, 26.

63 United Nations Security Council, 26; 'From the perspective of the Security Council's Charter objectives, it should focus first and foremost on the most pressing, large-scale armed conflicts'.: United Nations Security Council, '6005th Meeting', 29 October 2008, 15; United Nations Security Council, '6302nd Meeting', 16.

64 United Nations Security Council, '6180th Meeting', 7 August 2009, 14.

65 United Nations Security Council, 14; United Nations Security Council, '6195th Meeting', 11; United Nations Security Council, '6302nd Meeting', 16; United Nations Security Council, '6411th Meeting', 26 October 2010, 28; United Nations Security Council, '6453rd Meeting', 16 December 2010, 21.

66 United Nations Security Council, '5916th Meeting', 19 June 2008, 19.

within armed conflicts constituted a violation of international law, urging all parties to conflicts to 'abide by IHL and international human rights law'.[67] They ceded the point that sexual violence was deeply related to armed conflict, and thus within the Security Council's mandate for maintaining international peace and security;[68] however, given the interrelationship with armed conflict, they argued that it should not be dealt with as an independent issue.[69] Further, China repeatedly stressed that 'Governments bear the primary responsibility for protecting women in their respective countries'.[70] In line with this, China argued that the 'Security Council should focus on preventing and reducing instances of armed conflict, thereby decreasing the root causes of women's suffering'.[71]

Beyond their position that the Security Council should not deal with issues of sexual violence (outside of individual instances of it occurring as a part of an armed conflict they are addressing), China's position on violence against women and women's role in post-conflict rebuilding was somewhat paradoxical. China welcomed 'concepts such as gender equality, the empowerment of women and the prevention of and fight against sexual violence',[72] regularly condemning 'all acts of violence against women in conflict situations, including sexual violence';[73] conversely, China argued that the Security Council's role was to deal with threats to international peace and security, and that other UN

67 United Nations Security Council, '6195th Meeting', 14; See also: United Nations Security Council, '5916th Meeting', 19 June 2008, 19; United Nations Security Council, '6114th Meeting', 29 April 2009, 17; United Nations Security Council, '6453rd Meeting', 16 December 2010, 18.

68 United Nations Security Council, '5916th Meeting', 19 June 2008, 19; United Nations Security Council, '6005th Meeting', 29 October 2008, 26.

69 United Nations Security Council, '5916th Meeting', 19 June 2008, 19; United Nations Security Council, '6005th Meeting', 29 October 2008, 26.

70 United Nations Security Council, '6180th Meeting', 7 August 2009, 21; See also: United Nations Security Council, '5916th Meeting', 19 June 2008, 20; United Nations Security Council, '6114th Meeting', 29 April 2009, 18; United Nations Security Council, '6195th Meeting', 14; United Nations Security Council, '6411th Meeting', 26 October 2010, 29; United Nations Security Council, '6453rd Meeting', 16 December 2010, 18.

71 United Nations Security Council, '6195th Meeting', 14; See also: United Nations Security Council, '5916th Meeting', 19 June 2008, 19; United Nations Security Council, '6180th Meeting', 7 August 2009, 20; United Nations Security Council, '6411th Meeting', 26 October 2010, 29; United Nations Security Council, '6453rd Meeting', 16 December 2010, 18.

72 United Nations Security Council, '6180th Meeting', 7 August 2009, 20.

73 United Nations Security Council, '6195th Meeting', 14; See also: United Nations Security Council, '5916th Meeting', 19 June 2008, 19; United Nations Security Council, '6180th Meeting', 7 August 2009, 20; United Nations Security Council, '6411th Meeting', 26 October 2010, 29; United Nations Security Council, '6453rd Meeting', 16 December 2010, 18.

organs were responsible for action where such a threat did not exist.[74] Given this statement's positioning in relation to a debate on the issue of sexual violence as a tactic of war, this clearly implies that China did not consider this an issue of international security. However, at one point, they also stated the following:

> Unable to protect their personal security, women can hardly take an effective part in peace processes or political life. We attach great importance to this question … As the organ that bears the primary sponsor the for the maintenance of international peace and security, the Security Council should step up its efforts on the prevention and resolution of conflicts so that the root causes of women suffering in war can be removed.[75]

Thus, while China evidently attached great importance to the question, their statements betray an underlying assumption that casts doubt on their simultaneous statements of support for gender equality. By stating that women were incapable of protecting themselves, China revealed a view of women as passive victims lacking agency and requiring protection, rather than suffering oppression, sexual violence and exclusion from civil society as a result of endemic social structures that privilege men. By taking this view, China actually contributed to perpetuating these social structures rather than supporting gender equality. Their statements also reasserted their position that sexual violence in armed conflict was not a security issue.

4 Summary of Coding

This case study featured support for a finding of 'threat to the peace' from France, the US and the UK, with opposition from Russia and China. China's opposition was on the basis that Security Council action should accord with all relevant laws, and their interpretation that this situation was outside the Security Council's mandate. China also demonstrated a lack of faith in the proposed solution. Russia's opposition was based on the perception that the situation lacked sufficient gravity and their lack of faith in the proposed solution. The US used emotive rhetoric to implicitly argue that the gravity of

74 United Nations Security Council, '6195th Meeting', 14; United Nations Security Council, '6411th Meeting', 26 October 2010, 30; United Nations Security Council, '6453rd Meeting', 16 December 2010, 18.

75 United Nations Security Council, '6005th Meeting', 29 October 2008, 26.

the situation placed it within the Security Council's mandate, and that a finding of 'threat to the peace' would support the rule of law and the protection of human rights. The UK argued that the gravity of the situation made the existence of a 'threat to the peace' self-evident, placing it within the Security Council's mandate, and contending that such a finding would support the rule of law. France used emotive rhetoric to argue that the existence of a 'threat to the peace' was self-evident and that a finding would support the rule of law.

CHAPTER 22

Piracy: Somalia and Gulf of Guinea

1 Relevance to the Overall Project

As an issue, piracy has received a great deal of Security Council attention (14 resolutions in total, 12 related to Somali piracy,[1] and two related to Gulf of Guinea piracy by the end of time period of this project).[2] In spite of the large volume of resolutions and the amount of time spent dealing with this issue, at no stage has piracy been considered a 'threat to the peace' under Article 39. This seems particularly counterintuitive given that all 12 Somali piracy resolutions (in addition to featuring in general Somalia resolutions)[3] were made under Chapter VII (the Chapter VII action was possibly due to Somalia generally already constituting a 'threat to peace', and the piracy being seen as an extension and exacerbation of that situation), and the volume of international counter-piracy action that has taken place in the Horn of Africa region.[4] This case study thus enables examination of the reasons why an issue considered significant enough to generate such a strong and comprehensive international

---

1 'Resolution 1816 (2008)', S/RES/1816 (2008) UN Security Council (2008); 'Resolution 1838 (2008)', S/RES/1838 (2008) UN Security Council (2008); 'Resolution 1846 (2008)', S/RES/1846 (2008) UN Security Council (2008); 'Resolution 1851 (2008)', S/RES/1851 (2008) UN Security Council (2008); 'Resolution 1897 (2009)', S/RES/1897 (2009) UN Security Council (2009); 'Resolution 1918 (2010)', S/RES/1918 (2010) UN Security Council (2010); 'Resolution 1950 (2010)', S/RES/1950 (2010) UN Security Council (2010); 'Resolution 1976 (2011)', S/RES/1976 (2011) UN Security Council (2011); 'Resolution 2015 (2011)', S/RES/2015 (2011) UN Security Council (2011); 'Resolution 2020 (2011)', S/RES/2020 (2011) UN Security Council (2011); 'Resolution 2077 (2012)', S/RES/2077 (2012) UN Security Council (2012); 'Resolution 2125 (2013)', S/RES/2125 (2013) UN Security Council (2013).

2 'Resolution 2018 (2011)', S/RES/2018 (2011) UN Security Council (2011); 'Resolution 2038 (2012)', S/RES/2038 (2012) UN Security Council (2012).

3 'Resolution 1676 (2006)', S/RES/1676 (2006) UN Security Council (2006), para. Preamble; 'Resolution 1772 (2007)', S/RES/1772 (2007) UN Security Council (2007), para. Preamble & 18.

4 See generally: Paige, Tamsin Phillipa, 'The Impact and Effectiveness of UNCLOS on Counter-Piracy Operations', *Journal of Conflict and Security Law* 22, no. 1 (2017): 97–123, https://doi.org/10.1093/jcsl/krv028; Tamsin Phillipa Paige, 'How Building Prisons in Somalia Promoted the Rule of Law through East Africa', *Bingham Centre for the Rule of Law Global Rule of Law Exchange Papers*, June 2016, http://binghamcentre.biicl.org/ruleoflawexchange/documents/205_paige_practice_note.pdf?showdocument=1; Rob McLaughlin and Tamsin Phillipa Paige, 'The Role of Information Sharing in Counter Piracy in the Horn of Africa Region: A Model for Transnational Criminal Enforcement Operations', *Journal of International Law and International Relations* 12, no. 1 (Fall 2016): 82–119.

 DOI:10.1163/9789004391420_024

response was nevertheless not deemed sufficiently grave to warrant an independent Article 39 declaration of 'threat to the peace'. The *Repertoire of Practice of the Security Council* in relation to Gulf of Guinea piracy reveals that significant debate occurred among Security Council members on the question of Article 39, particularly in relation to characterising transnational organised crime as a 'threat to the peace'.[5] Regarding Somalia, the *Repertoire of Practice of the Security Council* concluded that much of the debate centred on the relationship between Somali state failure and piracy, particularly the manner in which piracy exacerbated the situation in Somalia (which was regarded as the situation that constituted the 'threat to the peace') and the broader implications of this relationship between situations and interdependent or subsidiary characterisations.[6]

2 Context of the Debates

The issue of piracy in Somalia was certainly on the Security Council radar (at least peripherally) before it began to feature consistently in country reports.[7] The reports before the Security Council that raise the issue of piracy began as general country briefings on Somalia before moving to piracy-specific reports.[8] The Security Council began dealing with Somali piracy separately from the issue of Somali state failure in response to requests from the international community.[9] The primary report before the Security Council on the factual

5 Repertoire of the Practice of the Security Council, '17th Supplement 2010–2011 Part VII: Actions with Respect to Threats to the Peace, Breaches of the Peace, and Acts of Aggression (Chapter VII of the Charter)' (United Nations), 25–27.

6 Repertoire of the Practice of the Security Council, '16th Supplement 2008–2009 Part VII: Actions with Respect to Threats to the Peace, Breaches of the Peace, and Acts of Aggression (Chapter VII of the Charter)' (United Nations), 21–23.

7 United Nations Security Council, 'Security Council, Sixtieth Year, 5302nd Meeting (S/PV.5302)', 9 November 2005, 3.

8 'Report of the Secretary-General on Somalia' (United Nations Security Council, 21 February 2006), paras. 15, 20, 30–33 & 37; 'Report of the Secretary-General on Somalia' (United Nations Security Council, 20 June 2006), paras. 40 & 45; 'Report of the Secretary-General on Somalia' (United Nations Security Council, 25 June 2007), para. 51; 'Report of the Secretary-General on Somalia' (United Nations Security Council, 7 November 2007), paras. 22 & 93; 'Report of the Secretary-General on Children and Armed Conflict in Somalia' (United Nations Security Council, 7 May 2007), para. 26; 'Report of the Secretary-General on Somalia' (United Nations Security Council, 14 March 2008), paras. 19, 22 & 48; 'Report of the Secretary-General on Somalia' (United Nations Security Council, 16 July 2008), paras. 17, 21, 23 & 86.

9 'Resolution A.979(24)', International Maritime Organization (2005), para. 24; United Nations Security Council, 'Security Council, Sixty-Second Year, 5805th Meeting (S/PV.5805)',

causes, history and influencing factors, along with recommendations addressing the problem of Somali piracy was delivered on 21 November 2008,[10] with the majority of subsequent reports focused either upon specialised issues,[11] or merely providing updates on the situation.[12] The rationale for dealing with Somali piracy, apart from Somali state failure, is evident in the reports before the Security Council indicating that piracy took root in the Puntland region—which had a relatively stable government, but lacked the financial infrastructure to engage in effective law enforcement—rather than the civil war region of South Central Somalia.[13] Piracy's primary driving factors were identified as poverty, high unemployment, environmental hardship and lack of regional law enforcement.[14]

In relation to Gulf of Guinea piracy, Nigeria raised this issue during their presidency,[15] first in a general West Africa report from the Secretary-General,[16] and then later in a specific fact-finding commission report from the Secretary-General.[17] These reports were orally summarised before the Council in the

17 December 2007, 14; Juan Antonio Yáñez-Barnuevo, 'Letter Dated 23 April 2008 from the Permanent Representative of Spain to the United Nations Addressed to the President of the Security Council' (United Nations Security Council, 23 April 2008), 2.

10 Ahmedou Ould-Abdallah, 'Piracy off the Somali Coast: Workshop Commissioned by the Special Representative to the Secretary General of the UN to Somalia – Final Report: Detailed Recommendations' (Nairobi: International Expert group on the Piracy off the Somali Coast, 21 November 2008); Ahmedou Ould-Abdallah, 'Piracy off the Somali Coast: Workshop Commissioned by the Special Representative to the Secretary General of the UN to Somalia – Final Report: Assessment and Recommendations' (Nairobi: International Expert group on the Piracy off the Somali Coast, 21 November 2008).

11 'Report of the Secretary-General on Specialized Anti-Piracy Courts in Somalia and Other States in the Region' (United Nations Security Council, 20 January 2012); Jack Lang, 'Report of the Special Adviser to the Secretary-General on Legal Issues Related to Piracy off the Coast of Somalia' (United Nations Security Council, 24 January 2011).

12 'Report of the Secretary-General Pursuant to Security Council Resolution 1950 (2010)' (United Nations Security Council, 25 October 2011); 'Report of the Secretary-General Pursuant to Security Council Resolution 2020 (2011)' (United Nations Security Council, 22 October 2012).

13 Ould-Abdallah, 'Piracy off the Somali Coast', 10–12.

14 Ould-Abdallah, 15.

15 U. Joy Ogwu, 'Letter Dated 17 October 2011 from the Permanent Representative of Nigeria to the United Nations Addressed to the Secretary-General' (United Nations Security Council, 17 October 2011).

16 'Report of the Secretary-General on the Activities of the United Nations Office for West Africa' (United Nations Security Council, 30 December 2011).

17 'Report of the United Nations Assessment on Piracy in the Gulf of Guinea (7 to 24 November 2011)' (United Nations Security Council, 19 January 2012).

meetings in which they were tabled.[18] It was suggested that piracy in the Gulf of Guinea was driven by a number of factors, including the civil war in Libya, food insecurity, youth unemployment and political instability in the northern parts of the region.[19] It was also suggested that wide income disparities in the region, and the illicit arms trade,[20] along with the continuing strengthening of transnational criminal organisations (with transnational organised crime perceived as inseparable from piracy)[21] were driving factors.[22]

3 Justificatory Discourse of the P5

The P5's justificatory discourse in response to piracy off the coast of Somalia in 2005 and 2006 was relatively unified. In both years, the President of the Security Council made a joint statement regarding the issue with the consent of all Security Council members. These statements were about Somalia generally, although they raised the issue of piracy originating in Somalia. In both cases, the Security Council called for regionally led solutions supported by the relevant international actors.[23] The P5's consistent and unified approach to the issue of piracy and 'threat to the peace' remained evident throughout their continuing statements in relation to Somali and Gulf of Guinea piracy.

The US drove the Security Council to address piracy as an issue apart from the broader issue of Somali state failure.[24] Their emotive justification for Security Council action against piracy can be broadly characterised as being on the basis of defending freedoms (commerce and navigation particularly) and pursuing justice. This can be clearly detected at the outset of their first substantive statement on the issue of 'the scourge of piracy',[25] where they

18 United Nations Security Council, 'Security Council, Sixty-Seventh Year: 6703rd Meeting (S/PV.6703)', 16 January 2012; United Nations Security Council, 'Security Council, Sixty-Seventh Year: 6717th Meeting (S/PV.6717)', 21 February 2012; United Nations Security Council, 'Security Council, Sixty-Seventh Year: 6723rd Meeting (S/PV.6723)', 27 February 2012.

19 United Nations Security Council, '6703rd Meeting', 3.

20 'Report of the United Nations Assessment on Piracy in the Gulf of Guinea (7 to 24 November 2011)', para. 64.

21 United Nations Security Council, '6717th Meeting', 3.

22 United Nations Security Council, 3.

23 United Nations Security Council, '5302nd Meeting', 3; United Nations Security Council, 'Security Council, Sixty-First Year, 5387th Meeting (S/PV.5387)', 15 March 2006, 3.

24 United Nations Security Council, '5805th Meeting', 14.

25 United Nations Security Council, 'Security Council, Sixty-Third Year, 6046th Meeting (S/PV.6046)', 16 December 2008, 9–10.

characterised the challenge as a 'threat to commerce, security and, perhaps most importantly, to the principle of the freedom of navigation of the seas'.[26] Their arguments for justice are evident in their bold declaration that '[w]e need to end the impunity of Somali pirates'.[27] While the US argued in favour of regional solutions,[28] they acknowledged that in Somalia's case, state failure rendered the need for Security Council action under Chapter VII necessary,[29] and that this action should thus be focused upon rebuilding Somalia.[30]

This parallel justification and approach to Security Council action on piracy was also evident in the US approach to the Gulf of Guinea. In this case, the US argued that piracy attacks 'threaten regional and maritime security and the safety of seafarers, as well is impede economic growth across Western Central Africa'.[31] They also stated that '[t]he scourge of piracy in the Gulf of Guinea has threatened the economies, Governments and peoples of the region for far too long'.[32] Again, the US favoured regional solutions with support from the international community,[33] and as there was no underlying state failure behind the Gulf of Guinea piracy, this was regarded as perhaps a more viable option in this situation. While the Gulf of Guinea statements were littered with calls to end impunity, similar appeals to the pursuit of justice can be found in the US statement that 'no price can be placed upon the loss of life as occurred on 13 February, when gunmen shot and killed the captain and chief engineer of a cargo ship off the coast of Nigeria'.[34]

The UK's statements on piracy were predominantly taciturn and grounded in practicality ('I think that this an important opportunity to discuss both the narrow issue of piracy and the wider situation in Somalia. I will try to do so briefly').[35] In relation to both geographical areas, the UK characterised piracy

26 United Nations Security Council, 9.

27 United Nations Security Council, 11.

28 United Nations Security Council, 10–11.

29 United Nations Security Council, 10–11.

30 United Nations Security Council, 10–11.

31 United Nations Security Council, 'Security Council, Sixty-Seventh Year: 6633rd Meeting (S/PV.6633)', 19 October 2011, 17; See also: United Nations Security Council, '6717th Meeting', 9.

32 United Nations Security Council, '6633rd Meeting', 18.

33 United Nations Security Council, 17; 'The United States believes that piracy in the Gulf of Guinea requires the strongest possible regional response, with international help': United Nations Security Council, '6723rd Meeting', 7.

34 United Nations Security Council, '6723rd Meeting', 8.

35 United Nations Security Council, '6046th Meeting', 4. The UK on the issue of piracy made statements totalling approximately 3 3/4 pages over 4 meetings. In comparison statements by the rest of the P5 were as follows: France, 6 3/4 pages over 7 meetings; Russia,

as a threat to international navigation, maritime safety and trade.[36] In the Gulf of Guinea, specifically, the UK called for regionally led solutions with international support;[37] in Somalia, they acknowledged that piracy was exacerbating an existing 'threat to the peace' and could consequently only be dealt with by addressing the broader problems faced by that state.[38]

French statements regarding piracy, both in Somalia and the Gulf of Guinea, had their basis in respect for law. They argued that piracy, along with other forms of transnational organised crime, was a symptom of weak governmental institutions, caused by problems in post-conflict rebuilding.[39] In relation to both Somalia and the Gulf of Guinea, they characterised piracy as a regional threat.[40] For the French, this meant that in the Gulf of Guinea, piracy constituted a threat to maritime security, trade and economic development,[41] while in Somalia, the threat was that '[e]very day, pirates are slowly killing the Somalian [sic] people'.[42] Similarly, in relation to the Gulf of Guinea, France argued that piracy required a regional response, with support from the international community;[43] but in Somalia, because of the ongoing civil war, they suggested that 'upstream assistance'[44] was required to deal with the problem.[45] In all circumstances, France argued that international law, particularly the United Nations Convention on the Law of the Sea (UNCLOS) and principles of state sovereignty, must be respected in Security Council responses to the issue.[46]

The Russian response to curbing the 'scourge'[47] of piracy can be characterised as an argument made on the basis of law and order. In relation to both

6 pages over 7 meetings; China, 5 1/2 pages over 6 meetings; and USA, 5 1/2 pages over 5 meetings.

36 United Nations Security Council, 4; United Nations Security Council, '6633rd Meeting', 14; United Nations Security Council, '6723rd Meeting', 13.

37 United Nations Security Council, '6633rd Meeting', 14–15; United Nations Security Council, '6723rd Meeting', 13.

38 United Nations Security Council, '6046th Meeting', 4.

39 United Nations Security Council, 12; United Nations Security Council, '6717th Meeting', 7.

40 United Nations Security Council, 'Security Council, Sixty-Third Year, 5987th Meeting (S/PV.5987)', 7 October 2008, 3; United Nations Security Council, '6723rd Meeting', 9.

41 United Nations Security Council, '6633rd Meeting', 7–8.

42 United Nations Security Council, '5987th Meeting', 4.

43 United Nations Security Council, '6723rd Meeting', 9.

44 United Nations Security Council, 'Security Council, Sixty-Second Year, 5749th Meeting (S/PV.5749)', 25 September 2007, 15.

45 United Nations Security Council, '6046th Meeting', 12–13.

46 United Nations Security Council, '5987th Meeting', 3; United Nations Security Council, '6633rd Meeting', 8.

47 United Nations Security Council, 'Security Council, Sixty-Third Year, 6026th Meeting (S/PV.6026)', 2 December 2008, 4.

Somalia and the Gulf of Guinea, Russia approached the question of piracy as a response to criminal activity,[48] albeit a criminal activity that constituted a threat to maritime security and economic wellbeing.[49] Thus, they suggested that in the Gulf of Guinea, piracy was an issue to be dealt with through regional law enforcement organisations, with the support of the international community.[50] In Somalia, however, they suggested 'that piracy and armed robbery at sea is just the tip of the iceberg'[51] of the problems faced, and that long-term solutions would only be possible through efforts to 're-establish peace and law and order in that country'.[52] For both locations, Russia called for the Security Council and the international community at large to respect all applicable international law, particularly the law of the sea, in all responses to these situations.[53]

China's response to the issue of piracy was grounded in respect for the principle of non-intervention, and for international law. Their respect for non-intervention is evident in their reference to requests for support from the Security Council from the Transitional Federal Government of Somalia (TFG),[54] and the Nigerian Government.[55] In relation to piracy itself, China argued that this challenge did pose a threat to international navigation and the global economy, and thus a threat to peace and security within the regions it which it was occurring.[56] In the case of the Gulf of Guinea, China argued that this therefore required regionally led solutions that should receive the support of the international community.[57] In relation to Somalia, however, they agreed that the 'scourge of piracy is a mere symptom of the profound political, economic, social and humanitarian crises confronting Somalia'[58] and could only be truly

48 United Nations Security Council, 4; United Nations Security Council, '6633rd Meeting', 9.

49 United Nations Security Council, '6633rd Meeting', 9.

50 United Nations Security Council, 10; United Nations Security Council, '6723rd Meeting', 12–13.

51 United Nations Security Council, '6046th Meeting', 3.

52 United Nations Security Council, '6026th Meeting', 4.

53 United Nations Security Council, '6046th Meeting', 3; United Nations Security Council, '6633rd Meeting', 8.

54 United Nations Security Council, 'Security Council, Sixty-Third Year, 5902nd Meeting (S/PV.5902)', 2 June 2008, 5.

55 United Nations Security Council, '6633rd Meeting', 12.

56 United Nations Security Council, '6026th Meeting', 2; United Nations Security Council, '6046th Meeting', 5; United Nations Security Council, '6633rd Meeting', 12; United Nations Security Council, '6723rd Meeting', 9.

57 United Nations Security Council, '6633rd Meeting', 12; 'The Gulf of Guinea countries bear the primary responsibility for dealing with piracy': United Nations Security Council, '6723rd Meeting', 9.

58 United Nations Security Council, '6046th Meeting', 5–6.

dealt with through on-land solutions targeting the Somali failed state.[59] For both Somalia and the Gulf of Guinea, China stated that all piracy solutions must accord with international law and the Security Council's mandate under the UN Charter for maintaining international peace and security.[60]

4 Summary of Coding

None of the P5 members supported a finding of 'threat to the peace' in relation to piracy. The UK and Russia offered few meaningful reasons; however, they articulated a preference for regional solutions. The US used emotive rhetoric to advocate for regional solutions that supported the rule of law. France argued that a finding of 'threat to the peace' would violate the affected states' right of non-interference and advocated for regional solutions. China argued that transnational organised crime in the form of piracy was outside the Security Council's mandate generally and that a finding of 'threat to the peace' would violate the affected states' right of non-interference; they advocated for regional solutions that accorded with all relevant laws.

59 United Nations Security Council, '5902nd Meeting', 5; United Nations Security Council, '6026th Meeting', 3; United Nations Security Council, '6046th Meeting', 6.

60 United Nations Security Council, '5902nd Meeting', 5; United Nations Security Council, '6046th Meeting', 5; United Nations Security Council, '6717th Meeting', 13–14.

CHAPTER 23

Civil War in Syria

1 Relevance to the Overall Project

The civil war in Syria is highly relevant to the question of how the P5 approach the concept of 'threat to the peace'. In the 67 years (1946–2013) of Security Council debate on 'threat to the peace' addressed in this book, the conflict in Syria has had three vetoes from China, which have only cast eight vetoes (across all Security Council issues) in that entire period.[1] Interestingly, although only one of those vetoed resolutions purported to be made under Chapter VII with a finding of 'threat to the peace',[2] two of the vetoed resolutions and two of the enacted resolutions were made under Chapter VI.[3] The contested nature of how to characterise this civil conflict in the Security Council offers exceptional insight into how the P5 members consider what constitutes a 'threat to the peace'. The *Repertoire of Practice of the Security Council* only references the chemical weapons debate (addressed below) as a significant Security Council debate in relation to 'threat to the peace' in Syria;[4] however, the debates

1 Dag Hammarskjöld Library, 'Security Council-Veto List', Dag Hammarskjöld Library Research Guides, 19 August 2018, http://research.un.org/en/docs/sc/quick/veto; United Nations Security Council, 'Security Council, Sixty-Sixth Year: 6627th Meeting (S/PV.6627)', 4 October 2011, 2; United Nations Security Council, 'Security Council, Sixty-Seventh Year: 6711th Meeting (S/PV.6711)', 4 February 2012, 2; United Nations Security Council, 'Security Council, Sixty-Seventh Year: 6810th Meeting (S/PV.6810)', 19 July 2012, 2.

2 United Nations Security Council, 'France, Germany, Portugal, United Kingdom of Great Britain and Northern Ireland and United States of America: Draft Resolution (S/2012/538)', 19 July 2012.

3 United Nations Security Council, 'France, Germany, Portugal and United Kingdom of Great Britain and Northern Ireland: Draft Resolution (S/2011/612)', 4 October 2011; United Nations Security Council, 'Bahrain, Colombia, Egypt, France, Germany, Jordan, Kuwait, Libya, Morocco, Oman, Portugal, Qatar, Saudi Arabia, Togo, Tunisia, Turkey, United Arab Emirates, United Kingdom of Great Britain and Northern Ireland and United States of America: Draft Resolution', 4 February 2012.

4 Repertoire of the Practice of the Security Council, '18th Supplement 2012–2013 Part VII: Actions with Respect to Threats to the Peace, Breaches of the Peace, and Acts of Aggression (Chapter VII of the Charter)' (United Nations), 23; The civil war in Syria is also absent from the 2010–2011 considerations: Repertoire of the Practice of the Security Council: Repertoire of the Practice of the Security Council, '17th Supplement 2010–2011 Part VII: Actions with Respect to Threats to the Peace, Breaches of the Peace, and Acts of Aggression (Chapter VII of the Charter)' (United Nations).

 | DOI:10.1163/9789004391420_025

themselves show that the chemical weapons debate was separate in nature and focus to the Syrian Civil War, and that both these issues were significantly addressed in terms of the question of 'threat to the peace'.

2 Context of the Debates

The Security Council's information on the Syria conflict came overwhelmingly in the form of oral briefings at the commencement of meetings.[5] This was supplemented on one occasion by a written report from the Arab League on their mission into the region,[6] although the salient points of this document were provided in an oral briefing at the commencement of that meeting.[7]

The information provided to the Security Council at the beginning of the debates in April 2011 suggested that civil unrest commenced in the form of peaceful protests in response to the government's detention of 15 school children for writing anti-government graffiti.[8] These protests quickly cascaded across the whole country,[9] and were met with a promise of governmental reforms on one hand, and violent repression on the other.[10] The country then descended rapidly into civil war, with military operations and violence on both sides;[11] however, Lynn Pascoe, Under-Secretary-General for Political Affairs, who provided the briefing, noted a lack of transparency in the information coming out of Syria,[12] rendering the Secretariat unable to verify most of the claims being made by either side in the conflict.[13]

This information was updated in January 2012 with a report from the Arab League's observation mission,[14] the salient points of which were provided to

5 United Nations Security Council, 'Security Council, Sixty-Sixth Year: 6524th Meeting (S/PV.6524)', 27 April 2011, 2–4; United Nations Security Council, 'Security Council, Sixty-Seventh Year: 6710th Meeting (S/PV.6710)', 31 January 2012, 2–9; United Nations Security Council, 'Security Council, Sixty-Seventh Year: 6734th Meeting (S/PV.6734)', 12 March 2012, 2–3.

6 United Nations Secretary-General, 'Letter Dated 24 January 2012 from the Secretary-General Addressed to the President of the Security Council' (United Nations, 30 January 2012).

7 United Nations Security Council, '6710th Meeting', 2–9.

8 United Nations Security Council, '6524th Meeting', 2.

9 United Nations Security Council, 2.

10 United Nations Security Council, 2.

11 United Nations Security Council, 2–3.

12 United Nations Security Council, 3.

13 United Nations Security Council, 3.

14 United Nations Secretary-General, 'Letter Dated 24 January 2012 from the Secretary-General Addressed to the President of the Security Council'.

the Security Council in the form of an oral briefing by Sheikh Al-Thani and Secretary-General Nabil Elaraby at the commencement of meeting 6710.[15] They reported that the Syrian Government had failed to meet the deadlines outlined by the Arab League's peace initiative, resulting in the Arab League applying sanctions.[16] Further, they reported that this failure was a result of stalling rather than frustrated implementation.[17] The observer mission also confirmed that the Syrian Government had committed crimes against humanity in the form of extrajudicial killings, arbitrary detention, enforced disappearances and acts of torture, including sexual violence as a tactic of war.[18] They suggested that opposition group violence was a response to government oppression, rather than the cause of governmental violence.[19] The Arab League characterised the situation in Syria as one of ongoing violence and a threat to the entire Middle East region;[20] however, they argued against foreign intervention, particularly foreign military intervention,[21] and called upon the Security Council to support the Arab League's initiatives and solutions rather than taking primary responsibility for the situation.[22] In March 2012, the UN Secretary-General briefed the Security Council on the Middle East generally,[23] and in relation to Syria, stated that the Syrian Government had failed in its responsibility to protect.[24] The 6 July 2012 Observer Mission report[25] confirmed that both government and opposition forces had engaged in targeting civilians,[26] noted the fractured and disorganised nature of the opposition groups,[27] and placed on record the continuing failure of both sides to cease violent engagement.[28]

15 United Nations Security Council, '6710th Meeting', 2–9.
16 United Nations Security Council, 3.
17 United Nations Security Council, 4.
18 United Nations Security Council, 5.
19 United Nations Security Council, 4.
20 United Nations Security Council, 5.
21 United Nations Security Council, 6; United Nations Secretary-General, 'Letter Dated 24 January 2012 from the Secretary-General Addressed to the President of the Security Council', 20–22.
22 United Nations Security Council, '6710th Meeting', 7.
23 United Nations Security Council, '6734th Meeting', 2–3.
24 United Nations Security Council, 2.
25 United Nations Secretary-General, 'Report of the Secretary-General on the Implementation of Security Council Resolution 2043 (2012)' (United Nations Security Council).
26 United Nations Secretary-General, paras. 10–11.
27 United Nations Secretary-General, para. 4.
28 United Nations Secretary-General, paras. 12–16.

3 Justificatory Discourse of the P5

With the exception of the agreement underpinning the presidential statement made in meeting 6598, and in Resolutions 2042 and 2043 (2012) (all of which condemn the violence, attacks on civilians, human rights violations and the lack of progress on political reforms that would allow peace, calling for an end to these breaches of international law and accountability for those who have caused them),[29] the justificatory discourse regarding whether the Syrian Civil War constituted a 'threat to the peace' has hinged on arguments over the primacy of different norms of international law. This can generally be characterised by, on one side, France, the US and the UK giving primacy to human rights norms and arguing that democracy is now a norm of international law that ought to receive primacy; and by contrast, Russia and China's arguments being underpinned by the principle of non-intervention and non-interference in the domestic affairs of states, and the pacific settlement of disputes in accordance with the Purposes and Principles of the UN Charter. The details of these arguments are now outlined in more detail.

The US employed a strong degree of emotive rhetoric when discussing the Syria situation, characterised by respect for human rights and defence of democracy. They referred to the conflict in Syria as, among other things, an 'outrageous and ongoing use of violence against peaceful protesters',[30] 'cries for freedom of expression, association, peaceful assembly and the ability to freely choose their leaders',[31] 'yearning for liberty and universal human rights'[32] and 'peaceful protesters crying out for freedom'.[33] They described the al-Assad regime's conduct as 'crimes against humanity',[34] 'a regime of thugs with guns that tramples human dignity and human rights',[35] a 'reign of terror',[36] 'abhorrent brutality',[37] a 'horrific campaign of violence that is shocking the conscience of the world',[38] as possessing a 'long record of broken promises, deceit and

29 United Nations Security Council, 'Security Council, Sixty-Sixth Year: 6598th Meeting (S/PV.6598)', 3 August 2011, 2; 'Resolution 2042 (2012)', S/RES/2042 (2012) UN Security Council (2012); 'Resolution 2043 (2012)', S/RES/2043 (2012) UN Security Council (2012).

30 United Nations Security Council, '6524th Meeting', 3.

31 United Nations Security Council, 4.

32 United Nations Security Council, '6627th Meeting', 8.

33 United Nations Security Council, 9.

34 United Nations Security Council, 8.

35 United Nations Security Council, 8.

36 United Nations Security Council, '6710th Meeting', 14.

37 United Nations Security Council, '6711th Meeting', 5.

38 United Nations Security Council, '6734th Meeting', 11.

disregard for the most basic standards of humanity'[39] and as '[persisting] in the slaughter of the Syrian people'.[40] Further, the US argued that all of the opposition factions in Syria were acting only 'in self-defence'.[41]

In justifying the position that the civil conflict in Syria constituted a 'threat to the peace',[42] the US contended that the al-Assad regime had failed in its responsibility to protect.[43] They also argued that the Arab Spring was evidence that civil society, the rule of law and democracy were not Western impositions, but indigenous to all humanity.[44] They further advocated the need for 'external pressure'[45] and 'meaningful consequences'[46] to be imposed upon the Syrian Government to end the conflict,[47] suggesting that it was the Security Council's responsibility to do so,[48] and that in failing to achieve this it 'has utterly failed to address the urgent moral challenge and growing threat to regional peace and security'.[49] In relation to the vetoes from China and Russia, the US argued that these were evidence of complicity and support for the al-Assad regime's actions, as well as being 'very destructive'[50] and 'dangerous and deplorable'.[51] The vetoes themselves left the US 'outraged' and 'disgusted';[52] at one stage they suggested that China and Russia were 'paranoid, if not disingenuous'.[53] The US also made it clear that in addition to the sanctions and arms embargo being advocated,[54] they (and their allies) were 'preparing for those actions that will be required', suggesting a willingness to engage in unilateral action.[55]

---

39 United Nations Security Council, 'Security Council, Sixty-Seventh Year: 6756th Meeting (S/PV.6756)', 21 April 2012, 10.

40 United Nations Security Council, 10.

41 United Nations Security Council, 'Security Council, Sixty-Seventh Year: 6751st Meeting (S/PV.6751)', 14 April 2012, 9.

42 United Nations Security Council, '6711th Meeting', 5.

43 United Nations Security Council, '6734th Meeting', 11.

44 United Nations Security Council, 12.

45 United Nations Security Council, '6756th Meeting', 10.

46 United Nations Security Council, 10.

47 United Nations Security Council, 10.

48 United Nations Security Council, '6627th Meeting', 8; United Nations Security Council, '6710th Meeting', 13; United Nations Security Council, '6711th Meeting', 5; United Nations Security Council, '6734th Meeting', 11; United Nations Security Council, '6751st Meeting', 9; United Nations Security Council, '6756th Meeting', 10; United Nations Security Council, '6810th Meeting', 10.

49 United Nations Security Council, '6627th Meeting', 8.

50 United Nations Security Council, '6810th Meeting', 10.

51 United Nations Security Council, 10.

52 United Nations Security Council, '6711th Meeting', 5.

53 United Nations Security Council, '6810th Meeting', 10.

54 United Nations Security Council, '6711th Meeting', 5.

55 United Nations Security Council, '6756th Meeting', 10.

The UK adopted a similar position to the US, grounded in respect for human rights, the responsibility to protect, ending impunity for crimes against humanity and defending democracy. While they had moments of impassioned rhetoric, their general approach was somewhat more detached. In relation to the conflict generally, the UK's descriptions included 'a systematic attempt to stifle the legitimate demands of the Syrian people through violence and oppression … We have witnessed the repeated and deliberate targeting of civilians and the use of tanks and other heavy weaponry against peaceful protesters',[56] and 'horrifying violence that has engulfed Syria … Which is an unmitigated tragedy for the people of that country and a real threat to international peace and security'.[57] The UK called for the Syrian Government to fulfil its 'responsibility to protect',[58] for the international community to condemn the Syrian Government's conduct,[59] and for independent investigations into the military's acts, including violence against civilians.[60] The UK argued that while models of democracy may differ from country to country, and culture to culture, the principle of democracy is a fundamental right that must be respected.[61] The UK's overall position was neatly encapsulated thus:

> We believe that today, nearly 6000 Syrians have died in appalling circumstances. That includes, as we have heard, 384 children. Between 30 and 100 people currently die every single day from violence in Syria. They will be dying as we speak. Thousands more are enduring torture, imprisonment and sexual violence, including the rape of children.[62]

While making very little direct reference to the Syrian Government, it was overwhelmingly clear that the UK held the government almost wholly responsible for the conflict, as evidenced by the statements above, and in what the UK asserted to be a disproportionately differential use of force between the government and rebel factions.[63] In relation to the vetoes from China and Russia, the

56 United Nations Security Council, '6524th Meeting', 5.
57 United Nations Security Council, '6710th Meeting', 16.
58 United Nations Security Council, '6524th Meeting', 5.
59 United Nations Security Council, 5.
60 United Nations Security Council, 5.
61 United Nations Security Council, '6734th Meeting', 4.
62 United Nations Security Council, '6710th Meeting', 17.
63 United Nations Security Council, '6627th Meeting', 7.

UK described their position as being 'deeply disappointed'[64] and 'appalled';[65] they expressed a belief that the vetoes signified an inability to put words into action for peace.[66] Further, the UK saw the vetoes as a failure of the Security Council.[67] In relation to Russia's concerns that the vetoed resolutions, had they passed, would have led to a Libya-style intervention and mission creep, the UK pointed out that two of the resolutions were to be made under Chapter VI,[68] and that a Chapter VII resolution was not necessarily a precursor to military intervention; they cited Sudan and South Sudan as evidence.[69]

The French position in relation to Syria, like that of the US and the UK, was grounded in respect for democracy, the defence of human rights and the ending of impunity for *jus cogens* violators. Their impassioned statements lie somewhere between the US and the UK in terms of emotive appeal. France described the conflict generally as emerging from a desire for 'peace and respect for their dignity',[70] and a situation where '[a] people has [sic] risen up to defend its liberty'[71] but where 'peace is threatened by the bloody downward spiral of a regime gasping its last'.[72] The French positions on the conflict, and on the al-Assad regime, were aptly summarised in their statements on the passing of Resolutions 2042 and 2043:

> The perpetrators of this barbaric repression of a peaceful civilian population will not go unpunished, I am happy that today, finally, the Security Council has been unanimous in recognising their criminal responsibility.[73]
>
> I would like to recall that our goal in deploying the mission is not just an end to repression; above all, it is the launching of a political transition in Syria towards a democratic system, so that the Syrian people can at last

64 United Nations Security Council, 7.

65 United Nations Security Council, '6711th Meeting', 6; United Nations Security Council, '6810th Meeting', 2.

66 United Nations Security Council, '6810th Meeting', 3.

67 United Nations Security Council, '6627th Meeting', 7; United Nations Security Council, '6710th Meeting', 17; United Nations Security Council, '6711th Meeting', 7; United Nations Security Council, '6810th Meeting', 3.

68 United Nations Security Council, '6711th Meeting', 7.

69 United Nations Security Council, '6810th Meeting', 3.

70 United Nations Security Council, '6710th Meeting', 14.

71 United Nations Security Council, 14.

72 United Nations Security Council, 14.

73 United Nations Security Council, '6751st Meeting', 6.

> freely choose their destiny ... We can wait no longer. More civilians are dying with each passing day.[74]

The French further argued that the crimes against humanity being committed in Syria were overwhelmingly to be laid at the door of the Syrian Government (with suggestions that violence from government opposition is in the vast minority,[75] and that the Syrian Government had 'lost all legitimacy by murdering their own people').[76] At one stage, France provided a summary to which they referred as 'this ghastly list',[77] arguing that '[b]etween bombardments, the regime sends its terrifying militias to cut throats, kidnap, rape and generate inter-communal fear among the civilian population'.[78] France has regularly called for action to end impunity for these crimes.[79] France described the Security Council's lack of response (aside from 'a mere presidential statement')[80] as 'the scandalous silence of the Security Council. Indeed, I call it scandalous';[81] 'shameful';[82] and 'a sad day for all the friends of democracy'.[83] In this vein, France thus described Russia's and China's vetoes as thwarting 'the legitimate aspirations of the Syrian people to democracy, the rule of law and respect for fundamental human rights',[84] and stalling rhetoric,[85] based on accusations 'of seeking regime change and preparing for military intervention' that were 'patently false',[86] and as 'a mockery of diplomatic action with de facto paralysis'.[87]

Russia's position on the Syrian Civil War was grounded in the principles of national sovereignty and territorial integrity, non-intervention in domestic affairs, self-determination and pacific settlement of disputes.[88] In relation to the conflict itself, they rejected characterisations of the violence being primarily

74 United Nations Security Council, '6756th Meeting', 3.
75 United Nations Security Council, '6710th Meeting', 15.
76 United Nations Security Council, '6627th Meeting', 3.
77 United Nations Security Council, '6810th Meeting', 3.
78 United Nations Security Council, 4.
79 United Nations Security Council, '6627th Meeting', 3; United Nations Security Council, '6734th Meeting', 7; United Nations Security Council, '6751st Meeting', 6; United Nations Security Council, '6810th Meeting', 4.
80 United Nations Security Council, '6711th Meeting', 3.
81 United Nations Security Council, '6710th Meeting', 14.
82 United Nations Security Council, '6711th Meeting', 3.
83 United Nations Security Council, 3.
84 United Nations Security Council, '6810th Meeting', 3.
85 United Nations Security Council, '6711th Meeting', 3–4.
86 United Nations Security Council, 4.
87 United Nations Security Council, '6810th Meeting', 4.
88 United Nations Security Council, '6627th Meeting', 3.

the Syrian Government's responsibility, arguing that opposition groups were just as culpable.[89] While they agreed that full-scale conflict in Syria would lead to destabilisation throughout the Middle East,[90] they made it clear that their continued veto was grounded in foundationally different approaches to the UK, US and France.[91] Russia consistently made it clear that they could support any action that could lead to a repeat of NATO's interpretation of the Security Council resolutions in relation to Libya,[92] arguing that in that case, an arms embargo led to a full-scale naval blockade and fuelled a fully-fledged civil war that transcended national boundaries.[93] Russia also contended that the use of sanctions would actually hinder rather than assist the peace process:

> We reject any sanctions, any attempts to employ the Council's instruments to fuel conflict or to justify any eventual foreign military interference … The Council cannot impose parameters for an internal political settlement. The Charter gives no such authority. The sides must be encouraged to engage in dialogue rather than being intimidated into doing so.[94]

Russia regularly asserted that the US, UK and France were pushing for regime change within Syria, beyond the Council's authority. At one stage they referred to these states as meddling 'Pharisees [that] have been pushing their own geopolitical intentions, which have nothing in common with the legitimate interests of the Syrian people',[95] and arguing that they were 'calling for regime change, encouraging the opposition towards power, indulging in provocation and nurturing the armed struggle'.[96] To this end, Russia argued that a draft resolution vote that took place

> should not have taken place at all … The Russian delegation has been very clear and consistently explained that we cannot accept a document, under

89 'One cannot disregard that the violence does not originate entirely from one side'.: United Nations Security Council, '6524th Meeting', 7; United Nations Security Council, '6627th Meeting', 4; United Nations Security Council, '6710th Meeting', 24; United Nations Security Council, '6734th Meeting', 10; United Nations Security Council, '6751st Meeting', 3; United Nations Security Council, '6810th Meeting', 9.
90 United Nations Security Council, '6710th Meeting', 23.
91 United Nations Security Council, '6627th Meeting', 3.
92 United Nations Security Council, 4; 'The Libyan model should remain forever in the past'.: United Nations Security Council, '6756th Meeting', 2.
93 United Nations Security Council, '6627th Meeting', 4.
94 United Nations Security Council, '6710th Meeting', 24.
95 United Nations Security Council, '6810th Meeting', 8.
96 United Nations Security Council, '6711th Meeting', 9.

> Chapter VII of the Charter of the United Nations, that would open the way for pressure of sanctions and later for external military involvement in Syrian domestic affairs.[97]

Russia noted that such action would simply 'fan the flames of extremists, including terrorist groups'.[98] Russia regularly pointed out that they considered the draft resolutions biased in their failure to recognise violence being perpetrated by opposition groups,[99] and that as far as the peace process was concerned, '[a]ny external influence imposed by us on that process could risk exacerbating the crisis'.[100] Russia regularly stated that it consistently advocated for a peaceful resolution and an end to violence,[101] and that its suggestions on this matter had been rejected.[102]

China's starting point for its engagement with the Syrian conflict was one of praise for investigation of the Syrian military's wrongdoing (inferring support for international criminal law),[103] and suggestions that the Arab Spring had generally had a negative effect on regional and world peace and security.[104] They were brief in their statements, supporting Russia's lead.[105] China's justification for its position on Syria can be summarised in the following statement:

> Most important, is [sic] should depend upon whether it complies with the Charter of the United Nations and the principle of non-interference in internal affairs of states—which has a bearing upon security and survival of developing countries, in particular small and medium-sized countries, and laws on world peace and stability.[106]

---

97 United Nations Security Council, '6810th Meeting', 8.

98 United Nations Security Council, 8.

99 United Nations Security Council, '6627th Meeting', 3; United Nations Security Council, '6711th Meeting', 9; United Nations Security Council, '6810th Meeting', 8–9.

100 United Nations Security Council, '6756th Meeting', 2.

101 United Nations Security Council, '6524th Meeting', 7; United Nations Security Council, '6627th Meeting', 4; United Nations Security Council, '6710th Meeting', 23; United Nations Security Council, '6711th Meeting', 9; United Nations Security Council, '6751st Meeting', 3; United Nations Security Council, '6810th Meeting', 8.

102 United Nations Security Council, '6710th Meeting', 25; United Nations Security Council, '6711th Meeting', 9; United Nations Security Council, '6810th Meeting', 9.

103 United Nations Security Council, '6524th Meeting', 7.

104 United Nations Security Council, 7–8.

105 'China supports the amendments proposed by the Russian Federation and has noted that the Russian Foreign Minister will visit Syria next week'.: United Nations Security Council, '6711th Meeting', 10. Further, in all meetings China spoke after Russia.

106 United Nations Security Council, '6627th Meeting', 5.

China consistently argued in a measured manner that all solutions must respect the principle of non-interference in a state's internal matters,[107] the Purposes and Principles of the UN Charter,[108] international law,[109] 'the sovereignty, independence and territorial integrity of Syria',[110] the freedom of self-determination,[111] and the pacific settlement of disputes.[112] While China has consistently condemned the violence occurring in Syria, they have justified their veto of various draft resolutions on the basis that they are unbalanced,[113] would undermine the above-mentioned principles,[114] and would 'not help to facilitate the easing of the situation in Syria'.[115] China's position on Syria can be aptly summarised in the following statement:

> China has consistently taken a cautious approach to sanctions. Sanctions, rather than assistance [sic] in resolving an issue, often lead to further complications of the situation. We firmly oppose the use of force to resolve the Syrian issue, as well as practices, such as forcibly pushing for regime change, that violate the purposes and principles of the United Nations Charter and the basic norms that govern international relations.[116]

---

107 United Nations Security Council, 5; United Nations Security Council, '6756th Meeting', 8; United Nations Security Council, '6810th Meeting', 8.

108 United Nations Security Council, '6524th Meeting', 8; United Nations Security Council, '6627th Meeting', 5; United Nations Security Council, '6710th Meeting', 25; United Nations Security Council, '6711th Meeting', 9; United Nations Security Council, '6734th Meeting', 19.

109 United Nations Security Council, '6710th Meeting', 25; United Nations Security Council, '6734th Meeting', 19.

110 United Nations Security Council, '6711th Meeting', 9.

111 United Nations Security Council, '6751st Meeting', 4; United Nations Security Council, '6756th Meeting', 8; United Nations Security Council, '6810th Meeting', 13.

112 United Nations Security Council, '6524th Meeting', 8; United Nations Security Council, '6627th Meeting', 5; United Nations Security Council, '6710th Meeting', 25; United Nations Security Council, '6711th Meeting', 9–10; United Nations Security Council, '6734th Meeting', 19; United Nations Security Council, '6751st Meeting', 4; United Nations Security Council, '6756th Meeting', 8; United Nations Security Council, '6810th Meeting', 13.

113 United Nations Security Council, '6711th Meeting', 9–10; United Nations Security Council, '6810th Meeting', 13.

114 United Nations Security Council, '6627th Meeting', 5; United Nations Security Council, '6711th Meeting', 9; United Nations Security Council, '6810th Meeting', 13.

115 United Nations Security Council, '6627th Meeting', 5.

116 United Nations Security Council, '6710th Meeting', 25.

4 Summary of Coding

This situation garnered opposition to a finding of 'threat to the peace' from China and Russia (coupled with vetoes from both), and support from France, the US and the UK. China's opposition (and vetoes) were grounded in their lack of faith in the proposed solution, which they saw as not conforming to the relevant laws, and as violating the Purposes and Principles of the Charter and Syria's rights to non-interference and self-determination. Russian opposition (and vetoes) were expressed through emotive rhetoric and based on a lack of faith in the proposed solution, which they saw as beyond the scope of the Security Council's mandate. They also argued that the proposed solution ran in opposition to the pacific settlement of disputes and Syria's rights to self-determination and non-interference. France used emotive rhetoric to argue that the gravity of the situation made the existence of a 'threat to the peace' self-evident, and that such a finding was necessary to protect human rights and defend democracy. The US used emotive rhetoric to argue that the situation in Syria was within the Security Council's mandate and that a finding of 'threat to the peace' was necessary because of the ongoing international law violations and the responsibility to protect. Further, the US argued that such a finding was essential for protecting human rights and defending democracy. The UK used formal legal arguments to state that the gravity of the situation and the ongoing international law violations made the existence of a 'threat to the peace' self-evident, and that such a finding was essential for defending democracy, promoting the rule of law and protecting human rights.

CHAPTER 24

Chemical Weapons (2013): Resolution 2118

1 Relevance to the Overall Project

Much like the East Timor intervention case study, this case study's value to the overall project of understanding how the P5 approach 'threat to the peace' is in the consensus they displayed in this instance. Further, the resolution itself is the only resolution to date where the declaration of 'threat to the peace' was not restricted in any geographical or temporal manner.[1] Operative paragraph 1 boldly declares 'that use of chemical weapons anywhere constitutes a threat to international peace and security'.[2] The *Repertoire of the Practice of the Security Council* for 2012–13 briefly notes the discussions and asserts that most states held the view that the use of chemical weapons clearly constituted a 'threat to the peace'.[3] The *Repertoire of Practice* also highlights the Security Council's self-awareness of the fact that they were creating an unfettered and ongoing finding.[4] Dissecting the basis of this consensus greatly illuminates the approaches applied to this concept, particularly when the ongoing internal strife

---

1 'Resolution 2118 (2013)', S/RES/2118 (2013) UN Security Council (2013); For example, the terrorism resolutions made in the wake of the 9/11 (Resolution 1368 and Resolution 1373) terrorist attacks find that 'such acts, like any act of international terrorism, constitute a threat to international peace and security'. This contains a geographical limiter and a contextual limiter, namely that the act be international in character (as opposed to domestic in nature) and that the act be terrorism (as opposed to an act of war or an apolitical crime, even though these acts may have the same outcome and appearance – even though Resolution 1269 condemns 'all acts of terrorism, irrespective of motive' Turk's work on terrorism makes it abundantly clear that the decision to categorise an act as terrorism is entirely political one). This can be contrasted with the declaration in Resolution 2118 that simply states that any use of chemical weapons, regardless of its geographical location, is a threat to the peace. It is this lack of geographical limitation (thereby bypassing potential future non-interference in domestic matters arguments) and the lack of qualifying context (all chemical weapons as opposed to requiring it to fit an abstract definition that goes to motivation) that makes it unique. 'Resolution 1269 (1999)', S/RES/1269 (1999) UN Security Council (1999); 'Resolution 1368 (2001)', S/RES/1368 (2001) UN Security Council (2001); 'Resolution 1373 (2001)', S/RES/1373 (2001) UN Security Council (2001); Austin Turk, 'Sociology of Terrorism', *Annual Review of Sociology* 30 (2004): 247.

2 Resolution 2118 (2013), para. 1.

3 Repertoire of the Practice of the Security Council, '18th Supplement 2012–2013 Part VII: Actions with Respect to Threats to the Peace, Breaches of the Peace, and Acts of Aggression (Chapter VII of the Charter)' (United Nations), 23.

4 Repertoire of the Practice of the Security Council, 23.

 DOI:10.1163/9789004391420_026

that formed the background to this resolution was not, separately, considered a 'threat to the peace'; the case study highlights areas where even a greatly divided Security Council can nevertheless take action when the background to a situation is dogged by stalemate.[5]

2 Context of the Debates

In relation to the ongoing conflict in Syria,[6] the Secretary-General ordered an investigation of allegations of chemical weapons use in the Syrian Arab Republic in the Ghouta area of Damascus on 21 August 2013.[7] This investigation took the form of a UN special mission (the Mission), supported by the World Health Organization and the Organisation for the Prohibition of Chemical Weapons. The legal authority for the Mission came from *General Assembly Resolution 42/37 C*,[8] and *Security Council Resolution 620 (1988)*.[9] The Mission landed in Damascus on 18 August 2013,[10] and was already in situ to investigate the 21 August incidents when the allegations of chemical weapons use arose.[11]

The mission conducted investigations in the affected region on 26 and 28–29 August under a tenuous ceasefire and, on one occasion, sniper fire.[12] The investigation consisted of medical, biomedical and scientific data collected in the region, supplemented by qualitative data in the form of interviews from more than 50 exposed survivors.[13] The medical data examined the symptoms and likely causes of injuries to the survivors (of the 80 presented to the Mission, 36

5 Previously the situation in Syria had been met with a veto on three occasion by both Russia and China; United Nations Security Council, 'Security Council, Sixty-Sixth Year: 6627th Meeting (S/PV.6627)', 4 October 2011, 2; United Nations Security Council, 'Security Council, Sixty-Seventh Year: 6711th Meeting (S/PV.6711)', 4 February 2012, 2; United Nations Security Council, 'Security Council, Sixty-Seventh Year: 6810th Meeting (S/PV.6810)', 19 July 2012, 2.

6 See previous case study on this conflict (Chapter 23) for details.

7 United Nations Secretary-General, 'Report of the United Nations Mission to Investigate the Use of Chemical Weapons in the Syrian Arab Republic on the Alleged Use of Chemical Weapons in the Ghouta Area of Damascus on 21 August 2013' (United Nations, 16 September 2013), para. 4.

8 'Chemical and Bacteriological (Biological) Weapons', A/RES/42/37 UN General Assembly (1987), para. C 4.

9 'Resolution 620 (1988)', S/RES/620 (1988) UN Security Council (1988), para. 2.

10 United Nations Secretary-General, 'Report of the United Nations Mission to Investigate the Use of Chemical Weapons in the Syrian Arab Republic on the Alleged Use of Chemical Weapons in the Ghouta Area of Damascus on 21 August 2013', 6.

11 United Nations Secretary-General, 6.

12 United Nations Secretary-General, 6.

13 United Nations Secretary-General, 6.

were subject to in-depth examination of their symptoms) and the deceased.[14] The scientific data concerned local weather during the incident, munitions delivery systems and environmental samples.[15] The biomedical samples consisted of blood, urine and hair samples from 34 of the 36 patients.[16] The overwhelming conclusion on the basis of all this combined evidence (including the presence of Sarin in the munitions and the blood samples) was that chemical weapons had been used as a part of the ongoing conflict, and that these weapons had been deployed against civilians and children.[17] The full report detailing these conclusions and methodologies formed the basis for the meeting statements made after the unanimous adoption of *Security Council Resolution 2118 (2013)*.[18] The Geneva communiqué of 30 June 2012 (annexed to *Security Council Resolution 2118*),[19] on the political resolution of the ongoing conflict in Syria, also featured in the meeting.

3 Justificatory Discourse of the P5

While the Secretary-General characterised *Resolution 2118 (2013)* as a victory, and a beacon of hope for the people of Syria,[20] the reality is that *Resolution 2118 (2013)* was not really about Syria or the ongoing conflict, but rather a non-proliferation resolution that just happened to fall within the Syrian conflict narrative.[21] That this resolution is, fundamentally, a non-proliferation resolution is highlighted by statements from Russia and China regarding conflict resolution and peace through political processes rather than violence.[22] The existence of a 'threat to the peace' by virtue of confirmed chemical weapons usage can thus be seen as being taken as a given in light of statements from the P5, and because voting on the issue was conducted (resulting in unanimous

14 United Nations Secretary-General, 7.
15 United Nations Secretary-General, 7.
16 United Nations Secretary-General, 8.
17 United Nations Secretary-General, 8.
18 United Nations Security Council, 'Security Council, Sixty-Eighth Year: 7038th Meeting (S/PV.7038)', 27 September 2013, 2.
19 Resolution 2118 (2013), 9–13.
20 United Nations Security Council, '7038th Meeting', 2.
21 This can be seen by the way in which Resolution 2118 echoes Resolution 1540 (which is dedicated to the non-proliferation of weapons of mass destruction generally) and by virtue of the fact that of the 22 operative paragraphs in Resolution 2118, only paras. 16 and 17 make are directed to the conflict generally; 'Resolution 1540 (2004)', S/RES/1540 (2004) UN Security Council (2004); Resolution 2118 (2013).
22 United Nations Security Council, '7038th Meeting', 4 & 9.

support) and followed by justificatory statements, rather than voting following the debate.

Russian support of *Resolution 2118 (2013)* was not obviously grounded in any clear ideology, but it can be inferred from their statements to have been based in respect for international law. Russia drove home its position that political resolution in Syria was the only legitimate option by immediately highlighting that this non-proliferation resolution was in accordance 'with the Russian-American agreements achieved in Geneva on 14 September'.[23] From this point, Russia turned its attention to the chemical weapons stockpiles and their usage in Syria. Their focus was on praising Syria for joining the Chemical Weapons Convention and highlighting the role of the Security Council and the international community in taking control of the 'chemical arsenals',[24] ensuring that they did not fall into the hands of extremists.[25] Of particular interest is Russia's assertion that the Security Council stood ready to take Chapter VII action in response to the use of chemical weapons in violation of *Resolution 2118 (2013)*;[26] however, they simultaneously claimed that *Resolution 2118 (2013)* itself did not fall under Chapter VII,[27] even though operative paragraph 1 clearly invokes Article 39,[28] and the rest of the P5 regarded it as a Chapter VII decision.[29] Throughout their statement, Russia made no direct claims for the basis of a 'threat to the peace' finding,[30] and only oblique references to the ongoing 'threat to the peace' declared in operative paragraph 1;[31] however, their entire statement strongly infers that use of chemical agents in direct opposition to prohibition of chemical weapons use, codified in the Chemical Weapons Convention,[32] was the basis for their support of this finding.

While Russia was very reserved in its statements regarding 'threat to the peace' and *Resolution 2118 (2013)*, the same cannot be said for the US, which made bold statements regarding notions of justice and respect for international law.

---

23 United Nations Security Council, 3.

24 United Nations Security Council, 3.

25 United Nations Security Council, 3–4.

26 United Nations Security Council, 4.

27 United Nations Security Council, 4.

28 Resolution 2118 (2013), para. 1.

29 China's position regarding Resolution 2118 and Chapter VII is not explicit but can be seen through inference in their statement; United Nations Security Council, '7038th Meeting', 5–7 & 9–10.

30 United Nations Security Council, 3–4.

31 'All similar cases will be immediately considered by the Security Council with the objective of taking the necessary measures': United Nations Security Council, 4.

32 'Convention on the Prohibition of the Development, Production, Stockpiling and Use of Chemical Weapons and on Their Destruction', 1974 UNTS 85 (1992).

Their statement began with graphic descriptions of the horrific aftermath of the Syrian chemical weapons attack, claiming forcefully that 'the world's conscience was shocked'.[33] They followed this with proclamations that *Resolution 2118 (2013)* was precedent-setting in nature (a particularly brazen and unsettling approach, given that international law does not recognise precedent in a legal sense),[34] and that

> for the first time, that the use of chemical weapons, which the world long ago determined to be beyond the bounds of acceptable human behaviour, is also a threat to international peace and security, anywhere they might be used, any time they might be used, under any circumstances.[35]

The basis for these sweeping claims in support of such a wide-ranging resolution with indeterminable reach and consequences was the US position that the Security Council bore a responsibility to 'defend the defenceless'[36] from people who believe 'that they can use weapons of mass destruction with impunity'.[37] While they made no secret of the fact that their primary goal was the disarmament of chemical weapons held by the Syrian military, through force if necessary,[38] the US statements indicated that they were positively buoyant about achieving 'even more' through peaceful means in this resolution.[39] The basis of US support for the finding of 'threat to the peace' was thus grounded in notions of justice,[40] that 'actions must have consequences',[41] that the world's patience must be short when it comes to governments murdering their own citizens and that when this occurs,[42] it is the world's responsibility to bear the burden of preventing or ending mass killings of this nature.[43] The final justification, and possibly the most telling line, is the US claim 'that international norms matter'.[44]

The UK's expressed justification for *Resolution 2118 (2013)*, particularly the ongoing 'threat to the peace' declaration in operative paragraph 1, was brief,

33 United Nations Security Council, '7038th Meeting', 4.
34 United Nations Security Council, 4.
35 United Nations Security Council, 4.
36 United Nations Security Council, 4.
37 United Nations Security Council, 4.
38 United Nations Security Council, 4–5.
39 United Nations Security Council, 5.
40 United Nations Security Council, 5.
41 United Nations Security Council, 5.
42 United Nations Security Council, 5.
43 United Nations Security Council, 5.
44 United Nations Security Council, 5.

clinical and detached, but abundantly clear. It was grounded in their interpretation of the use of chemical weapons as a breach of *jus cogens*. They began by characterising the 21 August chemical weapons attack as a *jus cogens* violation in the form of war crimes.[45] On this basis, they established their support for creating 'an important international norm'[46] by which 'any use of chemical weapons is a threat to international peace and security'[47] through *Resolution 2118 (2013)*. Their position that it is the Security Council's role to undertake Chapter VII action in the event of non-compliance with the prohibition of chemical weapons use,[48] in the name of preventing atrocities,[49] was also clear in their statement.

The French statement echoed that of the US—they too made calls for justice and compliance with international law. They began with an emotive appeal to recognise the gravity of Syria's violation of the prohibition of the use of chemical weapons,[50] insinuating that it is the Security Council's responsibility to safeguard against such violations of international law.[51] The wide-reaching nature of operative paragraph 1 was not lost on the French; rather, it was a source of celebration for the victory of justice:

> The resolution identifies the use of chemical weapons as a threat to international peace and security. The Security Council can therefore act on this issue at any time in the future and will be the guarantor of chemical disarmament. The resolution clearly states that those responsible for such crimes must be held accountable for their actions and brought to justice.[52]

France also made clear that they would not shy away from undertaking Chapter VII action in the future after any violations of *Resolution 2118 (2013)* and the prohibition of the use of chemical weapons.[53] The remainder of the French

45 United Nations Security Council, 5.
46 United Nations Security Council, 5.
47 United Nations Security Council, 5.
48 United Nations Security Council, 6.
49 United Nations Security Council, 6.
50 United Nations Security Council, 7.
51 United Nations Security Council, 7; Arguably it is the role of the Security Council to maintain international peace and security, not to police violations of international law, although often the two will overlap: Karel Wellens, 'The UN Security Council and New Threats to the Peace: Back to the Future', *Journal of Conflict and Security Law* 8, no. 1 (2003): 31–32; 'Charter of the United Nations', 1 UNTS XVI (1945) Article 24(1).
52 United Nations Security Council, '7038th Meeting', 7.
53 United Nations Security Council, 7–8.

statement was used as an opportunity to criticise the Security Council for its long-term lack of meaningful action in response to the Syrian conflict, particularly in the face of 'humanitarian catastrophe and repression',[54] irrespective of the fact that the resolution itself was not focused on this issue.

China's statements on *Resolution 2118 (2013)* were telling and terse, focused on respect for international law. They began by emphasising the need for the Security Council to always act within the Purposes and Principles of the Charter.[55] They confirmed this by reiterating their position of non-intervention in the affairs of other states, and their manifest preference for the pacific settlements of disputes.[56] Their support for *Resolution 2118 (2013)* was therefore made on the basis that it supported peaceful and political settlement of the Syrian crisis,[57] in addition to supporting international law in the form of the prohibition of the use of chemical weapons.[58] After making this brief statement regarding the grounds for their support of the resolution, China used the remainder of its statement to reaffirm the Chinese view that '[p]olitical settlement is the only way out for Syria'.[59]

4 Summary of Coding

All P5 members supported a finding of 'threat to the peace' in relation to the use of chemical weapons. Russia's support was made wholly on the basis that using these weapons constituted a violation of international law. The UK used formal legal arguments to state that a finding based on the use of chemical weapons constituting an international law violation was necessary to protect human rights. China's support was grounded in their desire for peaceful solutions in accordance with the Purposes and Principles of the Charter. France argued that the use of chemical weapons constituted a violation of the Purposes and Principles of the Charter and of international law more generally, placing it within the Security Council's mandate, and that a finding of 'threat to the peace' supported the rule of law and peaceful solutions to conflict in

54 United Nations Security Council, 8.
55 United Nations Security Council, 9.
56 'China opposes the use of force in international relations. We believe that military means cannot solve the Syrian issue; rather, they would lead to greater turmoil and disaster'.: United Nations Security Council, 9.
57 United Nations Security Council, 9.
58 United Nations Security Council, 9–10.
59 United Nations Security Council, 10.

accordance with all relevant laws. The US used a combination of formal legal arguments and emotive rhetoric to state that the use of chemical weapons constituted a violation of international law, and a finding of 'threat to the peace' was thus a natural consequence. They also argued that such a finding supported the rule of law and the protection of human rights.

PART 3

Meta-synthesis

CHAPTER 25

Meta-Synthesis Overview

At this point in the book, a strong set of case studies has articulated the diverse approaches that the P5 have taken to date in relation to the question of 'threat to the peace' within the confines of the Security Council. While individually, each is insightful in terms of the resolutions (or lack thereof) created by the Security Council, the broader question guiding this project is whether there is any pattern or consistency to these decisions. The remainder of the book focuses on this question; first, I must explain how this question is explored.

Lawyers have often sought to use the specific to articulate the general; indeed, this is the underlying basis of the concept of precedent within the common law legal system, where specific individual cases are used to create binding general legal propositions. With the exception of vague analogies to customary international law, such a principle does not exist in the domain of public international law. That said, it is equally clear that international lawyers have nevertheless sought methods by which to contextualise and parse specific situations to articulate general legal principles in an authoritative manner. Henderson, for example, did this in relation to Australian Defence Force (ADF) concepts of rank and competence levels within the legal corps.[1] He achieved this by taking a case study on specific roles undertaken by ADF lawyers and used a logical extrapolation of this specific case study to explain the general duties required by the different competence levels of military lawyers within the ADF. In doing so, he argued that the case study details demonstrated the more general concepts contained within the idea of competence levels in a manner very akin to common law methods of precedent. However, this method is completely unsuitable for this project, as it relies upon using a single case study to formulate the pinnacle definition of the general principles being articulated. Such a process is obviously inapplicable here, as the case studies demonstrate the varied and imprecise nature of the P5's justifications surrounding the concept of 'threat to the peace'.

McLaughlin also explores this idea of the relationship between the specific and the general when discussing the process of providing operational legal

1 Ian Henderson, 'Legal Officers in the Australian Defence Force: Functions by Rank and Competency Levels, along with a Case-Study on Operations', *Military Law and the Law of War Review* 50, no. 1 (2011): 37.

 DOI:10.1163/9789004391420_027

advice as a military lawyer.[2] He focuses intently upon practical outcomes that satisfy the demands of the law and the expectations of public policy, as well as the goals of the commander receiving the advice. This method is also unsatisfying and unhelpful when trying to understand how the P5 approach the question of 'threat to the peace', because McLaughlin's work in this instance concentrates on how best to translate clear and concrete general principles to specific situations that may not neatly mesh with these concepts. By contrast, the issue confronted in this book is that the specifics are clear, while the general is still uncertain.

Dickinson has also contributed to this field of work on understanding military lawyers' international law compliance in battlefield situations.[3] She uses organisational theory to understand how the monolithic organisation of the US military generally, and the various Judge Advocate General's Corps specifically, create an individually anchored culture of compliance within the organisation. While use of organisational theory is well accepted in many disciplines, it is not analogously appropriate to the current situation. This is because organisational theory presupposes and relies upon the concept of a monolithic organisation that exercises a measure of dominance, power and control over the individuals contained within it, which in turn shapes its members' culture and behaviour. While it could theoretically be argued that the UN is such an institution, to suggest that the P5 are controlled by the UN, rather than that the P5 control the UN—or at least the Security Council—themselves is a proposition that would be difficult to defend (although it could be wholly appropriate for a study on the UN Secretariat). Organisational theory is thus of little assistance in understanding the bigger picture created by the case studies included in this book.

While the general approaches lawyers use are unhelpful in making sense of P5 approaches to the concept of 'threat to the peace' as explored in the case studies here, sociology does provide a tool for such an exploration. Meta-synthesis, which was first used in 1994 (and is thus a relatively new form of analysis),[4] provides a framework through which groups of qualitative data studies can be used to explore more general principles. The concept of meta-synthesis hinges on the idea that the case studies represent 'multi-layered

2 Rob McLaughlin, '"Giving" Operational Legal Advice: Context and Method', *Military Law and the Law of War Review* 50 (2011): 99.

3 Laura A. Dickinson, 'Military Lawyers on the Battlefield: An Empirical Account of International Law Compliance', *American Journal of International Law* 104, no. 1 (2010): 1.

4 Janet Heaton, 'Secondary Analysis of Qualitative Data: An Overview', *Historical Social Research* 33, no. 3 (2008): 36.

context which can be peeled back to reveal generative processes of phenomena not glimpsed in standalone studies'.[5] Indeed, 'the purpose of a qualitative synthesis would be to achieve greater understanding and attain a level conceptual or theoretical development beyond that which is achieved in any empirical study'.[6] Such a method seems entirely appropriate for addressing the question of understanding to be gleaned from case studies of the P5's general approaches to the question of 'threat to the peace'. This is because it provides a method of understanding the bigger-picture themes that connect the individual case studies, and thus our understanding of the Security Council's operations and tendencies.

The concept of meta-synthesis emerged from qualitative researchers' desire to have within their methodological armoury a means of understanding the broader implications of multiple related studies, similar to the way in which quantitative researchers use meta-analysis. In line with this need, the methodology has been used extensively in medical sociology and anthropology to understand patterns in narrative and subjective areas of medical practice.[7] The primary difference between meta-synthesis and meta-analysis, however, is not the use of qualitative versus quantitative data, but the different goals and purposes of the two different types of analysis. While meta-analysis seeks to aggregate data to increase certainty in the conclusions of individual studies, meta-synthesis seeks to provide greater understanding and explanation for general phenomena.[8] While this methodology has generally been employed in the fields of medical sociology and medical anthropology, there is no reason it cannot be used as a tool of legal sociology to understand the phenomena of 'threat to the peace'.

5 Denis Walsh and Soo Downe, 'Meta-Synthesis Method for Qualitative Research: A Literature Review', *Journal of Advanced Nursing* 50, no. 2 (2005): 205.

6 Rona Campbell et al., 'Evaluating Meta-Ethnography: A Synthesis of Qualitative Research on Lay Experiences of Diabetes and Diabetes Care', *Social Science & Medicine* 56 (2003): 672.

7 See for example: Myfanwy Lloyd Jones, 'Role Development and Effective Practice in Specialist and Advanced Practice Roles in Acute Hospital Settings: Systematic Review and Meta-Synthesis', *Journal of Advanced Nursing* 49, no. 2: 191; K Whalley Hammell, 'Quality of Life after Spinal Cord Injury: A Meta-Synthesis of Qualitative Findings', *Spinal Cord* 45 (2007): 124; Donna Clemmens, 'Adolescent Motherhood: A Meta-Synthesis of Qualitative Studies', *American Journal of Maternal Child Nursing* 28, no. 2 (April 2003): 93; Hanne Aagaard and Elisabeth O.C. Hall, 'Mothers' Experiences of Having a Preterm Infant in the Neonatal Care Unit: A Meta-Synthesis', *Journal of Pediatric Nursing* 23, no. 3 (June 2008): e26; Katherine Salter et al., 'The Experience of Living with Stroke: A Qualitative Meta-Synthesis', *Journal of Rehabilitation Medicine* 40, no. 8 (September 2008): 595.

8 Walsh and Downe, 'Meta-Synthesis Method for Qualitative Research', 204–05.

Given its relative infancy when compared with other more established analysis methods, meta-synthesis lacks a fixed methodology.[9] However, the general qualitative sociological principles of analysis are still applied, albeit on a different layer. Rather than coding and analysing individual primary source material to create a coherent individual study (which has been done throughout the case studies here via the Security Council meeting transcripts), meta-synthesis treats the interpretations and explanations of the individual studies as its data source to then be coded and analysed.[10] In this project, this means that each of the included case studies represents the materials to be coded and then analysed within the meta-synthesis sections of the book. Thus, the interpretive explanations of the primary source material that created each individual case study then become the source material for the meta-synthesis. Through this process, the individual meanings in each case study are placed in a larger context, which assists in understanding the greater question of whether there is any pattern or consistency in the approaches of each individual P5 member state regarding the question of 'threat to the peace'.

Consequently, this meta-synthesis is a method of ordering and holistically assessing the coded justifications given by each P5 member in these case studies regarding their position on the existence, or lack thereof, of a 'threat to the peace'. The process of coding only categorises the P5 responses to the question of 'threat to the peace' into general themes of justification employed across all the case studies (the results of this coding can be found in Annex 1 and are summarised at the end of each case study). By then separating each of the case studies into the responses by each individual member, rather than by the Security Council as a whole, I have created a means to visualise the recurring general justifications of each P5 member. This required creating a categorisation system for each case study outcome, as previous studies on 'threat to the peace' have only examined positive findings.[11]

The intuitive categories of positive finding and negative finding are a false dichotomy, and unhelpful in terms of understanding each P5 member's approach to the existence of a 'threat to the peace'. This is because the position taken by an individual P5 state did not necessarily correlate with the eventual finding of the Security Council as a whole. This notionally created four separate categories of enquiry: positive finding where the state supported such a finding; positive finding where the state did not support such a finding; negative finding where the state supported such a finding; and negative finding

9 Nicky Britten et al., 'Using Meta Ethnography to Synthesise Qualitative Research: A Worked Example', *Journal of Health Services Research and Policy* 7, no. 4 (October 2002): 210.

10 Britten et al., 210.

11 See Chapter 1 for details.

where the state did not support such a finding. While notionally, these four categories exist, the goal of understanding how each individual P5 member approaches the question of 'threat to the peace' renders the actual outcome of the individual case studies irrelevant to the meta-synthesis. What is important to understanding the approach of each P5 member is the position that they took either in support of, or in opposition to, a finding of 'threat to the peace'. For example, it does not matter that there was a failure to determine that the US- and UK-led invasion of Iraq was a 'threat to the peace' when considering how France, Russia and China approach the possible existence of a 'threat to the peace'. What matters is that they all supported a finding, and the reasons each state gave for their support.[12] This is because my goal in this book is not to create a metric of when the Security Council decided if a 'threat to the peace' existed (this could be done in a matter of days with a spreadsheet and a lot of reading). Instead, my goal is to understand, based upon the justificatory discourse provided by the P5 states, how they make their decisions regarding the possible existence of a 'threat to the peace'. This renders the overall consensus outcome irrelevant. Two categories of enquiry thus emerge in the meta-synthesis related to each individual P5 member: whether they supported a finding of 'threat to the peace' or whether they did not. Through the meta-synthesis process, a third category emerged within the majority of P5 states: general approaches existing within both categories, such as the US using the gravity of the situation at hand to justify both support and opposition to a finding of 'threat to the peace' (discussed anon).

Further, a meta-synthesis of the Security Council's general approaches as a whole, which is particularly focused on creating context and the P5's responses to the Secretariat and other formal meeting sources of information, would not conform to these categories; rather, it addresses the role of the facts in justificatory discourse and the role of outside recommendations in decisions. Given the undefined nature of the meta-synthesis methodologies (and the fact that this is a first-of-its-kind study in the legal field, and into the P5's justificatory discourse), for the sake of consistency throughout the different meta-syntheses and varying contexts of the case studies, I have opted to require that justification occurs in at least three relevant instances and in at least 25% of the relevant instances to be considered recurring and pattern-forming.[13]

12 See Chapter 20 for details.

13 For example, should a member of the P5 find themselves in opposition to a finding of 'threat to the peace' in six of the case studies, for their justification to constitute a pattern, that justification will need to have been used in three of those six case studies to satisfy both the recurrence of a minimum of three times and a recurrence in at least 25% of the relevant case studies.

CHAPTER 26

General Meta-Synthesis Observations

1 Overview

In this chapter, I address the patterns that emerge in the context-forming sections of the case studies. The importance of this step is that each situation's context informed all the decisions made regarding that situation; thus, if patterns exist in how the context was formed and presented to the Security Council, this has a flow-on effect on how the P5 approach the question of 'threat to the peace'. The two main issues that arise from the context-forming sections of the case studies are the question of how the situation's facts were provided to the Security Council, and the recommendations made to the Security Council by the Secretary-General following the presentation of the facts. The discussion below focuses predominantly on the patterns that emerge and their effect; while I hypothesise the reason behind these patterns, ultimately, the question of why they exist is beyond the scope of this project. Rather, it is this project's goal to establish whether there are any patterns and consistency in how the Security Council approaches the concept of 'threat to the peace', so while the question of why patterns emerge is inherently and intensely interesting, it is less relevant for this analysis than the existence of the patterns themselves—the 'why' question in relation to these patterns is one for further study rather than for this book.

2 The Facts of the Matter

The question of how facts provided the context for Security Council meetings can be divided into three categories, although two of them are indistinguishable from each other. The first category is situations where all of the facts providing context for the meetings originated from a UN source, either from within the Secretariat or from a specially mandated fact-finding committee. The second of these categories, which, for practical matters, has no real difference from the first, is situations where the facts were presented from both a UN-mandated source and from other parties that had some involvement with the situation in question. The reason this bears little or no consideration separate from the question of facts from a UN source is that generally, in these situations, the facts from the non-UN-mandated source served to prompt the

 | DOI:10.1163/9789004391420_028

UN fact-finding mission, or expand upon the facts already presented by the UN from the affected party's perspective. The final category is situations where all of the facts providing context for the UN Security Council debates were derived from non-UN sources—often the parties to the situation themselves.

Situations where the factual context of the debates was provided by a UN-mandated fact-finding group, or in a hybrid manner from both UN sources and non-UN sources, constitute the vast majority of the case studies (15 of the 22 case studies, covering 19 situations). There is no pattern to these case studies suggesting that fact-finding from a UN source leads to a greater likelihood of a 'threat to the peace' finding. What is worth noting is the decline in situations that drew upon non-UN sources for establishing context of the debates. In the case studies covered in this project, every one after 1993 drew its context from UN sources, sometimes supplemented by non-UN sources, usually from parties intimately involved in the situation. For example, this is evident in relation to Syria, where a good portion of the factual context was provided by the League of Arab States regarding their efforts to implement a ceasefire and bring about peace,[1] or in relation to the WMD case studies and the DPRK's statements after their nuclear test.[2] The most likely explanation for the normalisation of UN-based fact-finding for the Security Council since the early 1990s is the well-documented expansion of Security Council activity since the end of the Cold War;[3] however, given the prevalence of UN-based fact-finding in situations where the question of 'threat to the peace' was not a foregone conclusion, this pattern, while interesting, seems to have no bearing on how the P5 make this decision.

The situation for case studies in which all context was provided by non-UN sources is less clear. Six of the 22 case studies in this project had their entire factual context provided by non-UN sources, usually the principal parties to the situation in question (although in the case of Iraq in 1991, it was provided by the states affected by the refugee flows resulting from the internal strife in Iraq). At first glance, there appears to be nothing of note when considering situations where the entire factual context was derived from non-UN sources.

1 See Chapter 23.
2 See Chapter 19.
3 See for example: Michael J. Glennon, 'Why the Security Council Failed', *Foreign Affairs* 82 (2003): 31; Christopher J. Le Mon and Rachel S. Taylor, 'Security Council Action in the Name of Human Rights: From Rhodesia to the Congo', *U.C. Davis Journal of International Law & Policy* 10, no. 2 (2004): 199–200; Inger Österdahl, *Threat to the Peace: The Interpretation by the Security Council of Article 39 of the UN Charter* (Uppsala: Iustus, 1998), 10–15; Karel Wellens, 'The UN Security Council and New Threats to the Peace: Back to the Future', *Journal of Conflict and Security Law* 8, no. 1 (2003): 28.

Of the five situations, three resulted in positive findings of 'threat to the peace' and the other two were not considered to warrant such a finding. This initial assessment suggests that—much like the situations where the facts were derived predominantly from UN sources—this has no real effect on how the P5 make their decisions. This is likely, but would need to be confirmed through further studies on situations where facts were provided by parties to a bilateral or multilateral dispute.

A closer examination of the three situations that resulted in positive findings, where all the facts were derived from non-UN sources, shows that each situation can be distinguished as unique. Consequently, this uniqueness led to the finding of 'threat to the peace', and distinguishes each of these situations from the rest of the case studies, where a positive finding occurred when the facts were presented solely by non-UN sources. In the case of Iraq in 1991,[4] the facts presented to the Security Council—leading to the finding of 'threat to the peace'—came from Turkey and were supplemented by Iran, with both commenting on high levels of internal Iraqi oppression of the civilian population causing refugee flows across their borders. While not present in this case study, entirely relevant, as it distinguishes it from others in this category, is the fact that about a week prior to these meetings, the Secretary-General provided the Security Council with a report on the effect of Iraq's occupation of Kuwait.[5] This report contained numerous mentions of the effects of the Iraqi repression during their occupation, and the high levels of displaced people generated as a result of this violence. Given that the report raised similar issues to those being raised by Turkey and Iran, but one week prior, and the fact that these issues were creating refugee flows akin to those seen in Kuwait, it is reasonable to suggest that Turkey and Iran's credibility in relation to these claims was significantly bolstered by the Secretary-General's report. Thus, while the case study relied upon facts only presented by non-UN sources, it actually bears greater resemblance to those case studies where the factual context was delivered by UN sources, although it was supported by facts from the affected parties.

The other two situations that can be distinguished as sui generis in terms of their factual context and the finding of 'threat to the peace' are the sanctions placed on Haiti in 1993,[6] and the action taken for Yugoslavia in 1991.[7]

4 See Chapter 10

5 United Nations Secretary-General, 'Report of the Secretary-General on Humanitarian Needs in Kuwait in the Immediate Post-Crisis Environment by a Mission to the Area Led by Mr. Martii Ahtisaari, Under-Secretary-General for Administration and Management, Dated 28 March 1991' (New York: United Nations, 28 March 1991).

6 See Chapter 12.

7 See Chapter 11.

In both these situations, the facts were presented to the Security Council by the head of state of the country affected by the finding. Further, in presenting the facts in both these situations, each head of state specifically requested Security Council action under Chapter VII, and thus a preconditional finding of 'threat to the peace', in relation to the ongoing situation in their state. In both situations, the Security Council's finding hinged on (respectively) Yugoslav and Haitian consent for Security Council Chapter VII action in relation to their internal conflicts. This distinguishes these situations from the three remaining case studies, where the facts were presented entirely by parties affected by the dispute who brought their versions of the facts before the Security Council.

In the two remaining case studies where facts were presented before the Security Council by parties to the dispute, it must be noted that both situations, the Security Council declined to make a finding of 'threat to the peace' and take Chapter VII action. In both situations, the facts were presented by opposing parties to an interstate dispute, ranging from border skirmishes[8] to full-blown invasion and purported establishment of a puppet government.[9] Both situations resulted in either a veto by one of the P5, or veiled and inferred threats of a veto by one of the P5. While there is not enough evidence to suggest a pattern of behaviour from the Security Council, these case studies suggest that further investigation would be valuable to determine if such a pattern might exist. While the use of UN-mandated fact-finding in Security Council deliberations seems to have no discernible influence on the outcome, its absence in bilateral and multilateral disputes may do so; however, further study would be required to determine if this is the case.

3 The Effect of Recommendations

The other key issue arising from the context sections of the case studies is the effect and role that fact-finding recommendations have upon the Security Council, particularly in terms of how the P5 deal with such recommendations. Eight of the twenty-two case studies featured recommendations from the Secretary-General or UN-appointed fact-finding body to inform the Security Council of the situation. Nominally, the Security Council followed three of these eight recommendations; however, two these situations (apartheid and Rwanda) can be distinguished because of the events surrounding the Security Council's decision to follow the recommendation (see immediately below).

8 See Chapter 5.

9 See Chapter 7.

Further, the remaining situation (the Spanish Franco regime) can also be distinguished, as it was the only situation that recommended the Security Council should not find a 'threat to the peace'.

The apartheid case study is distinguishable because of the huge time lag between the Security Council's decision to make a finding of 'threat to the peace', and the fact-finding body's recommendation that such a finding was appropriate and necessary.[10] The eventual finding of 'threat to the peace' and Chapter VII action against South Africa for its policy of apartheid occurred as a result of *Resolution 418 (1977)*. This stands in stark contrast to the recommendation that such a finding be made by the Special Committee on Apartheid in March 1964 and then again in May 1964. This gap of more than 13 years between recommendation and decision suggests that the recommendation had little or no bearing on the P5's eventual decision.

The Rwanda case study can also be distinguished because of the P5's decision to blatantly ignore the Secretary-General's recommendation for a finding of 'threat to the peace' and increased peacekeeping forces under a Chapter VII mandate.[11] This decision to ignore the Secretary-General's recommendation was reversed four weeks later after evidence of continuing heavy fighting as well as mass killings of civilians and exponential increases of internally displaced peoples as a result of the ongoing civil war and genocide. While the P5, and the Security Council as a whole, did eventually follow the Secretary-General's recommendation, it was only after glaring evidence that their decision to ignore the initial recommendation likely contributed significantly to the deterioration within Rwanda. As with the apartheid case study, it is difficult to characterise the decision to find a 'threat to the peace' in Rwanda being linked to the recommendations from the Secretary-General's fact-finding.

With the decisions on apartheid and Rwanda distinguished on the basis that factually, the fact-finding body's recommendations had little immediate influence on the P5's decisions, an interesting pattern emerges in relation to these recommendations. Of the remaining six recommendations within the case studies in this project, only one was followed by the Security Council: the situation of the Spanish Franco regime, where the fact-finding body recommended that no action be taken.[12] In the other five situations (Iran hostage crisis, small arms trade, US- and UK-led invasion of Iraq in 2003, sexual violence as a tactic of armed conflict and the Syrian Civil War),[13] recommendations were made to

10 See Chapter 6.
11 See Chapter 14.
12 See Chapter 3.
13 See Chapters 8, 17, 20, 21 and 23 respectively.

the Security Council that the situation before them should constitute a 'threat to the peace'. In each of these situations, the P5 found reasons to justify a determination that this was not, in fact, the case. Indeed, when taken holistically, it would seem that the act of recommending that the Security Council make a finding of 'threat to the peace' leads to the reverse outcome. While the justifications in each individual situation in which the Security Council ignored these recommendations may seem reasonable, when taken as a whole, the pattern suggests that the act of recommending that the Security Council make a positive finding of 'threat to the peace' causes the P5 to have a petulant and contrary reaction. A possible reason for this reaction is the Security Council's desire to reassert its power over the Secretariat by reminding the Secretary-General that the Security Council bears the responsibility for maintaining international peace and security; however, this would require a dedicated empirical study to determine, as it is a question beyond the scope of this book.

CHAPTER 27

Team America: World Police?

1 Overview

In this section, I analyse the US approaches to the concept of 'threat to the peace' under Article 39 of the UN Charter. As outlined in Chapter 25, the approaches identified in the case study data can be usefully classified into two separate categories of analysis of approach: situations where a finding of 'threat to the peace' was supported, and situations where a finding of 'threat to the peace' was opposed. Interestingly, in the case of the US, no case studies had a positive finding that the US opposed. Because of this, the data where the US opposed a finding of 'threat to the peace' is a much smaller sample (this is telling in and of itself; however, I address this anon). I also provide general observations on the approaches the US took regarding the question of 'threat to the peace', regardless of the outcome they advocated; by doing so in conjunction with their support and opposition justificatory discourse, I am able to provide a more complete picture of their approaches.

2 General Observations

When observing the overall data from the US in relation to 'threat to the peace' without noting whether they supported or opposed a finding, two general observations can be made regarding their approach to the question. The first observation is the style of argument that the US employed, beginning with legal formalism at the end of World War II and throughout the Cold War, but shifting to more emotive rhetoric in the 1990s. The second observation is the factor that seems key to US decision-making: the gravity of the situation.

When analysing the data as a whole, an interesting pattern arises regarding the US's argument style. The early case studies (indeed, up until 1980) indicate that stylistically, the US's arguments conformed closely to generally accepted ideas of legal formalism[1] in their structure and tone. In four of the six case

1 In the context of this book I refer to legal formalism as the standard legal practice of applying the relevant laws to the facts at hand in as objective and dispassionate way as possible in order to reach a logical conclusion based upon those rules. This is in line with the conceptions black letter law and legal positivism outline in Chapter 1.

 DOI:10.1163/9789004391420_029

studies between 1946 and 1983, the US used these formalistic legal arguments when making their case in the Security Council. The first instance was in relation to Palestine, where the US dissected the content of Article 39 of the Charter, arguing that the use of the word 'shall' placed a burden upon the Security Council to make a determination should one exist, rather than leaving them with an option to do so.[2] Similarly, formal legal arguments appear again in the Portuguese African territories case study, where the US discussed the correct procedure for Senegal to bring a complaint against Portugal in the Security Council.[3] Formal legal arguments were applied again in the early stages of the apartheid debates, where the US argued that in spite of their disagreement with South Africa over the policy of apartheid, Article 2(7) of the Charter prohibited Security Council action against South Africa.[4] Finally, formal legal arguments once more took centre stage in US justifications during the Iran hostage crisis, where they contended that the new Iranian Government could not seek the benefits of the law while they were also systematically violating it.[5] However, subsequent to this, and with the exception of a brief throwaway use of a legal maxim in the small arms debates ('hard cases do not make good law'),[6] the US did not employ formal legal arguments again after the Iran hostage crisis.

The US started commonly employing an argument style featuring more emotive rhetoric[7] to support their position with the Libya case study in 1992;[8] this approach continued with regularity from that point onwards. From its beginnings in 1992, the use of emotive rhetoric-style arguments appears in seven of the 12 case studies discussed in this volume. In the case of Libya, this approach is clearly evident in the language the US chose to characterise the Lockerbie bombing—they used emotive arguments as a basis to contend that

2 See Chapter 4.
3 See Chapter 5.
4 See Chapter 6.
5 See Chapter 8.
6 United Nations Security Council, 'Security Council, Sixty-Third Year: 5881st Meeting (S/PV.5881)' (United Nations, 30 April 2008), 15.
7 When discussing emotive rhetoric I refer to language that, *prima facie*, has been employed with the intent of appealing to the heart strings of the audience and convince them that the position being advocated through emotional manipulation rather than logical argument. I acknowledge that the existence of emotive rhetoric is a subjective interpretation of the transcripts and contextual in nature. With this in mind, I have included quotes that demonstrate the emotive rhetoric within the case studies and have included quotes where possible within the meta-synthesis chapters.
8 See Chapter 13.

ordinary legal procedures were inapplicable.[9] In the Afghanistan case study in 1999, the US's emotive rhetoric is most strongly apparent in their statements describing Osama bin Laden and the Taliban.[10] Similarly, this sort of language is also evident in the East Timor case study, particularly in the graphic language used to describe the plight of the East Timorese people at the hands of pro-Indonesian militia after the independence vote.[11] When arguing in the debates surrounding sexual violence as a tactic of war, emotive-style rhetoric is apparent in US descriptions of the plight of sexual violence victims in a wartime environment and the effect this has upon them and the community.[12] In relation to piracy, both in Somalia and the Gulf of Guinea, the US chose emotive rhetoric to describe the character of the pirates themselves and their effect upon society.[13] When discussing the Syrian Civil War, the US employed emotive rhetoric on two separate fronts: first, in relation to the violence within Syria itself, and second, in relation to the vetoes being deployed by China and Russia.[14] Finally, in the chemical weapons case study, the US used highly emotive rhetoric when describing the effect of chemical weapons attacks in the Syrian Civil War.[15]

While this shift in argument style is abundantly clear when the data are subjected to the meta-synthesis of all the case studies, what is not clear from this meta-synthesis is the cause of this shift. Given the timing of this change in argument style, it would be reasonable to suggest that the end of the Cold War and the collapse of the Soviet Union was the catalyst, if not a core reason, for the change (the period between Iran in 1980 and Iraq in 1991 is an uncertainty because of the lack of case studies during this time to more precisely ascertain the point of shift). This hypothesis supports Glennon's analysis of US

9 The US referred to the Lockerbie bombing as "ghastly" and as "Libya's wanton and criminal destruction of civil aviation". Above at Chapter 13.

10 For example: "[this resolution] will send a direct message to Usama bin Laden, and terrorists everywhere, 'you can run, you can hide, but you will be brought to justice'". Above at Chapter 15.

11 For example: "militia – clearly backed by elements of the military of Indonesia – took to the streets and began a murderous rampage". Above at Chapter 16.

12 For example: "When women and girls are preyed upon and raped, the international community cannot be silent or inactive. It is our responsibility to be their advocates and their defenders"; and "[the] troubling dynamic of men with guns forgiving other men with guns for crimes committed against women". Above at Chapter 21.

13 For example: "the scourge of piracy". Above at Chapter 22.

14 For example: "[the] outrageous and ongoing use of violence against peaceful protesters"; "cries for freedom of expression, association, peaceful assembly and the ability to freely choose their leaders"; and "yearning for liberty and universal human rights". Above at Chapter 23.

15 For example: "the world's conscience was shocked". Above at Chapter 24.

conduct in the Security Council after the end of the Cold War: that the fall of the Soviet Union left the US emboldened to conduct themselves as the moral authority of the world with little regard for international legal norms, treating the Security Council as a formality that could be ignored rather than a global authority.[16] However, as interesting as it is to dissect such a cultural shift within US international relations and foreign policy, this investigation is beyond the scope of this book.

The other area in which the general meta-synthesis of the US arguments regarding the concept of 'threat to the peace' reveals a distinct pattern, regardless of whether they supported or opposed a finding, is the idea of the gravity of the situation. The US used the argument that the situation was or was not sufficiently grave to warrant a finding of 'threat to the peace' by the Security Council in 10 of the 22 case studies. This figure represents approximately 45% of the case studies in this volume, and the percentage is relatively stable when considering situations where the US opposed such a finding as well as situations where the US advocated for such a finding. In three of the seven situations where the US opposed a finding of 'threat to the peace' (Spain in 1946, the Portuguese African territories in 1963 and apartheid before 1977),[17] a core argument was that the situation lacked sufficient gravity for Security Council action. Similarly, in seven of the 16 situations where the US supported a finding of 'threat to the peace' (Palestine in 1948, the Iran hostage crisis in 1979–80, civil war in Yugoslavia in 1991, the Rwandan Civil War and genocide in 1993–94, AIDS and peacekeeping in 2000–05, sexual violence in armed conflict 2008–10 and WMDs 2002–06),[18] the US deployed the core argument that the situation was sufficiently grave to warrant Security Council action. Their consistency in using this argument demonstrates that they consider it a key principle when approaching the question of a 'threat to the peace'; however, there is a lack of clarity surrounding what factors are taken into account when considering the gravity of any given situation.

3 Opposition to a Finding

Of the 26 situations covered in the 22 case studies, the US opposed a finding of 'threat to the peace' on seven separate occasions (totalling eight situations

16 See generally: Michael J. Glennon, 'Why the Security Council Failed', *Foreign Affairs* 82 (2003): 16.

17 See Chapters 3, 5 and 6 respectively.

18 See Chapters 4, 8, 11, 14, 18, 21 and 22 respectively.

overall): the Spanish Franco regime in 1946,[19] the Portuguese African territories in 1963,[20] apartheid prior to 1977 (although the US eventually supported a finding a 'threat to the peace' in relation to apartheid; their initial position was one of clear opposition to such a finding, and thus must be considered in this section),[21] the South African occupation of Namibia in 1981–83,[22] action against the small arms trade in 1999–2011,[23] the US- and UK-led invasion of Iraq in 2003[24] and piracy in Somalia and the Gulf of Guinea in 2008–12 (while Chapter VII action was taken against Somali piracy, this was done under the auspices of the 1992 resolutions relating to the civil war in the wake of the Barre regime's collapse, rather than against piracy itself).[25] This breakdown between support and opposition is telling, indicating the US's propensity to generally favour Security Council action in response to potential 'threats to the peace'. Within this dataset, a number of thematic arguments can be identified, although only four recur sufficiently to constitute a pattern. One of these is legal formalism as an argument style, as addressed above. The other themes can be classified as a lack of faith in the proposed solution, considerations regarding the gravity of the situation and advocating for a peaceful solution through negotiation and diplomacy. The effect of this predisposition is that while the US will use individual arguments in specific situations in which they oppose a finding, in line with context, these three recurring arguments provide a guiding baseline for helping to understand when the US will oppose a finding of 'threat to the peace'.

US arguments stating a lack of faith in the solution proposed occurred in relation to the Portuguese African territories in 1963, the South African occupation of Namibia in 1981–83 and action against the small arms trade in 1999–2011. In each of these situations, one of the core arguments used to defend the US position of opposition to a finding of 'threat to the peace' was that they did not believe the solutions being proposed under Chapter VII of the Charter would improve the situation, or lead to any meaningful change. Regarding the Portuguese African territories and the South African occupation of Namibia, the basis for this lack of faith was grounded in the supposition that Chapter VII

19 See Chapter 3.
20 See Chapter 5.
21 See Chapter 6.
22 See Chapter 9.
23 See Chapter 17.
24 See Chapter 20.
25 See Chapter 22.

action would escalate the situation and cause greater harm and suffering rather than resolve the problem. Regarding the small arms trade, this lack of faith was grounded in the position that a blanket, overarching response to the situation would be impractical and that measures had be implemented on a case-by-case basis through individual arms embargoes relating to specific conflict situations. This recurring lack of faith in the proposed solution in US arguments opposing a finding of 'threat to the peace' suggests that US support for a finding, and subsequent Security Council-based action, requires their being convinced that the action being proposed will bring about meaningful change and improve the situation.

The second argument that features frequently in US opposition to a finding of 'threat to the peace' is that the situation lacked sufficient gravity to warrant a finding and subsequent Chapter VII action. This position was taken in relation to the Spanish Franco regime in 1946, the Portuguese African territories in 1963 and apartheid prior to 1977. In each of these situations, the US argued that based on the facts before the Security Council, the situation did not meet the undefined gravity threshold to warrant and prompt Security Council action in the form of a finding of 'threat to the peace'. What is unclear from this collection of arguments is what in fact makes a situation sufficiently grave to warrant US support for a finding of 'threat to the peace'; however, what is clear (especially when considering that this argument crops up regularly in situations where the US support such a finding, as explored below) is that if the US is not convinced that a situation meets this amorphous gravity threshold, they will not support Security Council action.

The final argument consistently apparent when the US opposed a finding of 'threat to the peace' is the notion that a peaceful solution should be found through negotiation and diplomatic action. This position was advocated in relation to the Portuguese African territories in 1963, apartheid prior to 1977 and the South African occupation of Namibia in 1981–83. Interestingly, there is a positive correlation of arguments for a peaceful solution in two situations where the US did not find the situation to be sufficiently grave to warrant Chapter VII action (Portuguese African territories in 1963, and apartheid prior to 1977), and in two situations where the US lacked faith in the proposed solution (Portuguese African territories in 1963, and the South African occupation of Namibia in 1981–83). A close reading of these situations suggests that rather advocating for a peaceful solution being used as an independent argument against a finding of 'threat to the peace', the US instead posed this as an alternate solution to the situation when they were disinclined to support Security Council action under Chapter VII.

4 Support for a Finding

Of the 22 case studies, covering 26 different situations, the US supported a finding of 'threat to the peace' in 16 of these case studies (amounting to 19 of the 26 situations addressed in this book): Palestine in 1948,[26] apartheid after Black Wednesday in 1977,[27] the Vietnamese incursion into Cambodia in 1978–79,[28] the Iran hostage crisis in 1979–80,[29] Iraq in 1991,[30] the civil war in Yugoslavia in 1991,[31] Haiti in 1991–93,[32] Libya and the Lockerbie bombing in 1992,[33] the Rwandan Civil War and genocide in 1993–94,[34] Afghanistan in 1999,[35] East Timor independence in 1999,[36] AIDS and peacekeeping in 2000–05,[37] WMDs and non-proliferation in 2002–06,[38] sexual violence as a tactic of armed conflict in 2008–10,[39] the Syrian Civil War in 2011–13[40] and chemical weapons in 2013.[41] Before exploring the patterns that existed in their arguments in favour of 'threat to the peace' findings, it is worth observing that in situations where the existence of a 'threat to the peace' was not considered self-evident by the whole Security Council, the US predominantly spoke in favour of Security Council action on matters, evidenced by their tendency to support more than oppose a finding. Further, it is also worth noting that this preference for Security Council action has increased over time; the case studies show that in the Security Council's early stages, the US was disinclined to support findings of a 'threat to the peace', with this reluctance fading to almost nonexistence by the early 1990s.

26 See Chapter 4.
27 See Chapter 6.
28 See Chapter 7.
29 See Chapter 8.
30 See Chapter 10.
31 See Chapter 11.
32 See Chapter 12.
33 See Chapter 13.
34 See Chapter 14.
35 See Chapter 15.
36 See Chapter 16
37 See Chapter 18.
38 See Chapter 19.
39 See Chapter 21. Although the US did not openly support a finding of 'threat to the peace', their lack of opposition and their statements suggest that had there been sufficient support for a finding they would have lent their support.
40 See Chapter 23.
41 See Chapter 24.

This evidence supports the idea of US reluctance for action during the Cold War, which fell by the wayside with the collapse of the Soviet Union.[42]

While, over the course of the Security Council's history, the US has employed a number of arguments to justify their support for a finding of 'threat to the peace', only eight recur with sufficient significance to be considered core arguments the US have used for this matter: international law violations constituting a 'threat to the peace', the gravity of the situation leading to a finding, a finding of 'threat to the peace' being a consequence of a state's actions or failure to comply with a Security Council resolution, emotive rhetoric as an argument style (although this has been dealt with above, so is not addressed in this section), defending or promoting the rule of law, protecting human rights, defending democracy and the notion that the 'existence of a threat to the peace' is self-evident based on the facts. Of particular interest in these recurring arguments and themes is that they all broadly relate to the idea of enforcing and promoting law and defending and promoting human rights. This clearly demonstrates what the US thematically prioritises when considering the existence of a 'threat to the peace'.

In seven of the case studies, the US argued that the facts made the situation in question sufficiently grave to warrant a finding of 'threat to the peace' and, consequently, amenable to Chapter VII action. These situations were Palestine in 1948, the Iran hostage crisis in 1979–80, the civil war in Yugoslavia in 1991, the Rwandan Civil War and genocide in 1993–94, AIDS and peacekeeping in 2000–05, WMDs and non-proliferation in 2002–06 and sexual violence as a tactic of armed conflict in 2008–10. With the exception of the Iran hostage crisis, the basis of this gravity threshold seemed to be the violence in progress as a result of the situation (or the potential for mass violence, in the case of WMDs and non-proliferation). In the case of the Iran hostage crisis, the idea of 'gravity' was more abstract, focused upon the argument that Iran's actions placed one of the cornerstones of international law and international relations in jeopardy: the concept of diplomatic protection and inviolability of diplomatic premises. There is a strong correlation between this argument of gravity and the argument that the facts make the existence of a 'threat to the peace' self-evident. The US argued for this self-evidence on five separate occasions, four in conjunction with the argument of gravity: Palestine in 1948, the civil

42 Glennon, 'Why the Security Council Failed'; Christopher J. Le Mon and Rachel S. Taylor, 'Security Council Action in the Name of Human Rights: From Rhodesia to the Congo', *U.C. Davis Journal of International Law & Policy* 10, no. 2 (2004): 209–26; Inger Österdahl, *Threat to the Peace: The Interpretation by the Security Council of Article 39 of the UN Charter* (Uppsala: Iustus, 1998), 11; Karel Wellens, 'The UN Security Council and New Threats to the Peace: Back to the Future', *Journal of Conflict and Security Law* 8, no. 1 (2003): 67–68.

war in Yugoslavia in 1991, Libya and the Lockerbie bombing in 1992, AIDS and peacekeeping in 2000–05 and WMDs and non-proliferation in 2002–06. With the exception of Libya in 1992, all of these arguments of self-evidence were intrinsically linked to the notion of gravity, suggesting that what makes the situation grave enough for Security Council action, much like pornography, cannot be defined but is obvious when seen.[43]

The remaining five common arguments the US employed all possess a high degree of overlap within this group, and were often used in tandem. They all indicate the US's approach to international law in relation to the Security Council's role; prioritising the protection of human rights and democracy in conjunction with the idea of the rule of law's supremacy, and violations of law having consequences, thus lay at the heart of this approach. The idea that violations of international law in of themselves could lead to a finding of 'threat to the peace' was employed on six separate occasions: the Vietnamese incursion into Cambodia in 1978–79 (state sovereignty, territorial integrity and the principle of non-interference), the Iran hostage crisis in 1979–80 (laws regarding diplomatic relations), the civil war in Yugoslavia in 1991 (attempts to change borders through the use of force), WMDs and non-proliferation in 2002–06 (non-proliferation laws and terrorism), the Syrian Civil War in 2011–13 (various violations of the laws of armed conflict and other *jus cogens* violations) and chemical weapons in 2013 (the prohibition of the use of chemical weapons). In all these situations, the US argued that serious ongoing breaches of certain rules or international law norms were sufficient to justify Security Council action under Chapter VII. Similarly, on five different occasions, the US contended that the Security Council had a duty to promote and uphold the rule of law in situations where security was at risk: Libya in the Lockerbie bombing in 1992 (international terrorism), Afghanistan in 1999 (civil war and international terrorism), East Timor independence in 1999 (civil unrest and threats to democracy), sexual violence as a tactic of armed conflict in 2008–10 (systematic violence against women and armed conflict) and chemical weapons in 2013 (civil war).

Linked to the idea of the rule of law and the concept that ongoing breaches of international law can lead to a finding of 'threat to the peace', on five occasions, the US in favour of a finding of 'threat to the peace', and thus for Chapter VII action, on the basis of a failure to comply with previous Security Council resolutions, or that such a Security Council finding was an inevitable consequence of the target state's actions. This occurred in relation to the Iran hostage crisis in 1979–80, Libya and the Lockerbie bombing in 1992, Afghanistan

43 Jacobellis v Ohio, 378 United States Reports 179 (Ohio State Supreme Court 1964).

in 1999, WMDs and non-proliferation in 2002–06 and chemical weapons in 2013. In all these cases, the US argued that actions taken that clearly conflicted with important accepted international norms (including Security Council decisions) needed to have consequences to maintain the integrity of the international legal order.

The final two recurring arguments the US used are similar in nature, but often require different contexts to be used effectively. These are the protection of human rights and the defence of democracy, which were employed six and five times respectively in the studied material. The suggestion that the protection of human rights could be sufficient grounds for Security Council action arising from a finding of 'threat to the peace' was argued in relation to apartheid after Black Wednesday in 1977, Iraq in 1991, Haiti in 1991–93, sexual violence as a tactic of armed conflict in 2008–10, the Syrian Civil War in 2011–13 and chemical weapons in 2013. The idea that the Security Council should take action to defend democracy has significant crossover with the idea that they should take action to protect human rights. The defence of democracy featured as a core argument in relation to apartheid after Black Wednesday in 1977, Haiti in 1991–93, Afghanistan in 1999, East Timor independence in 1999 and the Syrian Civil War in 2011–13.

As briefly discussed above, this meta-synthesis of the case studies in which the US supported a finding of 'threat to the peace' by the Security Council, and action under Chapter VII stemming from this finding, provides some insight into the guiding principles that appear to inform the US approach to Article 39 (and international law generally). It thus seems clear that the US require satisfaction that the relatively amorphous threshold of gravity has been met, but that this threshold is often self-evident. This then forms a key starting point for US justifications. Once this intangible threshold of gravity has been met, the US tend to push for action on the basis the idea of the rule of law, promoting and protecting human rights and defending and promoting democracy. Further, the US's broad conceptions of these ideas mean that they are more likely than not to advocate for Security Council action in relation to a situation.

CHAPTER 28

London Calling

1 Overview

In this section, I parse the manner in which the UK has approached the idea of 'threat to the peace' under Article 39 of the UN Charter. First, I address a set of general observations regarding the UK approach, regardless of the outcome they advocated, to identify any recurring concepts or themes across all case studies. Once these general observations are detailed, I examine the case studies in which the UK opposed a finding of 'threat to the peace'. Interestingly, much like the US, there are no positive case studies in which the UK opposed such a finding (although their initial position on apartheid must be considered in this category; because of their eventual support of a finding, this cannot be considered a situation where 'threat to the peace' was found while being opposed by the UK). Finally, I examine the case studies in which the UK supported a finding of 'threat to the peace' to assess whether there is any pattern of approach in how they justified their decisions on this matter.

2 General Observations

When examining the data as a whole, rather than in its separate categories, two overarching patterns emerge in relation to the UK's approach to the concept of 'threat to the peace', regardless of their particular position in each instance. The first is an argument style, and methodological approach, to justification that centres on formal legal reasoning. The UK seems to have consistently adopted this approach—it is overtly present in nine of the 22 case studies, while also arguably forming a clear subtext in the remaining case studies. The other general observation is that, much like the US, the perceived gravity of the situation regularly presents as a key factor in the UK's decision-making process.

A legal formalist approach is present in UK arguments throughout the period being examined. This type of approach is subtly apparent in almost every case study; however, it is overtly present in four of the case studies where the UK opposed a finding of 'threat to the peace', and five of the case studies where the UK supported such a finding. In situations where the UK opposed a finding, formal legal reasoning was present in the arguments regarding Spain

 | DOI:10.1163/9789004391420_030

in 1946,[1] the Portuguese African territories in 1963,[2] apartheid prior to 1977[3] and AIDS and peacekeeping in 2000–05.[4] The situations where UK supported a finding of 'threat to the peace' were Palestine in 1948,[5] the Vietnamese incursion into Cambodia in 1978–79,[6] Libya and the Lockerbie bombing in 1992,[7] the Syrian Civil War in 2011–13[8] and chemical weapons in 2013.[9]

In relation to Spain in 1946, this formal legal reasoning is most clearly present in how the UK dissected the distinction between the phrase 'likely to endanger' and the concept of 'threat'. It can also be observed in their later interpretation of the right of self-determination as not prohibiting any particular form of government. When considering the Portuguese African territories in 1963, formal legal arguments were evident in the UK's comments regarding correct procedure for seeking Security Council action on an issue, and their equating the Security Council with the courts of equity regarding the requirement of clean hands when seeking redress. The arguments surrounding apartheid prior to 1977 also overtly demonstrate this formal legal reasoning: first, in the requirement that a state's territorial and political integrity must be threatened for the Security Council to lawfully take action, and second, with the idea that a blanket arms embargo against South Africa would have violated their right of self-defence under Article 51 of the Charter. When discussing AIDS and peacekeeping, legal formalism informed the UK's argument for a clear separation of powers and between the relevant mandates of different UN organs in dealing with the issue, suggesting that the issue of AIDS did not fall within the Security Council's mandate for direct action under Chapter VII.

In the Palestine case study, the UK's support for a finding arose directly from a formal legal reasoning approach demonstrating their interpretation of Article 39 of the UN Charter. In this case, the UK went through the process of treaty interpretation, in the same way a municipal lawyer would engage in statutory interpretation, to determine whether the phrase 'threat to the peace' should have the word 'international' read into it. They concluded, based upon the presence of the word 'international' with every other use of the word 'threat' in the UN Charter, that the omission was a drafting error and that

1 See Chapter 3.
2 See Chapter 5.
3 See Chapter 6.
4 See Chapter 18.
5 See Chapter 4.
6 See Chapter 7.
7 See Chapter 13.
8 See Chapter 23.
9 See Chapter 24.

'international' should be read into Article 39. On this basis, their support for a finding of 'threat to the peace' in relation to Palestine occurred only after such international elements had been established. In relation to the Vietnamese incursion into Cambodia in 1978–79, formal legal reasoning guided UK responses in terms of their interpretation of the right of sovereignty and territorial integrity. In spite of their blanket objections to the conduct of the Khmer Rouge, the UK interpretation of the primacy in international law of this right led them to support action against Vietnam following their military intervention into Cambodia. In the Lockerbie bombing case study, the UK's arguments regarding finding a 'threat to the peace' with respect to Libya for their failure to extradite suspects for prosecution is grounded entirely in the law of jurisdiction. When arguing in favour of a finding of 'threat to the peace' in relation to Syria in 2011–13, formal legal reasoning was again evident in how the UK characterised democracy as a fundamental human right, their arguments regarding the Assad regime's disproportionate use of force and their use of the idea of precedent to counter the justification for Russia's vetoes. Finally, the UK's use of formal legal reasoning can be observed in relation to chemical weapons in 2013, where they argued that the prohibition of the use of chemical weapons was an important international norm, and that a finding of 'threat to the peace' simply served to reinforce this point.

The suggestion that the UK's decision-making process, and thus argument style, is governed by formal legal reasoning is supported by other recurring elements in their arguments. One example is the way the UK justified its position as being a consequence of the state in question failing to heed calls to comply with international law, or previous Security Council directives, in almost all instances where that argument was logically available to them (Palestine in 1948, Apartheid in 1977, Libya and the Lockerbie bombing in 1992, WMDs and non-proliferation in 2002–06 and the US- and UK-led invasion of Iraq in 2003).[10] The regular reference to the idea that international law violations can constitute a 'threat to the peace' (the Iran hostage crisis in 1979–80, the civil war in Yugoslavia in 1991, Afghanistan in 1999, the Syrian Civil War in 2011–13 and chemical weapons in 2013),[11] and regular references to the Security Council's mandate (Palestine in 1948, apartheid prior to 1977, Libya and the Lockerbie bombing in 1992, AIDS and peacekeeping in 2000–05, WMDs and non-proliferation in 2002–06 and sexual violence as a tactic of armed conflict in 2008–10),[12] further support the assessment that legal formalism is the guiding

10 See Chapters 4, 6, 13, 19 and 20 respectively.

11 See Chapters 8, 11, 15, 23 and 24 respectively.

12 See Chapters 4, 6, 13, 18, 19 and 21 respectively.

force behind the UK's otherwise moderate approach to decision-making within the Security Council.

Similarly to the US, the UK regularly argued their position on any given situation on the basis of a perceived gravity threshold required for Chapter VII action. In nine of the 22 case studies in this book, the UK argued for the gravity of the situation in approximately 40% of those situations. From a statistical perspective, the argument features slightly more frequently in situations where the UK opposed a finding of 'threat to the peace' (three times in seven case studies, or 43%, compared with six times in 16 case studies, or 37.5%); however, given the UK's propensity for supporting a finding of 'threat to the peace', this difference is relatively insignificant. The details of how and why the UK argued in relation to the gravity of the situation are discussed below, but it is important to note that regardless of the UK's position, this notion of gravity is a frequently recurring benchmark when considering the existence of a 'threat to the peace'.

3 Opposition to a Finding

The UK opposed a finding of 'threat to the peace' in seven of the 22 case studies in this book, totalling eight situations out of the 26 covered: the Spanish Franco regime in 1946,[13] the Portuguese African territories in 1963,[14] Apartheid prior to 1977 (although the UK eventually supported a 'threat to the peace' finding in relation to apartheid, their initial position was one of clear opposition to such a finding, and thus must be considered in this section),[15] the South African occupation of Namibia in 1981–83,[16] AIDS and peacekeeping in 2000–05,[17] the US- and UK-led invasion of Iraq in 2003[18] and piracy in Somalia and the Gulf of Guinea in 2008–12 (as noted previously, while Chapter VII action was taken against Somali piracy, this was done under the auspices of the 1992 resolutions relating to the civil war in the wake the Barre regime's collapse rather than against piracy itself).[19] As noted above, the limited instances in which the UK opposed a finding of 'threat to the peace' demonstrate a clear preference for Security Council action where the existence of a 'threat' is in

13 See Chapter 3.
14 See Chapter 5.
15 See Chapter 6.
16 See Chapter 9.
17 See Chapter 18.
18 See Chapter 20.
19 See Chapter 22.

question. The only theme recurring with sufficient frequency to be considered a pattern within this opposition to a finding is the notion of gravity (legal formalism as an argument style and method of reasoning also occur with sufficient frequency, but this has been dealt with above).

The notion of gravity as the basis of an argument against a finding of 'threat to the peace' is not inherently bound to idea of the situation lacking sufficient gravity. In situations where the UK opposed Security Council action under Chapter VII, the argument of gravity was foundational on three occasions. In relation to the Spanish Franco regime in 1946, the UK employed the very technical legal argument that the fact-finding demonstrated that the regime was 'likely to endanger' international peace and security, and the fact-finders' decision to use this language instead of the language of Article 39 of the Charter—namely, 'threat to the peace'—thus demonstrated that the situation did not meet the threshold required for Security Council action under Chapter VII. When considering apartheid prior to 1977, the UK took a very similar approach, arguing that while the policy of apartheid was abhorrent, there was no evidence that it threatened the political and territorial integrity of any other state; thus, the policy did not meet the gravity threshold required for a finding of 'threat to the peace' under Article 39. The arguments of gravity when considering the US- and UK-led invasion of Iraq in 2003 were more reminiscent of arguments supporting a finding of 'threat to the peace'. Here, the UK argued that the threat posed by the Saddam Hussein regime in Iraq posed a sufficiently weighty threat to international peace and security, and that the invading actions of the coalition forces were therefore justified by Iraq's failure to comply with previous Security Council resolutions. The UK thus argued that a finding of 'threat to the peace' in relation to the coalition forces would undermine their actions against the existing threat that had already met the gravity threshold for Chapter VII action. While these arguments do not assist in defining a metric for assessing the gravity of the situation in relation to Article 39, they do demonstrate the crucial role this idea plays in the UK's decision-making process.

4 Support for a Finding

In the 16 case studies where the UK supported a finding of 'threat to the peace', three lines of argument were sufficiently recurring to be considered a pattern, in addition to the UK's regular use of formal legal reasoning discussed above: the gravity of the situation, linked to the idea that the existence of a 'threat to the peace' is self-evident, and the argument that violations of certain aspects of international law are sufficiently serious to lead to a Security Council finding of 'threat to the peace'. Alongside these patterns, three recurring arguments are noticeable, albeit not frequent enough to be necessarily considered patterns; rather, these arguments are most likely tied to the use of formal legal reasoning as a decision-making process and argument style. These are references to the UN Security Council's mandate, the protection of human rights and the idea that a finding of 'threat to the peace' is an inevitable consequence of failure to comply with previous Security Council resolutions or calls for conduct to accord with international law.

When arguing that the gravity of the situation in question led to a finding of 'threat to the peace', the UK almost exclusively made this argument in relation to the scale of violence occurring in the situation being addressed. The essence of this argument is evident in the following case studies: the Rwandan Civil War and genocide in 1993–94,[20] East Timor independence in 1999,[21] action against the small arms trade in 1999–2011,[22] sexual violence as a tactic of armed conflict in 2008–10[23] and the Syrian Civil War 2011–13.[24] In each of these situations, the UK argued that the death toll and scale of violence that was directly attributed to the matter being debated warranted a finding of 'threat to the peace', and thus the need for Security Council action under Chapter VII. In this notion of gravity being intrinsically linked with the scale of the violence taking place, there appears to be a strong correlation with the argument that the situation's facts make the existence of a 'threat to the peace' self-evident. The UK made this argument that a 'threat to the peace' was self-evident in relation to East Timor independence in 1999,[25] action against the small arms trade in 1999–2011,[26] WMDs and non-proliferation in 2002–06,[27] sexual violence as a tactic of armed conflict in 2008–10[28] and the Syrian Civil War in 2011–13.[29] In most of these situations, the argument that the existence of a 'threat to the peace' was self-evident occurred in conjunction with arguments relating to the gravity of the situation; however, regarding WMDs, the argument was that failure to take action to prevent the proliferation of WMDs would result in

20 See Chapter 14.
21 See Chapter 16.
22 See Chapter 17
23 See Chapter 21.
24 See Chapter 23.
25 See Chapter 16.
26 See Chapter 17.
27 See Chapter 19.
28 See Chapter 21.
29 See Chapter 23.

large-scale violence and atrocity, thus making it analogous to the correlation with the gravity arguments in the other case studies.

The other situation argued on the basis of gravity was the Iran hostage crisis in 1979–80.[30] In this situation, the UK contended that the international law violations being perpetrated by the new regime in Iran were so heinous and destabilising that they warranted Security Council action in the form of a finding of 'threat to the peace' and Chapter VII consequences. This situation was also the first time in the studied material that the UK began to argue that international law violations in and of themselves could lead to a finding of 'threat to the peace'. This notion that international law violations could lead to a finding of 'threat to the peace' subsequently occurred in relation to systematic IHL violations in the civil war in Yugoslavia in 1991,[31] Afghanistan in 1999[32] and the Syrian Civil War in 2011–13.[33] In each of these situations, this argument regarding violations stands very distinct from and separate to the notion of gravity, as it was not so much the volume and effect of the violence that prompted these arguments, but the nature of the violence itself—*jus cogens* violations, such as war crimes, and other crimes against humanity, such as genocide and the forced displacement of peoples. In this regard, the UK approach clearly identified systematic violations of the laws of war as sufficient for Security Council action under Chapter VII, even if such violations did not meet the 'standard' gravity threshold. When arguing that international law violations could lead to a 'threat to the peace' finding in relation to chemical weapons in 2013,[34] the fundamental rationale was the same, although its scope was much broader. In this case, the UK argued that the use of chemical weapons was a *jus cogens* violation, and breaches of *jus cogens* norms are of such intrinsically heinous nature that the Security Council should have a mandate to act against them whenever and wherever they occur.

Recurring arguments surrounding the Security Council's mandate (Palestine in 1948, Libya and the Lockerbie bombing in 1992, WMDs and non-proliferation in 2002–06 and sexual violence as a tactic of armed conflict in 2008–10), the protection of human rights (Iraq in 1991, East Timor independence in 1999, the Syrian Civil War in 2011–13 and chemical weapons in 2013), and that Security Council action is an inevitable consequence of failure to comply with previous Security Council resolutions or calls for conduct to accord with international

30 See Chapter 8.
31 See Chapter 11.
32 See Chapter 15.
33 See Chapter 23.
34 See Chapter 24.

law (Palestine in 1948, Apartheid in 1977, Libya and the Lockerbie bombing in 1992 and WMDs and non-proliferation in 2002–06) are not patterns in and of themselves. Rather, these arguments tend to reinforce the suggestion that the UK is governed predominantly by formal legal reasoning when making decisions about the existence, or lack thereof, of a 'threat to the peace'. This is because in each situation where these arguments were made, they were grounded in the faithful application of the international legal principles relevant to the situation at hand. While this does not provide a set of guiding principles regarding how the UK are likely to respond to a potential 'threat to the peace', as was the case with the US, it does reveal a method by which those well versed in the international law governing any situation should be able to predict how the UK are likely to position themselves by applying formal legal reasoning to the law and the facts of the situation.

CHAPTER 29

Vive la France

1 Overview

In this chapter, I address France's approach to the concept of 'threat to the peace' in Chapter VII of the UN Charter. Much like the US and UK, no case studies contained the finding of 'threat to the peace' where such a finding was opposed by France; however, France did initially oppose such a finding for apartheid in South Africa and the Rwandan Civil War and genocide before acquiescing to the notion that a 'threat to the peace' existed—both of these case studies are thus considered in terms of France's opposition as well as its support. First, I address the general observations, such as they are, that can be gleaned from France's arguments when considering both their opposition to and support for a finding of 'threat to the peace'. I then examine any patterns and trends apparent in the data for situations where France opposed a finding of 'threat to the peace' to understand the grounds likely to lead to such opposition. Finally, I address the trends and pattern the French displayed when arguing in favour of, or supporting, the existence of a 'threat to the peace' within the Security Council.

2 General Observations

France, unlike the UK and the US, displayed no overarching arguments in terms of style, decision-making method or recurring thematic justification in terms of their overall approach to the concept of 'threat to the peace'. This is not to say there is no pattern at all in their approach, for some patterns are indeed apparent in their justifications of opposition to a finding, and their justifications of support for a finding (all of which are discussed below); however, these varying patterns in support or opposition in no way appear to translate into an overarching approach. Of note when considering the French response across all the case studies is France's significant general preference to support a finding of 'threat to the peace'—they gave support for such a finding in 18 of the 22 case studies, demonstrating a significantly higher preference for Security Council action than any other P5 member.

 | DOI:10.1163/9789004391420_031

3 Opposition to a Finding

France opposed a finding of 'threat to the peace', at least initially, in six of the 22 case studies, addressing seven separate situations contained in this book: the Portuguese African territories in 1963,[1] apartheid prior to 1977,[2] the South African occupation of Namibia in 1981–83,[3] the initial stages of the Rwandan Civil War and genocide in 1993–94,[4] AIDS and peacekeeping in 2000–05[5] and piracy in Somalia and the Gulf of Guinea in 2008–12.[6] Across these six different situations, France employed eight general arguments to justify their position; however, only two of these recur sufficiently to be considered a pattern: the right of states to non-interference in domestic affairs, and the scope of the Security Council's mandate.

The right of non-interference in domestic affairs was a strong French justification in opposing Security Council action in response to the Portuguese African territories in 1963, apartheid prior to 1977 and piracy in Somalia and the Gulf of Guinea in 2008–12. The arguments regarding apartheid and the Portuguese African territories on the grounds of non-interference were essentially identical. When arguing that the right of non-interference precluded Security Council action in relation to the Portuguese African territories, France argued that while decolonisation was preferable, the pace at which it occurred (in the absence of significant violence) was an issue that fell within the colonising country's domestic mandate, which in turn placed the matter outside of Security Council authority. Similarly, when discussing apartheid, France argued that the South African Government's decisions on racial segregation and related apartheid fell wholly within that government's domestic jurisdiction, and any Security Council interference would be a violation of Article 2(7) of the UN Charter. In both these instances, the arguments against Security Council action on the basis of the right of non-interference in the domestic affairs of states were intrinsically linked with arguments about the scope of the Security Council's mandate. In both instances, France contended that to interfere in matters of a purely domestic nature, where another state's political and/or territorial integrity was not at risk, was beyond the scope of the Security Council's mandate, thus precluding them from supporting such an action.

1 See Chapter 5.
2 See Chapter 6.
3 See Chapter 9.
4 See Chapter 14.
5 See Chapter 18.
6 See Chapter 22.

The arguments invoking the right of non-interference in the domestic affairs of states in relation to the piracy case study mirrored the arguments invoked in relation to the Portuguese African territories and apartheid. When addressing piracy, France argued that the primary criminal jurisdiction for addressing the issue lay with the state from which the piracy was originating, and any Security Council action ran the risk of usurping this well-established criminal jurisdiction (although they were willing to overlook this for Somalia to expand the 1992 Chapter VII provisions in relation to the civil war to also address the issues of piracy). The arguments regarding the Security Council's mandate in relation to AIDS and peacekeeping operations were grounded in the fact that France did not perceive AIDS to be, intrinsically, a security issue, as it was being addressed by other UN organs; thus, while France advocated for Security Council support for these other UN organs, they believed it was outside the Security Council's mandate to maintain international peace and security.

4 Support for a Finding

When supporting a finding of 'threat to the peace', France employed numerous arguments to justify their support in 18 of the 22 case studies; however, only four of these arguments recur sufficiently to be considered a foundational pattern of approach to the question. Further, one of these arguments was more a coercive mechanism to assist compliance, rather than a justification of their position. These arguments were the right of self-determination, the gravity of the situation, the notion that a 'threat to the peace' was self-evident on the basis of the facts and that the situation should be resolved peacefully through diplomacy and political negotiation, rather than through the use of force.

Whereas for the US and UK, the notions of gravity and self-evidence were intrinsically linked in their arguments, this was not the case with France. While some correlation exists between the two arguments, France argued that a situation was self-evidently a 'threat to the peace' on more occasions than they argued that the gravity of the situation led to a finding of 'threat to the peace'. Further, there are instances where self-evidence was argued in the absence of gravity, and vice versa, suggesting that for France, these arguments are not co-dependent. The issue of gravity was argued in relation to the Spanish Franco regime in 1946,[7] Palestine in 1948,[8] Libya and the Lockerbie bombing in 1992,[9]

7 See Chapter 3.
8 See Chapter 4.
9 See Chapter 13.

the Rwandan Civil War and genocide in 1993–94,[10] action against the small arms trade in 1999–2011[11] and the Syrian Civil War in 2011–13.[12] In relation see the Spanish Franco regime, France argued that the very existence of a fascist, pro-Nazi regime in the wake of World War II was a matter of serious global concern, such that a 'threat to the peace' existed. In relation to Libya in 1992, France argued that evidence of state involvement in horrific acts of airline terrorism was sufficiently grave to warrant Security Council intervention to ensure that justice was served. In the remaining situations where the question of gravity was argued to justify a Security Council finding of a 'threat to the peace', French arguments related directly to the scale of violence involved with, or resulting from, the issue being considered. These findings of gravity correlate with the idea of self-evidence in French arguments regarding Palestine in 1948, Libya and the Lockerbie bombing in 1992, action against the small arms trade in 1999–2011 and the Syrian Civil War in 2011–13. In each of these situations, the argument of self-evidence and the argument of gravity, while distinguishable, operated along the same lines.

The argument of self-evidence deviated from the argument of gravity in the cases of East Timor independence in 1999,[13] WMDs and non-proliferation in 2002–06[14] and sexual violence as a tactic of armed conflict in 2008–10.[15] In relation to East Timor, France argued that pro-Indonesian militias' rejection of the East Timor independence ballot constituted a violation of the right of self-determination exercised through democratic ballot, which self-evidently warranted Security Council intervention. In relation to WMDs and non-proliferation, France simply contended that the continued production and proliferation of WMDs, particularly in relation to North Korea and non-state actors, was self-evidently a 'threat to the peace' and worthy of Security Council action. In relation to sexual violence as a tactic of armed conflict, France argued that because addressing wartime rape was crucial to ensuring lasting peace in post-conflict regions, this issue was self-evidently a 'threat to the peace'. Thus, while some correlation exists between the notion of gravity and the notion of the facts making a 'threat to the peace' self-evident in the French discourse surrounding what constitutes a 'threat to the peace', this seems more of a general catchall justification by France rather than an approach predicated upon strong links to the idea of gravity, as evident in the UK and the US approaches.

10 See Chapter 14.
11 See Chapter 17.
12 See Chapter 23.
13 See Chapter 16.
14 See Chapter 19.
15 See Chapter 21.

The other primary justificatory argument the French employed centred upon violations of the right of self-determination leading to a finding of 'threat to the peace' and Security Council action. This argument was employed in relation to the Spanish Franco regime in 1946,[16] civil war in Yugoslavia in 1991,[17] Haiti in 1991–93,[18] East Timor independence in 1999[19] and the UK- and US-led invasion of Iraq in 2003.[20] With the exception of the Spanish Franco regime, in each of these instances, France argued that the violent actions of one or more of the parties to the situation constituted an ongoing violation of the right of self-determination under Articles 1(2) and 2(7) of the Charter, which—as these articles are a core tenant of the UN system—therefore constituted a 'threat to the peace'. When discussing the Spanish Franco regime, the rationale was similar, but the way it was delivered was distinguishable. In this instance, France argued that as the Spanish Franco regime's rise to power was achieved through outside intervention by Nazi Germany and Fascist Italy, it constituted a violation of the rights self-determination, as the Franco Government did not represent the will of Spain's people, but rather of the governments of Germany and Italy.

French arguments based on the idea that situations should be resolved through peaceful diplomatic and political negotiation, rather than through the use of force, present not so much as a justification for their position, but rather as a coercive measure directed at the states in question. This approach was exercised in response to the Iran hostage crisis in 1979–80,[21] the civil war in Yugoslavia in 1991,[22] the Rwandan Civil War and genocide in 1993–94,[23] WMDs and non-proliferation in 2002–06[24] and chemical weapons in 2013.[25] In each of these situations, France argued that they were firmly in favour of peaceful solutions to the situation at hand, but should this approach not be successful, they were willing to engage in stronger enforcement measures permitted under Chapter VII to end the situation. In this regard, the argument for achieving peaceful solutions through negotiation was less a form of justificatory discourse, and more a regularly employed Sword of Damocles hovering over the parties to the dispute to coerce a solution.

16 See Chapter 3.
17 See Chapter 11.
18 See Chapter 12.
19 See Chapter 16.
20 See Chapter 20.
21 See Chapter 8.
22 See Chapter 11.
23 See Chapter 14.
24 See Chapter 19.
25 See Chapter 24.

CHAPTER 30

From Russia with Love

1 Overview

This chapter addresses Russian responses to the concept of 'threat to the peace', and how they justified their responses to this question. It is worth noting here that Russia has undergone a level of political turmoil not experienced by France, the UK and the US during the period being examined. The collapse of the Soviet Union in the late 1980s and early 1990s was formalised with the Russian Federation taking over as the successor state in the UN in 1991, which represents the key marker in this political upheaval.[1] This development was followed by erosions in Russian democracy under Vladimir Putin, commencing in late 1999, in favour of a more oligarchical style of government.[2] The effect, if any, of these political restructures is addressed in the general observations section of this chapter. Following these general observations, I analyse Russia's approaches to justifying its opposition to a finding of 'threat to the peace'. Finally, I address how Russia justified its support for a finding of 'threat to the peace', even in situations where no such finding was ultimately made. Of interest is the fact that Russia did not reverse their position in any of the case studies.

2 General Observations

An examination of the overall data for Russia reveals three general features, two of which seem related to the political upheaval noted above. The first is the argument style Russia employed in the Security Council, and the second is Russia's willingness to engage in Security Council action for any given situation. The final observation, which appears unrelated to the political upheaval, is a key factor in Russia's decision-making process across all situations: the right of self-determination.

A clear shift in Russia's argument style can be observed when contrasting their justificatory discourse before and after the collapse of the Soviet Union.

1 Russian Federation, 'History' <http://russiaun.ru/en/permanent_mission/istorija>.

2 Timothy J. Colton and Michael McFaul, 'Russian Democracy Under Putin', *Johnson's Russia List* 50, no. 4 (25 July 2003): 1–3.

 | DOI:10.1163/9789004391420_032

In the six case studies included in this book that took place while the Soviet Union was still intact (the Spanish Franco regime 1946, Palestine in 1948, the Portuguese African territories in 1963, apartheid prior to 1977, the Vietnamese incursion into Cambodia in 1978–79, the Iran hostage crisis in 1979–80 and the South African occupation of Namibia in 1981–93),[3] Russia argued their position with heavy use of overtly emotive rhetoric in four of these situations.[4] By contrast, after the fall of the Soviet Union, Russia only employed emotive rhetoric to make its point on one occasion: the Syrian Civil War in 2011–13.[5] While this resurgence of emotive rhetoric may be a manifestation of Vladimir Putin's consolidation of power, there is not enough evidence within the case studies here to support such a hypothesis.[6] However, what is clear is that Russia's use of emotive rhetoric in justificatory discourse went into hibernation (perhaps until very recently) with the fall of the Soviet Union, resulting in a much less bombastic argument style when addressing the question of 'threat to the peace'.

The second general observation regarding Russia in the Security Council is their willingness to find a 'threat to the peace' over time. Where France, the UK and the US demonstrated an increased willingness over time to support Security Council action in situations where 'threat to the peace' was not a foregone conclusion, Russia's trajectory was exactly the opposite. The case studies demonstrate a restrictive view of what constitutes a 'threat to the peace' by France, the UK and the US up until the early 1990s, after which these states appear to favour a more expansive approach to determining the concept. Conversely, Russia took an extremely expensive approach during the first four and a half decades, advocating heavily for Security Council action up until the fall of the Soviet Union, and then supporting unified Security Council action throughout the majority of the 1990s, before shifting approach to a much more restricted view of Security Council action. Indeed, up until the small arms trade case study, which commenced in 1999, the case studies reveal Russian opposition to a finding of 'threat to the peace' on only two occasions: the Vietnamese incursion into Cambodia in 1978–79, and the Iran hostage crisis in 1979–80.[7]

3 See Chapters 3–9.

4 These case studies also correlated with some form of Western colonisation: See Chapters 4–6 and 9 for details of this emotive rhetoric.

5 See Chapter 23.

6 While there is insufficient evidence within this project for this hypothesis, the resurgence of emotive rhetoric correlates with Vladimir Putin's consolidation of power and his boisterous, hyper-masculine persona. It is a project worth pursuing in more detail as a dedicated enterprise.

7 See Chapters 7–8.

In contrast to this trend, since Vladimir Putin's rise to power at the end of 1999, Russia opposed the push for Security Council action in five of the eight case studies.[8] This restrictive view of what constitutes a 'threat to the peace', coinciding with the consolidation of Vladimir Putin's power in Russia, may be coincidental, but this seems unlikely.

The final general observation relating to Russia is the emphasis it placed upon the right of self-determination in the justificatory discourse relating to 'threat to the peace'. In eight of the 22 case studies, Russia opposed a finding three times and supported a finding five times; a core reason for their position was how the current situation and Security Council action would affect the right of self-determination for the state in question.[9] In situations where Russia opposed a finding of 'threat to the peace' on these grounds, they generally held the opinion that Security Council action undermined the right of self-determination within that state. Similarly, in situations where they supported Security Council action on these grounds, it was because they believed that the right of self-determination was currently being violated, and the onus was thus upon the Security Council to respond to this violation and facilitate an unfettered exercise of this right. These arguments are discussed more comprehensively below; however, it is clear that the right of self-determination forms a cornerstone of Russia's position in relation to the existence of a 'threat to the peace'.

3 Opposition to a Finding

Within the cases addressed in this book, Russia opposed a finding of 'threat to the peace' on seven different occasions: the Vietnamese incursion into Cambodia in 1978–79,[10] the Iran hostage crisis in 1979–80,[11] action against the small arms trade in 1999–2011,[12] AIDS and peacekeeping in 2000–05,[13] sexual violence as a tactic of armed conflict in 2008–10,[14] piracy in Somalia and the Gulf of Guinea in 2008–12[15] and the Syrian Civil War in 2011–13.[16] From these case

8 See Chapters 17–18, and 21–23.
9 See Chapters 5–9, 12, 16, and 23.
10 See Chapter 7.
11 See Chapter 8.
12 See Chapter 17.
13 See Chapter 18.
14 See Chapter 21.
15 See Chapter 22.
16 See Chapter 23.

studies, three different grounds for opposition emerge as substantially recurring in the justificatory discourse. The first is the premise that Russia's opposition was inherently grounded in lack of faith in the solutions being proposed to the Security Council for the situation at hand. The second is that a finding of 'threat to the peace' would be beyond the bounds of the Security Council's mandate. The third is the idea that Security Council action following a finding of 'threat to the peace' would lead to a violation of the right of self-determination.

Opposition to a finding of 'threat to the peace' on the grounds of lack of faith in the proposed solution was raised in four of the seven case studies where Russia opposed the finding: the Iran hostage crisis in 1979–80, action against the small arms trade in 1999–2011, sexual violence as a tactic of armed conflict in 2008–10 and the Syrian Civil War in 2011–13. In each of these situations, this argument was relatively straightforward: Russia was unconvinced that the action proposed before the Security Council would assist in offering an adequate resolution to the situation. In relation to the specific disputes for which this argument was deployed (the Iran hostage crisis and the Syrian Civil War), Russia argued that the proposition before the Security Council would not only fail to bring about a resolution, but also exacerbate the dispute. When Russia used this argument in relation to general thematic problems before the Security Council (the small arms trade and sexual violence as a tactic of armed conflict), they contended that the solutions being proposed were impractical and would only detract from the Security Council's broader responsibilities. Even though the basis for their lack of faith in the proposed solution differed when dealing with specific and general issues, the fact remains that this justificatory basis forms the key reason for Russia's opposition to a finding of 'threat to the peace'.

Russia's arguments relating to the Security Council's mandate to oppose a finding of 'threat to the peace' were also quite straightforward in their basis and application. This argument was used for the small arms trade, AIDS and peacekeeping operations and the Syrian Civil War. In relation to the small arms trade, Russia argued that Security Council action with direct connection to ongoing conflicts on the Security Council agenda would be permissible; however, they asserted that attempts to address this issue generally within the Security Council under Chapter VII would be beyond the scope of the Security Council's mandate. In relation to AIDS and peacekeeping operations, Russia suggests that as this issue was being handled by the Economic and Social Council and the General Assembly, it was improper and outside the Security Council's mandate to take Chapter VII action. Instead, Russia advocated for Security Council support for actions taken by these other arms of the UN. When discussing the Syrian Civil War, Russia simply asserted that the Security Council's mandate did not permit interference in an internal armed conflict within a state. All these different interpretations of the relationship between the Security Council's mandate and the situation being debated clearly demonstrate that the scope of the Security Council's mandate operates as a restraining force in terms of what Russia regards as permissible action in relation to Chapter VII.

Russia's final recurring justification in opposing a finding of 'threat to the peace' was the belief that Security Council action would negatively affect the right of self-determination of the state in question. This argument was raised in relation to the Vietnamese incursion into Cambodia, where Russia suggested that Security Council intervention to reinstate the Pol Pot regime would violate the Khmer people exercising their right of self-determination by toppling Pol Pot's Government; the Iran hostage crisis, where Russia argued that any Security Council action would unduly undermined the newly established Iranian Government; and the Syrian Civil War, where Russia argued that outside interference in the multilateral internal armed conflict would result in a government established in violation of the right of self-determination. Perhaps more notable is Russia's willingness to veto any Security Council action they felt would violate this right of self-determination, which occurred in each of these case studies. This consistent resistance to a finding of 'threat to the peace' when Russia believed that the right of self-determination would be threatened by that finding demonstrates the importance Russia places upon this right.

4 Support for a Finding

Russia supported Security Council action under Chapter VII in the remaining 15 case studies considered in this book, and these case studies feature a number of themes that recur often enough to warrant mention: the idea of the gravity of the situation warranting a finding of 'threat to the peace', the notion that the facts made the existence of a 'threat to the peace' self-evident, that violations of the right of self-determination created a 'threat to the peace', that international law violations led to such a finding, that a finding of 'threat to the peace' was a legitimate consequence of a failure to comply with Security Council resolutions and that the international nature of any given situation was a key factor in Russian support.

Russia's most commonly used argument to support a finding of 'threat to the peace' was that the gravity of the situation warranted Chapter VII action by the Security Council. This argument was raised for Palestine in 1948,[17] the

17 See Chapter 4.

Portuguese African territories in 1963,[18] the Rwandan Civil War and genocide in 1993–94,[19] East Timor independence in 1999,[20] WMDs and non-proliferation in 2002–06[21] and the US- and UK-led invasion of Iraq in 2003.[22] In every case, Russia argued that the actual or potential violence caused directly by, or flowing from, each of these situations met the amorphous threshold of gravity warranting a finding of 'threat to the peace'. This threshold of likely or actual violence seems to be the key defining feature in Russia's considerations of gravity in any given situation; however, with the exception of references to genocide in the Portuguese African territories case study, and references to attacks on civilians in East Timor, Russia did not appear to clearly articulate a point at which the violence was sufficient to possess this gravity element.

Often linked to arguments surrounding the gravity of the situation were arguments that the facts made a situation self-evidently a 'threat to the peace'. This argument was used for Palestine,[23] the Portuguese African territories,[24] Libya and the Lockerbie bombing in 1992[25] and WMDs and non-proliferation.[26] In relation to Palestine and WMDs and non-proliferation, the idea that the facts made a 'threat to the peace' self-evident was clearly and intrinsically linked with the notion of gravity discussed above. In relation to the Portuguese African territories, a connection was evident between the idea of self-evidence and the notion of gravity; however, this argument was intrinsically linked to Russian positions regarding colonial ideologies, and thus to attribute this outcome solely to the notion of gravity would be a mistake. When discussing self-evidence in relation to the Lockerbie bombing, the idea was intrinsically linked to Russian views on terrorist actions—namely that, in Russia's view, all terrorist actions have the potential to constitute a 'threat to the peace' by their intrinsic nature. This argument was echoed in the WMD and non-proliferation debates.

Russian arguments about the right of self-determination leading to a finding of 'threat to the peace' and Security Council action were all relatively similar and straightforward in manner. This argument was raised in relation to the Portuguese African territories in 1963, apartheid prior to 1977, the South African

18 See Chapter 5.
19 See Chapter 14.
20 See Chapter 16.
21 See Chapter 19.
22 See Chapter 20.
23 See Chapter 4.
24 See Chapter 5.
25 See Chapter 13.
26 See Chapter 19.

occupation of Namibia in 1981–83, Haiti in 1991–93 and East Timor independence in 1999. In each of these situations, Russia argued that the actions under scrutiny by the Security Council constituted a violation of the right of self-determination held by the affected peoples and that this created a 'threat to the peace'. Russia did not specify precisely how they interpreted this right of self-determination, but the context and nature of their statements suggests that they understand it as the right of all states to determine their form of government, free of interference from external forces.[27] While arguments were made in relation to the democratically elected officials in Haiti and the right of self-determination, for the Russians, the right self-determination and notions of democracy are not linked. This slightly undermines arguments that democracy constitutes an emerging customary norm in international law in relation to permissible forms of government.[28]

Russian arguments that international law violations could lead to a finding of 'threat to the peace' arose in relation to the South African occupation of Namibia,[29] Afghanistan in 1999,[30] WMDs and non-proliferation in 2002–06,[31] the US- and UK-led invasion of Iraq in 2003[32] and chemical weapons in 2013.[33] In relation to Namibia and Iraq, Russia argued that following the acts of aggression that had taken place, the Security Council had an onus to end to such egregious international law violations. When discussing chemical weapons and WMDs, Russia made reference to various sources of non-proliferation law that had been violated, prompting their support for these resolutions. In relation to Afghanistan, Russia argued that the international law violations hinged on Taliban involvement in terrorism and transnational narcotics trafficking. All of these instances demonstrate that Russia's conception of which international law violations can lead to a finding of 'threat to the peace' are broad in nature; however, each of the instances cited constitutes a serious international law violation, suggesting that even in this argument, the notion's subtext is possibly one of gravity.

Related to this argument that international law violations can lead to a finding of 'threat to the peace' was Russia's insistence that some findings of 'threat to the peace' were a direct consequence of failure to comply with previous

---

27 James Crawford, *The Creation of States in International Law*, 2nd ed (Oxford: New York: Clarendon Press; Oxford University Press, 2006), 126.

28 See Chapter 1, page 18 for an overview of these arguments.

29 See Chapter 9.

30 See Chapter 15.

31 See Chapter 19.

32 See Chapter 20.

33 See Chapter 24.

Security Council resolutions. This argument was used in relation to Libya and the Lockerbie bombing in 1992,[34] Afghanistan in 1999,[35] WMDs and non-proliferation in 2002–06[36] and the US- and UK-led invasion of Iraq in 2003.[37] In each of these situations, Russia justified their support for a finding of 'threat to the peace' by citing previous Security Council resolutions that were being violated by the targeted states. In every case, this ongoing violation of a Security Council resolution was a central element of Russia's position; indeed, Russia clearly argued that the Security Council had no choice but to respond with a finding of 'threat to the peace' and Chapter VII action in the face of flagrant violations of previous resolutions.

Russia's final key argument when supporting a finding of 'threat to the peace' was the idea that the situation was international in nature. This is particularly interesting given that Article 39 makes no reference to the requirement of 'international' in its text; nonetheless, Russia regularly argued that the international nature of the situation permitted them to support such a finding. This justification was used for Iraq in 1991,[38] Yugoslavia in 1991,[39] Libya and the Lockerbie bombing in 1992[40] and the US- and UK-led invasion of Iraq in 2003.[41] In each of these situations, Russia was at pains to point out that the situation being discussed was not a purely domestic matter, but had international repercussions, and that these allowed the Security Council to act under Article 39 and Chapter VII. Given that Article 39 proffers no requirement as to the international nature of the situation (apart from the threat having some international consequence), Russian arguments along these lines were more likely related to their regular overtures about respect for the right of non-interference, even though the right of non-interference did not feature as a significant argument in either their support for, or opposition to, findings of 'threat to the peace'.

34 See Chapter 13.
35 See Chapter 15.
36 See Chapter 19.
37 See Chapter 20.
38 See Chapter 10.
39 See Chapter 11.
40 See Chapter 13.
41 See Chapter 20.

CHAPTER 31

Enter the Dragon

1 Overview

In this final analysis chapter, I address the themes that appear in the case studies in relation to China's approaches to the question of 'threat to the peace'. It is worth noting that, much like Russia, China experienced political upheaval in the form of the Communist Revolution, circa 1950. However, the result of this for the Security Council was delayed, since the People's Republic of China only replaced the Republic of China on the Security Council in 1971.[1] There are insufficient case studies to determine whether this political transition had any meaningful effect upon China's justificatory discourse, although there is no discernible difference in the justificatory discourse used in the case study that straddles this change in representation: apartheid prior to 1977.[2] In this chapter, I first address some general observations arising from the justificatory discourse throughout the case studies. This is followed by an assessment of the themes surrounding China's opposition to a finding of 'threat to the peace'. Finally, I address those themes that arise in relation to China's support for a finding of 'threat to the peace'.

2 General Observations

When considering all 22 case studies without regard to China's position in each, four overarching themes emerge from the data. The first is the respect for the right of non interference in domestic affairs enjoyed by states. The second is the requirement that all 'threat to the peace' findings fall within the scope of the Security Council's mandate. The third is the requirement that any Security Council action will effectively work towards a peaceful resolution to the problem at hand. The final theme is the requirement that any action taken in relation to 'threat to the peace' must accord with all relevant law.

1 United Nations, *The Yearbook of the United Nations 1971*, vol. 25, The Yearbook of the United Nations (United Nations, 1974), 132–33.

2 See Chapter 6.

 DOI:10.1163/9789004391420_033

China directly invoked the right of non-interference in domestic affairs in seven different case studies.[3] In the majority of these case studies, this right was invoked as the basis for opposing any Security Council action (this is explored more fully below); however, it was also invoked on one occasion of a 'threat to the peace' finding on the basis that Vietnam had violated Cambodia's right of non-interference by manufacturing a coup. Beyond these direct invocations, there is clear subtext regarding the right of sovereignty, territorial integrity and non-interference in domestic affairs that is also evident in several other case studies in which this issue was not directly raised—these include apartheid prior to 1977,[4] the civil war in Yugoslavia in 1991,[5] Haiti in 1991–93,[6] Afghanistan in 1999[7] and chemical weapons in 2013.[8] This regular use of the concept of sovereignty and territorial integrity, and the right of non-intervention in domestic affairs, is not only a pillar of Chinese justificatory discourse, but also—when used by China in tangential asides—indicates the emphasis that China obviously places upon this concept when considering the existence of a 'threat to the peace'.

The second major theme appearing throughout China's justificatory discourse is that any finding of 'threat to the peace', and action stemming from this finding, must fall within the scope of the Security Council's mandate. While the specifics of how this concept was applied in relation to China's support or opposition to any particular finding is discussed in more detail below, it is important to note that this argument was raised in eight of the 22 case studies.[9] In each of these, China's support for or opposition to Security Council action under Chapter VII was firmly grounded in whether they perceived the proposed action to fall within the scope of the Security Council's mandate as articulated within the UN Charter: the maintenance of international peace and security. This overarching theme is intrinsically linked to the third theme mentioned above—that any Security Council action must be the catalyst for a peaceful resolution of the situation at hand. China most frequently employed this justification when supporting a finding of 'threat to the peace' on the basis that the proposed Security Council action would, to their mind, directly lead to a peaceful resolution (which is discussed below); however, China also used this argument to oppose Security Council action in relation to Palestine in

3 See Chapters 7–8, 10, 16–17, and 22–23.

4 See Chapter 6.

5 See Chapter 11.

6 See Chapter 12.

7 See Chapter 15.

8 See Chapter 24.

9 See Chapters 4, 7, and 16–21.

1948, and Libya and the Lockerbie bombing in 1992. On both these occasions, a core aspect of China's opposition to Security Council action and the finding of 'threat to the peace' was the belief that the action proposed would exacerbate the situation, leading to greater violence, rather than diffuse it and result in a peaceful outcome.

The final general theme that emerges from the case studies relating to China's justificatory discourse is the notion that all Security Council action stemming from a finding of 'threat to the peace' must conform to all relevant international law. This argument was employed seven times throughout the 22 case studies,[10] four times as a basis for opposition to a finding and three times in support of a finding. When this argument was used for Chinese opposition to a finding of 'threat to the peace', it was implicitly tied to the idea that China believed the proposed Security Council action would in some way violate relevant international law. Likewise, when it was invoked in support of the existence of a 'threat to the peace', it was done so on the basis that China believed the finding and consequential action met all requirements under (generally unspecified, or only nominally specified) international law governing the situation.

3 Opposition to a Finding

China opposed a finding of 'threat to the peace' in half the case studies examined in this book. This demonstrates China's much more restrained approach to the use of Chapter VII compared with any other P5 member. The situations where China opposed a finding of 'threat to the peace' were the Spanish Franco regime in 1946,[11] Palestine in 1948,[12] the Portuguese African territories in 1963,[13] the Iran hostage crisis in 1979–80,[14] Iraq in 1991,[15] Libya and the Lockerbie bombing in 1992,[16] action against the small arms trade in 1999–2011,[17] AIDS and peacekeeping in 2000–05,[18] sexual violence as a tactic of armed conflict

10 See Chapters 13, 16, 19, and 21–24.
11 See Chapter 3.
12 See Chapter 4.
13 See Chapter 5.
14 See Chapter 8.
15 See Chapter 10.
16 See Chapter 13
17 See Chapter 17.
18 See Chapter 18.

in 2008–10,[19] piracy in Somalia and the Gulf of Guinea in 2008–12[20] and the Syrian Civil War in 2011–13.[21] Throughout these 11 case studies, five different argumentative approaches recur within the Chinese justificatory discourse: the right of non-interference in a state's domestic affairs, a lack of faith in the proposed solution, the scope of the Security Council's mandate, that any action accord with the relevant international law and the idea that the situation lacked sufficient gravity to warrant a finding of 'threat to the peace'. In addition to these five recurring arguments, China also frequently abstained from voting when its opposition to a finding of 'threat to the peace' was not shared by the remaining P5 members. These abstentions occurred for Palestine in 1948, the Iran hostage crisis in 1979–80, Iraq in 1991 and Libya and the Lockerbie bombing in 1992. Although Russia vetoed Chapter VII action for the Iran hostage crisis, this preference for choosing abstention rather than veto suggests that although China is much more conservative and restrained than the rest of the P5 in their approach to the idea of 'threat to the peace', they are much more willing to compromise on this issue.

China's most common basis for opposing a finding of 'threat to peace' and ensuing Chapter VII action by the Security Council was the notion that such a finding would violate the right of the state in question to non-interference in its domestic affairs. This argument was raised for the Iran hostage crisis in 1979–80, Iraq in 1991, action against the small arms trade in 1999–2011, piracy in Somalia and the Gulf of Guinea in 2008–12 and the Syrian Civil War in 2011–13. The nature of the argument was consistent across all of these case studies, and can be summarised as follows: wherever China argued that the situation in question was purely of a domestic nature, they also asserted that any Security Council action would be a violation of Article 2(7) of the UN Charter. The consistency of this argument, and the frequency of its use, clearly demonstrates that for China to support the suggestion that a situation represents a 'threat to the peace', they must be convinced that such a finding would not violate this right. Further, this assessment highlights the prime position that this right holds in Chinese interpretations of, and approaches to, international law.

Similar to this predisposition to prioritise respect for the right of non-interference was the Chinese view that a finding of 'threat to the peace' must fall within the scope of the Security Council's mandate to maintain international peace and security. This argument was raised in relation to Palestine in 1948, action against the small arms trade in 1999–2011, AIDS and peacekeeping

19 See Chapter 21.
20 See Chapter 22.
21 See Chapter 23.

in 2000–05, sexual violence as a tactic of armed conflict in 2008–10 and piracy in Somalia and the Gulf of Guinea in 2008–12. When this argument was raised in relation to the small arms trade, AIDS and peacekeeping operations and sexual violence as a tactic of armed conflict, the essence of China's argument was that these issues were peripheral to maintaining international peace and security, were being dealt with by other UN bodies and thus were outside the ambit of Security Council competence. The argument used in relation to piracy was that the Security Council's mandate to maintain international peace and security did not authorise violations of the right of non-interference in domestic affairs. Finally, in relation to Palestine, China argued that the Security Council's mandate did not extend to authorising the use of force where such use would not bring about a peaceful solution to the conflict. This varied approach to understanding the Security Council mandate not only provides insight into the importance placed upon this notion when considering the question of 'threat to the peace', but also provides an idea of China's understanding of the scope of the mandate.

Equally as common as cries for Security Council action to be within the scope of the mandate was China's opposition to a finding of a 'threat to the peace' on the grounds that they had little or no faith in the proposed solution. This argument was raised in relation to Palestine in 1948, the Iran hostage crisis in 1979–80, Libya and the Lockerbie bombing in 1992, sexual violence as a tactic of armed conflict in 2008–10 and the Syrian Civil War in 2011–13. In each of these situations, except for sexual violence as a tactic of armed conflict, China argued that any attempt to bring about a peaceful resolution to the situation through using force or applying sanctions would be ineffective, and would likely exacerbate the problem rather than assist in resolving it. In relation to sexual violence as a tactic of armed conflict, China argued that this situation was a byproduct of armed conflict, and that focusing upon the sexual violence generally—rather than addressing the source of each of the armed conflicts on the Security Council agenda—would constitute an ineffective use of resources, and would be unlikely to bring about any effective change. While this consistently employed argument does not readily provide insight as to what China would consider an effective solution, it does highlight China's need to be convinced that the proposed solution will be effective before they support Chapter VII action arising from a finding of 'threat to the peace'.

Perhaps the least well-defined of China's recurring arguments in opposition to a finding of 'threat to the peace' was the idea that any Security Council action had to be taken in accordance with the relevant international law. Statements regarding this position were made in relation to Libya and the Lockerbie bombing in 1992, sexual violence as a tactic of armed conflict in 2008–10, piracy in Somalia and the Gulf of Guinea in 2008–12 and the Syrian Civil War in 2011–13. In none of these statements did China clarify what their concern was; instead, they placed the onus on the Security Council members to understand, through inference, that China was not convinced that a finding of 'threat to the peace' and any Security Council action under Chapter VII would be lawful under the circumstances. Thus, while the specificity of China's concerns regarding the lawfulness of the proposed Security Council action in these situations was often unclear or expressed only in general terms, the regular use of this argument suggests that for China to support a finding of 'threat to the peace', they must be convinced that the proposed action will accord with international law.

The final recurring argument in China's justificatory discourse, as evidenced in the case studies, is the proposition that for a finding of 'threat to the peace' to be made, the situation in question had to be sufficiently grave. This argument was used for the Spanish Franco regime in 1946, the Portuguese African territories in 1963 and AIDS and peacekeeping in 2000–05. Much like the rest of the P5, China did not provide any insight into how it understood or defined this amorphous notion of gravity when considering Chapter VII action; what is clear is that China required convincing that the situation met this undefined threshold. This said, when compared with the other requirements necessary to avoid Chinese opposition to a finding of 'threat to the peace', the question of gravity presents as much less significant.

4 Support for a Finding

China supported a finding of 'threat to the peace' in the remaining 11 case studies; however, there is less clarity regarding their support for this finding than is available for their opposition to such a finding. The case studies in which China supported a finding were apartheid prior to 1977,[22] the Vietnamese incursion into Cambodia in 1978–79,[23] the South African occupation of Namibia in 1981–83,[24] the civil war in Yugoslavia in 1991,[25] Haiti in 1991–93,[26] the Rwandan Civil War and genocide in 1993–94,[27] Afghanistan in 1999,[28] East Timor

22 See Chapter 6.
23 See Chapter 7.
24 See Chapter 9.
25 See Chapter 11.
26 See Chapter 12.
27 See Chapter 14.
28 See Chapter 15.

independence in 1999,[29] WMDs and non-proliferation in 2002–06,[30] the US- and UK-led invasion of Iraq in 2003[31] and chemical weapons in 2013.[32] The Chinese justificatory discourse for these situations highlights those patterns that seem to affect China's support for a finding of 'threat to the peace': that the dispute should be resolved in a peaceful manner, the upholding of the Purposes and Principles of the UN Charter, that Security Council action must accord with the relevant international law and that Security Council action must be within the scope of the Security Council's mandate to maintain international peace and security.

In the case studies, China's most frequently argued position in favour of Security Council action was that the situation should be resolved through peaceful means. Of the 11 case studies where China supported a finding of 'threat to the peace', this argument featured in the justificatory discourse in six situations: Apartheid, Haiti in 1991–93, the Rwandan Civil War and genocide in 1993–94, Afghanistan in 1999, WMDs and non-proliferation in 2002–06 and chemical weapons in 2013. Their arguments in each of these case studies relating to peaceful solutions, and their support for a finding of 'threat to the peace', were quite simply that China believed the proposed action before the Security Council would assist in bringing about a peaceful resolution to the situation. While the details varied in each situation, the general argument was the same. This suggests a great deal of pragmatism in China's approach to the question of 'threat to the peace'. Further, when combined with China's view that all Security Council action must be firmly grounded in respect for international law, Chinese practice clearly suggests that so long as all relevant international law is respected, and the solution before the Council is one that China is convinced is likely to bring about a peaceful resolution, then China will either support, or at least not object to, a finding of 'threat to the peace'.

Similarly, it appears that China's view that Security Council action must be within the scope of the Security Council's mandate, and that such action must accord with relevant international law, are closely related arguments, although they were only argued concurrently for WMDs and non-proliferation. The more specific argument that a finding of 'threat to the peace' must be within the scope of the Security Council's mandate was also proposed for the Vietnamese incursion into Cambodia and the US- and UK-led invasion of Iraq. In all these instances, China argued that the situation before the Security Council

29 See Chapter 16.
30 See Chapter 19.
31 See Chapter 20.
32 See Chapter 24.

threatened international peace and security, and was thus within the scope of the Security Council's mandate. The more vague argument that a finding of 'threat to the peace' existed because of breaches of international law was deployed for East Timor, chemical weapons and WMDs and non-proliferation. While this argument was not clearly articulated, its influence is inferred through China's support of a finding of 'threat to the peace' in each of these instances, while they asserted that any action being taken must accord with international law and their belief that Chapter VII action in each situation complied with all of the various possible international laws at play. In China's justificatory discourse, both of these arguments present less as grounds for their support of a finding of 'threat to the peace' than as precursors to that support.

The final recurring argument in the justificatory discourse evident in the case studies in which China supported a finding of 'threat to the peace' is that situations violating the Purposes and Principles of the Charter constitute such a threat. This argument was made for Apartheid, the US- and UK-led invasion of Iraq in 2003 and chemical weapons in 2013. In relation to the South African apartheid regime, China argued that the systematic policy of racism within South Africa was a violation of South Africa's obligations under Article 1(3) of the Charter. When this argument was made to oppose the US- and UK-led invasion of Iraq, China posited that the invasion itself constituted a violation of the prohibition of the use of force enshrined in Article 2(4). Finally, when China used this argument in the chemical weapons debates, asserting that Security Council action under Chapter VII against a category of weapon already banned by treaty and custom at international law bolstered the Purposes and Principles of the Charter generally, and China thus supported this action. These combinations of arguments in relation to the Purposes and Principles of the Charter suggest that where a systematic violation of Chapter I of the Charter exists, or where Security Council action would positively promote the Purposes and Principles of the Charter, then China is likely willing to support that action.

Conclusion

The question at the heart of this volume is this: are Security Council decisions relating to 'threat to the peace' in Article 39 of the UN Charter as arbitrary as commentators have suggested (without testing), or is there some form of internal definition of what constitutes a 'threat to the peace' evident in the patterns and consistency of approach behind these seemingly arbitrary decisions? The answer is invariably more nuanced and complicated than a simple yes or no; and relies upon the approach taken to the question itself. If the Security Council is perceived as a single, monolithic, coherent entity, then the answer is simply no—there is no pattern or consistency to the decisions, although there is some consistency to the process by which those decisions are made. However, if the Security Council is viewed as a complicated and fractious collective decision-making forum, with each member operating independently and with its own agenda, then consistency and patterns are visible, and thus so is an internal definition of the phrase 'threat to the peace' for each member. I adopt this latter perspective throughout this book. This is because the Security Council structure is grounded in partisan geopolitics, requiring consensus from the five permanent members (in conjunction with the majority of all members) to take action. Given that all members maintain their national ties while executing their duties on the Security Council, it would be naive to suggest that the Security Council is an independent and coherent body operating free from these partisan geopolitical and cultural influences.

Given this apparently fractious and partisan nature, it is entirely understandable why commentators have previously declared that Security Council decisions are essentially arbitrary and political,[1] while neglecting to rigorously test this conclusion. The first-of-its-kind testing I have conducted in this book indicates, perhaps surprisingly, that such claims regarding the Security

1 Amy Eckert, 'The Non-Intervention Principle and International Humanitarian Interventions':, *International Legal Theory* 7, no. 1 (2001): 56; Christopher J. Le Mon and Rachel S. Taylor, 'Security Council Action in the Name of Human Rights: From Rhodesia to the Congo', *U.C. Davis Journal of International Law & Policy* 10, no. 2 (2004): 198; Inger Österdahl, *Threat to the Peace: The Interpretation by the Security Council of Article 39 of the UN Charter* (Uppsala: Iustus, 1998), 103; Jennifer Welsh, Carolin Thielking, and S. Neil MacFarlane, 'The Responsibility to Protect: Assessing the Report of the International Commission on Intervention and State Sovereignty', *International Journal* 57 (2002): 502; N. D White, *Keeping the Peace: The United Nations and the Maintenance of International Peace and Security* (Manchester; New York; New York: Manchester University Press; Distributed exclusively in the USA and Canada by St. Martin's Press, 1993), 44.

 | DOI:10.1163/9789004391420_034

Council's fickle nature are relatively unfounded. The patterns and consistencies that exist within the Security Council sit mostly at the level of how the individual member state will approach the question of 'threat to the peace'; however, there are also consistencies in how the Security Council as a whole frames the question when considering the existence of a 'threat to the peace'. This study flips all the untested hypotheses made by other commentators relating to the Security Council's decision-making process by demonstrating empirically that there is in fact a strong degree of pattern and consistency in how the P5 make and justify decisions in the Security Council, and showing that each P5 member does indeed have a definition and understanding of what 'threat to the peace' actually means. This fills the significant hole in thinking regarding the relationship between international law and international relations in the context of the Security Council. Further, it empirically illustrates that, at least within the Security Council, if not international relations generally, international law is the language used to express and negotiate power. I first address how the Security Council frames the question of 'threat to the peace' before moving to how each member of the P5 approaches this question in a relatively stable manner, and thus in a manner that allows greater insight into the sorts of decisions these member states will likely take. This is all important because knowing how the P5 are likely to respond to any given situation based upon consistent past conduct will create greater predictability of Security Council actions, and thus enable greater preparedness for responding.

A key factor in every case study included in this book was the question of how the Security Council determined the context of the situation being addressed. Within this question of context, two key factors revealed the Security Council's pattern of approach as a whole. These were the manner in which the facts before the Security Council were determined, and the fact-finders' impact in making recommendations to the Security Council.[2] In relation to determining the facts, the case studies show that the Security Council as a whole clearly prefer facts gathered and verified by a UN source, usually the Secretary-General.[3] The approach of all Security Council members suggests that they find facts from a partisan source inherently less trustworthy than facts from a UN source. The most likely reason for this is the perception (or actuality) of bias when facts are presented by a party with a vested interest in the situation being addressed. This was most distinctly articulated by China in relation to the Portuguese

2 See above at Chapter 26.

3 For a greater understanding of the process of fact-finding (particularly in the context of human rights investigations) see Philip Alston and Sarah Knuckey, eds., *The Transformation of Human Rights Fact-Finding* (New York, NY: Oxford University Press, 2016).

African territories case study, where they argued that both parties to the dispute may be presenting the truth as they understood it, but that neither was a reliable source because of their vested interest and the perspectives that governed them.[4] This preference for neutral fact-finders in framing the context of a question of 'threat to the peace' stands in stark contrast to the lack of value placed upon fact-finder recommendations to the Security Council. In the case studies addressed in this book, only one recommendation from fact-finders was actually followed, and that was a recommendation to do nothing.[5] The reason for the Security Council consistently acting in opposition to, or merely disregarding, the recommendations of expert fact-finders is unclear; however, I believe it would be valuable to engage in an empirical study along similar lines to this one to illuminate the reasoning further.[6]

At the level of the individual states, rather than the Security Council as a whole, the P5 members all displayed patterns of approach that allow for greater understanding of how each of them conducts themselves in response to the question of 'threat to the peace'. None of these patterns of approach are certainties, particularly in light of the vast variety of situations that may be considered in relation to 'threat to the peace'; however, they do provide insight into the decision-making process and values prioritised when these decisions are made. By understanding the values prioritised by each P5 member, we can employ this insight to better predict how each P5 member will likely respond to a question of 'threat to the peace'. Similarly, such insight may allow those seeking to influence the P5 to better tailor their arguments pertaining to such a question when dealing with each state individually. As Johnston argues, the 'better argument' (i.e., the argument that has the most logical coherence with conduct and the international law) is the one that will usually win in the long term in matters of international security.[7] The question of what constitutes a better argument requires an understanding of how values and issues of international law are prioritised by each party; I humbly submit that the case studies, and the meta-synthesis I have conducted of these case studies, provide substantial insight into that issue. Further, the consistent use of international

4 United Nations Security Council, 'Security Council, Eighteenth Year: 1033rd Meeting (S/PV.1033)', 24 April 1963, 15.

5 See Chapters 3, 8, 17, 20, 21 and 23; see also Chapter 26 p. 235–237.

6 I would suggest that it is most likely (as with all activities within the Security Council) an exercise of power and dominance by the P5 to remind the factfinders, and the rest of the world, of the position of power and prominence they hold in matters of global security. See above at Chapter 26 p. 237.

7 See generally: Ian Johnstone, 'Security Council Deliberations: The Power of the Better Argument', *European Journal of International Law* 14, no. 3 (2003): 437–80.

law as the common language of diplomacy within the Security Council confirms my theory, presented in Chapter 1, that international law is the language of power and diplomacy.

This theory began with the work of numerous international law scholars, most notably Koskenniemi and Johnstone, who argue that the role of international law is to act as a restraining power on the self-interest of states in diplomatic relations. From this starting point, I synthesised this helpful but unsatisfying approach with the work of sociologists, notably Turk and Butler, on the relationship between law and power—namely that the law acts as the arm that is used to express power within society, intertwined and interdependent with other aspects of power. This synthesis led me to conclude that in diplomatic discourse, law does not act as a related and parallel restraining power on state self-interest, but rather as the common language through which states conduct diplomatic discourse.

When understanding how the US approaches the question of 'threat to the peace', an overarching first question must be addressed before the more detailed nuance of the situation becomes relevant. This question relates to the gravity of the situation—is the situation being put before the Security Council of sufficient gravitas to warrant their attention? When the US considers this issue, it usually involves the scale and effect of the violence underway rather than any other factor. Particularly clear is that the US considers this question of gravity to be a factual prerequisite to any Security Council powers and obligations found in Chapter VII and stemming from Article 39.[8] Once this question of gravity has been considered, the US tendency towards Security Council action is better understood, as are the likely reasons that the US will provide when expressing this preference for Security Council action. The US shows a definite tendency for using the Security Council to defend democracy,[9] protect

8 See for example: 'It is clear to my delegation that the application of sanctions under Chapter VII in the situation now before us would be both bad law and bad policy. It will be bad law because the extreme measures provided in Chapter VII where never intended and cannot reasonably be interpreted to apply to situations of this kind. The founders of the United Nations were very careful to reserve the right of the Organization to employ mandatory coercive measures in situations where there was an actuality of international violence or such a clear and present threat to peace as to leave no reasonable alternative but to resort to coercion. We do not have that kind of situation here'.: United Nations Security Council, 'Security Council, Eighteenth Year: 1052nd Meeting (S/PV.1052)' (United Nations, 2 August 1963), 16.

9 See for example: '[C]ries for freedom of expression, association, peaceful assembly and the ability to freely choose their leaders' United Nations Security Council, '6524th Meeting', above n 1245, 4; 'This unconstitutional and violent seizure of power denies the people of Haiti their right of self-determination. These violent and illegal action must not, and will not, succeed. The inalienable right of all of the people of Haiti to democracy and constitutional

human rights,[10] promote and maintain the rule of law,[11] and punish international law violations.[12] When these factors are considered in conjunction with the US preference for supporting a finding of 'threat to the peace', should the US be convinced that finding of 'threat to the peace' will support one or more of these factors, it is likely that they will support such a finding. These tendencies also demonstrate the areas of international law that are given primacy.

Much like the US, the UK's starting point when addressing the question of 'threat to the peace' is whether a situation possesses the required gravity indicating the need for Security Council attention.[13] Once this amorphous gravity threshold has been met, the UK process seems to be less governed by specific

---

rule must be restored'.: United Nations Security Council, 'Security Council, Forty-Sixth Year: 3011th Meeting (S/PV.3011)' (United Nations, 3 October 1991), 34.

10 See for example: '[T]he council's condemnation of the Iraqi government's continued violence towards its own people. The resolution insists that Iraq meet its humanitarian responsibilities'.: United Nations Security Council, '2982nd Meeting', above n 593, 58; 'When women and girls are preyed upon and raped, the international community cannot be silent or inactive. It is our responsibility to be their advocates and their defenders': United Nations Security Council, 'Security Council, Sixty-Third Year: 5916th Meeting (S/PV.5916)' (United Nations, 19 June 2008), 4; '[Y]earning for liberty and universal human rights': United Nations Security Council, 'Security Council, Sixty-Sixth Year: 6627th Meeting (S/PV.6627)', 4 October 2011, 8.

11 See for example: '[The US call on the Taliban to surrender bin Laden] to authorities in a country where he will be brought to justice'.: United Nations Security Council, 'Security Council, Fifty-Fourth Year: 4051st Meeting (S/PV.4051)', 15 October 1999, 3; 'It is time for all of us to assume our responsibility to go beyond condemning this behaviour and take concrete steps to end it, to make it socially unacceptable, to recognise that it is not cultural; it is criminal'.: United Nations Security Council, 'Security Council, Sixty-Fourth Year: 6195th Meeting (S/PV.6195)' (United Nations, 30 September 2009); '[I]nternational norms matter'.; United Nations Security Council, 'Security Council, Sixty-Eighth Year: 7038th Meeting (S/PV.7038)', 27 September 2013, 5.

12 See for example: 'That fact led us to the conclusion that the solution to the problem we are discussing is clear. Viet Nam must immediately withdraw its armed forces from Kampuchea, must respect that country's territorial integrity and must make credible its intention to respect the territorial integrity of other States in the region'.: United Nations Security Council, 'Security Council, Thirty-Fourth Year: 2110th Meeting (S/PV.2110)' (United Nations, 13 January 1979), 7; '[Iran] has placed itself in conflict with the structure of law and with the machinery of peace all of us have painstakingly built'.: United Nations Security Council, 'Security Council, Thirty-Fourth Year: 2182nd Meeting (S/PV.2182)' (United Nations, 29 December 1979), 2; '… for the first time, that the use of chemical weapons, which the world long ago determined to be beyond the bounds of acceptable human behaviour, is also a threat to international peace and security, anywhere they might be used, any time they might be used, under any circumstances'.: United Nations Security Council, '7038th Meeting', 4.

13 See for example: '[The UK has no quarrel with Iran beyond the] flagrant violation of the Vienna Convention on Diplomatic Relations, of other United Nations conventions, of

ideals and more by the process of formal legal reasoning.[14] While the case studies show the UK's propensity to act in response to situations it feels fall within the Security Council's mandate,[15] to protect human rights[16] and as enforcement action for failures to comply with previous Security Council resolutions or general international law,[17] these tendencies are intrinsically related to the UK's decision-making methods, rather than operating as driving ideals. While this provides less insight into the cultural values that shape the UK's interpretation of international law, it does provide a stable basis for understanding how they approach the question of 'threat to the peace'. The UK approaches a finding of 'threat to the peace' as a question of fact that the Security Council is legally obligated to make where the facts demonstrate that such a situation exists. To fulfil this obligation, the UK approaches each situation by applying the law to the relevant facts to determine whether such a threat exists, and then

general international law and long-standing diplomatic practices of States': United Nations Security Council, '2182nd Meeting', 3.

14 See for example: 'I know it may be said that these are legal quibbles, but I cannot accept that. It seems to me to be of prime importance to define exactly the scope and powers of the United Nations in matters of this kind'.: United Nations Security Council, 'Security Council, First Year: 46th Meeting (S/PV.46)' (United Nations, 17 June 1946), 347; 'This, I am bound to say, seems to us an exceptionally shocking argument. It is not only clearly contrary to the provisions and spirit of the Charter, but it offends against one of the most important and widespread principles of natural justice, namely, that he who comes to a court of law seeking equity should come with clean hands'.: United Nations Security Council, 'Security Council, Eighteenth Year: 1045th Meeting (S/PV.1045)', 26 July 1963, 9; 'We must, therefore, distinguish between a situation which has engendered international friction and one which constitutes a threat to peace. There is no evidence before us that the actions of the South African Republic, however repellent they may be to us all, are actions which threaten the territorial integrity of political independence of any member country ... The Council does not in these circumstances have the power to impose sanctions. To attempt to do so would, as the representative of the United States has said, be both bad law and bad policy'.: United Nations Security Council, 'Security Council, Eighteenth Year: 1054th Meeting (S/PV.1054)' (United Nations, 6 August 1963), 19–20; 'Whatever is said about human rights in Kampuchea, it cannot excuse Viet Nam, whose own human rights record is deplorable, for violating the territorial integrity of Democratic Kampuchea, an independent State Member of the United Nations ... Respect for the sovereignty, territorial integrity and political independence of Member States is one of the cornerstones of the Charter and of the United Nations system'.: United Nations Security Council, '2110th Meeting', 6–7; '[Libya has taken] no serious steps towards compliance with these requests': United Nations Security Council, 'Security Council, Forty-Seventh Year: 3063rd Meeting (S/PV.3063)' (United Nations, 31 March 1992), 68.

15 See Chapter 3; Chapter 13; Chapter 19; Chapter 21; Chapter 28.

16 See Chapter 10; Chapter 16; Chapter 23; Chapter 24; Chapter 28.

17 See Chapter 4; Chapter 7; Chapter 8; Chapter 11; Chapter 13; Chapter 15; Chapter 19; Chapter 20; Chapter 23; Chapter 24; Chapter 28.

positions itself accordingly. The UK thus appears to be less driven by passions and ideologies and more animated by obligations that they see as legally binding by virtue of their position as a permanent member of the Security Council. This assessment also means that those familiar with common-law-derived processes of formal legal reasoning should generally be able to predict how the UK will approach any situation, should they possess sufficient facts to make an analysis. In terms of understanding the competing provisions of international law to which the UK will give primacy, their statements in the Security Council provide little insight and suggest that on this front, they are moderates who will assess which norm is owed primacy on the basis of the facts.

The French appear to be the moderates, in the truest sense of the word, in that they are governed by law but not driven by it (in contrast to the UK). This supposition is based on the fact that France is the least predictable of any P5 member; the French seem to simply take each case on its individual merits, and apply the facts of that situation to all relevant law to reach their conclusion. As moderates (as opposed to middle-of-the-road centrists),[18] they do not appear driven by any concrete ideological position in relation to the question of 'threat to the peace'; indeed, there is no telling what they will choose to care about on any given day, which was most clearly demonstrated in the Rwanda case study.[19] This does not mean that no patterns emerge from the case studies regarding French approaches to 'threat to the peace', although perhaps the strongest pattern is France's overwhelmingly consistent willingness to make a positive finding of 'threat to the peace' leading to Security Council action.[20] The case studies show that of all P5 members, France most actively supported positive findings and Security Council action stemming from such findings. Perhaps the only ideological considerations that truly factor into the French decision-making process are that conflict situations should be resolved in a peaceful manner,[21] and that the right of self-determination of states should always be respected.[22] This moderate nature bequeaths upon France the title of least predictable of the P5; however, it also renders them the most open to being convinced that the situation is (or is not, as the case may be) a 'threat to the peace' without prejudice or judgement—a notion demonstrated by their overwhelming tendency to support positive findings. For much the same

18 See generally Chapter 29.

19 See Chapter 14 p. 139–40 for a strong example of the fickle change of positions by the French.

20 See Chapter 29.

21 See Chapter 8; Chapter 11; Chapter 14; Chapter 19; Chapter 24; Chapter 29.

22 See Chapter 3; Chapter 11; Chapter 12; Chapter 16; Chapter 20; Chapter 29.

reasons as the UK, these tendencies offer little insight into how the French will resolve conflicts of international law and to which norms they will give primacy; however, I suspect that much like their approach to the question of 'threat to the peace', this will depend entirely on the facts of each individual situation.

The data in the case studies suggest that Russia is perhaps the most practical of all the P5 members when considering the existence of a 'threat to the peace'. This is clearly demonstrated by the fact that Russia's most common argument against a finding of 'threat to the peace' was a lack of faith in the proposed solution.[23] Tied to this tendency is Russia's view that all Security Council action must fall within the Security Council's mandate to maintain international peace and security.[24] These two ideas, in conjunction with a view of the supremacy of the right of self-determination (and the right of non-interference in domestic affairs as a component of the right of self-determination)[25] in international law (highlighting a view of international law that the rights of states are to be given primacy over the rights of individuals), that underpin Russia's decision-making processes in relation to 'threat to the peace'. This pragmatism is combined with—and perhaps illustrated by—Russia's evident willingness

23 See for example: '[T]he dearth of necessary political will also makes it impossible to regulate that sphere appropriately'.: United Nations Security Council, 'Security Council, Sixty-Third Year: 5881st Meeting (S/PV.5881)' (United Nations, 30 April 2008), 12; 'Any external influence imposed by us on that process could risk exacerbating the crisis'.: United Nations Security Council, 'Security Council, Sixty-Seventh Year: 6756th Meeting (S/PV.6756)', 21 April 2012, 2.

24 See for example: 'With respect to the role of the Security Council, it is our conviction that the Council must focus its attention primarily on those instances in which the illicit trade in small arms and light weapons is directly linked to conflict situations that are on the Council's agenda'.: United Nations Security Council, 'Security Council, Fifty-Seventh Year: 4623rd Meeting (S/PV.4623)' (United Nations, 11 October 2002), 17; 'The Council cannot impose parameters for an internal political settlement. The Charter gives no such authority'.: United Nations Security Council, 'Security Council, Sixty-Seventh Year: 6710th Meeting (S/PV.6710)', 31 January 2012, 24.

25 See for example: 'The fundamental interests of the peoples of Africa – and not only of Africa – and the lofty principles of the United Nations Charter required that the struggle of the peoples of African countries for their freedom and independence and against colonialism and aggression should be supported by deeds'.: United Nations Security Council, '1033rd Meeting', 19; 'Peking's propaganda slanders the Kampuchean Patriots. That slander cannot hide an obvious fact: the Khmer people has waged a struggle in its territory for its own freedom. If there is an intervention from outside in the internal affairs of Kampuchea it is and continues to be carried out by Peking hegemonists'.: United Nations Security Council, 'Security Council, Thirty-Fourth Year: 2108th Meeting (S/PV.2108)' (United Nations, 11 January 1979), 17; 'Namibia is a territory illegally occupied by the South African racists': United Nations Security Council, 'Security Council, Thirty-Sixth Year: 2263rd Meeting (S/PV.2263)' (United Nations, 30 January 1981), 6.

to veto resolutions that it believes will violate any of these very practical ideals. In the Security Council's early years—the years of decolonisation—this tendency was displayed through Russia's great willingness to support Security Council action. Since Vladimir Putin's rise to power, these ideals have been characterised by a significant restraint on Security Council action under Chapter VII. However, regardless of this difference of approach, the reasons underpinning their approach to 'threat to the peace' remain the same: that Security Council action must support the right of self-determination of states, lead to practical solutions rather than exacerbate situations and be within the Security Council's mandate for maintaining international peace and security.

China, more than any other P5 member, takes a very narrow view of what constitutes a 'threat to the peace', a view that is more defined by what it will not tolerate in a finding, rather than the situations in which it will support a finding. China tends to oppose findings of 'threat to the peace' where it perceives the situation as lacking in gravity, and thus not warranting Security Council attention.[26] This is perhaps the only trait that China's approach shares with those of the US and UK. Much like Russia, China displays an unwillingness to support a finding of 'threat to the peace' where such a finding would constitute a violation of the right of non-interference in the domestic affairs of a state,[27] where the proposed solution would not bring about peace (while lending their full support to proposals they believed would result in peace)[28] or where the

26 See for example: '[AIDS is an issue to be addressed by other] relevant international bodies': United Nations Security Council, 'Security Council, Fifty-Eighth Year: 4859th Meeting (S/PV.4859)', 17 November 2003, 16.

27 See for example: '[The invasion and annexation of Cambodia by Viet Nam is] an important step in Viet Nam's strategy of establishing a colonial empire called the "Indo-Chinese Federation" under its armed control for further expansion of its sphere of influence in South-East Asia'.: United Nations Security Council, '2108th Meeting'; 'According to paragraph 7 of article 2 of the Charter, Security Council should not consider or take action on questions concerning the internal affairs of any state ... Based on the position I have just set out, we abstained in the vote on the resolution'.: United Nations Security Council, 'Security Council, Forty-Sixth Year: 2982nd Meeting (S/PV.2982)' (United Nations, 5 April 1991), 56; 'Most important, is [sic] should depend upon whether it complies with the Charter of the United Nations and the principle of non-interference in internal affairs of states – which has a bearing upon security and survival of developing countries, in particular small and medium-sized countries, and laws on world peace and stability'.: United Nations Security Council, '6627th Meeting'; 'National Governments bear the primary responsibility to fight the illicit trade in arms'.: United Nations Security Council, 'Security Council, Sixty-Eighth Year: 7036th Meeting (S/PV.7036)' (United Nations, 26 September 2013), 17.

28 See for example: '[China's vote is grounded in its] sincere desire to create conditions for the early restoration of peace and security in that country'.: United Nations Security

situation is outside the Security Council's mandate for maintaining international peace and security.[29] These tendencies demonstrate China's position that the associated state rights of non-interference and self-determination, in accordance with the Charter, are to be given primacy over all other norms of international law. However, unlike Russia, China shows a much greater willingness to compromise on their positions, as demonstrated by the case studies in which they objected to a positive finding, but then acquiesced to that outcome by abstaining from voting when the rest of the P5 were in support. The grounds for supporting positive findings of 'threat to the peace' are akin to their grounds for opposition: namely, should China be convinced that situation is within the Security Council's mandate, and that the proposed action will support peaceful solutions in accordance with all relevant international law, then they are quite willing to vote in favour of such a finding.

While many scholars have an inherent, and anecdotally understandable, tendency to think of the Security Council as a monolithic institution that possesses the ability to authorise proactive violence at the global level, a failure to comprehensively examine the conduct, across time, of the key individual entities that make up the institution has led to the perhaps incorrect assertion that Security Council findings of 'threat to the peace' are fluid, arbitrary and fickle. When the focus shifts from the collective endpoint decisions and moves instead to the manner in which the individual P5 states make those decisions and approach the problem, the perspective changes dramatically. No longer are Security Council decisions relating to 'threat to the peace' simply political, fluid and arbitrary; indeed, this raises questions around the conclusions that have been reached on the basis of those assertions. Instead, the decisions made by the individual states that form the core of the Security Council follow patterns that are grounded in each of those state's individual cultural approaches

Council, 'Security Council, Forty-Ninth Year: 3377th Meeting (S/PV.3377)' (United Nations, 16 May 1994), 9; 'China has consistently taken a cautious approach to sanctions. Sanctions, rather than assistance [sic] in resolving an issue, often lead to further complications of the situation. We firmly oppose the use of force to resolve the Syrian issue, as well as practices, such as forcibly pushing for regime change, that violate the purposes and principles of the United Nations Charter and the basic norms that govern international relations'.: United Nations Security Council, '6710th Meeting', 25. See also Chapter 4; Chapter 6; Chapter 8; Chapter 12; Chapter 13; Chapter 14; Chapter 15; Chapter 19; Chapter 21; Chapter 23; Chapter 24; Chapter 31.

29 See for example: 'Governments bear the primary responsibility for protecting women in their respective countries'.: United Nations Security Council, 'Security Council, Sixty-Fourth Year: 6180th Meeting (S/PV.6180)' (United Nations, 7 August 2009), 21. See also Chapter 4; Chapter 17; Chapter 18; Chapter 21; Chapter 22; Chapter 31.

to international law and the Security Council's role. This in turn provides great insight into how each of the veto nations will likely conduct themselves in relation to any given situation where the very existence of a 'threat to the peace' is substantially in question. This insight is founded upon an analysis of how the states have behaved in the past, and by using this analysis as a guide to how they will likely behave in the future. It is by no means a perfect metric and will need regular updating as time passes, but it does provide a better benchmark for the question of what constitutes a 'threat to the peace' in Article 39 of the UN Charter than has previously existed. The working Security Council definition exists as a middle ground that satisfies each of these separate approaches or, more frequently, does not encroach on their individual core values in an unacceptable manner.

Annex

Potential Case Studies

Positive Case Studies		
Name	**Year**	**Summary of Subject Matter**
Palestine	1948	Unrest and Religious/ Racial Conflict
Apartheid	1963–77	Racial Discrimination
Cyprus	1964–74	Armed Conflict
South Rhodesia	1963	Civil Unrest
Angola	1987	Acts of Aggression
Iraq	1991	Repression of a civilian population
Former Yugoslavia	1991–92	Civil war and genocide
Somalia	1992	Civil War
Libya	1992	State sponsored terrorism
Haiti	1993	Civil war and the defence of democracy
Rwanda	1994	Civil war and genocide
Ethiopia/Sudan/Egypt	1996	Assassination attempts
Great Lakes	1996	Civil war
Central African Republic	1997	Civil war
Angola	1997	Peace process concerns
Democratic Republic of Congo	1999	Civil war
Afghanistan	1999	Failure to comply with Security Council Resolution
East Timor	1999	Civil Unrest
Targeting of civilians	2000	Targeting of civilians in armed conflict
9/11 bombings	2001	Terrorism
Iraq	2002	WMDs

 | DOI:10.1163/9789004391420_035

Positive Case Studies

Name	Year	Summary of Subject Matter
Lebanon	2004	Internal political instability
Sudan	2004–06	Civil war and cross-border conflict
WMDs and non-state actors	2004	WMDs
Iran	2006	WMDs
North Korea	2006	WMDs
Chemical weapons	2013	Violation of jus cogens and other international law

Negative Case Studies

Name	Year	Summary of Subject Matter
Spain	1946	Fascism
Greek frontier incidents	1947	Border skirmishes
Portuguese African territories	1963	Decolonisation
Cambodia/Vietnam	1979	Vietnamese ousting of Pol Pot
Iran/USA	1979	Iran hostage crisis
Israeli occupation of the Syrian Golan Highlands	1981	Foreign military occupation
Namibia	1981–1984	Foreign military occupation
Burundi	1993	Internal unrest and coup
Small arms trade	1999–2011	Arms trade and 'threat to the peace'
AIDS and peacekeeping	2001–05	AIDS pandemic in Africa
Israel/Palestine/Middle East	2001–03	Continued unrest
Iraq/USA/UK	2003	Invasion of Iraq by Coalition of the willing

Children and armed conflict	2004	Child Soldiers
Myanmar	2006	Internal unrest
Piracy in Somalia	2007–12	Maritime Piracy
Georgia	2008	Civil unrest and aggression
Sexual violence as armed conflict	2008–10	Military sexual violence
Israel	2010	Incursion on the protest flotia
Piracy in West Africa	2011–12	Maritime Piracy
Conflict in Syria	2012–Ongoing	Multi-party internal armed conflict

Coding Results Tables

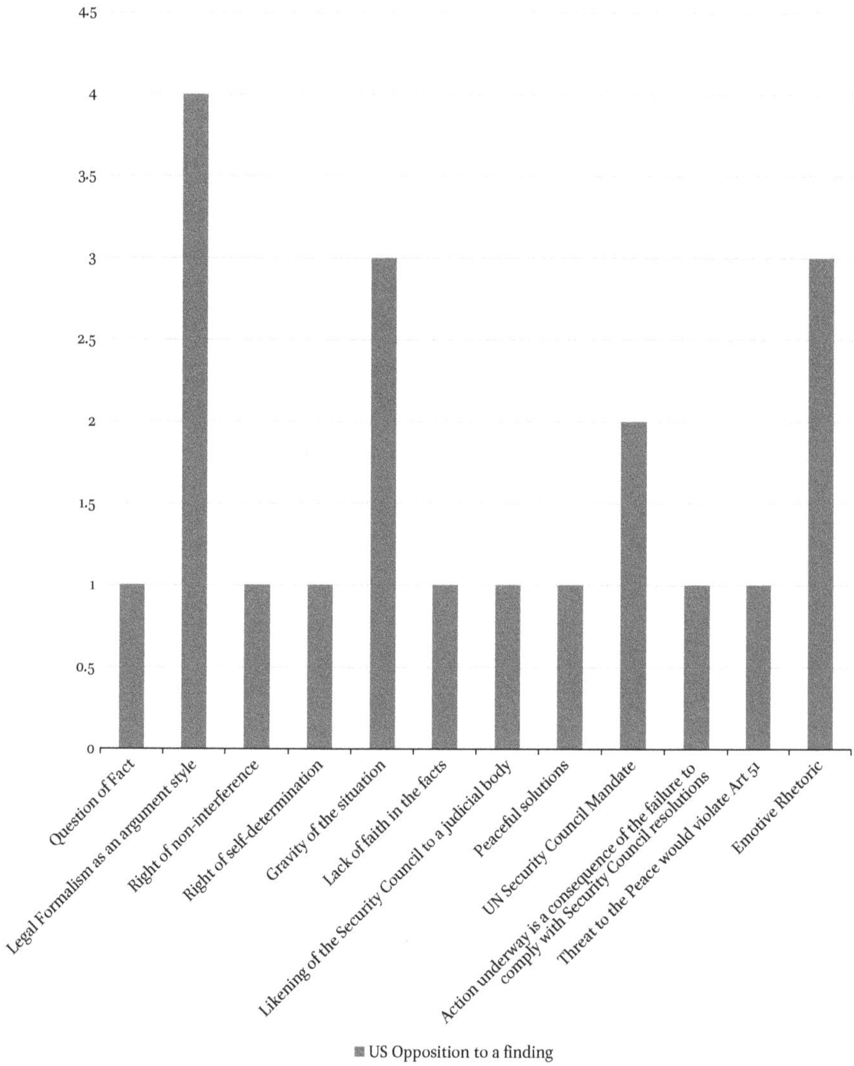

 | DOI:10.1163/9789004391420_036

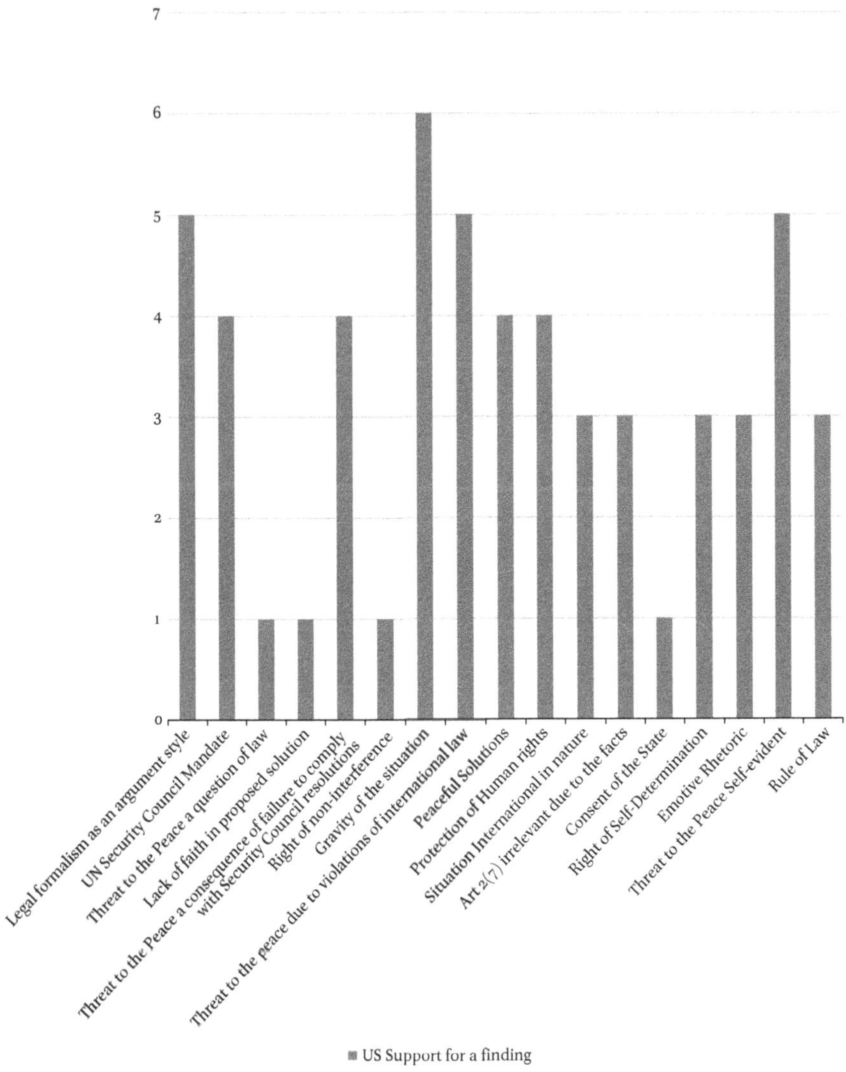
7
6
5
4
3
2
1
0
Legal formalism as an argument style
UN Security Council Mandate
Threat to the Peace a question of law
Lack of faith in proposed solution
Threat to the Peace a consequence of failure to comply with Security Council resolutions
Right of non-interference
Gravity of the situation
Threat to the peace due to violations of international law
Peaceful Solutions
Protection of Human rights
Situation International in nature
Art 2(7) irrelevant due to the facts
Consent of the State
Right of Self-Determination
Emotive Rhetoric
Threat to the Peace Self-evident
Rule of Law
US Support for a finding

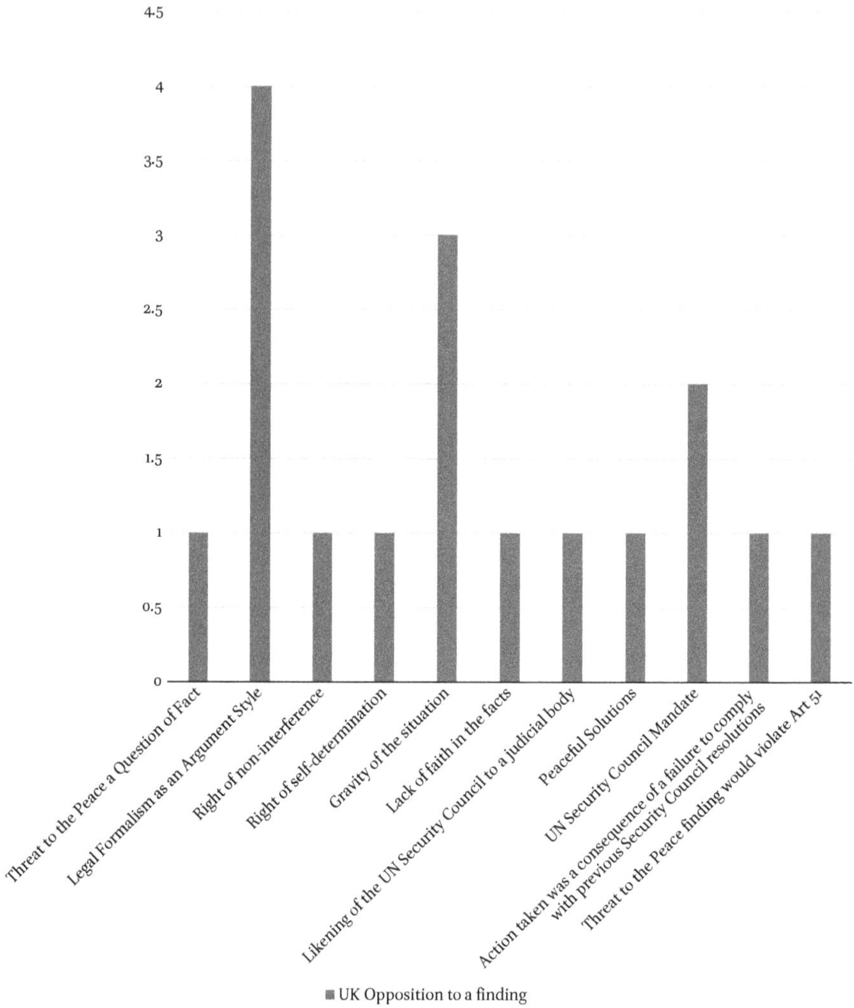
4.5
4
3.5
3
2.5
2
1.5
1
0.5
0
Threat to the Peace a Question of Fact
Legal Formalism as an Argument Style
Right of non-interference
Right of self-determination
Gravity of the situation
Lack of faith in the facts
Likening of the UN Security Council to a judicial body
Peaceful Solutions
UN Security Council Mandate
Action taken was a consequence of a failure to comply with previous Security Council resolutions
Threat to the Peace finding would violate Art 51
UK Opposition to a finding

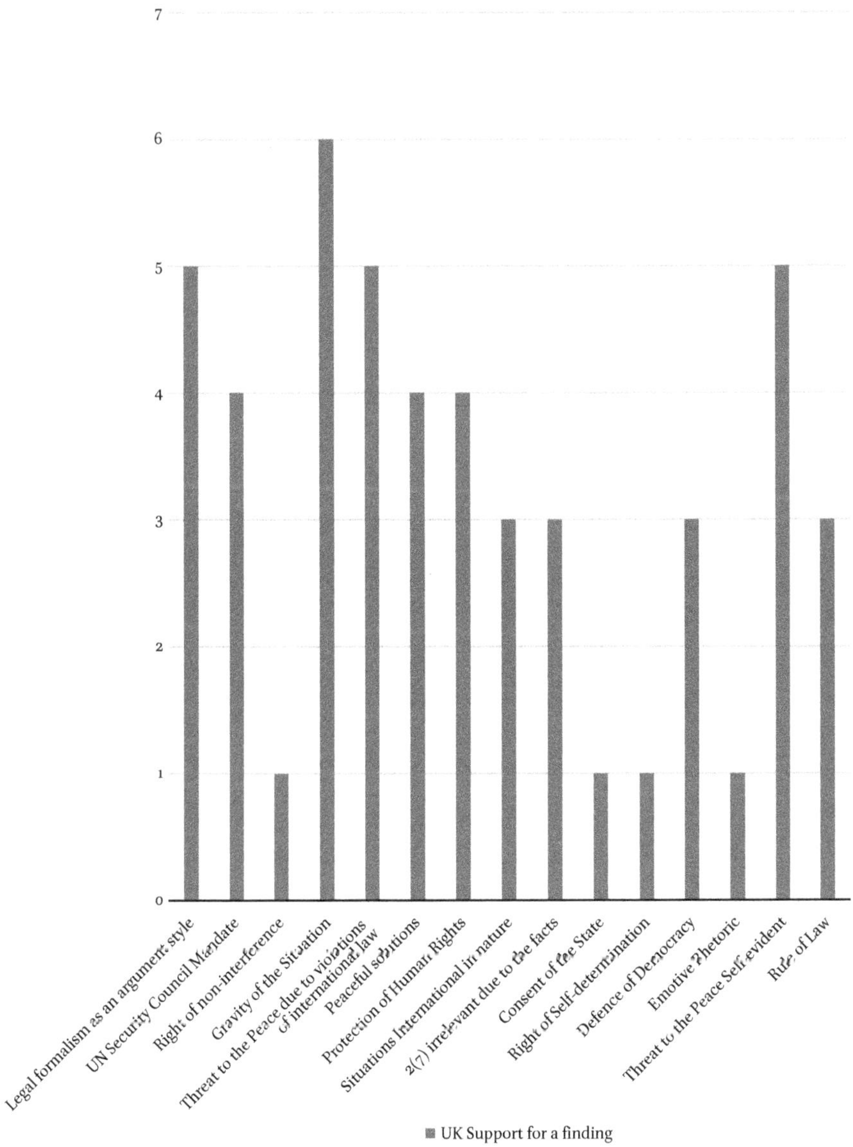
7
6
5
4
3
2
1
0
Legal formalism as an argument style
UN Security Council Mandate
Right of non-interference
Gravity of the Situation
Threat to the Peace due to violations of international law
Peaceful solutions
Protection of Human Rights
Situations International in nature
2(7) irrelevant due to the facts
Consent of the State
Right of Self-determination
Defence of Democracy
Emotive Rhetoric
Threat to the Peace Self-evident
Rule of Law
UK Support for a finding

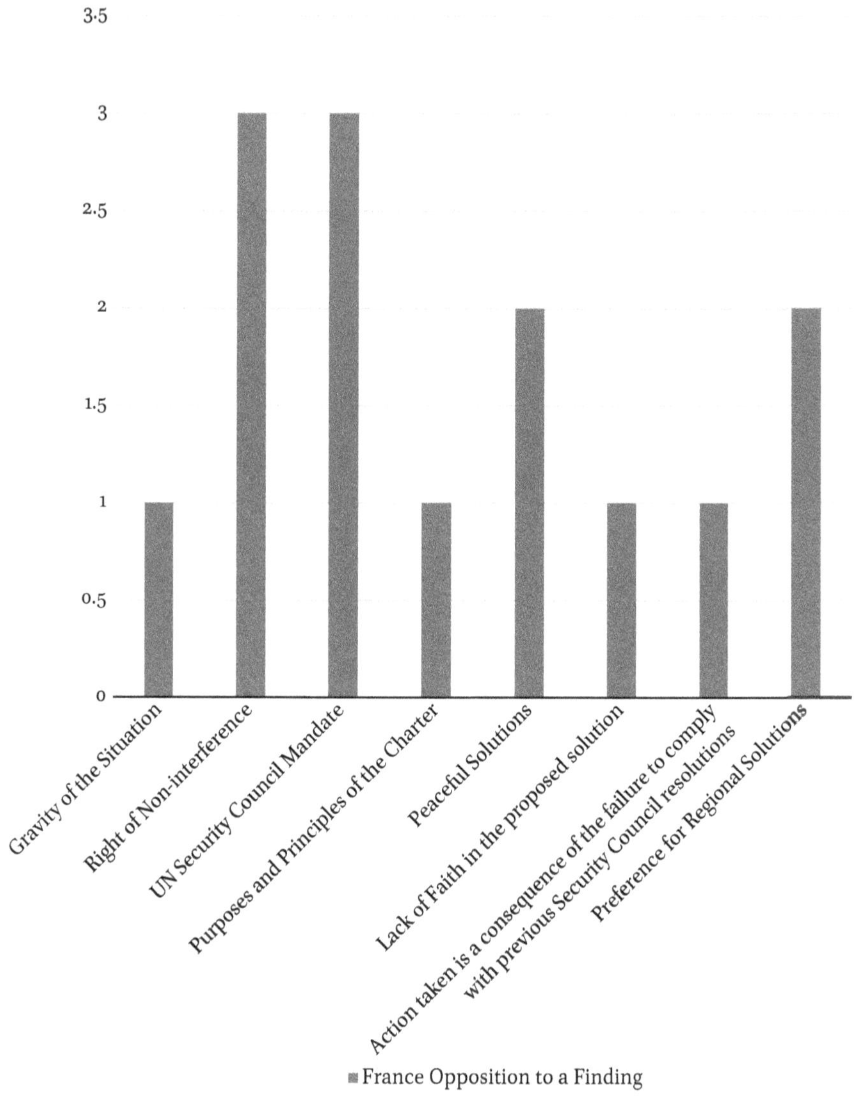
3.5
3
2.5
2
1.5
1
0.5
0
Gravity of the Situation
Right of Non-interference
UN Security Council Mandate
Purposes and Principles of the Charter
Peaceful Solutions
Lack of Faith in the proposed solution
Action taken is a consequence of the failure to comply with previous Security Council resolutions
Preference for Regional Solutions
France Opposition to a Finding

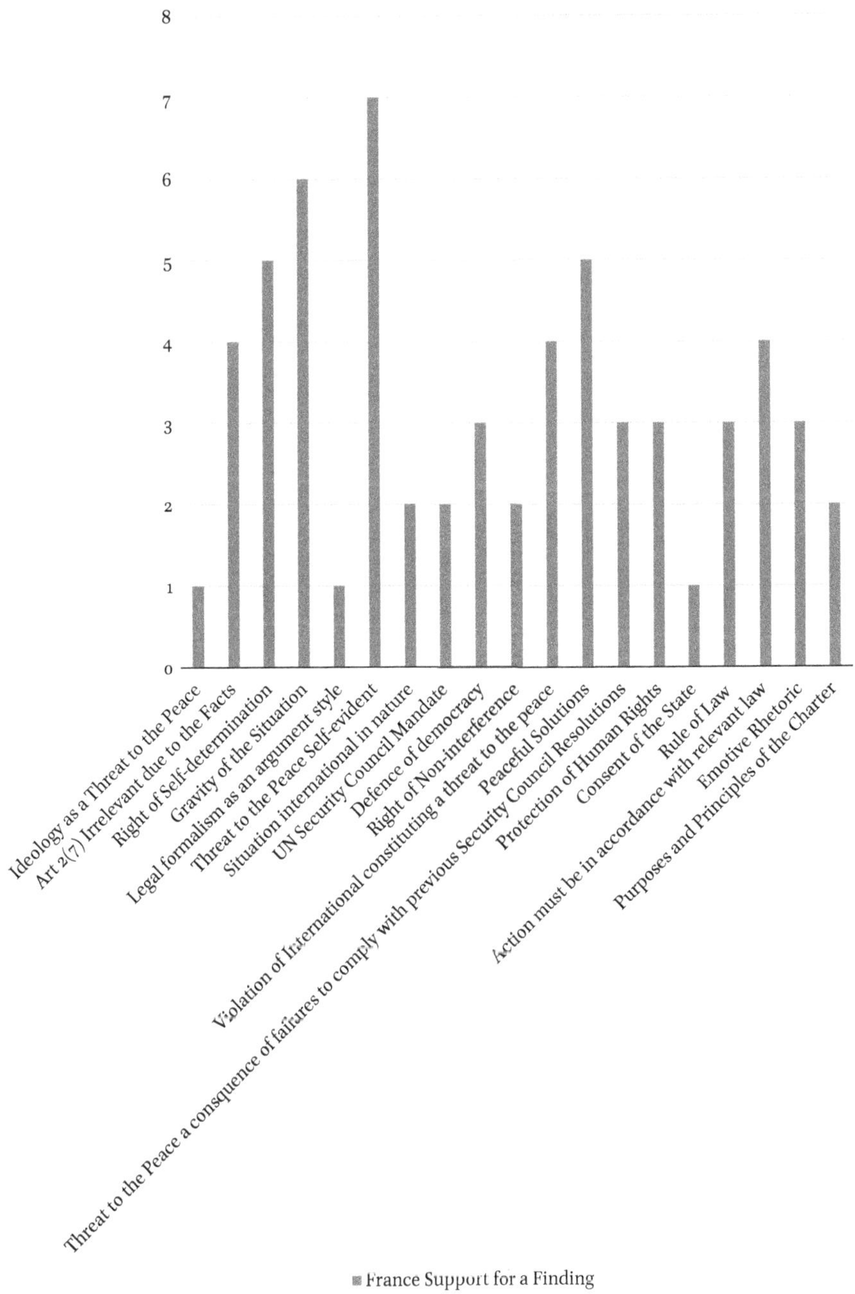
0
1
2
3
4
5
6
7
8
Ideology as a Threat to the Peace
Art 2(7) Irrelevant due to the Facts
Right of Self-determination
Gravity of the Situation
Legal formalism as an argument style
Threat to the Peace Self-evident
Situation international in nature
UN Security Council Mandate
Defence of democracy
Right of Non-interference
Violation of International constituting a threat to the peace
Peaceful Solutions
Threat to the Peace a consquence of failures to comply with previous Security Council Resolutions
Protection of Human Rights
Consent of the State
Rule of Law
Action must be in accordance with relevant law
Emotive Rhetoric
Purposes and Principles of the Charter
France Support for a Finding

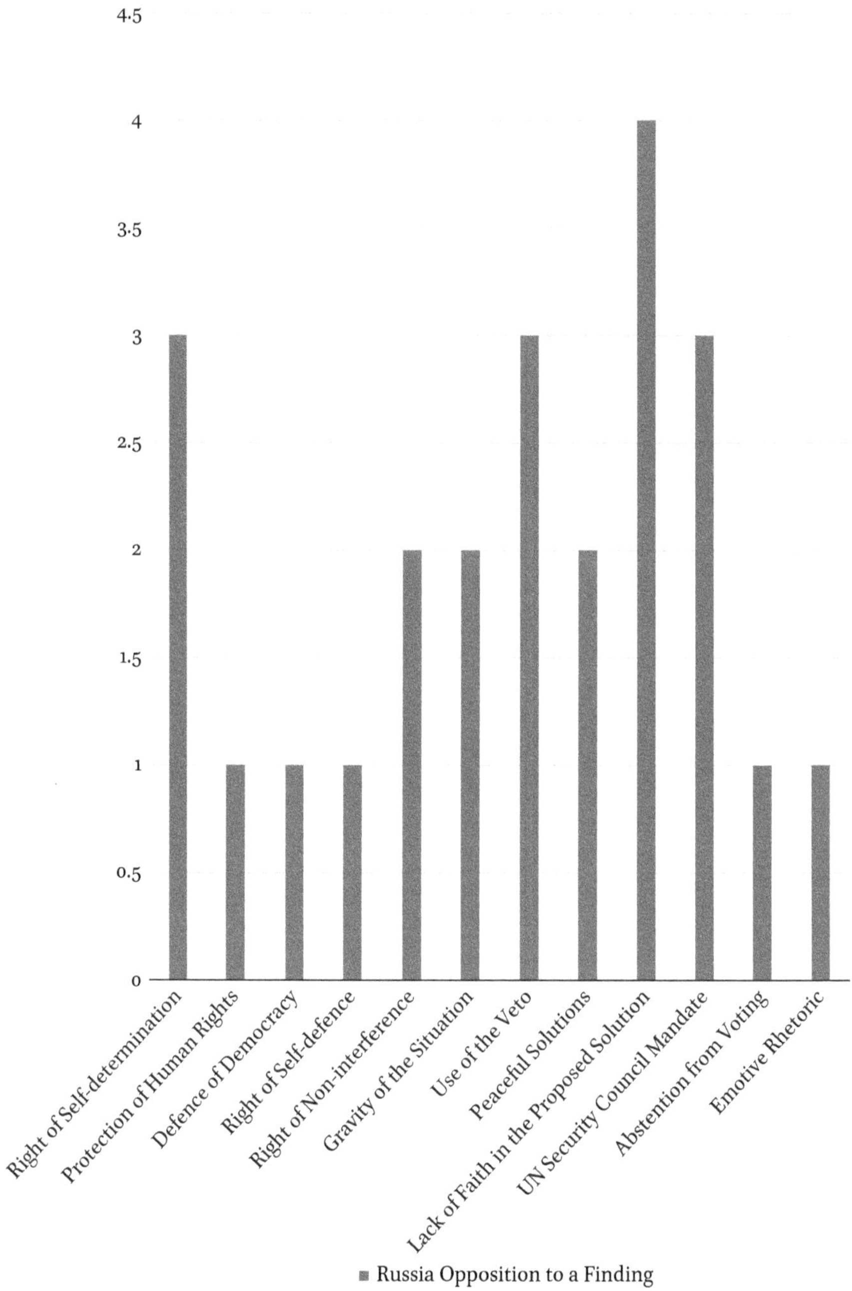
4.5
4
3.5
3
2.5
2
1.5
1
0.5
0
Right of Self-determination
Protection of Human Rights
Defence of Democracy
Right of Self-defence
Right of Non-interference
Gravity of the Situation
Use of the Veto
Peaceful Solutions
Lack of Faith in the Proposed Solution
UN Security Council Mandate
Abstention from Voting
Emotive Rhetoric
Russia Opposition to a Finding

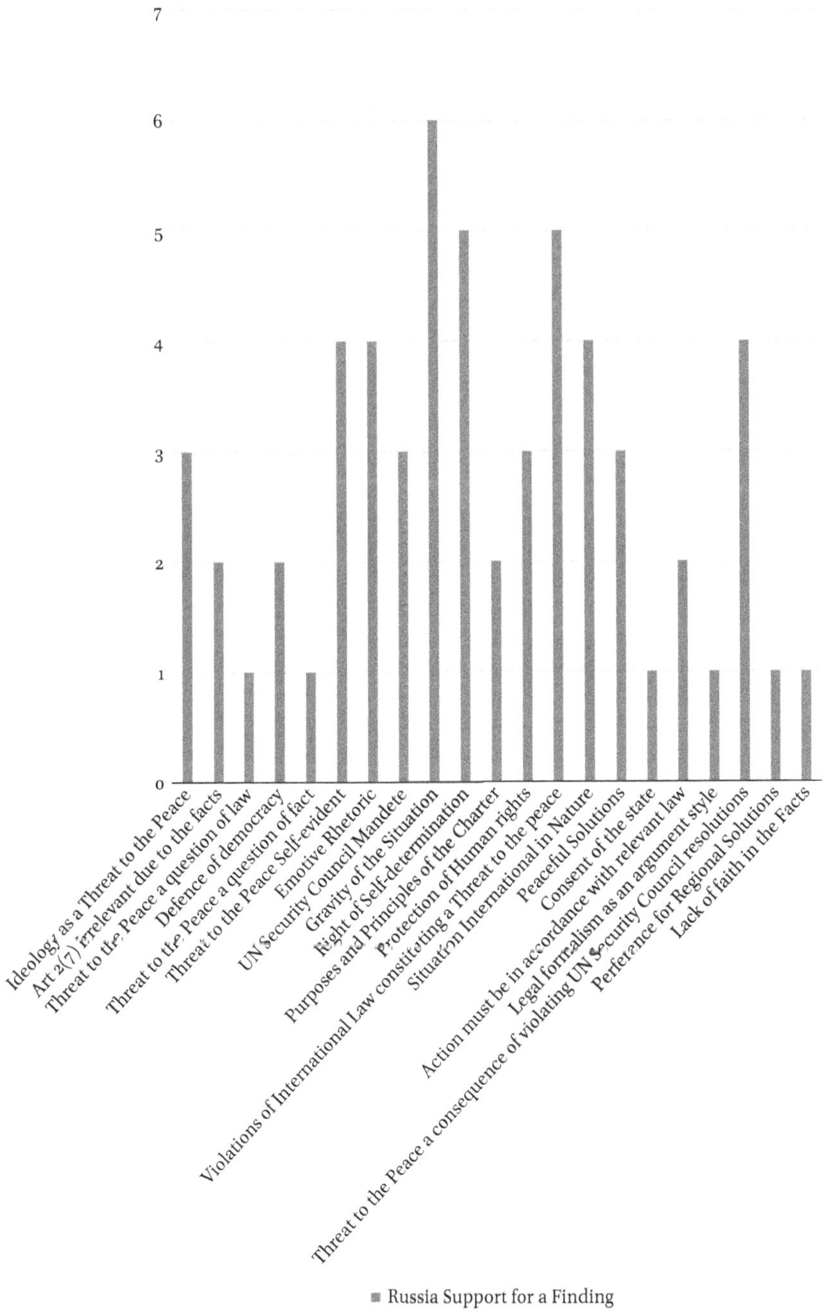
7
6
5
4
3
2
1
0
Ideology as a Threat to the Peace
Art 2(7) irrelevant due to the facts
Threat to the Peace a question of law
Defence of democracy
Threat to the Peace a question of fact
Threat to the Peace Self-evident
Emotive Rhetoric
UN Security Council Mandete
Gravity of the Situation
Right of Self-determination
Purposes and Principles of the Charter
Protection of Human rights
Violations of International Law constituting a Threat to the peace
Situation International in Nature
Peaceful Solutions
Consent of the state
Action must be in accordance with relevant law
Legal formalism as an argument style
Threat to the Peace a consequence of violating UN Security Council resolutions
Perference for Regional Solutions
Lack of faith in the Facts
Russia Support for a Finding

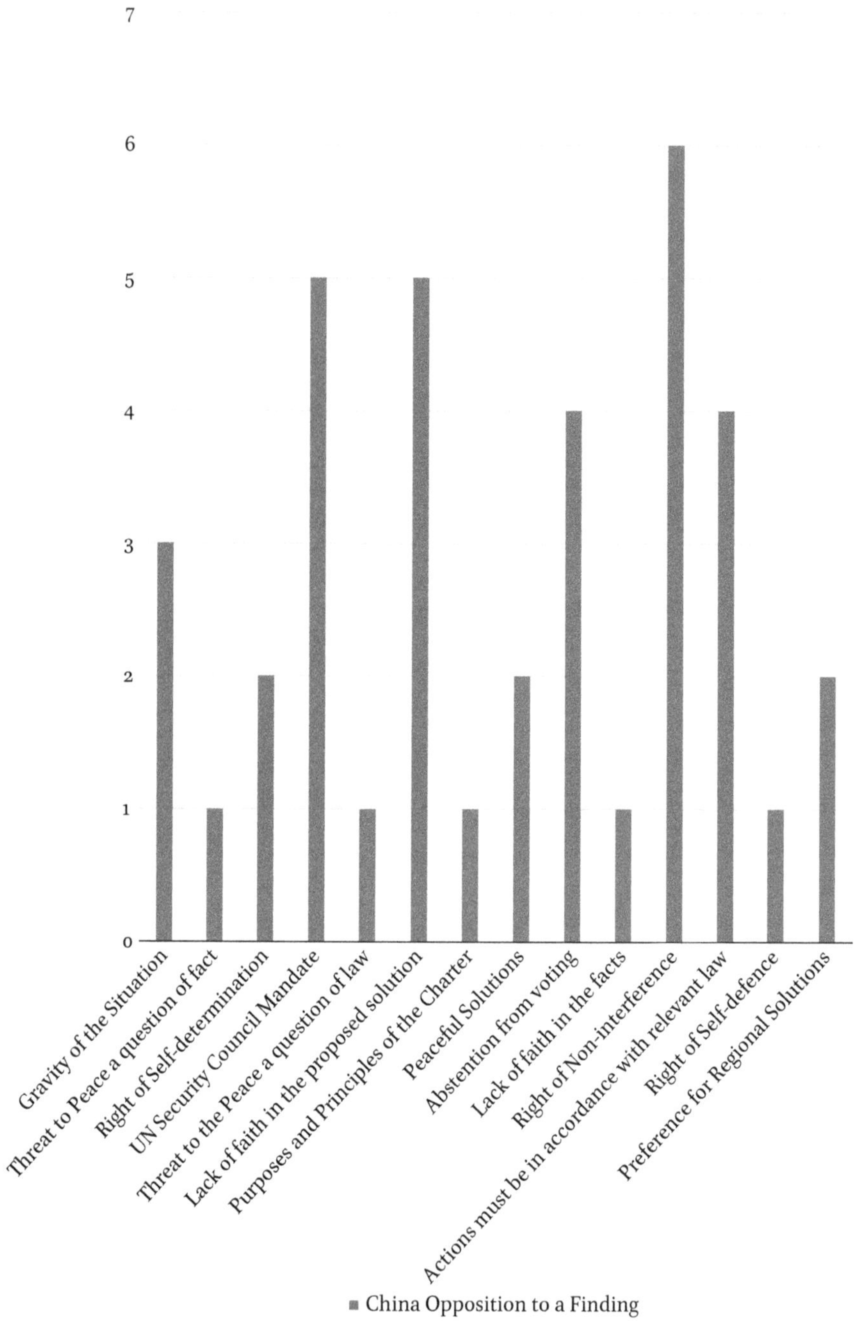
7
6
5
4
3
2
1
0
Gravity of the Situation
Threat to Peace a question of fact
Right of Self-determination
UN Security Council Mandate
Threat to the Peace a question of law
Lack of faith in the proposed solution
Purposes and Principles of the Charter
Peaceful Solutions
Abstention from voting
Lack of faith in the facts
Right of Non-interference
Actions must be in accordance with relevant law
Right of Self-defence
Preference for Regional Solutions
China Opposition to a Finding

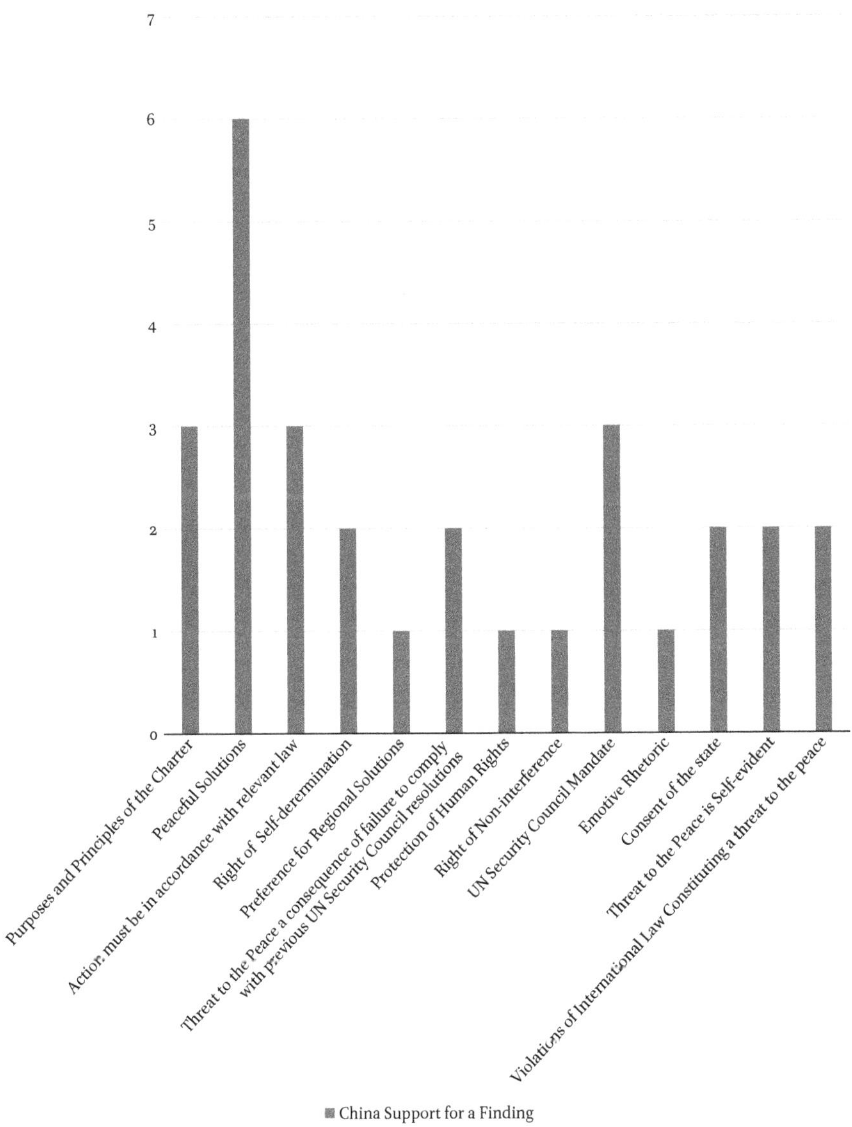
7
6
5
4
3
2
1
0
Purposes and Principles of the Charter
Peaceful Solutions
Action must be in accordance with relevant law
Right of Self-deremination
Preference for Regional Solutions
Threat to the Peace a consequence of failure to comply with previous UN Security Council resolutions
Protection of Human Rights
Right of Non-interference
UN Security Council Mandate
Emotive Rhetoric
Consent of the state
Threat to the Peace is Self-evident
Violations of International Law Constituting a threat to the peace
China Support for a Finding

Bibliography

Books

Alston, Philip and Sarah Knuckey (eds), *The Transformation of Human Rights Fact-Finding* (Oxford University Press, 2016).

Butler, Judith, *Antigone's Claim: Kinship between Life and Death* (Columbia University Press, 2000).

Cotterrell, Roger, *The Sociology of Law: An Introduction* (Butterworths, 2nd ed, 1992).

Cotterrell, Roger, *Law's Community: Legal Theory in Sociological Perspective* (Clarendon Press; Oxford University Press, 1995).

Cotterrell, Roger, *The Politics of Jurisprudence: A Critical Introduction to Legal Philosophy* (Oxford University Press, 2nd ed, 2003).

Cotterrell, Roger, *Law, Culture and Society: Legal Ideas in the Mirror of Social Theory* (Ashgate Pub. Co, 2006).

Crawford, James, *The Creation of States in International Law* (Clarendon Press; Oxford University Press, 2nd ed, 2006).

Farrall, Jeremy Matam, 'Impossible Expectations? The UN Security Council's Promotion of the Rule of Law after Conflict' in Hilary Charlesworth and Brett Bowden (eds), *The role of international law in rebuilding societies after conflict: great expectations* (Cambridge University Press, 2009) 134.

Fine, Bob, Democracy and the Rule of Law: Liberal Ideals and Marxist Critiques (Pluto Press, 1984).

Foucault, Michel, Discipline and Punish: The Birth of the Prison (Allen Lane, 1977).

Foucault, Michel and Colin Gordon, Power/Knowledge (Pearson Education: Longman, 1980).

Foucault, Michel, The History of Sexuality (Penguin, 1990) vol 1.

Glaser, Barney G. and Anselm L Strauss, The Discovery of Grounded Theory: Strategies for Qualitative Research (Aldine, 1967).

Golder, Ben and Peter Fitzpatrick, *Foucault's Law* (Routledge, 2009).

Goodrich, Leland M, *Charter of the United Nations; Commentary and Documents* (Columbia University Press, 3d and rev. ed, 1969).

Hart, HLA, *The Concept of Law* (Oxford University Press, 1972).

Hirst, Paul Q., *Law, Socialism, and Democracy* (Allen & Unwin, 1986).

Hollis, Duncan B., 'Defining Treaties' in Duncan B Hollis (ed), *The Oxford guide to treaties* (Oxford University Press, 1st ed, 2012) 11.

Hunt, Alan and Gary Wickham, *Foucault and Law: Towards a Sociology of Law as Governance* (Pluto Press, 1994).

Kafka, Franz, *The Trial* (Penguin, 2000).

Koskenniemi, Martti, The Gentle Civilizer of Nations: The Rise and Fall of International Law, 1870–1960 (Cambridge University Press, 2002).

Lauterpacht, Hersch, *The Function of Law in the International Community* (Oxford University Press, 1st pbk. ed, 2011).

Miéville, China, 'Multilateralism as Terror: International Law, Haiti and Imperialism' [2009] *London: Birkbeck ePrints* <http://eprints.bbk.ac.uk/783>.

Orwell, George, *Animal Farm* (The University of Adelaide, eBook, 2008).

Österdahl, Inger, *Threat to the Peace: The Interpretation by the Security Council of Article 39 of the UN Charter* (Iustus, 1998).

Paige, Tamsin Phillipa, 'The Maintenance of Heteronormativity' in Dianne Otto (ed), *Queering International Law: Possibilities, Alliances, Complicities, Risk* (Routledge, 2017a).

Reisigl, Martin and Ruth Wodak, 'The Discourse-Historical Approach (DHA)' in Ruth Wodak and Michael Meyer (eds), *Methods of critical discourse analysis* (SAGE, 2nd ed, 2009) 87.

Santos, Boaventura de Sousa, Toward a New Legal Common Sense: Law, Globalization, and Emancipation (Butterworths LexisNexis, 2002).

Schlink, Bernhard, *The Reader* (Vintage Books, 1998).

Simpson, Gerry J, Great Powers and Outlaw States: Unequal Sovereigns in the International Legal Order (Cambridge University Press, 2004).

Sophocles, The Three Theban Plays (Penguin Books, 1984).

Turk, Austin, *Criminality and the Legal Order* (Rand McNally & Company, 1969).

Van Dijk, Teun A, 'Critical Discourse Analysis' in D Tannen, D Schiffrin and H Hamilton (eds), *Handbook of Discourse Analysis* (Blackwell, Second Edition, 2013) 352.

Venzke, Ingo, *How Interpretation Makes International Law: On Semantic Change and Normative Twists* (Oxford University Press, 1st ed, 2012).

White, ND, *The United Nations and the Maintenance of International Peace and Security* (Manchester University Press; Distributed in the USA and Canada by St. Martin's Press, 1990).

White, ND, *Keeping the Peace: The United Nations and the Maintenance of International Peace and Security* (Manchester University Press; Distributed exclusively in the USA and Canada by St. Martin's Press, 1993).

Wodak, Ruth and Michael Meyer, 'Critical Discourse Analysis: History, Agenda, Theory and Methodology' in Ruth Wodak and Michael Meyer (eds), *Methods of Critical Discourse Analysis* (SAGE, 2nd ed, 2009a) 1.

Wodak, Ruth and Michael Meyer (eds), *Methods of Critical Discourse Analysis* (SAGE, 2nd ed, 2009b).

Journal Articles

Aagaard, Hanne and Elisabeth OC Hall, 'Mothers' Experiences of Having a Preterm Infant in the Neonatal Care Unit: A Meta-Synthesis' (2008) 23(3) *Journal of Pediatric Nursing* e26.

Alvarez, Jose E, 'Judging the Security Council' (1996) 90(1) *The American Journal of International Law* 1.

Banakar, Reza, 'Can Legal Sociology Account for the Normativity of Law?' *University of Westminster School of Law Research Paper No.13-03* http://papers.ssrn.com/sol3/papers.cfm?abstract_id=2229241.

Beck, Anthony, 'Foucault and Law: The Collapse of Law's Empire' (1996) 16(3) *Oxford Journal of Legal Studies* 489.

Binder, Martin and Monika Heupel, 'The Legitmacy of the UN Security Council: Evidence from Recent General Assembly Debates' (2015) 59(2) *International Studies Quarterly* 238.

Blommaert, Jan and Chris Bulcaen, 'Critical Discourse Analysis' (2000) 29 *Annual Review of Anthrology* 447.

Britten, Nicky et al., 'Using Meta Ethnography to Synthesise Qualitative Research: A Worked Example' (2002) 7(4) *Journal of Health Services Research and Policy* 209.

Campbell, Rona et al., 'Evaluating Meta-Ethnography: A Synthesis of Qualitative Research on Lay Experiences of Diabetes and Diabetes Care' (2003) 56 *Social Science & Medicine* 671.

Chan, Phil, 'A Keen Observer of the International Rule of Law? International Law in China's Voting Behaviour and Argumentation in the United Nations Security Council' (2013) 26(4) *Leiden Journal of International Law* 875.

Chesterman, Simon, 'UNaccountable? The United Nations, Emergency Powers, and the Rule of Law' (2009) 42 *Vanderbilt Journal of Transnational Law* 1509.

Clemmens, Donna, 'Adolescent Motherhood: A Meta-Synthesis of Qualitative Studies' (2003) 28(2) *American Journal of Maternal Child Nursing* 93.

Cryer, Robert, 'The Security Council and Article 39: A Threat to Coherence?' (1996) 1 *Journal of Armed Conflict* 161.

Deitelhoff, Nicole, 'The Discursive Process of Legalization: Charting Islands of Persuasion in the ICC Case' (2009) 63(1) *International Organization* 33.

Dickinson, Laura A, 'Military Lawyers on the Battlefield: An Empirical Account of International Law Compliance' (2010) 104(1) *American Journal of International Law* 1.

Eckert, Amy, 'The Non-Intervention Principle and International Humanitarian Interventions': (2001) 7(1) *International Legal Theory* 49.

Ewald, François, 'Norms, Discipline, and the Law' (1990) 30(Spring) *Representations* 138.

Glennon, Michael J, 'Why the Security Council Failed' (2003) 82 *Foreign Affairs* 16.

Hammell, K Whalley, 'Quality of Life after Spinal Cord Injury: A Meta-Synthesis of Qualitative Findings' (2007) 45 *Spinal Cord* 124.

Heaton, Janet, 'Secondary Analysis of Qualitative Data: An Overview' (2008) 33(3) *Historical Social Research* 33.

Hehir, Aidan, 'NATO's "Humanitarian Intervention" in Kosovo: Legal Precedent or Aberration?' (2009) 8 *Journal of Human Rights* 245.

Henderson, Ian, 'Legal Officers in the Australian Defence Force: Functions by Rank and Conpetency Levels, along with a Case-Study on Operations' (2011) 50(1) *Military Law and the Law of War Review* 37.

Henkin, Louis, 'Kosovo and the Law of "Humanitarian Intervention"' (1999) 93(4) *The American Journal of International Law* 824.

Hirsch, Moshe, 'The Sociology of Interntional Law: Invitation to Study International Rules in Their Social Context' (2005) 55(4) *University of Toronto Law Journal* 891.

Hirsch, Moshe, 'The Sociology of International Economic Law: Sociological Analysis of the Regulation of Regional Agreements in the World Trading System' (2008) 19(2) *European Journal of International Law* 277.

Johnstone, Ian, 'Security Council Deliberations: The Power of the Better Argument' (2003) 14(3) *European Journal of International Law* 437.

Jones, Myfanwy Lloyd, 'Role Development and Effective Practice in Specialist and Advanced Practice Roles in Acute Hospital Settings: Systematic Review and Meta-Synthesis' 49(2) *Journal of Advanced Nursing* 191.

Kennedy, Duncan, 'The Stakes of Law, or Hale and Foucault' (1991) 15(4) *Legal Studies Forum* 327.

Koskenniemi, Martii, 'The Place of Law in Collective Security' (1996) 17 *Michigan Journal of International Law* 455.

Koskenniemi, Martii, 'The Mystery of Legal Obligation' (2011) 3(2) *International Theory* 319.

Le Mon, Christopher J and Rachel S Taylor, 'Security Council Action in the Name of Human Rights: From Rhodesia to the Congo' (2004) 10(2) *U.C. Davis Journal of International Law & Policy* 197.

Linter, JE, 'Humanitarian Intervention: Legitimising the Illegal?' (2005) 5(2) *Defence Studies* 271.

Mason, Mark, 'Sample Size and Saturation in PhD Studies Using Qualitative Interviews' (2010) 11(3) *Forum: Qualitative Social Research* http://www.qualitative-research.net/index.php/fqs/article/view/1428/3027.

McLaughlin, Rob, '"Giving" Operational Legal Advice: Context and Method' (2011) 50 *Military Law and the Law of War Review* 99.

McLaughlin, Rob and Tamsin Phillipa Paige, 'The Role of Information Sharing in Counter Piracy in the Horn of Africa Region: A Model for Transnational Criminal

Enforcement Operations' (2016) 12(1) *Journal of International Law and International Relations.*

Paige, Tamsin, 'Piracy and Universal Jurisdiction' (2013) 12 *Macquarie Law Journal* 131.

Paige, Tamsin Phillipa, 'How Building Prisons in Somalia Promoted the Rule of Law through East Africa' [2016] *Bingham Centre for the Rule of Law Global Rule of Law Exchange Papers* <http://binghamcentre.biicl.org/ruleoflawexchange/documents/205_paige_practice_note.pdf?showdocument=1>.

Paige, Tamsin Phillipa, 'The Impact and Effectiveness of UNCLOS on Counter-Piracy Operations' (2017b) 22(1) *Journal of Conflict and Security Law* 97.

Pickard, Daniel, 'When Does Crime Become a Threat to International Peace and Security?' (1998) 12(1) *Florida Journal of International Law* 1.

Reisman, W Michael, 'International Law-Making: A Process of Communication' (1981) Paper 713 *Yale Law School Faculty Scholarship Series* 101.

Rose, Nikolas and Mariana Valverde, 'Governed By Law?' (1998) 7 *Social & Legal Studies* 541.

Salter, Katherine et al., 'The Experience of Living with Stroke: A Qualitative Meta-Synthesis' (2008) 40(8) *Journal of Rehabilitation Medicine* 595.

Turk, Austin, 'Psychiatry vs. The Law – Therefore?' (1967) 5 *Criminologica* 30.

Turk, Austin, 'Sociology of Terrorism' (2004) 30 *Annual Review of Sociology* 271.

Wallensteen, Peter and Patrik Johansson, 'Security Council Decisions in Perspective' in David E Malone (ed), *The UN Security Council: From the Cold War to the 21st Century* (Lynne Rienner Publishers, 1st ed, 2004) 17.

Walsh, Denis and Soo Downe, 'Meta-Synthesis Method for Qualitative Research: A Literature Review' (2005) 50(2) *Journal of Advanced Nursing* 204.

Wellens, Karel, 'The UN Security Council and New Threats to the Peace: Back to the Future' (2003) 8(1) *Journal of Conflict and Security Law* 15.

Welsh, Jennifer, Carolin Thielking and S Neil MacFarlane, 'The Responsibility to Protect: Assessing the Report of the International Commission on Intervention and State Sovereignty' (2002) 57 *International Journal* 489.

Wheeler, Nicholas J., 'Reflections on the Legality and Legitimacy of NATO's Intervention in Kosovo' (2000) 4(3–4) *The International Journal of Human Rights* 144.

Letters and Reports

Algeria et al., 'Letter Dated 11 July 1963 Addressed to the President of the Security Council by the Representatives of Algeria, Burundi, Cameroon, Central African Republic, Chad, Congo (Brazzaville), Congo (Leopoldville), Dahomey, Ethiopia, Gabon, Ghana, Guinea, Ivory Coast, Liberia, Libya, Madagascar, Mali, Mauritania, Morocco, Niger, Nigeria, Rwanda, Senegal, Sierra Leone, Somalia, Sudan, Tanganyika, Togo,

Tunisia, Uganda, United Arab Republic and Upper Volta' (S/5347, United Nations, 11 July 1963a).

Algeria et al., 'Letter Dated 11 July 1963 Addressed to the President of the Security Council by the Representatives of Algeria, Burundi, Cameroon, Central African Republic, Chad, Congo (Brazzaville), Congo (Leopoldville), Dahomey, Ethiopia, Gabon, Ghana, Guinea, Ivory Coast, Liberia, Libya, Madagascar, Mali, Mauritania, Morocco, Niger, Nigeria, Rwanda, Senegal, Sierra Leone, Somalia, Sudan, Tanganyika, Togo, Tunisia, Uganda, United Arab Republic and Upper Volta' (S/5348, United Nations, 11 July 1963b).

Democratic Kampuchea, 'Telegram Dated 31 December 1978 from the Deputy Prime Minister in Charge of Foreign Affairs of Democratic Kampuchea Addressed to the President of the Security Council' (S/13001, United Nations, 31 December 1978).

Democratic Kampuchea, 'Telegram Dated 3 January 1979 from the Deputy Prime Minister in Charge of Foreign Affairs of Democratic Kampuchea Addressed to the President of the Security Council' (S/13003, United Nations, 3 January 1979).

Democratic People's Republic of Korea, 'Letter Dated 11 October 2006 from the Representative of the Democratic People's Republic of Korea Addressed to the President of the Security Council' (S/2006/801, United Nations, 11 October 2006).

France, 'Letter Dated 4 April 1991 from the Charge D'Affaires A.I. of the Permanent Mission of France to the United Nations Addressed to the President of the Security Council' (S/22442, United Nations, 4 April 1991a).

France, 'Letter Dated 20 December 1991 from the Permanent Representative of France to the United Nations Addressed to the Secretary-General' (S/23306, United Nations, 20 December 1991b).

Haiti, 'Letter Dated 30 September 1991 from the Permanent Representative of Haiti to the United Nations Addressed to the President of the Security Council' (S/23098, United Nations, 30 September 1991).

Haiti, 'Letter Dated 7 June 1993 from the Permanent Representative of Haiti to the United Nations Addressed to the President of the Security Council' (S/25958, United Nations, 16 June 1993).

Iran, 'Letter Dated 13 November 1979 from the Charge D'Affairs of the Permanent Mission of Iran to the United Nations Addressed to the Secretary-General' (S/13626, United Nations, 13 November 1979).

Lang, Jack, 'Report of the Special Adviser to the Secretary-General on Legal Issues Related to Piracy off the Coast of Somalia' (S/2011/30, United Nations Security Council, 24 January 2011).

Ogwu, U Joy, 'Letter Dated 17 October 2011 from the Permanent Representative of Nigeria to the United Nations Addressed to the Secretary-General' (S/2011/644, United Nations Security Council, 17 October 2011).

Ould-Abdallah, Ahmedou, 'Piracy off the Somali Coast: Workshop Commissioned by the Special Representative to the Secretary General of the UN to Somalia – Final Report: Detailed Recommendations' (International Expert group on the Piracy off the Somali Coast, 21 November 2008a).

Ould-Abdallah, Ahmedou, 'Piracy off the Somali Coast: Workshop Commissioned by the Special Representative to the Secretary General of the UN to Somalia – Final Report: Assessment and Recommendations' (International Expert group on the Piracy off the Somali Coast, 21 November 2008b).

Permanent Mission of the United Kingdom of Great Britain and Northern Ireland to the United Nations, 'Women Targeted or Affected by Armed Conflict: What Role for Military Peacekeepers? (Conference Summary)' (S/2008/402, United Nations, 18 June 2008).

'Question of East Timor: Report of the Secretary-General' (S/1999/513, 5 May 1999).

'Report of the Secretary-General on Children and Armed Conflict in Somalia' (S/2007/259, United Nations Security Council, 7 May 2007).

'Report of the Secretary-General on Somalia' (S/2006/122, United Nations Security Council, 21 February 2006).

'Report of the Secretary-General on Somalia' (S/2006/418, United Nations Security Council, 20 June 2006).

'Report of the Secretary-General on Somalia' (S/2007/381, United Nations Security Council, 25 June 2007).

'Report of the Secretary-General on Somalia' (S/2007/658, United Nations Security Council, 7 November 2007).

'Report of the Secretary-General on Somalia' (S/2008/178, United Nations Security Council, 14 March 2008).

'Report of the Secretary-General on Somalia' (S/2008/466, United Nations Security Council, 16 July 2008).

'Report of the Secretary-General on Specialized Anti-Piracy Courts in Somalia and Other States in the Region' (S/2012/50, United Nations Security Council, 20 January 2012).

'Report of the Secretary-General on the Activities of the United Nations Office for West Africa' (S/2011/811, United Nations Security Council, 30 December 2011).

'Report of the Secretary-General pursuant to Security Council Resolution 1950 (2010)' (S/2011/662, United Nations Security Council, 25 October 2011).

'Report of the Secretary-General pursuant to Security Council Resolution 2020 (2011)' (S/2012/783, United Nations Security Council, 22 October 2012).

'Report of the United Nations Assessment on Piracy in the Gulf of Guinea (7 to 24 November 2011)' (S/2012/45, United Nations Security Council, 19 January 2012).

Senegal, 'Letter Dated 10 April 1963 from the Acting Charge D'Affairs of the Permanent Mission of Senegal Addressed to the President of the Security Council' (S/5279, United Nations, 10 April 1963).

South Africa, 'Letter Dated 28 January 1981 from the Permanent Representative of South Africa to the United NAtions Addressed to the Secretart-General' (S/14346, 29 January1981).

Special Committee on the Policies of Apartheid of the Government of the Republic of South Africa, 'Report of the Special Committee on the Policies of Apartheid of the Government of the Republic of South Africa' (S/5621, United Nations, 25 March 1964).

Special Committee on the Policies of Apartheid of the Government of the Republic of South Africa, 'Report of the Special Committee on the Policies of Apartheid of the Government of the Republic of South Africa' (S/5717, United Nations, 25 May 1964).

'Summary Report of Tenth Meeting of Committee III/2' 12(72) *Documents on the United Nations Conference on International Organisations* 1.

Tunisia, 'Letter Dated 20 October 1977 from the Permanent Representative of Tunisia to the United Nations Addressed to the President of the Security Council' (S/12420, United Nations Security Council, 20 October 1977).

Turkey, 'Letter Dated 2 April 1991 from the Permanent Representative of Turkey to the United Nations Addressed to the President of the Security Council' (S/22435, United Nations, 2 April 1991).

United Kingdom of Great Britain and Northern Island, 'Letter Dated 20 December 1991 from the Permanent Representative of United Kingdom of Great Britain and Northern Ireland to the United Nations Addressed to the Secretary-General' (S/23307, United Nations, 20 December 1991).

United Nations, *The Yearbook of the United Nations 1971* (United Nations, 1974) vol 25.

United Nations Palestine Commission, 'Letter from the Chairman of the United Nations Palestine Commission to the President of the Security Council Dated 30 January 1948' (S/663, United Nations Security Council, 30 January 1948a).

United Nations Palestine Commission, 'Letter from the Chairman of the United Nations Palestine Commission to the President of the Security Council Dated 16 February 1948' (S/676, United Nations Security Council, 16 February 1948b).

United Nations Secretary-General, 'Report of the Secretary-General in Pursuance of the Resolution Adopted by the Security Council at Its 1078th Meeting on 4 December 1963 (S/5471)' (S/5658, United Nations, 20 April 1964).

United Nations Secretary-General, 'Report of the Secretary-General Concerning Implementation of Security Council Resolution 457 (1979)' (S/13704, United Nations Security Council, 22 December 1979).

United Nations Secretary-General, 'Further Report of the Secretary-General Concerning the Implementation of Security Council Resolutions 435 (1978) and 439 (1978)

Concerning the Question of Namibia' (S/14333, United Nations Security Council, 19 January 1981).
United Nations Secretary-General, 'Further Report of the Secretary-General Concerning the Implementation of Security Council Resolutions 435 (1978) and 439 (1978) Concerning the Question of Namibia' (S/15776, United Nations Security Council, 19 May 1983a).
United Nations Secretary-General, 'Further Report of the Secretary-General Concerning the Implementation of Security Council Resolutions 435 (1978) and 439 (1978) Concerning the Question of Namibia' (S/15943, United Nations Security Council, 29 August 1983b).
United Nations Secretary-General, 'Report of the Secretary-General on Humanitarian Needs in Kuwait in the Immediate Post-Crisis Environment by a Mission to the Area Led by Mr. Martii Ahtisaari, Under-Secretary-General for Administration and Management, Dated 28 March 1991' (S/22409, United Nations, 28 March 1991).
United Nations Secretary-General, 'Report of the Secretary-General pursuant to Paragraph 4 of Security Council Resolution 731 (1992)' (S/23574, United Nations Security Council, 11 February 1992a).
United Nations Secretary-General, 'Further Report of the Secretary-General pursuant to Paragraph 4 of Security Council Resolution 731 (1992)' (S/23672, United Nations Security Council, 3 March 1992b).
United Nations Secretary-General, 'Interim Report of the Secretary-General on Rwanda' (S/25810, United Nations, 20 May 1993a).
United Nations Secretary-General, 'Report of the Secretary-General on Rwanda' (S/26488, United Nations, 24 September 1993b).
United Nations Secretary-General, 'Report of the Secretary-General on the United Nations Assistance Mission for Rwanda' (S/26927, United Nations, 30 December 1993c).
United Nations Secretary-General, 'Second Progress Report of the Secretary-General on the United Nations Assistance Mission for Rwanda' (S/1994/360, United Nations, 30 March 1994a).
United Nations Secretary-General, 'Special Report of the Secretary-General on the United Nations Assistance Mission for Rwanda' (S/1994/470, United Nations, 20 April 1994b).
United Nations Secretary-General, 'Report of the Secretary-General on the Situation in Rwanda' (S/1994/565, United Nations, 13 May 1994c).
United Nations Secretary-General, 'The Situation in Afghanistan and Its Implication for International Peace and Security' (A/53/695-S/1998/1109, United Nations, 23 November 1998).
United Nations Secretary-General, 'Small Arms: Report of the Secretary-General' (S/2005/69, United Nations, 7 February 2005).

United Nations Secretary-General, 'Letter Dated 8 March 2006 from the Secretary-General Addressed to the President of the Security Council' (S/2006/150, United Nations, 9 March 2006).

United Nations Secretary-General, 'Small Arms: Report of the Secretary-General' (S/2008/258, United Nations, 17 April 2008a).

United Nations Secretary-General, 'Women and Peace and Security: Report of the Secretary-General' (S/2008/622, United Nations Security Council, 25 September 2008b).

United Nations Secretary-General, 'Children and Armed Conflict: Report of the Secretary-General' (A/63/785-S/2009/158, United Nations, 26 March 2009a).

United Nations Secretary-General, 'Report of the Secretary-General pursuant to Security Council Resolution 1820 (2008)' (S/2009/362, United Nations Security Council, 20 August 2009b).

United Nations Secretary-General, 'Women and Peace and Security: Report of the Secretary-General' (S/2010/173, United Nations Security Council, 6 April 2010a).

United Nations Secretary-General, 'Women and Peace and Security: Report of the Secretary-General' (S/2010/498, United Nations Security Council, 28 September 2010b).

United Nations Secretary-General, 'Report of the Secretary-General pursuant to Security Council Resolutions 1820 (2008) and 1888 (2009)' (A/65/592-S/2010/604, United Nations Security Council, 24 November 2010c).

United Nations Secretary-General, 'Letter Dated 24 January 2012 from the Secretary-General Addressed to the President of the Security Council' (S/2012/71, United Nations, 30 January 2012).

United Nations Secretary-General, 'Report of the United Nations Mission to Investigate the Use of Chemical Weapons in the Syrian Arab Republic on the Alleged Use of Chemical Weapons in the Ghouta Area of Damascus on 21 August 2013' (A/67/997-S/2013/553, United Nations, 16 September 2013).

United Nations Secretary-General, 'Report of the Secretary-General on the Implementation of Security Council Resolution 2043 (2012)' (S/2012/523, United Nations Security Council).

United Nations Security Council, 'The Report of the Sub-Committee on the Spanish Question Appointed by the Security Council on 29 April 1946' (S/75, United Nations, 1 June 1946a).

United Nations Security Council, 'Factual Findings Concerning the Spanish Situation: Supplementary Memorandum to the Report of the Sub-Committee Appointed by the Security Council on 29 April 1946' (S/76, United Nations, 1 June 1946b).

United Nations Security Council, 'Bahrain, Colombia, Egypt, France, Germany, Jordan, Kuwait, Libya, Morocco, Oman, Portugal, Qatar, Saudi Arabia, Togo, Tunisia, Turkey,

United Arab Emirates, United Kingdom of Great Britain and Northern Ireland and United States of America: Draft Resolution'.

United Nations Security Council, 'China: Draft Resolution' (S/13022, 11 January 1979).

United Nations Security Council, 'France, Germany, Portugal and United Kingdom of Great Britain and Northern Ireland: Draft Resolution (S/2011/612)'.

United Nations Security Council, 'France, Germany, Portugal, United Kingdom of Great Britain and Northern Ireland and United States of America: Draft Resolution (S/2012/538)'.

United Nations Security Council, 'Note by the President of the Security Council' (S/23500, United Nations, 31 January 1992).

United Nations Security Council, 'Note by the President of the Security Council' (S/2006/270, United Nations, 28 April 2006).

United Nations Security Council, 'Statement by the President of the Security Council (S/PRST/1999/21)'.

United Nations Security Council, 'Statement by the President of the Security Council (S/PRST/1999/28)'.

United Nations Security Council, 'Statement by the President of the Security Council (S/PRST/2000/10)'.

United Nations Security Council, 'Statement by the President of the Security Council (S/PRST/2001/21)'.

United Nations Security Council, 'Statement by the President of the Security Council (S/PRST/2002/30)'.

United Nations Security Council, 'Statement by the President of the Security Council (S/PRST/2002/31)'.

United Nations Security Council, 'Statement by the President of the Security Council (S/PRST/2004/1)'.

United Nations Security Council, 'Statement by the President of the Security Council (S/PRST/2005/7)'.

United Nations Security Council, 'Statement by the President of the Security Council (S/PRST/2006/38)'.

United Nations Security Council, 'Statement by the President of the Security Council (S/PRST/2007/3)'.

United Nations Security Council, 'Statement by the President of the Security Council (S/PRST/2007/24)'.

United Nations Security Council, 'Statement by the President of the Security Council (S/PRST/2007/42)'.

United Nations Security Council, 'Statement by the President of the Security Council (S/PRST/2008/43)'.

United Nations Security Council, 'Statement by the President of the Security Council (S/PRST/2009/20)'.

United Nations Security Council, 'Statement by the President of the Security Council (S/PRST/2010/6)'.
United Nations Security Council, 'Statement by the President of the Security Council (S/PRST/2012/16)'.
United Nations Security Council, 'United States of America: Draft Resolution'.
United States of America, 'Letter Dated 23 December 1991 from the Acting Permanent Representative of United States of America to the United Nations Addressed to the Secretary-General' (S/23317, United Nations, 23 December 1991).
Viet Nam, 'Letter Dated 9 January 1979 from the Permanent Representative of Viet Nam to the United Nations Addressed to the President of the Security Council' (S/13013, United Nations Security Council, 9 January 1979a).
Viet Nam, 'Letter Dated 11 January 1979 from the Permanent Representative of Viet Nam to the United Nations Addressed to the President of the Security Council' (S/13020, United Nations Security Council, 11 January 1979b).
Yugoslavia, 'Letter Dated 24 September 1991 from the Permanent Representative of Yugoslavia to the United Nations Addressed to the President of the Security-Council' (S/23069, United Nations, 24 September 1991).

Cases

Case Concerning Application of the Convention on the Prevention and Punishment of the Crime of Genocide (Bosnia and Herzegovina v Yugoslavia (Serbia and Montenegro)) (2007) 2007 International Court of Justice Reports of Judgments, Advisory Opinions and Orders.
Case Concerning the Arrest Warrant of 11 April 2000 (Democratic Republic of Congo v Belgium) (Joint separate opinion of Judges Higgins, Kooijmans and Buergenthal) [2002] ICJ Reports.
Case Concerning United States Diplomatic and Consular Staff in Tehran (United States of America v Iran): Request for the Indication of Provisional Measures (1979) 1979 International Court of Justice Reports of Judgments, Advisory Opinions and Orders.
Jacobellis v Ohio (1964) 378 United States Reports 179.
Legal Consequences for States of the Continued Presence of South Africa in Namibia (South West Africa) notwithstanding Security Council Resolution 276 (1970) (Unreported, International Court of Justice, 21 June 1971).
Prosecutor v Dusko Tadic a/k/a 'Dule' (Decision on the Defence Motion for Interlocutory Appeal on Jurisdiction) [1995] International Criminal Tribunal for the Former Yugoslavia, Appeals Chamber.
The Prosecutor v Joseph Kanyabashi (Decision on the Defence Motion on Jurisdiction) [1997] International Criminal Tribunal for Rwanda.

Treaties and Legal Instruments

Agreement between the Republic of Indonesia and the Portuguese Republic on the Question of East Timor 1999.
Amendment to the Rome Statute of the International Criminal Court on the Crime of Aggression, Articles 8bis, 15bis and 15ter (2187 UNTS 90).
Charter of the United Nations 1945 (1 UNTS XVI).
Chemical and Bacteriological (Biological) Weapons 1987 (UN General Assembly).
Convention on the Prohibition of the Development, Production, Stockpiling and Use of Chemical Weapons and on Their Destruction 1992 (1974 UNTS 85).
East Timor Popular Consultation 1999.
Statute of the International Court of Justice 1945 (1 UNTS 993).
The Arms Trade Treaty 2013 (UNTC Chapter XXVI 8).
United Nations Convention on the Law of the Sea 1982 (1833 UNTS 3).
Vienna Convention on the Law of Treaties 1969 (1155 UNTS 18232).

Resolutions

Resolution 4 (1946) 1946 (UN Security Council).
Resolution 50 (1948) 1948 (UN Security Council).
Resolution 54 (1948) 1948 (UN Security Council).
Resolution 161 (1961) 1961 (UN Security Council).
Resolution 180 (1963) 1963 (UN Security Council).
Resolution 182 (1963) 1963 (UN Security Council).
Resolution 186 (1964) 1964 (UN Security Council).
Resolution 217 (1965) 1965 (UN Security Council).
Resolution 218 (1965) 1965 (UN Security Council).
Resolution 232 (1966) 1966 (UN Security Council).
Resolution 307 (1971) 1971 (UN Security Council).
Resolution 353 (1974) 1974 (UN Security Council).
Resolution 418 (1977) 1977 (UN Security Council).
Resolution 439 (1978) 1978 (UN Security Council).
Resolution 532 (1983) 1983 (UN Security Council).
Resolution 539 (1983) 1983 (UN Security Council).
Resolution 573 (1985) 1985 (UN Security Council).
Resolution 620 (1988) 1988 (UN Security Council).
Resolution 678 (1990) 1990 (UN Security Council).
Resolution 688 (1991) 1991 (UN Security Council).
Resolution 713 (1991) 1991 (UN Security Council).

Resolution 731 (1992) 1992 (UN Security Council).
Resolution 733 (1992) 1992 (UN Security Council).
Resolution 748 (1992) 1992 (UN Security Council).
Resolution 827 (1993) 1993 (UN Security Council).
Resolution 841 (1993) 1993 (UN Security Council).
Resolution 912 (1994) 1994 (UN Security Council).
Resolution 918 (1994) 1994 (UN Security Council).
Resolution 1054 (1996) 1996 (UN Security Council).
Resolution 1078 (1996) 1996 (UN Security Council).
Resolution 1214 (1998) 1998 (UN Security Council).
Resolution 1267 (1999) 1999 (UN Security Council).
Resolution 1269 (1999) 1999 (UN Security Council).
Resolution 1308 (2000) 2000 (UN Security Council).
Resolution 1368 (2001) 2001 (UN Security Council).
Resolution 1373 (2001) 2001 (UN Security Council).
Resolution 1514 (XV) 1960 (UN General Assembly).
Resolution 1540 (2004) 2004 (UN Security Council).
Resolution 1676 (2006) 2006 (UN Security Council).
Resolution 1772 (2007) 2007 (UN Security Council).
Resolution 1816 (2008) 2008 (UN Security Council).
Resolution 1820 (2008) 2008 (UN Security Council).
Resolution 1838 (2008) 2008 (UN Security Council).
Resolution 1846 (2008) 2008 (UN Security Council).
Resolution 1851 (2008) 2008 (UN Security Council).
Resolution 1882 (2009) 2009 (UN Security Council).
Resolution 1888 (2009) 2009 (UN Security Council).
Resolution 1897 (2009) 2009 (UN Security Council).
Resolution 1918 (2010) 2010 (UN Security Council).
Resolution 1950 (2010) 2010 (UN Security Council).
Resolution 1960 (2010) 2010 (UN Security Council).
Resolution 1976 (2011) 2011 (UN Security Council).
Resolution 2015 (2011) 2011 (UN Security Council).
Resolution 2018 (2011) 2011 (UN Security Council).
Resolution 2020 (2011) 2011 (UN Security Council).
Resolution 2038 (2012) 2012 (UN Security Council).
Resolution 2042 (2012) 2012 (UN Security Council).
Resolution 2043 (2012) 2012 (UN Security Council).
Resolution 2077 (2012) 2012 (UN Security Council).
Resolution 2117 (2013) 2013 (UN Security Council).
Resolution 2118 (2013) 2013 (UN Security Council).

Resolution 2125 (2013) 2013 (UN Security Council).
Resolution A.979(24) 2005 (International Maritime Organization).

Meeting Records

United Nations Security Council, 'Security Council, First Year: 34th Meeting (S/PV.34)'.
United Nations Security Council, 'Security Council, First Year: 35th Meeting (S/PV.35)'.
United Nations Security Council, 'Security Council, First Year: 37th Meeting (S/PV.37)'.
United Nations Security Council, 'Security Council, First Year: 44th Meeting (S/PV.44)'.
United Nations Security Council, 'Security Council, First Year: 45th Meeting (S/PV.45)'.
United Nations Security Council, 'Security Council, First Year: 46th Meeting (S/PV.46)'.
United Nations Security Council, 'Security Council, First Year: 48th Meeting (S/PV.48)'.
United Nations Security Council, 'Security Council, Third Year: 253rd Meeting'.
United Nations Security Council, 'Security Council, Third Year: 262nd Meeting'.
United Nations Security Council, 'Security Council, Third Year: 271st Meeting'.
United Nations Security Council, 'Security Council, Third Year: 270th Meeting'.
United Nations Security Council, 'Security Council, Third Year: 274th Meeting'.
United Nations Security Council, 'Security Council, Third Year: 277th Meeting'.
United Nations Security Council, 'Security Council, Third Year: 283rd Meeting'.
United Nations Security Council, 'Security Council, Third Year: 287th Meeting'.
United Nations Security Council, 'Security Council, Third Year: 292nd Meeting'.
United Nations Security Council, 'Security Council, Third Year: 293rd Meeting'.
United Nations Security Council, 'Security Council, Third Year: 295th Meeting'.
United Nations Security Council, 'Security Council, Third Year: 296th Meeting'.
United Nations Security Council, 'Security Council, Third Year: 297th Meeting'.
United Nations Security Council, 'Security Council, Third Year: 298th Meeting'.
United Nations Security Council, 'Security Council, Third Year: 302nd Meeting'.
United Nations Security Council, 'Security Council, Third Year: 305th Meeting'.
United Nations Security Council, 'Security Council, Third Year: 306th Meeting'.
United Nations Security Council, 'Security Council, Third Year: 308th Meeting'.
United Nations Security Council, 'Security Council, Third Year: 307th Meeting'.
United Nations Security Council, 'Security Council, Third Year: 310th Meeting'.
United Nations Security Council, 'Security Council, Third Year: 309th Meeting'.
United Nations Security Council, 'Security Council, Third Year: 317th Meeting'.
United Nations Security Council, 'Security Council, Third Year: 333rd Meeting'.
United Nations Security Council, 'Security Council, Third Year: 334th Meeting'.
United Nations Security Council, 'Security Council, Third Year: 336th Meeting'.
United Nations Security Council, 'Security Council, Third Year: 338th Meeting'.

United Nations Security Council, 'Security Council, Eighteenth Year: 1027th Meeting (S/PV.1027)'.

United Nations Security Council, 'Security Council, Eighteenth Year: 1028th Meeting (S/PV.1028)'.

United Nations Security Council, 'Security Council, Eighteenth Year: 1032nd Meeting (S/PV.1032)'.

United Nations Security Council, 'Security Council, Eighteenth Year: 1033rd Meeting (S/PV.1033)'.

United Nations Security Council, 'Security Council, Eighteenth Year: 1040th Meeting (S/PV.1040)'.

United Nations Security Council, 'Security Council, Eighteenth Year: 1041st Meeting (S/PV.1041)'.

United Nations Security Council, 'Security Council, Eighteenth Year: 1043rd Meeting (S/PV.1043)'.

United Nations Security Council, 'Security Council, Eighteenth Year: 1042nd Meeting (S/PV.1042)'.

United Nations Security Council, 'Security Council, Eighteenth Year: 1044th Meeting (S/PV.1044)'.

United Nations Security Council, 'Security Council, Eighteenth Year: 1045th Meeting (S/PV.1045)'.

United Nations Security Council, 'Security Council, Eighteenth Year: 1046th Meeting (S/PV.1046)'.

United Nations Security Council, 'Security Council, Eighteenth Year: 1047th Meeting (S/PV.1047)'.

United Nations Security Council, 'Security Council, Eighteenth Year: 1048th Meeting (S/PV.1048)'.

United Nations Security Council, 'Security Council, Eighteenth Year: 1049th Meeting (S/PV.1049)'.

United Nations Security Council, 'Security Council, Eighteenth Year: 1050th Meeting (S/PV.1050)'.

United Nations Security Council, 'Security Council, Eighteenth Year: 1052nd Meeting (S/PV.1052)'.

United Nations Security Council, 'Security Council, Eighteenth Year: 1053rd Meeting (S/PV.1053)'.

United Nations Security Council, 'Security Council, Eighteenth Year: 1054th Meeting (S/PV.1054)'.

United Nations Security Council, 'Security Council, Eighteenth Year: 1056th Meeting (S/PV.1056)'.

United Nations Security Council, 'Security Council, Eighteenth Year: 1077th Meeting (S/PV1077)'.

United Nations Security Council, 'Security Council, Eighteenth Year: 1078th Meeting (S/PV1078)'.

United Nations Security Council, 'Security Council, Nineteenth Year: 1127th Meeting (S/PV1127)'.

United Nations Security Council, 'Security Council, Nineteenth Year: 1128th Meeting (S/PV1128)'.

United Nations Security Council, 'Security Council, Nineteenth Year: 1130th Meeting (S/PV1130)'.

United Nations Security Council, 'Security Council, Nineteenth Year: 1131st Meeting (S/PV1131)'.

United Nations Security Council, 'Security Council, Nineteenth Year: 1133rd Meeting (S/PV1133)'.

United Nations Security Council, 'Security Council, Nineteenth Year: 1135th Meeting (S/PV1135)'.

United Nations Security Council, 'Security Council, Twenty-Fifth Year: 1546th Meeting (S/PV1546)'.

United Nations Security Council, 'Security Council, Twenty-Fifth Year: 1547th Meeting (S/PV1547)'.

United Nations Security Council, 'Security Council, Twenty-Fifth Year: 1548th Meeting (S/PV1548)'.

United Nations Security Council, 'Security Council, Twenty-Fifth Year: 1549th Meeting (S/PV1549)'.

United Nations Security Council, 'Security Council, Thirty-Second Year: 1999th Meeting (S/PV1999)'.

United Nations Security Council, 'Security Council, Thirty-Second Year: 2037th Meeting (S/PV2037)'.

United Nations Security Council, 'Security Council, Thirty-Second Year: 2039th Meeting (S/PV2039)'.

United Nations Security Council, 'Security Council, Thirty-Second Year: 2045th Meeting (S/PV2045)'.

United Nations Security Council, 'Security Council, Thirty-Second Year: 2044th Meeting (S/PV2044)'.

United Nations Security Council, 'Security Council, Thirty-Second Year: 2046th Meeting (S/PV2046)'.

United Nations Security Council, 'Security Council, Thirty-Fourth Year: 2108th Meeting (S/PV.2108)'.

United Nations Security Council, 'Security Council, Thirty-Fourth Year: 2109th Meeting (S/PV.2109)'.

United Nations Security Council, 'Security Council, Thirty-Fourth Year: 2110th Meeting (S/PV.2110)'.

United Nations Security Council, 'Security Council, Thirty-Fourth Year: 2112th Meeting (S/PV.2112)'.

United Nations Security Council, 'Security Council, Thirty-Fourth Year: 2114th Meeting (S/PV.2114)'.

United Nations Security Council, 'Security Council, Thirty-Fourth Year: 2115th Meeting (S/PV.2115)'.

United Nations Security Council, 'Security Council, Thirty-Fourth Year: 2116th Meeting (S/PV.2116)'.

United Nations Security Council, 'Security Council, Thirty-Fourth Year: 2117th Meeting (S/PV.2117)'.

United Nations Security Council, 'Security Council, Thirty-Fourth Year: 2118th Meeting (S/PV.2118)'.

United Nations Security Council, 'Security Council, Thirty-Fourth Year: 2129th Meeting (S/PV.2129)'.

United Nations Security Council, 'Security Council, Thirty-Fourth Year: 2172nd Meeting (S/PV.2172)'.

United Nations Security Council, 'Security Council, Thirty-Fourth Year: 2175th Meeting (S/PV.2175)'.

United Nations Security Council, 'Security Council, Thirty-Fourth Year: 2178th Meeting (S/PV.2178)'.

United Nations Security Council, 'Security Council, Thirty-Fourth Year: 2182nd Meeting (S/PV.2182)'.

United Nations Security Council, 'Security Council, Thirty-Fourth Year: 2184th Meeting (S/PV.2184)'.

United Nations Security Council, 'Security Council, Thirty-Fifth Year: 2191st Meeting (S/PV.2191)'.

United Nations Security Council, 'Security Council, Thirty-Sixth Year: 2263rd Meeting (S/PV.2263)'.

United Nations Security Council, 'Security Council, Thirty-Sixth Year: 2271st Meeting (S/PV.2271)'.

United Nations Security Council, 'Security Council, Thirty-Sixth Year: 2272nd Meeting (S/PV.2272)'.

United Nations Security Council, 'Security Council, Thirty-Sixth Year: 2275th Meeting (S/PV.2275)'.

United Nations Security Council, 'Security Council, Thirty-Sixth Year: 2277th Meeting (S/PV.2277)'.

United Nations Security Council, 'Security Council, Thirty-Eighth Year: 2439th Meeting (S/PV.2439)'.

United Nations Security Council, 'Security Council, Thirty-Eighth Year: 2447th Meeting (S/PV.2447)'.

United Nations Security Council, 'Security Council, Thirty-Eighth Year: 2448th Meeting (S/PV.2448)'.

United Nations Security Council, 'Security Council, Thirty-Eighth Year: 2484th Meeting (S/PV.2484)'.

United Nations Security Council, 'Security Council, Thirty-Eighth Year: 2485th Meeting (S/PV.2485)'.

United Nations Security Council, 'Security Council, Thirty-Eighth Year: 2488th Meeting (S/PV.2488)'.

United Nations Security Council, 'Security Council, Thirty-Eighth Year: 2492nd Meeting (S/PV.2492)'.

United Nations Security Council, 'Security Council, Forty-Sixth Year: 2982nd Meeting (S/PV.2982)'.

United Nations Security Council, 'Security Council, Forty-Sixth Year: 3009th Meeting (S/PV.3009)'.

United Nations Security Council, 'Security Council, Forty-Sixth Year: 3011th Meeting (S/PV.3011)'.

United Nations Security Council, 'Security Council, Forty-Seventh Year: 3033rd Meeting (S/PV.3033)'.

United Nations Security Council, 'Security Council, Forty-Seventh Year: 3063rd Meeting (S/PV.3063)'.

United Nations Security Council, 'Security Council, Forty-Eighth Year: 3183rd Meeting (S/PV.3183)'.

United Nations Security Council, 'Security Council, Forty-Eighth Year: 3238th Meeting (S/PV.3238)'.

United Nations Security Council, 'Security Council, Forty-Eighth Year: 3244th Meeting (S/PV.3244)'.

United Nations Security Council, 'Security Council, Forty-Eighth Year: 3288th Meeting (S/PV.3288)'.

United Nations Security Council, 'Security Council, Forty-Ninth Year: 3326th Meeting (S/PV.3326)'.

United Nations Security Council, 'Security Council, Forty-Ninth Year: 3358th Meeting (S/PV.3358)'.

United Nations Security Council, 'Security Council, Forty-Ninth Year: 3368th Meeting (S/PV.3368)'.

United Nations Security Council, 'Security Council, Forty-Ninth Year: 3377th Meeting (S/PV.3377)'.

United Nations Security Council, 'Security Council, Fifty-Fourth Year: 4039th Meeting (S/PV.4039)'.

United Nations Security Council, 'Security Council, Fifty-Fourth Year: 4041st Meeting (S/PV.4041)'.

United Nations Security Council, 'Security Council, Fifty-Fourth Year: 4042nd Meeting (S/PV.4042)'.
United Nations Security Council, 'Security Council, Fifty-Fourth Year: 4043rd Meeting (S/PV.4043)'.
United Nations Security Council, 'Security Council, Fifty-Fourth Year: 4048th Meeting (S/PV.4048)'.
United Nations Security Council, 'Security Council, Fifty-Fourth Year: 4051st Meeting (S/PV.4051)'.
United Nations Security Council, 'Security Council, Fifty-Fourth Year: 4057th Meeting (S/PV.4057)'.
United Nations Security Council, 'Security Council, Fifty-Fifth Year: 4087th Meeting (S/PV.4087)'.
United Nations Security Council, 'Security Council, Fifty-Fifth Year: 4087th Meeting (S/PV.4087) (Resumption 1)'.
United Nations Security Council, 'Security Council, Fifty-Fifth Year: 4172nd Meeting (S/PV.4172)'.
United Nations Security Council, 'Security Council, Fifty-Sixth Year: 4259th Meeting (S/PV.4259)'.
United Nations Security Council, 'Security Council, Fifty-Sixth Year: 4355th Meeting (S/PV.4355)'.
United Nations Security Council, 'Security Council, Fifty-Seventh Year: 4623rd Meeting (S/PV.4623)'.
United Nations Security Council, 'Security Council, Fifty-Seventh Year: 4625th Meeting (S/PV.4625)'.
United Nations Security Council, 'Security Council, Fifty-Seventh Year: 4625th Meeting (S/PV.4625 Resumption 3)'.
United Nations Security Council, 'Security Council, Fifty-Seventh Year: 4644th Meeting (S/PV.4644)'.
United Nations Security Council, 'Security Council, Fifty-Eighth Year: 4709th Meeting (S/PV.4709)'.
United Nations Security Council, 'Security Council, Fifty-Eighth Year: 4709th Meeting (S/PV.4709) (Resumption 1)'.
United Nations Security Council, 'Security Council, Fifty-Eighth Year: 4717th Meeting (S/PV.4717)'.
United Nations Security Council, 'Security Council, Fifty-Eighth Year: 4717th Meeting (S/PV.4717) (Resumption 1)'.
United Nations Security Council, 'Security Council, Fifty-Eighth Year: 4726th Meeting (S/PV.4726)'.
United Nations Security Council, 'Security Council, Fifty-Eighth Year: 4726th Meeting (S/PV.4726) (Resumption 1)'.

United Nations Security Council, 'Security Council, Fifty-Eighth Year: 4859th Meeting (S/PV.4859)'.

United Nations Security Council, 'Security Council, Fifty-Ninth Year: 4896th Meeting (S/PV.4896)'.

United Nations Security Council, 'Security Council, Fifty-Ninth Year: 4950th Meeting (S/PV.4950)'.

United Nations Security Council, 'Security Council, Fifty-Ninth Year: 4956th Meeting (S/PV.4956)'.

United Nations Security Council, 'Security Council, Sixtieth Year: 5127th Meeting (S/PV.5127)'.

United Nations Security Council, 'Security Council, Sixtieth Year: 5228th Meeting (S/PV.5228)'.

United Nations Security Council, 'Security Council, Sixtieth Year, 5302nd Meeting (S/PV.5302)'.

United Nations Security Council, 'Security Council, Sixty-First Year, 5387th Meeting (S/PV.5387)'.

United Nations Security Council, 'Security Council, Sixty-First Year: 5390th Meeting (S/PV.5390)'.

United Nations Security Council, 'Security Council, Sixty-First Year: 5500th Meeting (S/PV.5500)'.

United Nations Security Council, 'Security Council, Sixty-First Year: 5551st Meeting (S/PV.5551)'.

United Nations Security Council, 'Security Council, Sixty-Second Year, 5749th Meeting (S/PV.5749)'.

United Nations Security Council, 'Security Council, Sixty-Second Year, 5805th Meeting (S/PV.5805)'.

United Nations Security Council, 'Security Council, Sixty-Third Year: 5881st Meeting (S/PV.5881)'.

United Nations Security Council, 'Security Council, Sixty-Third Year, 5902nd Meeting (S/PV.5902)'.

United Nations Security Council, 'Security Council, Sixty-Third Year: 5916th Meeting (S/PV.5916)'.

United Nations Security Council, 'Security Council, Sixty-Third Year: 5916th Meeting (S/PV.5916) (Resumption 1)'.

United Nations Security Council, 'Security Council, Sixty-Third Year, 5987th Meeting (S/PV.5987)'.

United Nations Security Council, 'Security Council, Sixty-Third Year: 6005th Meeting (S/PV.6005)'.

United Nations Security Council, 'Security Council, Sixty-Third Year: 6005th Meeting (S/PV.6005) (Resumption 1)'.

United Nations Security Council, 'Security Council, Sixty-Third Year, 6026th Meeting (S/PV.6026)'.

United Nations Security Council, 'Security Council, Sixty-Third Year, 6046th Meeting (S/PV.6046)'.

United Nations Security Council, 'Security Council, Sixty-Fourth Year: 6114th Meeting (S/PV.6114)'.

United Nations Security Council, 'Security Council, Sixty-Fourth Year: 6114th Meeting (S/PV.6114) (Resumption 1)'.

United Nations Security Council, 'Security Council, Sixty-Fourth Year: 6180th Meeting (S/PV.6180)'.

United Nations Security Council, 'Security Council, Sixty-Fourth Year: 6180th Meeting (S/PV.6180) (Resumption 1)'.

United Nations Security Council, 'Security Council, Sixty-Fourth Year: 6195th Meeting (S/PV.6195)'.

United Nations Security Council, 'Security Council, Sixty-Fifth Year: 6302nd Meeting (S/PV.6302)'.

United Nations Security Council, 'Security Council, Sixty-Fifth Year: 6411th Meeting (S/PV.6411)'.

United Nations Security Council, 'Security Council, Sixty-Fifth Year: 6411th Meeting (S/PV.6411) (Resumption 1)'.

United Nations Security Council, 'Security Council, Sixty-Fifth Year: 6453rd Meeting (S/PV.6453)'.

United Nations Security Council, 'Security Council, Sixty-Fifth Year: 6453rd Meeting (S/PV.6453) (Resumption 1)'.

United Nations Security Council, 'Security Council, Sixty-Sixth Year: 6524th Meeting (S/PV.6524)'.

United Nations Security Council, 'Security Council, Sixty-Sixth Year: 6598th Meeting (S/PV.6598)'.

United Nations Security Council, 'Security Council, Sixty-Sixth Year: 6627th Meeting (S/PV.6627)'.

United Nations Security Council, 'Security Council, Sixty-Seventh Year: 6633rd Meeting (S/PV.6633)'.

United Nations Security Council, 'Security Council, Sixty-Seventh Year: 6703rd Meeting (S/PV.6703)'.

United Nations Security Council, 'Security Council, Sixty-Seventh Year: 6710th Meeting (S/PV.6710)'.

United Nations Security Council, 'Security Council, Sixty-Seventh Year: 6711th Meeting (S/PV.6711)'.

United Nations Security Council, 'Security Council, Sixty-Seventh Year: 6717th Meeting (S/PV.6717)'.

United Nations Security Council, 'Security Council, Sixty-Seventh Year: 6723rd Meeting (S/PV.6723)'.

United Nations Security Council, 'Security Council, Sixty-Seventh Year: 6734th Meeting (S/PV.6734)'.

United Nations Security Council, 'Security Council, Sixty-Seventh Year: 6751st Meeting (S/PV.6751)'.

United Nations Security Council, 'Security Council, Sixty-Seventh Year: 6756th Meeting (S/PV.6756)'.

United Nations Security Council, 'Security Council, Sixty-Seventh Year: 6810th Meeting (S/PV.6810)'.

United Nations Security Council, 'Security Council, Sixty-Eighth Year: 7036th Meeting (S/PV.7036)'.

United Nations Security Council, 'Security Council, Sixty-Eighth Year: 7038th Meeting (S/PV.7038)'.

Other Resources

Colton, Timothy J and Michael McFaul, 'Russian Democracy Under Putin' (2003) 50(4) *Johnson's Russia List* 1.

Dag Hammarskjöld Library, 'Security Council – Veto List' http://research.un.org/en/docs/sc/quick/veto.

Paige, Tamsin Phillipa, *The Role of the Law in the Rise and Fall of Piracy* (Master of Philosophy (Law), The Australian National University, 2014).

Repertoire of the Practice of the Security Council, 'Chapter XI: Considerations of Chapter VII the Charter (1946–51)'.

Repertoire of the Practice of the Security Council, 'Chapter XI: Considerations of Chapter VII the Charter (1952–55)'.

Repertoire of the Practice of the Security Council, 'Chapter XI: Considerations of Chapter VII the Charter (1956–58)'.

Repertoire of the Practice of the Security Council, 'Chapter XI: Considerations of Chapter VII the Charter (1959–63)'.

Repertoire of the Practice of the Security Council, 'Chapter XI: Considerations of Chapter VII the Charter (1964–65)'.

Repertoire of the Practice of the Security Council, 'Chapter XI: Considerations of Chapter VII the Charter (1966–68)'.

Repertoire of the Practice of the Security Council, 'Chapter XI: Considerations of Chapter VII the Charter (1969–71)'.

Repertoire of the Practice of the Security Council, 'Chapter XI: Considerations of Chapter VII the Charter (1972–74)'.

Repertoire of the Practice of the Security Council, 'Chapter XI: Considerations of Chapter VII the Charter (1975–80)'.

Repertoire of the Practice of the Security Council, 'Chapter XI: Considerations of Chapter VII the Charter (1981–84)'.

Repertoire of the Practice of the Security Council, 'Chapter XI: Considerations of Chapter VII the Charter (1985–88)'.

Repertoire of the Practice of the Security Council, 'Chapter XI: Considerations of Chapter VII the Charter (1989–92)'.

Repertoire of the Practice of the Security Council, 'Chapter XI: Considerations of Chapter VII the Charter (1993–95)'.

Repertoire of the Practice of the Security Council, 'Chapter XI: Considerations of Chapter VII the Charter (1996–99)'.

Repertoire of the Practice of the Security Council, 'Chapter XI: Considerations of Chapter VII the Charter (2000–03)'.

Repertoire of the Practice of the Security Council, 'Chapter XI: Considerations of Chapter VII the Charter (2004–07)'.

Repertoire of the Practice of the Security Council, '16th Supplement 2008–2009 Part VII: Actions with Respect to Threats to the Peace, Breaches of the Peace, and Acts of Aggression (Chapter VII of the Charter)'.

Repertoire of the Practice of the Security Council, '17th Supplement 2010–2011 Part VII: Actions with Respect to Threats to the Peace, Breaches of the Peace, and Acts of Aggression (Chapter VII of the Charter)'.

Repertoire of the Practice of the Security Council, '18th Supplement 2012–2013 Part VII: Actions with Respect to Threats to the Peace, Breaches of the Peace, and Acts of Aggression (Chapter VII of the Charter)'.

Russian Federation, 'History' http://russiaun.ru/en/permanent_mission/istorija.

United Nations, 'Security Council Meeting Records: Meetings Conducted by the Security Council in 2013 (in Reverse Chronological Order)' http://www.un.org/en/sc/meetings/records/2013.shtml.

Dag Hammarskjöld Library, 'Security Council – Veto List' <http://research.un.org/en/docs/sc/quick/veto>.

Index

www.ingramcontent.com/pod-product-compliance
Lightning Source LLC
LaVergne TN
LVHW020633300926
849161LV00004B/685